Transforming Women's Education

MUSIC IN AMERICAN LIFE

A list of books in the series appears at the end of this book.

Transforming Women's Education

Liberal Arts and Music in Female Seminaries

JEWEL A. SMITH

UNIVERSITY OF ILLINOIS PRESS
Urbana, Chicago, and Springfield

Library of Congress Control Number: 2018051866
ISBN 978-0-252-04224-9 (hardcover), 978-0-252-08400-3
(paperback), 978-0-252-05107-4 (e-book)

To Dr. Karin Pendle, professor and mentor

Contents

List of Illustrations   ix

Acknowledgments   xi

Introduction   1

1   Philosophies of Women's Education in the United States   11

2   Beyond an Accomplishment: A Philosophy of Music
Education   25

3   The Dawn of a New Era in Women's Education   37

4   Seminary Structure: A Comparison   59

5   Curricula: Academic and Ornamental   72

6   Music Education for a Young Lady   92

7   Instrumental Music at the Seminaries   114

8   Singing Ladies: Vocal Repertoire at the Seminaries   142

Afterword   172

Notes   175

Bibliography   239

Index   251

Illustrations

Figures

3.1 Sarah Pierce 38
3.2 Litchfield Female Academy 41
3.3 Emma Hart Willard 42
3.4 Troy Female Seminary 47
3.5 Mary Lyon 48
3.6 Mount Holyoke Female Seminary 52
3.7 Orramel Whittlesey and Music Vale Seminary Faculty 53
3.8 Whittlesey Pianos 54
3.9 Music Vale Seminary 56
5.1 Examination Room, Troy Female Seminary 86
7.1 Concert Program, Troy Female Seminary, February 1, 1853 118
7.2 S. B. Mills, "Saltarello," op. 26, title page 134
8.1 Orramel Whittlesey, "Harp of the Wild Wind," title page 144
8.2 "The Old English Gentleman," title page 156

Musical Examples

7.1 George W. Warren's "La Fête des Fées," op. 13, mm. 46–61 125
7.2 Sigismond Thalberg, "Home! Sweet Home!," op. 72,
mm. 37–41 126
7.3 James M. Wehli, "Home Sweet Home," mm. 73–81 127

7.4 Oscar Comettant, "Gabrielle: Etude d'Expression pour Piano," mm. 45–57   129

7.5 Rudolphe Kreutzer, "The Celebrated Overture to *Lodoïska*," mm. 81–111   131

7.6 S. B. Mills, "Saltarello," op. 26, mm. 149–187   135

7.7 "The Celebrated One Finger'd Sliding Waltz," mm. 1–18   136

8.1 Orramel Whittlesey, "Harp of the Wild Wind," mm. 29–45   145

8.2 Hymn 66, Isaac Watts, "Joy of Saints"   148

8.3 Karl Anton Florian Eckert, "The Celebrated Swiss Song," mm. 46–56   160

8.4 Faustina Hasse Hodges, "The Alp Horn," mm. 11–24   162

Tables

4.1 Annual Expense Chart   70

5.1 A Comparison of Academic Subjects at the Schools   82

6.1 Musical Instruments/Vocal Instruction Offered at the Seminaries   98

Acknowledgments

During the academic year of 2004–2005, I was fortunate to hold a research position at the Five College Women's Studies Research Center (hereafter FCWSRC), located on the Mount Holyoke College campus, which served as the launching point for this book. I sincerely appreciate the encouragement of my fellows who listened to me as I struggled to find the right path for my project. I am grateful to Ruth Solie for her advice in narrowing the geographic region to the Northeast in the initial phase. Judith Tick deserves a special thank-you for her support and belief in my topic, from the preliminary stage in applying for a National Endowment for the Humanities (NEH) grant to the completion of the manuscript.

Librarians and other professionals at Mount Holyoke College, Litchfield Historical Society, Emma Willard School, and Music Vale Seminary Archives graciously assisted me in obtaining materials. Patricia Albright, Mount Holyoke College Archives librarian, was helpful in aligning the focus of Mary Lyon's career, and Jennifer Gunter King, head of Archives and Special Collections, showed special interest in my work from the beginning. Louise Litterick, musicologist on the faculty of Mount Holyoke College, volunteered to serve as my mentor while I was a fellow at the FCWSRC; her reassurance proved invaluable in the early stages as we discussed my work over lunches and various meetings. Nancy Iannucci, archivist and history instructor, and Barbara Wiley, librarian (now retired), Emma Willard School, not only aided me in locating numerous artifacts concerning Troy Female Seminary, but they also drove in excess of two hours to attend a lecture recital that Tami Morris (my piano duet partner) and I gave while I was a fellow at the FCWSRC. I am grateful that Tami traveled to South Hadley, Massachusetts, to perform with me in two recitals in the area. Linda Hocking, curator of Library and Archives, Litchfield Historical Society, has supplied many documents concerning Litchfield Female Academy and provided answers to numerous emails. Benjamin Bradley, an intern at the Historical Society (now Discovery librarian, University of Maryland Libraries), spent many hours scanning pages of music books. I found a warm welcome from the Music Vale Seminary Archives staff, who helped me uncover noteworthy documents. William Schultz and David Wordell, friends of the archives, have contributed high-resolution scans of images that otherwise were not available and have been enthusiastic about this project.

I was fortunate to obtain a full-year grant from the NEH (2007) and a postdoctoral full-year fellowship from the American Association of University Women (2008). The financial support of both organizations came at a vital time when I was working on initial drafts of many chapters and needed relief from teaching obligations.

Tom Merrill, then chairman of the music department at Xavier University, Cincinnati, Ohio, deserves heartfelt thanks for providing financial assistance so that I could obtain high-resolution scans of numerous images from the Litchfield Historical Society. He also helped make it possible for me to attend conferences to talk with my editor, Laurie Matheson. I owe her a big debt of gratitude for her patience and hand-holding through this process. She was interested in my work from our initial conversation and reading my approved NEH grant proposal. Laurie's assistant, Julie Laut, has never failed to lend a helping hand, answering emails, even when she was not in the office. I could not have asked for a more supportive publisher than University of Illinois Press. I am truly grateful. As a reader for UIP, Nancy Newman provided copious insightful suggestions on the first and second drafts. Her comments helped to clarify problematic portions of the manuscript.

I want to thank the staff at various libraries for helping me obtain musical examples and images: University of Virginia; University of Kentucky, Lexington; Princeton Seminary; William L. Clements Library, University of Michigan; New York State Library, Albany; Sibley Music Library, Eastman School of Music, University of Rochester; and Sheridan Libraries, Johns Hopkins University. The staff at each of these libraries responded quickly and efficiently, making this part of the process move along smoothly. Deborah Richards, Special Collections archivist, and James Gehrt, digital projects lead in Digital Assets and Preservation Services, Mount Holyoke College, helped me obtain images and responded to emails at the end of this project. I owe special thanks to David Sandor, circulation supervisor, and Paul Cauthen, assistant music librarian, College-Conservatory of Music Library, University of Cincinnati, who helped with research difficulties as I was searching for music scores.

My acknowledgments would not be complete without mentioning the valuable support of Robert Zierolf, Karin and Frank Pendle, and Nell Stemmermann. Robert Zierolf provided vital encouragement when I was working on the NEH grant submission. The late Frank Pendle, a master historian, completed a close reading of my manuscript just a few weeks before his untimely death. I feel that I could not have begun this effort without the essential advice and expertise of Karin Pendle and her knowledge of women in music. She has read multiple versions of chapters with an eagle eye, offering substantial suggestions. Nell Stemmermann, a longtime close friend and likewise a superb reader, assisted in unraveling research snags and spent endless hours with me as we discussed my work. Both of these women deserve to be repaid far beyond my capability.

Friends have listened, encouraged, and provided hospitality when I was in their area conducting research. Wes and Wanda Knapp cordially opened their home to me in upstate New York when I worked at the Emma Willard School Archives in Troy. Ken and Carol Anne Edmonds welcomed me to stay with them in New Britain, Connecticut, while I was working at Music Vale Seminary Archives in Salem. I sincerely thank the congregation of Bible Baptist Church in West Springfield, Massachusetts, for their love and concern as I acclimated to the Northeast while I conducted research. Don and the late Donna Backstrom, and Kent, Deborah, Anna, and Katie Anastasia accepted me as part of their family on holidays and numerous other occasions.

In conclusion, I must acknowledge the unfailing support of my sister and brother-in-law, Ruth and Gene Taylor. Without their tremendous moral support and encouragement, this project would not have been possible. I also thank my niece, Jennifer Schmitz, for always being there when I had computer issues. I must mention Mimi, my constant companion Boston terrier, who has remained faithfully by my side through the ups and downs that are inevitable through this long process. Next to last, the members of Norwood Baptist Church, where I am pianist and director of music, have always offered a shoulder to lean on when I needed it. Above all, I thank God, who gave me the desire for this project and the faith and determination to see it through to completion.

Transforming Women's Education

Introduction

During the late eighteenth century, daughters of American upper-class families had the opportunity of being educated at female seminaries and academies.[1] Such institutions were attractive if they could offer from twenty to forty or more "English" (academic) subjects as well as such ornamental arts as music, painting, and embroidery. Apparently many parents considered a school's popularity more important than its level of instruction. Advocates of women's education, including Emma Willard and Mary Lyon, rising up in opposition to the courses that offered little depth, laid the groundwork for the female seminary movement. The seminaries offered comprehensive academic education, which often prioritized quality music instruction; educators regarded music as one of the few accomplishments appropriate for women and argued that music had intrinsic value. Since employment prospects for women were limited, music instruction opened a door for graduates to find jobs as teachers or governesses should working for pay become necessary. A woman who would need to provide for her own financial support, or to help with family finances in the event of a father's or husband's illness or death, could rely on a thorough music education with a solid academic foundation as the basis for a respectable career.

Why a book about the female seminaries and academies? Given the importance of these institutions as launching pads for many degree-offering women's colleges, it is surprising that the standard histories of American music, including *Music in the New World*, *America's Music: From the Pilgrims to the Present*, and *America's Musical Life: A History*, have neglected them.[2] Instead, the authors of these works begin with instruction provided in the singing schools of the mid- to late eighteenth century and then leap to the achievements of Lowell Mason (the founder of public school music education) in the 1830s. This lacuna testifies to the limited scholarship available on institutions for women that offered musical training. The lack of interest in women's education has likely contributed to the omission of these schools from scholarly works.[3] Another reason for this gap is that relevant archival documents are widely dispersed and fragmentary and are often not well cataloged or indexed, making basic historical research difficult. I am fortunate to have conducted research at the Emma Willard School (Troy Female Seminary), Litchfield Historical Society (Litchfield Female Academy), Mount Holyoke College (Mount Holyoke Female Seminary), and Music Vale Seminary archives, which house such valuable documents as school catalogs, letters, diaries, journals, programs, and music books.

Further, the seminaries have been given minimal, if any, treatment in the histories of American music education, such as *A History of American Music Education.*[4] As would be expected, considerable attention is given to the singing schools, Pestalozzian music instruction, and Lowell Mason, but seminaries and academies are not mentioned. *A History of Music Education in the United States* includes a brief discussion of female seminaries and academies, but only marginal attention is allotted to the level of music study and repertoire at these institutions.[5]

Much scholarship has been published on the history of women's education, focusing on the establishment of women's schools and their curricula. Examples include *A History of Women's Education in the United States*; *Women's Education in the United States, 1780–1840*; and *Learning to Stand and Speak: Women, Education, and Public Life in America's Republic.*[6] These sources provide critical documentation of the history, curricula, pedagogy, and philosophy of the academy and seminary in the chronological development of women's education. They do not, however, expound on the value of music beyond its function as a social accomplishment or as part of women's higher education.

Because women in antebellum America generally did not enjoy public concert careers, and scholarship documenting music education at the better female seminaries and academies is grossly deficient, the music studied and performed at these institutions has been overlooked in recounting American music history. Seminaries and academies that promoted a quality academic education encouraged women to develop their talents fully but did not prepare them for the concert stage. An investigation of the piano repertoires studied and performed reveals that some American students at these progressive schools played the same repertoires performed in European salons and concert halls by artists such as Henri Herz, Sigismond Thalberg, and Louis Moreau Gottschalk. Why were these institutions rigorously and intensely training their students if a professional career was not open to them? While some nineteenth-century women's advocates, ministers, advice writers, and educators believed music education for women should do more than allow them to reach only a level of mediocrity, the value of this level of instruction needs to be assessed.

The Importance of This Book

In this book I examine the role of the seminaries as major institutions in the progress of women's higher education, particularly the treatment of music as a subject of artistic value, not merely one representing a social accomplishment. This book is a salient contribution to the existing literature on women's academic and music instruction in higher education. Although private teachers and music societies likely provided alternative sources of instruction, my study does not consider those venues.

In the process of narrating this neglected history, I address several broad issues within the context of middle- to upper-class American women: the importance of education as related to gender, education as women's ticket to intellectual and financial success, the level of instruction afforded by the seminaries, women's role in society, and performance venues open to them. Since most of my research concerns the years before the Civil War and women of color did not attend the schools under examination, I do not address the issues of slavery or of African American students.[7] Further, given that such pioneers as Willard and Lyon were opposed to the inequality of academic education available to women rather than music instruction, I do not include a comparison of music training accessible to both sexes.

Transforming Women's Education is a sequel to my book *Music, Women, and Pianos: The Moravian Young Ladies' Seminary in Antebellum Bethlehem, Pennsylvania* (2008), the first study to document not only the academic and music curricula offered at this distinguished female seminary but also the importance of piano study from a sociological viewpoint and music-making in a gendered environment. In researching and writing the earlier book, I became aware that further research and publication were necessary to illuminate issues surrounding women's academic and music education.[8]

The Need for Female Seminaries and Academies

After the American Revolution, political leaders realized the necessity of an educated citizenry if the new republic was to survive and advance as a nation. In postrevolutionary America, words such as "independence" and "self-reliance" now had personal as well as political implications.[9] Preserving the republic became as much an educational as a political responsibility; revolutionary leaders needed assurance that successive generations would continue to uphold the beliefs set forth in the Constitution. Since a mother was responsible for educating her children to become good citizens, she herself needed to be properly educated.[10] Further, emerging from a barter system to a market system, propelled by the Industrial Revolution, Americans needed more education than their ancestors had received.[11]

Numerous grammar schools, academies, seminaries, and other collegiate institutions for men, such as Harvard (1636), Yale (1701), and Princeton (1746), were established well before the Revolutionary War.[12] Colonial society deemed men's education a necessity: "from the guardian care of Legislatures, the presidencies and professorships of our colleges are some of the highest objects to which the eye of ambition is directed."[13] Female education, however, had been relegated to the "mother's knee," town schools (providing instruction when boys were in the field or otherwise unavailable), and "the mercy of private adventurers" eager to profit.[14] Many of the formal institutions for women were finishing schools that earned a discreditable reputation from those who valued education. Rather than focusing on young women's education, these schools became business enterprises. Emma Willard's biographer, John Lord, aptly describes the level of education offered at these popular seminaries:

> Daughters of ignorant people, suddenly enriched, attend for a year or two, to "finish" an education never earnestly begun; where girls of seventeen are put to the study of books which are only used in colleges for senior students, and this when these girls can neither spell correctly, nor write legibly, nor talk grammatically; when they are signally deficient in the very rudiments of knowledge such as are taught in common schools; when these girls, thoughtless, inattentive, ignorant, are grossly flattered and indulged and amused, so that their time may pass pleasantly; where their overindulgent parents are grossly deceived as to the advance made by their daughters; where study after study is pressed upon them, nominally—either to gain commissions on the articles sold, or to satisfy the demands of ignorant parents, who think the more books their daughters have looked into the greater is their proficiency;

where holidays and amusements of all sorts are freely given—any thing to please the girls—any thing to seduce them to return—smiles, favors, rewards.[15]

Such an education did not produce knowledgeable, literate women prepared to instruct their own children, manage the home, or benefit society. According to Lord, although a young woman who received this level of education was purportedly trained to entertain suitors in her parlor with a few choice piano selections and French idioms, no one seemed surprised when her marriage failed due to inadequate preparation.[16]

Nineteenth-Century Women's Advocates

While the Moravian Young Ladies' Seminary in Bethlehem, Pennsylvania, founded in 1742, should be regarded as a superior institution compared to any other school available for women in mid-eighteenth-century America, it remained for nineteenth-century educators and female institutions in the Northeast to advance women's education for the nation at large. The meritorious efforts of such advocates as Sarah Pierce, Emma Willard, and Mary Lyon to promote higher education need to be acknowledged. Unlike the Young Ladies' Seminary, the institutions established by Pierce (Litchfield Female Academy, Litchfield, Connecticut, 1792), Willard (Troy Female Seminary, Troy, New York, 1821), and Lyon (Mount Holyoke Female Seminary, South Hadley, Massachusetts, 1837) did not have the financial backing of a religious organization. Thus these educators found it necessary not only to appeal to the public for support but also to educate society regarding the importance of women's education.

Pierce, Willard, and Lyon deplored the meager instruction offered in the fashionable schools and contended that a woman needed an education comparable to that offered at men's colleges. Thanks to the trailblazing work of these women, a new type of educational institution was established in the early nineteenth century; most of these schools were founded between 1830 and 1860.[17] Emma Willard presented *A Plan for Improving Female Education* to the members of the New York Legislature in 1819. This plan helped to provide a foundation for the "female seminary movement," outlining the education and facilities Willard deemed appropriate for women.[18]

An examination of the accomplishments of Willard, Lyon, and Pierce illuminates the challenges they experienced in their struggle to convince society of the necessity for women's higher education. Using these three institutions as case studies sheds light on the curricula and organization of prominent schools in the development of the seminary movement. The inclusion of Orramel Whittlesey's Music Vale Seminary (Salem, Connecticut, ca. 1835) is crucial, since it is recognized as the first music conservatory in the nation and established exclusively for women. Whereas each of these institutions is distinct in its own right, they also shared the belief that women's intellectual ability was equal to that of their male counterparts.

Since Mount Holyoke did not open its doors until 1837, one might question how this school fits into the history of the seminary movement. In the early nineteenth century, daughters of the middle class often did not have the wherewithal to attend a seminary or academy. Lyon's objective was to establish an endowed institution in order to offer an education to those of lesser means.

My initial intention in describing the female seminaries and their philosophies of music was to focus on the antebellum era. However, I needed to make adjustments based on available sources. For example, I conclude my examination of Litchfield Female Academy in 1833. Although the school continued until 1844, its history, including Sarah Pierce's involvement, is sketchy beyond 1833. Under Pierce's leadership this institution achieved recognition as a prominent school for women in the late eighteenth and early nineteenth centuries and served as an important predecessor to the nineteenth-century female seminary movement.[19] Documentation for Troy and Mount Holyoke is more complete than that of Litchfield, with the exception of music programs at Mount Holyoke. Describing the history, curriculum, and music performances at Music Vale proved to be challenging because of sparse and haphazard programs, catalogs, and historical documentation, none of it cataloged. Thus, I found it necessary to expand the time period beyond the Civil War in order to obtain a coherent picture of the repertoire studied and performed at Music Vale.

Outline of the Book

Chapter 1 traces the views of women's education from the time the colonists came to America to the establishment of the female seminary movement. In order to understand the struggles that women's advocates faced, it is necessary to provide an outline of the slow development. Given that the home was believed to be their sphere, women initially received a limited education. As the population grew during the seventeenth and eighteenth centuries, women began to take on responsibilities outside the home as men assumed positions in the workforce, business, and leadership. The importance of religion and the establishment of churches also accelerated the progress of literacy, since the majority of churchgoers were women. At a minimum, women needed to be able to read the Bible.[20]

Though the demand for women's instruction seemed apparent, convincing the public of the need for higher education proved to be a battlefield. Much of society feared that schooling would make a woman discontented with her place in it. The elite members of society believed that, rather than solid academics, their daughters should receive a "finished education" that would make them marketable for marriage. After the American Revolution, women's roles continued to expand with the emergence of a middle-class society. The meager instruction women had received in previous decades was no longer sufficient for the "real" woman, who was now expected to assume multiple roles: mother, wife, educator, and, if necessary, breadwinner to support herself or her family.[21]

Chapter 2 challenges the common view of music as an accomplishment. A comparison of the philosophy of music study at the finishing schools to that at such respected institutions as those mentioned above reveals dramatic differences and provides a solid basis for music education. I argue that these institutions treated music instruction as comparable to an academic subject, and I examine the benefits of music beyond the finishing school mentality.

Chapter 3 explores the lives of Sarah Pierce, Emma Willard, Mary Lyon, and Orramel Whittlesey and their contributions to the growth of women's education. It also includes material on the establishment of Litchfield Female Academy, Troy and Mount Holyoke Female Seminaries, and Music Vale Seminary. The founding of each school is not only entwined with the accomplishments of prominent leaders in women's education but is also associated with the history of women's education. Whereas it is common to include Willard and Lyon in scholarship dealing with the history of women's education, Pierce is less familiar. Pierce made a name for herself with the opening of her academy in Litchfield; however, the work of noted Congregational minister Lyman Beecher and the first law school in the nation (founded by Judge Tapping Reeve), both in Litchfield, have eclipsed Pierce's accomplishments. Nevertheless, Pierce deserves attention, given her life and school in Litchfield, one of the cultural centers of the new nation.

Emma Willard's impact on this narrative is profound. While conducting a female school in Middlebury, Vermont, she became desirous of expanding educational opportunities for women in order to compete with those available for men at such institutions as Middlebury College. It was at that time Willard began to write *A Plan for Improving Female Education*, which changed the course of women's education and remained influential for decades. Her school in Troy, New York, became a model for female seminaries, attracting visitors who came out of curiosity to witness this advancement for women.[22]

Like Pierce and Willard, Lyon could be called a woman ahead of her time; she devoted herself to the cause of women's education and courageously pleaded for support to build Mount Holyoke Female Seminary. She became convinced that in order for a seminary to endure, it must be financially endowed. Moreover, Lyon was aware of the necessity of educating middle-class women.

Rather than making a noted contribution to women's academic education, Orramel Whittlesey played a vital part in training young women to become music teachers and performers beyond the level practiced at the finishing schools. His philosophy of music education concurred with that of Willard, Lyon, and Pierce: music was a subject in its own right and deserved quality instruction.

Chapter 4 considers the governance of the institutions. An examination of the personnel, student body, admission and retention polices, and expenses are all part of the cultural context.

Chapter 5 provides a comparison of the academic and ornamental curricula at the four schools. Ornamental courses included painting, elocution, languages, and the like. These subjects and the level of instruction offered reveal the emphasis placed on higher education for women. Analysis of the examination exercises affords a window on the assessment of students' knowledge and the examiners' views of women's education.

In chapters 6 through 8, I explore music instruction and repertoire at these institutions. In chapter 6, I examine music education by comparing the number, gender, and qualifications of the music teachers, music instruction (instruments, fees, and methods), music courses (aside from private instruction), performance opportunities for students, guest recitals, and the use of music in seminary life (such as recreation, calisthenics, and religious training, including church services). Although the amount and level of instruction varied at Litchfield, Troy, and Mount Holyoke, music education was nonetheless emphasized. Students who were privileged to attend Music Vale for one year received intense music instruction.

Chapters 7 and 8 cover instrumental and vocal repertoire, respectively, organized by genre, studied at the four schools. Piano was the chief instrument for young women to study. Troy and Music Vale over time also included lessons on the guitar, harp, and cabinet organ. In addition, students attending Troy from 1847 to 1850 could study violin. Mount Holyoke focused solely on vocal music, though students who had studied piano before entering the seminary received permission to continue studying on their own. Extant programs at Mount Holyoke prior to 1869 do not include piano performances. An examination of the piano literature found in student diaries, music books, school catalogs, and on programs reveals that the institutions kept abreast of current publications. Students were encouraged to develop their talents to the fullest, studying repertoires from a variety of genres by over 120 European and American composers.

The study of vocal music closely rivaled that of piano instruction at the seminaries and academies. While Troy and Music Vale offered private voice lessons, students attending Mount Holyoke and Litchfield had the opportunity to receive class instruction. Students sang sacred and secular compositions from various genres scored for diverse vocal parts. Like the instrumental repertoire, vocal literature was composed by Americans and Europeans. An investigation of the repertoire and performance reviews indicates that students were challenged to cultivate their abilities and to study literature presented by professional singers.

The importance of the female seminary movement, as illustrated by developments in these schools, cannot be underestimated in relation to the progress of women's education in general, the advancement of music education for women, and music-making in America. Without a consideration of the music curricula and the performances at such institutions as Troy, Music Vale, Mount Holyoke, and Litchfield, we miss a vital link in the history of American music and music education in America.

1

Philosophies of Women's Education
in the United States

When the British colonists came to America, they brought traditions from the old country, including their views on women's roles and their education. Colonial women lived under British law and social conventions such as "coverture," which included a male-dominated family where women were subservient to their husbands. Colonists assumed subordination of women to be a natural way of life endorsed by tradition and religion. Although women found their lives circumscribed by this restrictive culture, from the time of their arrival in the New World their circumstances contained seeds of societal change.[1]

The unstable economic status of the American colonies required all members of a family to work in order to ensure its survival.[2] The prevailing opinion was that the home, woman's sphere, included not only raising a "quiver full" of children to populate the vast wilderness but also fulfilling numerous other domestic duties—a requirement if the colonists were to endure the hardships of their new environment. Colonial women earned respect for their strength and ability to participate in the rigorous new lifestyle.[3]

Most women were minimally educated. Teaching her children became an integral part of a mother's responsibility in preparation for their future stations in life. The home served as a training ground where daughters were taught necessary domestic skills for homemaking. Based on these conditions and requirements, colonists argued that women needed little book knowledge, since they would not be engaged in work outside the home.[4] Though colonists perceived women as being less intelligent than men, New England laws required parents to teach their daughters to read. In 1647 the Massachusetts Bay Colony and in 1650 its sister colony, Connecticut, passed laws commanding towns of fifty families or more to provide elementary schools and towns of one hundred families to establish Latin grammar schools—both restricted to educating young men. Young women were rarely permitted to attend elementary schools until after the Revolutionary War.[5]

Religious leaders deemed Bible reading an important means of attaining piety and considered it essential for both women and men. Thus the mandates of ministers and Yankee commerce hastened the growth of literacy.[6] "Dame schools" for boys and girls, part of the British culture that colonists brought with them, became necessary, because some parents were either too busy or were themselves illiterate and unable to teach their children. Many of these private schools were conducted in the teacher's home; for example, an older woman might take responsibility for teaching children in her kitchen. This meager education consisted of reading, sometimes writing, rarely arithmetic, reciting the Lord's Prayer and portions of the Westminster Catechism, and proper etiquette.[7] Though girls could attend dame schools, their main purpose was to offer basic education to young boys in preparation for the town schools.[8]

Postcolonial Progression

Around the turn of the eighteenth century, occupations considered suitable for women broadened to include managing dry goods shops, keeping taverns, making furniture, and printing and publishing.[9] The wave of revivals known as the Great Awakening, which began to sweep the colonies in the 1730s and 1740s through the inspiration of English minister George Whitefield, challenged "religious authority and church hierarchy" and thus fostered a new equality among men and women.[10] During much of the eighteenth century, women, accustomed to a submissive lifestyle, accounted for the majority of New England churchgoers. As men became progressively involved in business, trade, and politics, their interest in religion began to wane. This enabled women to use religion as a means of leadership and to obtain more independence than they had previously enjoyed. Shifts from men's to women's responsibilities in the home and the church, along with the growth of the population and the economy, aided the development of women's education in the upper levels of colonial society.[11]

Enlightenment Philosophers' Views

Those favoring women's education found support in the writings of Enlightenment philosophers John Locke, René Descartes, and François Poullain de la Barre. Locke envisioned the child's mind as a tabula rasa, or blank slate, upon which to write the beliefs and goals of society, thus shaping a child's character. Locke's philosophy did not distinguish between male and female; rather, it disputed the current view of women's intellectual inferiority. French mathematician Descartes supported women's reasoning ability and advocated a proper education that would erase doubts as to the mental competence of the sexes. After studying human anatomy, ex-Jesuit scientist Poullain de la Barre declared that the brain had no sex and that the only difference between the male and female anatomy was their reproductive organs.[12]

The battle over women's intellectual ability, however, raged. Those who upheld women's mental inferiority gained validation from such philosophers as Jean-Jacques Rousseau, who argued that the reproductive organs controlled every part of the human being. Thus, he alleged that along with every other part of the body, the brain was also sexed. Rousseau's supporters expanded the concept of sexual differences and contended that equality for women existed solely through achievements appropriate for their sex.[13]

Standards for refinement, upheld by elite society, continued to supersede the anticipation of progress in women's learning during the Enlightenment. Wealthy Americans agreed that their daughters should have the same opportunity for education as their sons only if they proceeded to become ladies in the European sense as their brothers could become gentlemen.[14] Apprehension ultimately persisted concerning the effect education might have on young women, making them discontented to live as submissive wives.[15]

Mid- to Late Eighteenth Century

By the 1740s schools known as "adventure" or "venture" schools, operating as "select" schools, became popular. They received this title simply because their proprietors saw education as a business venture, offering instruction for daughters of elite families.[16] Another type of school, known as the "private day" or "boarding" school, was also established, mainly for girls of the upper class. Influenced by the philosophy of women's education in England, these schools used instruction methods comparable to those of notable British boarding schools, emphasizing the feminine accomplishments of French, music, dancing, drawing, and needlework. From 1750 to 1860 these day and boarding schools, which became known as female seminaries and academies, flourished as the primary type of women's educational institution. Although a few schools established in the early to mid-eighteenth century, such as the Ursuline Convent for women in New Orleans (1727) or the Moravian Young Ladies' Seminary in Bethlehem, Pennsylvania (1742), provided a solid academic education, many of the seminaries offered only a smattering of basic instruction along with showy accomplishments.[17]

Reactions to women's education varied. Affluent parents became less concerned about their daughters' receiving an academic education, preferring training that would prepare them for marriage. Men who had begun to acquire some wealth and to imitate the lifestyle of upper-class Europeans wanted their daughters to be taught such subjects as the social graces, music, and French. Consequently, many parents welcomed the proliferation of seminaries and academies that specialized in the ornamental arts.[18] These institutions became known as "finishing" or "fashionable" schools. Some parents, however, recognized the need for their daughters to be educated in order to be self-supporting should they remain single. With a surplus of women in some communities, it was likely that not all of them would marry.[19]

Given the thriving American economy at the end of the eighteenth century, men could be selective in their choice of wives. They found a woman particularly attractive if she could bring a large dowry to the marriage and sufficient skills to complement her husband in society. Limited employment choices made it difficult for single women to be self-supporting. Thus, those from the upper class found it essential to attract a well-to-do husband. In order to do so, women of means devoted their attention to becoming ladies of fashion like their counterparts in England. Once this trend began with the elite, it was difficult to reverse.[20] A common opinion among conservative minds held that "a woman needed to know only 'chemistry enough to keep the pot boiling, and geography enough to know the location of the different rooms in her house.'"[21] Despite prominent writers who defended women's intellectual abilities, opposing views of women's education remained strong.

Common schools for both boys and girls opened in 1770. In larger cities, school sessions lasted six months, while those in the smaller towns ran for two to four months. These schools provided a minimal education: spelling, reading, writing, and "rarely even the first rules of arithmetic."[22] As late as 1783, girls in the common schools still had limited prospects for education: "Females over ten years of age, in populous towns, were sometimes, though rarely, placed in the common schools, and taught to write a good hand, compose a little, cipher, and know something of history."[23] This appeared to represent significant progress in the development of women's education. In many instances, though, women had to wait until the revolutionary period to acquire instruction in anything beyond the basic academic subjects and the "fine arts."[24]

The American Revolution

With the outbreak of the Revolutionary War, women's responsibilities and domains increased, and women became accepted in both the private and the public spheres. They performed the duties of men on farms and in shops and served in the capacities of patriots or loyalists, "disguised as soldiers, spies, and camp followers."[25] Nevertheless, some male patriots had no intention of advancing women's rights or their education. Along with less educated Americans, they feared the results if a woman should receive an academic education and argued that if women learned to write, they might forge their husbands' signatures. Rather than increase their intellectual capabilities, men wanted their daughters to become noteworthy housewives who upheld the colonial traditions of "piety, modesty, frugality, and fertility."[26]

Girls in some locations were able to attend school from 5:00 to 7:00 A.M. or 6:00 to 8:00 P.M.. In some areas schools were also open to them for a few weeks in the summer, when their male counterparts worked on the farms or at dockyards. Considering the earlier restrictions on women's education, this was a major step forward and would have been momentous had more teachers been available. Frequently, however, young women tried to learn what they could without any help.[27] Such was the impoverished state of education for women at the time of the revolution; 90 percent of the white men in New England could write, but fewer than half of the white women were able to do so.[28]

As a result of the American Revolution, the concept of equality was embedded in the Constitution. The proposition that "all men are created equal" became the political promise of society. Eventually women questioned if all men are created equal, why women should be excluded.[29] Not only did the Declaration of Independence fail to provide women with the same egalitarianism as their male counterparts, but also further divisions arose in women's education—class began to establish the boundaries. While girls from the upper class received training in the ornamental arts, those from lower economic strata continued to consider themselves fortunate if they learned to read, write, and do basic arithmetic. Women from the upper class no longer received admiration and respect for their strength and domestic capabilities as did women of earlier generations; rather, these duties were relegated to the middle and lower classes.[30]

In addition to class issues, the quality of institutions that the wealthy patronized needs to be understood. After the revolution, many seminaries aspired to train young women to be accomplished so that they could embellish the home and appear respectable in the society of their husbands.[31] In order to seem attractive, some schools offered as many as forty subjects.[32] Women's advocates rose up in opposition to the vast number of courses offered with little depth. Inadequate supplies of materials, overworked teachers, and few endowments contributed to the dubious permanence of most seminaries.[33]

Postrevolutionary Struggles and Advancements in Women's Education

While the revolution brought political independence and the birth of a new nation, it simultaneously created the need for an educated populace. Formal education was no longer a luxury for the elite. An unprecedented way of life that resulted from American industrialization—a progression that radically changed the young nation's financial system and generated new levels of status, manufacturing, and ways of living—demanded a literate citizenry.[34]

Despite the embryonic stage of women's education in the postrevolutionary period, women reformers continued to face strong objections from those who were prejudiced against learned women.[35] Popular periodicals, such as the *Evening Fire-side; or, Literary Miscellany*, published articles that expressed widely held opinions: "A woman who is conscious of possessing, more intellectual power than is requisite in superintending the pantry, and in adjusting the ceremonials of a feast, and who believes she is conforming to the will of the giver, in improving the gift, is by the wits of the other sex denominated a learned lady. She is represented as disgustingly slovenly in her person, indecent in her habits, imperious to her husband, and negligent of her children."[36] Much of society condemned instruction as an unpardonable sin rather than a benefit to society. Many feared education would encourage a false sense of refinement and bolster a desire to remain single.

Advocates fought an intense battle for women's education. Arguments for and against this heated issue during the Early Republic (ca. 1780–1830) proved advantageous to women, bringing their significance to light while further shaping their lives. Benjamin Rush spoke out strongly on the need to rectify the appalling deficiencies of female education.[37] His address "Thoughts upon Female Education," delivered at the 1787 graduation exercises of the

Philadelphia Academy, became the most popular American paper quoted with regard to female education before 1790. Rush commented, "Let the ladies of a country be educated properly, and they will not only make and administer its laws, but form its manners and character."[38] He realized the significance of a woman's influence in the home and in society and recognized the necessity of instruction that would enable her to rightfully exert her authority.

As Rush contended, life in America was different from that in the old country and therefore required a change in educational philosophy: "It is high time to awake from this servility—to study our own character—to examine the age of our country—and to adopt manners in every thing, that shall be accommodated to our state of society and to the forms of our government."[39] The fashionable women of England were not considered appropriate models for American women. At best they were "ornamental" and at worst, degrading. American women had a greater responsibility in maintaining household affairs than ladies of the same status in England. As the family purchased additional property and its status increased, women needed proper training as stewards and managers of their husbands' lands. Given that men in America were created equal, women needed to possess the knowledge to educate their sons for future professions in government.[40]

In a concluding prayer, Rush pleads for the increase of seminaries that offered an education for women beyond the superficial studies: "O MOST HIGH! Without whose aid, nothing can prosper,—we beseech thee to regard with favour every Seminary of sound Learning! May they answer fully the purposes of their appointment; and let the number of them be increased! From them, may knowledge flow in living streams! In them, let multitudes be receiving continually impressions, which will secure the usefulness of each individual, and lay a firm foundation for private and public Virtue!"[41] Women could no longer be relegated to receiving the same level of education as their mothers. The lack of institutions offering solid intellectual instruction demanded urgent attention.

The views of Abigail Adams, wife of President John Adams (1797–1801), paralleled those of Benjamin Rush. Adams spoke freely to her husband about the need to reform women's education: "If we mean to have Heroes, Statesmen, and Philosophers, we should have learned women."[42] Further, she insisted, "It is very certain that a well-informed woman, conscious of her nature and dignity[,] is more capable of performing the relative duties of life, and of engaging and retaining the affections of a man of understanding, than one whose intellectual endowments rise not above the common level."[43] Adams could identify with many women given her responsibility of managing the affairs of the home, which included buying and selling property and supervising the farmhands in her husband's absence. She reminded her husband that according to the Constitution, all men, implying all human beings, were born equal. Political egalitarianism would not eliminate the need to educate women for their responsibilities in the home.[44]

Judith Sargent Murray (1751–1820) was as forceful, if not more so, as Abigail Adams. Writing "On the Equality of the Sexes," Murray maintained that women were men's intellectual equals and contended it was a woman's right to develop her mind. She declared that properly educated women would not desire such nonsense as trifles, gossip, and fashions, but rather would be better wives and more content in their domestic sphere than those with meager schooling.[45] Murray claimed that the disparity between the intellectual developments of the sexes could be traced to the difference in education. If a woman was a rational creature, she asked, should she "be so degraded as to be allowed no ideas other than those which are suggested by the mechanics of a pudding, or the sewing of the seams of a garment?"[46] To be denied an education was to undermine her worth.

In Great Britain the writings of Mary Astell (1666–1731) and Mary Wollstonecraft (1759–1797) also served as powerful arguments for the cause of women's education. Astell became the "first English woman of letters."[47] Her first three books were addressed to women. Astell believed in the intellectual equality of men and women and staunchly proclaimed that women deserved to be educated: "For, since GOD has given Women as well as Men intelligent Souls, why should they be forbidden to improve them? Since he has not denied us the faculty of Thinking, why shou'd we not (at least in gratitude to him) employ our Thoughts on himself their noblest Object, and not unworthily bestow them on Trifles and Gaities and secular Affairs?"[48] Women not only deserved but were obliged to develop their mental capabilities.

The assumption that education would unsex women and lead them to forsake their duties dovetailed with the idea that a woman could never concurrently be a scholar and a housekeeper. Wollstonecraft's *Vindication of the Rights of Woman* (London, 1792) was the most highly regarded source concerning the worth of women in her generation and what they could become if given the opportunity. While it cannot be confirmed that her book immediately influenced American thought, it was reprinted in Philadelphia shortly after its original publication and seemingly agreed with those who supported women's intellectual accomplishments. Wollstonecraft reasoned that educated women, as opposed to those taught to depend on frivolity and ignorance, would make better wives and mothers. Further, she argued that women could achieve financial security apart from marriage.[49]

The ideal of "Republican Motherhood" served as a further rationale for women's education. Exemplary Republican women displayed competence, compassion, and reliability.[50] The ideals of this woman and the lady of leisure were not found in the same person. Women's advocates recognized such women as Cornelia (mother of the Gracchi), Queen Elizabeth I of England, Empress Catherine the Great of Russia, and nineteenth-century British progressive thinkers like Hannah Moore and Mary Wollstonecraft as role models. They urged women of the younger generation to follow in their footsteps, though the formation of these icons in America would become "a major educational challenge."[51]

Besides such established institutions as Harvard, Yale, and Princeton, many grammar schools, academies, seminaries, and smaller colleges opened their doors to men long before the American Revolution, while American mothers still taught their daughters. Few schools founded before the late eighteenth century offered women a solid academic education. The Moravian Young Ladies' Seminary in Bethlehem, Pennsylvania, was an exception. The Philadelphia Academy, opened in 1787, was the first female academy established by a charter of incorporation in the United States, possibly in the world. Sarah Pierce's Litchfield Female Academy, founded in Connecticut in 1792, and Susanna Rowson's academy in Boston, established in 1797, can be regarded as two of the most remarkable precursors of prominent nineteenth-century female seminaries.[52]

Educational opportunities for women increased in the years immediately following the revolution, though the number of schools for young women did not equal those for their male counterparts. The success of these late eighteenth- and early nineteenth-century schools for women attests to the momentous development in the history of education in the Early Republic. By providing a quality higher education without endangering women's proper role in American society, these schools helped to lay the groundwork for the seminary movement (1830–1860), the organization of coeducational public high schools, and the opportunity for women to attend college.[53]

Women's Advocates

After the Revolutionary War, several men joined Benjamin Rush in promoting women's education. Chief supporters included DeWitt Clinton, Charles Burroughs, Thomas Gallaudet, Joseph Emerson, George B. Emerson, Horace Mann, Henry Barnard, William Russell, and William C. Woodbridge.[54] During the early nineteenth century, Clinton was active in New York's political affairs and promoted women's education. In 1819 he publicly deplored the current condition of women's learning: "Beyond initiatory instruction, the education of the female sex is utterly excluded from the contemplation of our laws."[55]

Charles Burroughs, rector of St. John's Church in Portsmouth, New Hampshire, gave an address concerning female education on October 26, 1827, vehemently arguing against the superficial training that women received at some seminaries and academies. He spoke of the purpose of women's education and assured listeners that the objective was not to make them philosophers or scientific lecturers: "When we speak of the extent of female education . . . we speak only in relation to its practical utility, and to its importance, as connected with the virtues and happiness of females, and with the general interests of society."[56] This address appeared in the January 1828 issue of the *American Journal of Education*, edited from 1826 to 1831 by William Russell. William C. Woodbridge, editor of *American Annals of Education* (1831–1839), also conveyed his support by welcoming articles discussing advanced education for women—an education that would prepare women for maternal and domestic responsibilities.[57]

Around the same time, educational reformer Thomas Gallaudet, best known for his work with the deaf, vigorously attacked the type of rote learning that was predominant in women's seminaries and instead encouraged a utilitarian training providing practical knowledge that would be useful in students' daily lives.[58] He declared that a mother's influence was inferior only to God's and contended it affected her family's destiny. At his seminary's dedication in 1822, Rev. Joseph Emerson stressed the importance of women's education for their sons' sakes.[59] George B. Emerson, associated with the American Institute of Instruction and principal of Boston's first high school (the English Classical School, for boys), stressed the need for women to be educated in order to perform their duties. In 1823 Emerson relinquished his position as principal to found a private secondary school for girls.[60]

Beyond motherhood, exponents of women's education emphasized the significance of women's influence over men both inside and outside the home. Burroughs argued that education would enable women to generate a "mass of moral energy," which in turn would help push society toward reform. Given their strong support of women's education, Horace Mann and Henry Barnard were recognized as pioneers in the field. Though they did not defend women's rights of suffrage and equal opportunity, they maintained that women's calling was to teach, insisting they understood the young mind better than men and thus could guide it more effectively. Mann and Barnard agreed that if only one gender would be educated, it should be women. At the least, women deserved an education equal to that given to men.[61]

While a few men such as those discussed above promoted women's education, the main support came from women who fought to ensure the establishment of female institutions and to raise their standards. New England produced the first group of women advocates: Sarah Pierce, Emma Willard, Mary Lyon, and Almira Phelps.[62] It appears that each accepted the constraints society placed on women but at the same time contended that women needed an education to properly fulfill their roles.[63] While these advocates recognized that women of all classes should be educated, they focused on the upper class, except for Mary Lyon, who concentrated on the middle class.

The early nineteenth century remained a troubled time for women's education. When Emma Willard introduced her *Plan for Improving Female Education* in 1818, the disparity between the possibilities of education for men and women persisted. Those who strove to advance educational opportunities for women faced continuing skepticism. By and large the intellectual world of the new nation relentlessly criticized female learning, equating it with aggressiveness and masculinity.[64]

The New Nineteenth-Century Woman

The American middle class that emerged between the revolution and the 1830s created a new type of family life: husbands worked outside the home and provided for the family while wives remained in the home, managing domestic affairs. The middle-class family became a "refuge from the commercial ethos, an antidote to the materialism and competition of the outside world."[65] As the middle-class home achieved its own status, the woman who ran it became important in her own right.[66]

While her position as overseer of the home gave a woman her own identity, she was reluctant to relinquish her independence. Along with the transition to married life, a woman faced many challenges: she automatically incurred domestic responsibilities; possibly encountered a geographic move that meant separation from family and breaking emotional ties; assumed the responsibility of child rearing, ensuring her children would not stray from the middle-class standing of their parents; and, most important, assumed the role of spiritual counselor to her children. Spacious homes needed additional attention, possibly requiring one or two servants, and necessitated supervisory responsibilities.

In 1831 renowned French politician and historian Alexis de Tocqueville observed the American lifestyle: "In no country has such constant care been taken as in America to trace two clearly distinct lines of action for the two sexes, and to make them keep pace with the other." He noted further, "American women never manage the outward concerns of the family, or conduct a business, or take a part in political life; nor are they, on the other hand, ever compelled to perform the rough labor of the fields, or to make any of those laborious exertions, which demand the exertion of physical strength. No families are so poor as to form an exception to this rule."[67] Countless women, however, including those from underprivileged families, destitute widows, mill girls in the North and slaves in the South, negate Tocqueville's assertions. The ideology of separate classes was not as clearly defined as Tocqueville described; rather, the lines of demarcation varied according to the demands placed on women.[68]

The newly achieved status of the middle-class family and women's innovative position became important issues in printed form, such as Lydia Maria Child's *The Frugal Housewife* (1829).[69] Changes in women's status led to greater expectations, requiring advancement in their education. The new image of middle- or upper-class American women, known as "the cult of true womanhood," became the nineteenth-century model.[70] Such women represented stability and possessed piety, integrity, passivity, and domesticity.[71] Society's standards for the new woman were much like religious customs. The term "woman's sphere" came to embody physical traits with specific connotations requiring no explanation. Altering this ideology, meticulously constructed over the past two hundred years, could prove hazardous.[72]

Since it was inappropriate for a woman to exercise her influence in public, she exerted her authority over her children through a close identity with her husband. By 1868 acclaimed nineteenth-century editor Sarah J. Hale stressed that "the home, not the public arena, was woman's battleground; her weapons were education, conversation, delicacy, femininity, and the power to persuade; and her role was that of God's moral agent on Earth."[73] The impact of the domestic circle proved to be of inestimable value rather than a restriction. Belief in a woman's guidance gave her a rare privilege: that of "having one's cake and eating it too." She could remain in her sphere and still receive praise from society.[74]

Rationales and Reforms in Women's Education

Women's increased activity in the church allowed for an enlarged, pervasive influence. Various new female societies sprang up as a result of the revival movement known as the Second Great Awakening, which occurred during the late eighteenth and early nineteenth centuries. Women became more involved in religious and charitable organizations such as Sunday schools,

schools for the poor and for black children, and missionary efforts at home and abroad.

New responsibilities for women helped to erase fears concerning the conflict between learning and domestic duties. Middle- and upper-class society valued the home too highly to allow it to be trusted to the uneducated.[75] Rather than encourage demarcation, advocates intended education to unite women and help to dissolve lines of class.[76] In addition, advocates saw women's roles as all-encompassing. Emma Willard claimed that women were well suited to teach (and could be hired at lower salaries than men).[77]

A letter from Mary Lyon to her mother, dated May 12, 1834, supports the argument for women's education:

> The course of instruction adopted [at Ipswich], and the course which I have endeavored to adopt when I have instructed among my native hills, I believe is eminently suited to make good mothers as well as teachers. I have had the pleasure of seeing many, who have enjoyed these privileges, occupying the place of mothers. I have noticed with peculiar interest the cultivated and good common sense, the correct reasoning, the industry and perseverance, the patience, meekness, and gentleness of many of them. I have felt, that if all our common farmers, men of plain good common sense, could go through the country and witness these mothers in their own families, and compare them with others in similar circumstances, they would no longer consider the money expended on these mothers as thrown away.
>
> . . . . O how immensely important is this work of preparing the daughters of the land to be good mothers! If they are prepared for this situation, they will have the most important preparation which they can have for any other; they can soon and easily become good teachers, and they will become, at all events, good members of society. The false delicacy, which some young ladies indulge, will vanish away as they see most of the companions of their childhood and youth occupying the solemn and responsible situation of mothers. It will no longer appear like a subject for which no care should be taken in the training of daughters.[78]

Such an education as Lyon proposed would replace a false sense of security with a firm foundation that prepared women for their most important responsibility: the training of their children.

Conclusion

The philosophy rooted in "Republican Motherhood" and the integral advances in women's education broke new ground.[79] The seeds of liberation sown in the colonists' environment in the New World finally began to germinate. Although arguments against women's education were strong, they did not thwart its development; instead, they aided its advancement and brought women's importance to light. In addition, the political revolution and the Industrial Revolution facilitated the progress of women's education. From the confidence displayed in the American Revolution concerning the virtue of its citizens, society demonstrated its belief that Americans would continue to uphold the values set forth in the Constitution. To that end, female academies and seminaries were defended on the basis that they served a new purpose.

Between 1830 and 1860 a new type of secondary school known as the female seminary or academy sprang up from Maine to Georgia and as far west as frontier towns. This enormous expansion created opportunities for women that they had not previously experienced and also foreshadowed those of the later nineteenth century. Sarah Pierce, as well as other founders of early female academies, appropriated the theory of "Republican Motherhood," giving domesticity the status of a vocation and motherhood that of a profession. Some schools appeared before 1800, such as the Ursuline Convent, the Moravian Young Ladies' Seminary, and Sarah Pierce's Litchfield Female Academy, but the greatest increase in the number of these schools occurred during the antebellum period. The founding of female academies and seminaries that stressed a quality education testifies that training young women solely in the ornamental arts was no longer meeting their needs. Rather, an education that embellished the mind and prepared women for a separate destiny became essential.[80] Along with a strong academic education, women's advocates valued the importance of music instruction, affording it the status of an intellectual subject. An examination of the philosophy of music instruction in the following chapter will reveal its value as part of a young woman's higher education.

2

Beyond an Accomplishment

A Philosophy of Music Education

As Americans in the late eighteenth and nineteenth centuries began to accumulate wealth, they desired to emulate the British lifestyle.[1] For a woman to be considered a fashionable lady, as in upper-class Britain, she needed to be "accomplished." Finishing schools such as Jedidiah Morse's in New Haven and Jane Voyer's in Charleston, had the reputation for offering an education that would prepare women to enter genteel society. These schools emphasized instruction in music, dancing, painting, fancy needlework, and French—subjects that would make a woman accomplished and therefore marketable for marriage.[2] "Like 'dress,' music was part of one's presentation to the world; like needlework, it was a useful craft." Furthermore, it was deemed a venue in which a woman could portray herself as a lady and display graceful, delicate, and tasteful feminine traits.[3]

A comparison of the philosophy of music education at the finishing schools with that of Litchfield Female Academy, Troy, Mount Holyoke, and Music Vale Seminaries, and an examination of the benefits of music study, is critical to understanding the significance of music beyond that of an accomplishment.[4] Although both types of schools valued music as an indispensable part of the curriculum, the level of instruction was based on their objectives.

Competing Philosophies of Music Education

Music at finishing schools was regarded as an ornamental subject, which characterized it as an "accomplishment." Educators, physicians, advice writers, ministers, and parents who endorsed women's higher education, however, insisted that music study was more than a social accomplishment and carried benefits equal to those of academic subjects.

Contemporary periodicals included articles reprimanding the finishing school mentality of music and defending its status as an intellectual subject. Ipse Vidi, writing in the *American Annals of Education*, contended that music had inherent distinctions beyond "the mere instrument of gratifying the senses." As long as music is reduced to a fashionable art with no connection to intellectual attainments, he argued, "it will be perverted to the ignoble purpose of a transient gratification to those who are not able to estimate its best qualities and purposes." Vidi chided those who supported this level of music education, claiming they must be viewed "as an inferior class of beings" in comparison to polite society.[5] An anonymous author discussing "The Beauties of Music," in *Ladies' Garland and Family Wreath Embracing Tales, Sketches, Incidents, History, Poetry, Music*, maintained that people who deem music "merely as subservient to amusement, or, at most, to that cultivation of mind which *emollit mores, nec sinit esse feros* (insists that social customs be genteel and cannot bear the slightest degree of coarseness)," unquestionably regard it as a lower art form.[6]

Perhaps the defining argument concerning the philosophies can be traced to the definitions of "accomplishment" and "ornament." The Reverend Edward W. Hooker, writing in 1841, claimed that these words are associated with that which "adorns"—the purpose of music instruction in the finishing schools' curricula. Conversely, founders of Litchfield, Troy, Mount Holyoke, and Music Vale maintained that music study had emotional, physical, and intellectual advantages. Reverend Hooker argued that music has been erroneously identified "as an accomplishment, or simply as an ornamental branch of female education," like dancing, calisthenics, or embroidery. If the intention of music instruction is to "*accomplish* a young lady," Reverend Hooker retorted, it has been degraded to a level far beneath its value.[7] Furthermore, he countered that those who confined music as merely part of a fashionable woman's education failed to embrace its intellectual and moral benefits.[8]

Not everyone agreed that women should be rigorously educated; some affluent parents preferred finishing schools for their daughters. Along with meager academic training, finishing schools often provided inadequate music instruction, which gave music education a negative connotation. Students were encouraged to practice only enough to play simple "ditties" in the parlor rather than to develop their talents.[9] Young women who could afford private lessons learned to play fashionable music and sing songs with sentimental or amatory texts.[10]

The superficial teaching of academic subjects and emphasis on accomplishments in the finishing schools led Emma Willard and Mary Lyon to stress academic subjects and devote less attention to music as a performing art. Willard encouraged her students to study music but did not consider it vital for a young woman to attain the level of her teacher.[11] Lyon wrote the following regarding the value of vocal music:

> Ever since vocal music was introduced into our seminary, I have had an increasing sense of its great practical importance. By our influence, and the influence of our pupils on this subject, probably hundreds may be benefited, for a succession of generations. Those who have been able to sing from childhood, do not know by experience the feelings which *some* have who cannot sing. When passing near the music-room last summer, and thinking that a large part of the choir, probably, had no more of a natural voice than myself, I found it necessary to restrain, with firm determination, a rising murmur. I have sometimes felt, that I would have given six months of my time, when I was under twenty, and defrayed my expenses, difficult as it was to find time or money, could I have enjoyed the privileges for learning vocal music that some of our pupils enjoy.[12]

Although Lyon regretted not having the privilege of a music education, she realized the importance of providing the opportunity for young women. Based on Lowell Mason's advice, Lyon did not encourage piano instruction at Mount Holyoke Female Seminary, yet she did not oppose it; instead she promoted vocal music.[13]

The principle of including music in the curriculum determined the type of music that students studied and the level to which they aspired. While finishing schools regarded music as a means of social entertainment, fashionable music—for example, dances, pieces based on operas, and marches—was most appropriate and desirable for young women to learn, since they would spend numerous hours in the parlor entertaining their guests. Though students at Music Vale, Troy, Litchfield, and Mount Holyoke also played this repertoire, they studied and performed sonatas, etudes, rondos, and concerti—the same literature performed in European salons and on concert stages by such artists as Henri Herz, Sigismond Thalberg, Clara Schumann, and Franz Liszt.[14] The degree of emphasis placed on music training differed among these schools, yet the rationale for including music in the curriculum was unanimous and remained a strong undercurrent alongside a solid academic curriculum.

The views about women's education as offered in the finishing schools led many parents to question the validity of music education for their daughters.

The pros and cons of this issue were intensely debated. In 1841 the *Musical Reporter* reflected the attitudes of many parents: music was simply an accomplishment or one of the ornamental arts; it was expensive, with regard to both time and money. It was one of the finer arts ("luxury") reserved for the upper class. Young women, especially from the middle class, would possibly not perform it after marriage.[15]

Although music was a satisfying art that brought enjoyment to the home, it was not considered a necessity of life. Some young women were deemed not to have enough talent to be worth the time and money necessary for lessons; for others it took years of instruction and practice to play well. Much of the music available was not considered appropriate for young women—especially pieces composed for the piano "associated with poetry of a light and frivolous character, and overcharged with sickly sentimentalism." According to Reverend Hooker, music was frequently combined with poetry that reflected "immoral character"; thus, music of this type would be detrimental to a young woman's religious devotion and morals when she studied it. Christian parents should not spend money on anything associated with the "accomplishments" when it should be designated for use in spreading the gospel.[16]

Benefits of Music Education

The notion that music, when made part of higher education, had useful qualities countered the sole purpose of music as practiced in the finishing schools. While Music Vale, Troy, Mount Holyoke, and Litchfield did not encourage students to pursue concert careers, educators and supporters of such institutions recognized the significance of inspiring young women to fulfill their potential. Numerous articles appeared in educational journals and popular magazines advocating the study of music as part of higher education—for example, benefit to physical, emotional, and mental health; refinement of sentimentality; use in religious worship at home and in church; and increase in employment qualifications.

PHYSICAL HEALTH

Since many American women suffered from chronic diseases, women's health became a grave concern to physicians and educators.[17] Physician Benjamin Rush stipulated that vocal music should be required in women's education, given that singing would exercise the lungs and improve health. He recommended that singing be practiced daily in order to receive the most benefits from this art.[18] William Alcott, another physician, concurred with Rush's advice and extended music's value to training the mind and morals.[19]

Considering its advantages for promoting good health, vocal music was deemed one of the most important branches of physical education.[20] Mary Lyon had the students at Mount Holyoke Female Seminary sing as they participated in calisthenics; Emma Willard incorporated singing for the practical purpose of increasing bodily activity to add warmth. During the cold winters in Vermont, when the fireplace at the Middlebury Female Academy could not produce sufficient heat, Willard arranged a contra dance for the students to invigorate the circulation of their blood. The young ladies who were able began singing while Willard, with a partner, led the dance; others followed in rapid succession.[21]

EMOTIONAL WELL-BEING

The emotional stability of young women ranked a close second to health concerns; physicians and educators regarded music as a panacea that could provide relief from a troubled mind. Lydia Sigourney, writer of advice books for women, stressed music's angelic power. She related the incident of a clergyman who, having taught his daughters the concepts of music and singing, reported that music served to cure their unhappiness.[22]

Musical harmony was often regarded as the "medicine of the mind," having the potential to renew one's spirit by affecting the ears and reaching the arteries of the heart, as portrayed by physicians William Alcott and Benjamin Rush, advice writer Mrs. L. G. Abell, and educator William C. Woodbridge.[23] Alcott doubted whether music had been recognized for its ability to calm agitated spirits "which haunt the path of human life."[24] A musically trained daughter could provide a calming atmosphere for her father after a demanding day at work, Abell insisted, and could relieve her mother's anxieties and depression.[25] Rush agreed, promoting vocal music as an antidote during stressful days caused by an ill-tempered husband, irritable children, and difficult times. According to Woodbridge, music could provide tranquility for the mind unlike any other art.[26]

Music also served as a remedy for loneliness and boredom—subsidiary themes of emotional concerns—often associated with a lady's lot in life. The Reverend George Burnap, nineteenth-century minister and advice writer, contended that music had almost magical powers in assisting women:

> When the spell of Music is upon us, the bad passions are hushed in profound repose, and the good affections awake and entrance the soul with visions of

whatever of good and great and tender, and beautiful we have ever experienced or imagined. Then pass before us, with the distinctness and reality of a dream, the long lost scenes of youth and home. Then forms and faces reappear that have long since been hid in darkness, and eyes beam upon us with more than living tenderness and intelligence, which now are quenched in death. The soul for a moment is freed from the dominion of what is most painful and depressing in our condition, and revels in all the joys of the past, the present, and the future. Sickness forgets its pains, sorrow suspends its sigh, age loses the consciousness of wrinkles and gray hairs, . . . and the soul, freed in some measure from the environments of time and space, catches glimpses, more perfect, perhaps, than at any other time.[27]

Although Burnap's description of music's capability seems overstated, he was likely referring to the benefits of music as promoted by educators, physicians, and advice writers supporting the level of instruction in higher education.

INTELLECTUAL BENEFITS

Intellectual inactivity was thought to make a young woman susceptible to emotional and mental maladies; the practice of music helped to hone and purify the mind.[28] In a series of articles appearing in the *Boston Musical Gazette* on the subject of music as a science, the author argued that the "application of these principles" is adequate to challenge "the utmost power of the mightiest mind."[29] The views of William Nixon, as presented in "A Guide to Instruction on the Pianoforte," concurred with the idea of music as a science and claimed that those who regarded music merely as an accomplishment inferred it was incapable of having any intellectual benefit.[30]

Attention to music study was regarded as beneficial for the gifted but especially profitable for those of lesser intellectual ability. It increased the attention span—the basis for all intellectual studies; reinforced memory, given that students were required to memorize the rules of music; developed the ability to recall information quickly; and enlarged one's comprehension.[31] Susanna Rowson, founder of the Young Ladies Academy in Boston in 1797, opined that music study should be included in the training of a "well-informed and cultivated mind" rather than regarded as a root cause of evil.[32] The anonymous writer of "Thoughts on Music" echoed Rowson's opinion, maintaining that singing improves the mind by "quickening [one's] sensibilities," thereby refining the insight of "mental as well as natural objects."[33] These applications of music were taught in such institutions as Music Vale, Mount Holyoke, Troy, and Litchfield.

G. C. Hill, Esq., member of and reporter for the examining committee at Troy Female Seminary, applauded the benefits of music as taught at the school:

> The Musical Education which the pupils of this Seminary have within their reach, is by no means the least of the advantages to be derived from a course of study here. Music is evidently made much of, and held to be something higher than a mere accomplishment. The Principals introduced it freely into the Examination exercises, as if they believed in its blessed power to elevate the thoughts, refine the sentiments, and increase the health of the whole being. Its influence was easily discernible over the entire body of the pupils. . . . We found it holding a prominent place in the studies of the Troy Female Seminary, and record the discovery with unaffected pleasure. In the future of our systems of popular education, there is no doubt that this branch will enter much more largely than it ever yet has into the pupil's intellectual and spiritual development.[34]

Elocution—the study of reading with expression—was an important part of a young woman's education. Emma Willard's sister, Almira Hart Lincoln Phelps (1793–1884), author and educator, affirmed that music was beneficial in training the ear to distinguish sounds that aided the student in learning to convey the sentiments implied in language.[35] Thus vocal music instruction was the best preparation for learning to speak and read clearly.[36] Since music is capable of demonstrating emotions, it qualified as the ultimate tool for perfecting those emotions.[37] An anonymous educator, writing on "Music, as a Branch of Common Education," published in the *American Annals of Education*, claimed that the student who "has not habituated [her] organs to the sudden and precise variations which they [musical tones] require, cannot understand perfectly the modern rules of elocution," necessary for reaping the full benefits of instruction in this art.[38]

REFINING WOMEN'S SENTIMENTALITY

As stated in the above report from the examining committee at Troy, music had a profound effect on woman's sentiments; without the capacity to feel, one would not be able to express emotion.[39] Young women who cultivated music naturally improved their taste and character, thus embellishing their minds.[40] A young woman who had acquired such a refined taste had an unusual influence in society, a "secret attractive charm" that "softens the feelings of the heart like those benign" powers beyond one's jurisdiction.[41]

In addition to offering a solid academic education, the seminaries continued to emphasize the training of young women to become refined young ladies. In 1857 the examining committee at the Troy Female Seminary commended the school on its devotion to aesthetic culture, maintaining "its vital importance in the training of the mind and the formation of the character, especially the female character, where want of taste is the 'unpardonable sin.'"[42] Young women needed to be instructed to enter genteel society in their accepted realm and to be complements to their husbands. Rather than an accomplishment, music was valued as an art that would give finesse and delicacy to female emotions and serve as an effective means to elevate one's character and offset insensitive passions.[43] If music study was governed by this philosophy, women would be a benefit to society rather than a mere adornment.

RELIGIOUS OBLIGATIONS AND REWARDS

Instead of regarding music as a woman's entrance into societal circles, ministers, educators, and advice writers proclaimed it was a gift from God and stressed that the highest employment of this art should be in praise to him. Almira Phelps concluded it was disheartening to observe a gifted musician who had never learned to employ her talents as an offering of thanksgiving.[44] Woodbridge concurred with Phelps, contending that vocal music was the most expressive language through which to communicate one's feelings of praise to God, whether in solitude or united with those of like beliefs.[45]

Music as part of religious devotions proved to be an additional palliative for emotions. Reverend Hooker determined that the employment of music in private devotions produced positive results in a woman's emotional state and thus was considered "an art of high utility."[46] Simply said, music had limitless ramifications for the student who devoted herself to study and the application of its principles. The importance of music instruction was extended beyond the individual and family to the church environment. An author referred to as "Amicus" pointed out, in an article titled "The Influence of a Musical Education," that society's lack of interest in prayer may be traced to an improper or deficient education in music. In order to be able to enlighten others, one first has to receive proper training.[47]

EMPLOYMENT

Women frequently needed financial support before they married or if by choice remained single; some found it necessary to contribute to the family's finances even after marriage.[48] Advice writers and educators admonished mothers not to assume their daughters would marry or acquire substantial money; thus, having an education in the arts could prove beneficial to women who needed employment.[49] Beginning around 1830 many seminaries and common schools across the country began to employ female teachers. Nineteenth-century advice writers, such as T. S. Arthur, encouraged women to pursue an education in which they had an interest and were qualified. Arthur maintained that a young woman who was well trained in music would have no difficulty finding employment.[50] Schools and families hiring teachers or governesses repeatedly requested that the candidate have musical training.[51] Parents and guardians realized that such an education enhanced their daughters' or wards' ability to find employment as schoolteachers or governesses. For instance, in his letter of inquiry to Mary Lyon, Daniel Wright, guardian of a young woman who was interested in attending Mount Holyoke, described his ward as someone who "wants to be fited for a music teacher as she has a natural taste for that branch."[52] Likewise, the seminaries received requests for music instructors. Susannah Fitch from Hamilton, Ohio, a former student at Mount Holyoke, appealed to Mary Lyon in 1848. Lyon responded to Fitch offering several suggestions for teachers, one of whom was recent graduate Emily Norcross: "She has devoted considerable time to music."[53] Given Lyon's standard of excellence, she would not have recommended Norcross if she had not had a high regard for her ability to teach music.

Although some women came from wealthy homes, there was no guarantee their parents would be able to provide for their daughters until they married. Arthur recounted a narrative titled "The Young Music Teacher" describing two daughters from an upper-class family who would have been left destitute after their parents' deaths were it not for the music education that enabled them to become independent and self-supporting.[54]

Arguments For and Against Music Education

While arguments supporting music education appeared convincing, those against such instruction were equally intense. Parents not disposed to having their daughters pursue music held to such problematic issues as time and expense, neglect of music after marriage, or music as an art reserved for the upper class.

TIME AND EXPENSE

Those opposed to music education frequently perceived it as a luxury rather than a necessity. A common contention lingered that some women had no musical talent, and for those who did, acquiring musical skills required too much time. Woodbridge claimed there were "degrees" of talent.[55] Nonetheless, some parents were reluctant to pay for their daughters' music instruction unless they demonstrated unusual talent. Although music education, including private lessons and a pianoforte or organ, was costly, the anonymous author of "Suggestions to Parents on Female Education" reminded parents that the purpose of music education was to train young women to become admirable citizens. Anything that advanced this objective was worthwhile, while that which did not was detrimental.[56]

Benjamin Rush emphasized the value of vocal music over instrumental, objecting to the cost of the instruments in addition to the instruction. Reverend Hooker, however, took the position that although lessons and an instrument were "somewhat expensive," this was not a substantial argument, given that in a short time many families wasted the price of an instrument on clothing, "superfluities of the table," or other unnecessary items. He reasoned further that the decision between purchasing expensive clothing, which within a year is outdated, or an instrument built to last a lifetime should not be difficult.[57]

Along with expense, parents were concerned about the amount of time necessary to become musically proficient. Rush agreed that to perform well required two to four hours of daily practice, and he therefore did not encourage young women who had limited time to study instrumental music. He was not opposed, however, if one had talent and the means: "Let it not be supposed from these observations that I am insensible of the charms of instrumental music, or that I wish to exclude it from the education of a lady where a musical ear irresistibly disposes to it, and affluence at the same time affords a prospect of such an exemption from the usual cares and duties of the mistress of a family, as will enable her to practice it. These circumstances form an exception to the general conduct that should arise upon this subject, from the present state of society and manners in America."[58] Rush realized that many young women attending an institution such as Mount Holyoke would not have the financial support to remain in school long enough to graduate and therefore needed to devote their time to other studies.

NEGLECT OF MUSIC AFTER MARRIAGE

Given the expense of providing an education for their daughters, parents could be hesitant to incur additional fees for private music lessons, since young women often neglected their talent after marriage. Those who supported music education, however, retorted that the blame should be laid on the young woman who did not comprehend its value. By not cultivating her musical abilities, she manifests dissatisfaction with her father's sacrifices to give her a music education.[59] Educator Gail Hamilton, writing in the 1860s, issued a compelling declamation:

> One hears much complaint of the direction and character of female education. It is dolefully affirmed that young ladies learn how to sing operas, but not how to keep house,—that they can conjugate Greek verbs, but cannot make bread,—that they are good for pretty toying, but not for homely using. Doubtless there is foundation for this remark, or it would never have been made. But I have been in the East and the West, and the North and the South; I know that I have seen the best society; and I am sure I have seen very bad, if not the worst; and I never met a woman whose superior education, whose piano, whose pencil, whose German, or French, or any school-accomplishments, or even whose novels, clashed with her domestic duties. I have read of them in books; I did hear of one once; but I never met one,—not one.

While Hamilton recognized the existence of negative arguments concerning music and higher education, she refuted them. She contended that a woman who did not continue to develop her mental faculties, including music, would waste away and soon be worthless.[60]

Although a married woman had responsibilities she had not previously held, music should still occupy an important place in her life. Sarah J. Hale, editor of *Godey's Lady's Book* from 1837 to 1877, asserted in her advice book, *Happy Homes and Good Society All the Year Round*, that music should be used for domestic purposes rather than to attract a romantic suitor. Hale argued that the mother or teacher has often been at fault in training a young woman to believe that music is simply a showy accomplishment.[61]

CLASS AND FASHION

Reverend Hooker refuted the claim that music education was appropriate only for young ladies of the upper class. Instead, he argued, class is irrelevant; music "belongs wherever there is love for it, and taste for its cultivation and enjoyment; and wherever there are fine feelings of the soul, susceptible of being moved and swayed by it," regardless of financial status.[62]

While finishing schools catered to the upper class, women's advocates and educators decried the frivolities and evils of music taught as an accomplishment. Phelps criticized the training of young women for a fashionable life, asserting that such instruction would encourage them to assume distasteful airs. If music was regarded "as an agreeable and refined amusement," which provides pleasure for oneself and one's friends, she countered, then "we should not see so much parade and fluttering when a young lady is requested to sing or play in company."[63] Phelps, Willard, and other like-minded educators observed that music taught as an accomplishment, along with other superficial instruction, did not produce refined young women benefiting society.

Conclusion

Arguments in defense of music instruction had significant merit and impact on families during the nineteenth century. If music was considered simply an accomplishment, why did the founders of such institutions as Litchfield, Troy, and Mount Holyoke, offering a stringent academic education, insist that music have a vital place in their curricula? Young women who were privileged to receive music instruction as part of their education could attest that it had useful benefits rather than simply training them to become fashionable ladies. Music education based on this philosophy was advantageous to all women, regardless of class. A discussion of the music instruction offered at Litchfield, Troy, Mount Holyoke, and Music Vale Seminaries (chapters 6, 7, and 8) affirms the value of music beyond that of a mere social accomplishment.

3

The Dawn of a New Era
in Women's Education

While Emma Willard and Mary Lyon have long been recognized as pioneers in women's education as we know it today in the United States, an investigation of its development reveals the seed was sown as early as 1742 with the founding of the Moravian Young Ladies' Seminary in Bethlehem, Pennsylvania, one of the most prestigious schools for young women at that time.[1] The paucity of scholarship that had been devoted to this school can possibly be attributed to its name. Perhaps scholars assumed it focused on religious training rather than a seminary offering young women academic and music instruction.

Changes in the newly formed republic provided the impetus for advancement in women's education. George Washington insisted that the public be enlightened in order to preserve the nation's virtue. As the education of men was considered important for this purpose, women's education also began to be deemed necessary to produce an honorable citizenry. The intellectually trained mind could offer an alternative to one of the problems of aging—an educated woman could still be attractive to society when her youthful charm had faded.[2] Unfortunately, acceptance of this philosophy progressed slowly. In spite of the prosperity the Moravian Young Ladies' Seminary enjoyed, only a marginal number of the new nation's citizens appreciated the value of educated women.

A description of the establishment of Litchfield Female Academy, Troy and Mount Holyoke Female Seminaries, and Music Vale Seminary illuminates the importance of these schools in helping to lay the foundation for women's academic and music education. Without a detailed account of the sacrifices and contributions of Sarah Pierce, Emma Willard, Mary Lyon, and Orramel Whittlesey, it is not possible to understand why these schools and educators are revered as cornerstones and pioneers in the history of American women's higher education.

Sarah Pierce and Litchfield Female Academy (1792)

Sarah Pierce (fig. 3.1) earned the recognition of her contemporaries and followers as one of the earliest advocates of American women's education after the revolution.[3] Pierce's talents as an educator and reformer marked her as an inspiration and model for women of the next generation.

Although little is recorded about Pierce's early training, she grew up in a family and a community that valued education. She was exposed to education through contact with several college-educated men in her mother's family, and her two brothers were apparently well educated.[4] Pierce's mother died when Sarah was three; two years later her father remarried. Her stepmother fully supported women's education and defined her position by joining a

Fig. 3.1. Sarah Pierce (1767–1853). Courtesy of the Collection of the Litchfield Historical Society, Litchfield, Connecticut.

group of women who petitioned the Litchfield School Board to grant girls the same educational privileges as those for boys. Pierce's father served as a member of the Litchfield School Committee for several terms, confirming interest in his children's education.[5]

As early as 1725, the town voted to retain school masters and dames to teach children to read and write; thus it can be assumed they attended dame schools from an early age. However, educational opportunities for Sarah Pierce in rural New England towns, such as Litchfield, were haphazard. For example, the school committee hired young college graduates to teach for two terms while they pursued other careers; women taught only during the summer. Pierce attended Ashbel Baldwin's school—a private school open to children whose parents could afford the tuition. Although Baldwin's school was coeducational, the curriculum differed somewhat: the girls studied reading, writing, English grammar, and arithmetic, while the boys were afforded such subjects as Greek and Latin. Despite the academic restrictions, the education offered at Baldwin's school superseded that for girls at most New England schools before the revolution.

Pierce's father died when she was sixteen; her older brother, John, became the family guardian. Since Sarah and some of her sisters needed to become self-supporting in order to help with family expenses, John encouraged them to become teachers. The new private schools established in the 1780s in cities such as New York had begun offering academic courses while still emphasizing ornamental subjects including needlework, dancing, and social graces and refinement.[6] Therefore, many Connecticut families considered fashionable female boarding schools in New York as the best option for their daughters' educations. It is not certain where Pierce furthered her education. Legend has it that John sent Sarah and one of her sisters to New York City; he realized the necessity of acquiring an education that would enable them to offer both academic and ornamental subjects for a successful school. Further, John had connections with leading New York families.[7] He died at the early age of thirty-five; Sarah's two older sisters married, leaving her with the responsibility of caring for her stepmother and three younger siblings.[8]

Sarah Pierce became appalled at the limited instruction offered to women and devoted her life to the intellectual improvement of her sex.[9] Although Litchfield was a small town, it was the fourth largest in the state and had a history of "town-supported schooling." As the county seat in 1751, Litchfield attracted many professional and college-educated men and promoted itself as a prosperous commercial center where some businessmen participated in the China trade.[10] In 1784 Judge Tapping Reeve opened the nation's first law school, which became widely recognized; several graduates later held prominent political positions.[11]

The presence of a distinguished law school brought an aura of esteem to Litchfield, thereby providing fertile ground for the founding of a female school. This thriving community induced numerous families to send their daughters to Litchfield Female Academy, accompanied by a relative attending the law school. Many parents preferred a rural setting as a place to educate their daughters without the distractions of the city.[12] Litchfield's location at the center of some of the main transportation routes made it readily accessible to students coming from a distance.[13] Local resident J. Deming Perkins documents his recollection of Pierce's decision to establish her school in Litchfield:

> I remember when a boy, after population had begun to center in a few towns, to have inquired of Miss Pierce why she started her school in Litchfield, why she did not move to some of the larger towns or cities of the State? She replied, "I did think of doing so, but Litchfield at that time was one of the leading Towns of the State, and I did as I have always been in the habit of doing when seeking assistance, went to my Bible. On opening it, my eyes fell first on a verse in the Psalms, Dwell in the Land, and verily thou shalt be fed. (XXXVII-3) And I at once decided that my school should be established in Litchfield."[14]

Pierce was obviously aware of the citizens' opinion of women's education and had the foresight and faith to believe her efforts would not be in vain when she founded the academy.

By 1798 the school had attracted the attention of twenty-five prominent leaders in the community who pledged their financial assistance to construct a suitable building; at that time the school received its official name (fig. 3.2).[15] The shareholders' backing revealed their confidence in Pierce's ability to administrate, to teach their children, and to develop a school that would uphold Litchfield's reputation.[16]

Between 1800 and 1803, Sarah and her sister Mary (Pierce's assistant in the school) built a home large enough to accommodate several students. The academy grew from its meager beginning in Pierce's dining room to a new school building and a house for some boarding students within a few years.[17]

The academy did not fit the mold of many early female seminaries "as small, ephemeral, academically unchallenging and therefore of little importance to the history of women's education."[18] Rather, it was a transitional institution—beginning, as did many late eighteenth-century private schools,

Fig. 3.2. Litchfield Female Academy, 1798. Courtesy of the Collection of the Litchfield Historical Society, Litchfield, Connecticut.

with one teacher and offering a few academic and ornamental courses, and gradually expanding to include a full staff of teachers and a curriculum that foreshadowed the development of the female seminary movement. Sarah Pierce was not an accomplished musician, but she recognized the importance of including music instruction in the curriculum, maintaining the same high standards for musical performances as she did for academic subjects.[19]

Emma Hart Willard and Troy Female Seminary (1821)

Emma Hart Willard (fig. 3.3) was destined to become a pioneer in women's higher education.[20] She saw herself as born for a special purpose ordained by God, a mission that would require her to move outside the accepted boundaries of "women's sphere."[21] Willard received many accolades for her work in education in general and for her revolutionary work in women's education in particular.

Emma Hart had a thirst for knowledge; by age twelve she was teaching herself geometry. Her family's interest in education and literature, and the instruction she received in the district and public schools in Berlin, Connecticut, continued to whet her appetite. She began teaching school at seventeen in her hometown village of Lower Lane and alternated teaching engagements between periods of furthering her education. In 1807 she accepted responsibility for the Middlebury Female Academy in Vermont.[22] While there she became aware of the discrepancy in instruction offered for women compared to that available for men at Middlebury College.[23] Hart perceived it as an unjustifiable inequality.

Two years later Emma married Dr. John Willard, twenty-eight years her senior, who had withdrawn from an esteemed medical practice for a career

Fig. 3.3. Emma Hart Willard (1787–1870). Courtesy of Emma Willard School Archives, Emma Willard School, Troy, New York.

in politics and public office. Although Emma cheerfully fulfilled her domestic duties, she continued to study to qualify herself as her husband's companion, investigating his medical library, exploring physiology and geometry, and reading Locke's "Essays Concerning Human Understanding."[24] John's nephew lived with them while attending Middlebury College. After studying his textbooks, she asked him to examine her progress; he found she had mastered the material. This encounter with instruction provided for young men further opened her eyes concerning educational deprivations of her sex. Pondering these setbacks, she searched for a solution.

Following the War of 1812, Emma decided to open a boarding school in her home to contribute to the family finances and to establish a better school for women than those in the vicinity. Sarah J. Hale, editor of *Godey's Lady's Book*, attested that Emma Willard was raising women's education to a level heretofore unattained in the nation.[25] One year later Willard realized the need to establish a school to train teachers and argued that women were as intellectually competent as men, limiting women's inferiority to physical capabilities.[26] Further, she claimed that the combination of domestic training with a "college" education would equip young women to work in a suitable profession and enable them to be better teachers and mothers.[27]

In order to fully acquaint herself with the academic standards and teaching methods at Middlebury College, Willard requested permission to attend the examination exercises. Not only was her appeal denied, but her students were not allowed to audit college courses. Rather than accepting this as a negative affirmation of women's intelligence, she taught the same subjects to herself and then to her students.[28] An anonymous author writing in the February 1893 issue of the *Journal of Education* claimed that Willard's school at Middlebury had launched a permanent revolution in women's education, but not without extreme opposition:

> It was in Middlebury that she inaugurated a work that will go forward so long as civilization shall endure. Her success was all the more praiseworthy because of the inertia and conservatism of the times. Many of the noblest, most godly men of the day believed it revolutionary. It was openly denounced as a crazy freak everyway detrimental to the public good. What was to become of fireside peace and religious tranquillity if women learned science and Greek. Many otherwise clear-headed, large-hearted men honestly thought that the designs and will of God would be frustrated if women became learned. It is a well-authenticated tradition that one devout farmer exclaimed, "Well, if they are going to educate the girls I shall expect to see them educate the cows!"[29]

Obviously, much of society feared women would become discontent with their positions in the home if allowed to receive a higher education. However, according to historian Colleen McDannell, women were the religious teachers of their children and needed a knowledge of history, geography, and chronology to instruct biblical truths.[30]

PLAN FOR IMPROVING FEMALE EDUCATION

During 1817 and 1818, Willard became desirous of establishing a school with the same support in administrative positions and the aid of legislative bodies enjoyed by many men's colleges in the country. According to John Lord, Willard's first biographer, no other female schools at that time had legislative supervision and support. Confident of women's intellectual capabilities, she began to devise her plan of education.[31] Lord claimed that her *Plan for Improving Female Education* was "the foundation of the female colleges of this country." Whatever her school would be called, "in all essential respects it was a college." As Lord argues, Willard's proposal for educating the "female mind to the utmost perfection of its nature" was "in harmony with the educational notions of the great thinkers of antiquity." Furthermore, using superior "method[s] of instruction" would render "better wives and mothers."[32]

Willard intended her plan to convince the public that current methods of women's education needed revision. Although the idea of a seminary shared a natural association with a college, she alleged that this school would be unlike institutions for men, given that the character and duties of women differed.[33] She addressed four main topics in her plan: (1) problems with the current mode of women's education, (2) recommendations for a new system of education, (3) the plan for a female seminary, and (4) the benefits to society from such schools.[34] Willard contended that women should be educated by their own sex, since they would understand their students' physical limitations, cultural expectations, and domestic obligations.[35] Furthermore, if "housewifery" was regarded as a profession and received a solid education, she argued, it would make women's sphere appealing even to the upper class.[36] Willard also addressed the necessity of boarding schools in her plan. Given the status of many schools—temporary institutions founded by individuals to make money—they could provide neither suitable accommodations nor proper instruction.[37]

Willard worked on her plan for several years, not informing her husband until one year after it was completed. She feared being viewed as a woman ahead of her time: "I knew that I should be regarded as visionary almost to insanity, should I utter the expectations which I secretly entertained in connection with it. But it was not merely on the strength of my arguments that I relied. I determined to inform myself and increase my personal influence and fame as a teacher, calculating that in this way I might be sought for in other places, where influential men would carry my project before some legislature, for the sake of obtaining a good school."[38] Although Willard recognized that many people would not understand her dedication to women's higher education, she forged ahead.

Emma Willard began to search for a name for the school she envisioned in her plan, but given that women were not allowed to attend college, she elected not to call it one. The name came to her as she heard a Dr. Merrill pray for "our seminaries of learning."[39] She decided, "I will call it a Female Seminary. That word, while it is as high as the highest, is also as low as the lowest, and will not create a jealousy that we mean to intrude upon the province of the men."[40] Thus, "Female Seminary," adopted by Willard, gradually became associated with institutions of higher learning for young women.[41]

In 1818 General Jacobus Van Schoonhoven, a wealthy citizen of Waterford, New York, whose adopted daughter attended Willard's school in Middlebury, encouraged Willard to send her plan to Governor DeWitt Clinton of New York.[42] Later that year, she published it at her own expense in a pamphlet titled *An Address to the Public; Particularly to the Members of the Legislature of New York, Proposing a Plan for Improving Female Education.* The following year she sent it to other prominent men, including President James Monroe, Thomas Jefferson, John Adams, and various members of Congress.[43]

In the spring of 1819 General Van Schoonhoven and several leading citizens encouraged Willard to move her school to Waterford.[44] The residents showed their endorsement by appointing a board of trustees who leased the Mansion House—a large three-story brick building regarded as the finest in Saratoga County—for the seminary. The time seemed appropriate for Willard to solicit help from the New York legislature. In addition to Governor Clinton's support, she received favorable comments from principal statesmen. After moving to Waterford, she had an opportunity to read her plan to several influential members of the legislature and on one occasion to a large group of people.[45] Addressing her views on women's higher education, she "was probably the first woman lobbyist," yet she astounded her audiences "as a noble woman inspired by a great ideal."[46] Flattering comments for her efforts and Governor Clinton's appeals, however, were not sufficient to break down barriers in the legislature. Although the Senate passed a bill granting her school two thousand dollars, it failed in the lower house. Willard found the decision devastating: "To have had it decently rejected, would have given me comparatively little pain, but its consideration was delayed and delayed until the session passed away. The malice of open enemies, the advice of false friends, and the neglect of others, placed me in a situation mortifying in the extreme. I felt it almost to frenzy; and even now, though the dream is long past, I cannot recall it without agitation. Could I have died a martyr to the cause, and thus have insured its success, I should have blessed the fagot and hugged the stake."[47] A false sense of encouragement proved to be more overwhelming to Willard than if influential men had never initially given their approval.

Nonetheless Willard became well known through her plan, which was distributed across the country and abroad.[48] It established the standard of schooling for women and had a profound influence on future developments in women's education. Historians regard it as a seminal document in the history of American culture, outlining a prescribed set of principles and beliefs so convincingly that it "has appropriately been called the Magna Carta of women's education."[49] Willard's *Plan for Improving Female Education* ranks alongside Mary Wollstonecraft's *Vindication of the Rights of Woman*, published twenty-seven years earlier.[50]

MOVE TO TROY, NEW YORK

In 1821 several prominent men of Troy, New York, urged Willard to move her school to their city and offered financial assistance. Given that the lease for the building in Waterford expired in May, and monetary provision to renew it was not forthcoming from either the citizens of Waterford or the state legislature, Dr. and Mrs. Willard accepted the offer. Troy was one of the most thriving cities outside of New England; its forward-looking industrialization with cotton mills, nail factory, paper mill, soap factory, tanneries, and potteries made it a major manufacturing center in the United States.[51]

On March 26, 1821, the common council of Troy initiated a special tax to raise four thousand dollars to purchase or construct a suitable building for the seminary. Private subscriptions provided additional monies needed for purchase and repairs.[52] Never before had Willard witnessed patrons demonstrate enthusiasm so efficiently.[53] Since the building was not ready for occupancy, classes were taught in the lecture room of the Troy Lyceum of Natural History. With renovation completed in September, the seminary found its permanent home centrally located in front of the square and adjacent to churches and public buildings (fig. 3.4).[54] By 1846 the main building had been enlarged twice.[55]

Fig. 3.4. Troy Female Seminary. Courtesy of Emma Willard School Archives, Emma Willard School, Troy, New York.

The seminary attracted distinguished visitors to this interesting American experiment in women's education. General Lafayette, for example, was an honored guest during his visit to the United States in 1824 and 1825 and offered high compliments to Willard and the seminary. The news of his visits spread quickly and greatly enhanced the seminary's reputation. He spoke avidly in France of this "unique" venture in female education.[56]

Emma Willard had a vested interest in every part of the seminary, including organizing the curriculum, selecting the books, and prescribing the menu.[57] She determined that the school would be the best institution for women's education in the country and offered a curriculum that was equal but pedagogically superior to that found in New England men's colleges.[58] The seminary soon achieved a legendary reputation; some students enrolled for a brief period under the influence of the school's name.[59] Like Sarah Pierce, it appears Emma Willard was not an accomplished musician, although she maintained that music was a vital part of a young woman's education and wrote texts for some of the songs performed at the school.[60]

Mary Lyon and Mount Holyoke Female Seminary (1837)

Mary Lyon (fig. 3.5), educator, author, and founder of Mount Holyoke Female Seminary, South Hadley, Massachusetts, grew up in a strong Christian

Fig. 3.5. Mary Lyon (1797–1849). Courtesy of Mount Holyoke College Archives and Special Collections, South Hadley, Massachusetts.

environment in Buckland, Franklin County, Massachusetts. From childhood she was interested in the welfare of others—a characteristic that would apparently consume her throughout her life.[61] According to her first biographer, close friend, and member of the initial board of trustees of Mount Holyoke Female Seminary, the Reverend Dr. Edward Hitchcock, she was "remarkable for a solidity of mind and sobriety of deportment rarely found in the volatile season of youth." She also possessed an unusual sense "of the ludicrous, and a power of humorous description," making her a coveted and honored friend.[62]

EDUCATION AND TEACHING PURSUITS

Although Lyon's family was known for intelligence and scholarship, her opportunities for formal education were limited. From the time Lyon could walk one mile to the district school, she attended when it was in session and then only occasionally after the school moved two miles away. In order to continue her education, she found it necessary to reside with families in Buckland and to work as an assistant for her board. Little is known of Lyon's early career except that in 1814 she began teaching summer school for children, presumably in her native village, where she "boarded round."

She took her first teaching job near Shelburne Falls, Massachusetts, in 1817, launching a new chapter in her life that alternated with periods of teaching and advancing her own studies.[63]

In the fall of 1817 Lyon entered Sanderson Academy at Ashfield, paying for her schooling with the meager sum she earned from housekeeping for her brother and from spinning and weaving. Her capability as a student became evident: "Her whole appearance at that time was so unique, her progression in study so unprecedented, her broad intelligent face so inviting, that no one who was then a member of the academy will ever forget her; nor how the scholars used to lay aside their books when she commenced her recitation. . . . In the rough specimen, they [her friends] could see a diamond of uncommon brilliancy, and knew that it needed only to be polished to shine with peculiar luster."[64] Early on she earned the respect of fellow scholars for her tenacity. Lyon's finances were soon depleted; she seriously considered returning to her previous employments when the trustees of the academy offered her free tuition. She resolved to pursue a teaching career and sold all of her possessions to pay for room and board. As a devoted scholar, Lyon spent her waking hours studying, taking hurried meals. The greater the challenge, the more she attained. News of her educational preparation spread, and she began to receive requests to teach.[65]

Lyon furthered her studies at Amherst Academy, where she studied chemistry with the renowned Amos B. Eaton.[66] In 1821, at age twenty-four, she moved to Byfield, near Newburyport, Massachusetts, to attend Rev. Joseph Emerson's female seminary.[67] Lyon's roommate described her zeal for studying as "gaining knowledge by the handfuls."[68] While attending Emerson's seminary, Lyon became increasingly aware of the true purpose of education: that of preparing one to be useful to society. She was challenged by the unequal opportunities for men and women and by the need to advance the education of her own sex.[69] After two terms she returned to the Sanderson Academy and became an assistant teacher—the first woman to hold this position at the school and the only female teacher employed.[70]

Mary Lyon served as Zilpah Grant's assistant at the Adams Female Academy in Derry, New Hampshire, during the summers from 1824 through 1827.[71] This school was possibly the first endowed institution for women in the country and the world and was the first female seminary in America to grant diplomas to its students.[72] Since the school was not in session from November to April, Lyon returned to Buckland or Ashfield to teach during the intervening months.[73] Even after Grant moved the school from Derry to Ipswich, Massachusetts, in the spring of 1828, Lyon taught at Ipswich during the summer and at Buckland in the winter. After two years it proved too difficult for Lyon to continue teaching at both schools, and thus she devoted herself to Ipswich for the next four years—a pivotal choice in her career advancement.[74]

WORK AT IPSWICH FEMALE SEMINARY

Lyon spent most of her time and energy at Ipswich as assistant principal. Her duties included assigning roommates, helping with admissions, arranging and attending recitations, counseling young teachers, keeping order in the seminary building, and acquainting herself with the character, progress, and needs of each student. Grant's health required that she take sabbaticals periodically, during which she relinquished the seminary's leadership to Lyon.[75]

Although Lyon prized the opportunity of working at Ipswich, she found the high tuition fees a detriment to advancing women's education. Many of the Ipswich students came from affluent families, while those of lesser means could not attend.[76] In response to this dilemma, she wrote: "My thoughts have turned not to the higher, not to the poorer, but to the middle classes, which contain the main-springs and main wheels which are to move the world. My heart has yearned over the young women in the common walks of life, till it has sometimes seemed as though a fire were shut up in my bones."[77] Empathetic to their situation, Lyon resolved to find a solution.

COMMITMENT TO WOMEN'S HIGHER EDUCATION

In 1832 she gave up the idea of marriage and devoted all of her attention to the advancement of female education.[78] In a letter to the Reverend Professor Hitchcock of Amherst, dated February 4, Lyon confessed, "Could I be permitted to labor in the portico, and spend my days in clearing the ground for that which is destined to continue, and to exert an extensive and salutary influence on female education and on religion from generation to generation, it would be the height of my ambition."[79] She relentlessly gave of herself in plowing new ground. During the summer of 1833, for example, she traveled by stagecoach as far as western New York and Detroit to discuss her ideas with women and educators. On August 9 she called on Emma Willard during a one-night stay in Troy. The trip must have been physically taxing, some days traveling up to fifty miles, as well as overnight journeys.[80]

In the fall of 1834, Lyon relinquished her duties at Ipswich in order to dedicate herself full time to founding a permanent seminary. Since together she and Grant could not establish an endowed institution at Ipswich, Lyon decided she could accomplish more on her own than remaining with Grant.

Realizing the tremendous hurdles to overcome if such an institution were to be established, she commented, "I do believe such a work will be effected at some future day, perhaps some twenty or fifty years from this time." She claimed that she was involved in an endeavor for God: "I never had a prospect of engaging in any labor, which seemed so directly the work of the Lord as this. It is very sweet, in the midst of darkness and doubt, to commit the whole to his guidance."[81] Lyon was a devout Christian, committed to establishing a seminary with a solid religious foundation.

Traversing the same path Emma Willard had previously covered, Lyon came to the same conclusion: in order to have a school where women could receive an education comparable to that of men, an endowment was essential.[82] "The cost of a single year in the better girls' schools of the time was often twice that of a man's entire college course."[83] Lyon set strategic goals to bring her plan to fruition: her seminary would not begin in a private home but should commence as an endowed institution through individual petitions.[84]

FOUNDING OF MOUNT HOLYOKE FEMALE SEMINARY

The seeds for Mount Holyoke Female Seminary were sown on September 6, 1834, when a few invited gentlemen gathered in Lyon's parlor to hear her plan for the proposed institution. They appointed a committee to begin work on the project until a permanent board of trustees could be formed.[85] Within two months Lyon had collected one thousand dollars from various sources for the new venture, which expressed her passion as well as the interests of many benefactors.[86]

The committee hired the Reverend Roswell Hawks as permanent agent. Traveling through Massachusetts and Connecticut, he strove to awaken the public to the need for such a seminary and to solicit funds for the land and building.[87] Lyon became involved with numerous details, including composing letters and circulars, and often accompanied Reverend Hawks as he traveled about the country.[88] Fund-raising efforts revealed the public's negative attitudes toward women's education, which Lyon admitted to be extremely trying "because I knew that my reasons for doing it were not understood."[89] She persistently knocked on doors and was usually cordially received but at other times rudely rejected. Rather than being discouraged by refusals, they seemed to strengthen her resolve. In her estimation "every donor was a prospective student, not naturally in person, but in influence." Each donation was important, whether it was five or fifty cents or one or one thousand dollars.[90]

Like Pierce and Willard, Lyon established herself as an unusual woman for her time. Reputable publications included derogatory comments regarding her plan. The Reverend Dr. Hitchcock found some of the disparagements so unkind that he offered to defend her but never received permission.[91] Rather than retaliate, Lyon responded, "I am doing a great work. I cannot come down. . . . No one can be more sensitive to such criticisms. I feel them keenly, . . . but I receive them as a severe yet indispensable test of my character."[92] Even the best men of the times could not comprehend the views of a woman with unselfish motives. While they might otherwise approve of such a school, they feared it would not endure. In discussing her plan with Professor Emerson of Andover, he remarked, "Who shall he be that cometh after the King? Will it not die with you?" Lyon replied, "No, it will not, we shall raise up our own teachers and it will go on."[93] Lyon had the foresight to see that her efforts would be fruitful.

On January 8, 1835, the committee confirmed South Hadley as the location, provided the pledged amount would be increased to eight thousand dollars. The following April 15, the seminary was named. On February 10, 1836, the school was incorporated; the governor signed the charter the following day. The first cornerstone of Mount Holyoke Female Seminary was laid on October 3, 1836, with religious ceremonies.[94] On September 6, 1837, nearly three years after the first meeting in her parlor, Lyon wrote, "Our building is going on finely. The seal to everything is soon to be fixed. My head is full of closets, shelves, doors, sinks, tables, etc." Mount Holyoke Female Seminary opened its doors on November 8, 1837 (fig. 3.6).[95]

Fig. 3.6. Mount Holyoke Female Seminary. Courtesy of Mount Holyoke College Archives and Special Collections, South Hadley, Massachusetts.

Orramel Whittlesey and Music Vale Seminary (ca. 1835)

Unknown to most scholars and musicians today, Music Vale Seminary, the first music conservatory in the nation and established for women, was founded in Salem, Connecticut.[96] The history of Music Vale is entwined with the biography of Orramel Whittlesey (fig. 3.7), composer and founder of the school. Whittlesey grew up in Salem, Connecticut, where he and his brothers Henry and John worked in their father's ivory factory during their youth.[97] From an early age they were interested in learning to play the piano but studied under adverse circumstances. Their mother supported them; their father, initially unsympathetic, later helped them buy a "crude second hand piano."[98] Since Mr. Whittlesey found their practicing offensive, the boys had to practice between 8:00 P.M. and 2:00 A.M. in a small shed removed from the house. They traveled some distance to take weekly lessons, arriving home at 5:30 A.M. for breakfast and farm chores.[99]

Whittlesey and his brothers began building pianos in Salem in 1826. Soon thereafter they attempted, but failed, to establish a business in New York City. After marrying Charlotte Maconda Morgan (1805–1865) that year, Orramel and his brothers moved to Buffalo and began manufacturing pianos. The brothers apparently excelled as piano builders, doing all of the fine workmanship—hand sawing the ivories, inlaying mother-of-pearl letters and ornamentation in cabinet design (fig. 3.8). Seven years later they moved the business back to Salem, closer to New York City (the principal market for their pianos), and in their amiable hometown environment.

Fig. 3.7. Orramel Whittlesey (1801–1876) and Music Vale Seminary Faculty, 1865. Courtesy of William Schultz, Salem Historical Society, Salem, Massachusetts.

Fig. 3.8. Whittlesey Pianos. Courtesy of William Schultz, Salem Historical Society, Salem, Massachusetts.

The move back to Salem proved beneficial to Whittlesey, who had obtained some measure of fame as a local musician. Shortly after his return, families from Salem and the nearby towns of Norwich and New London began requesting his services as a music teacher. Whittlesey soon became more interested in teaching than in building pianos; his immediate success attracted students from beyond the vicinity.[100]

FOUNDING OF MUSIC VALE

Orramel Whittlesey had no intention of establishing a school or accepting students as boarders until two young women arrived on a stormy night in 1835 and insisted on hospitality: "Well, we have come to study with you and you can't send us back [on] such a night like this."[101] By the following spring twelve students had come to study with Whittlesey.[102] The date for the seminary's founding is uncertain: 1835 when Whittlesey first accepted boarding students; 1836 on a memento; 1838 on a school photograph; and 1839 on a diploma.[103] Initially it was called "Mr. Whittlesey's Music School." Sometime afterward Whittlesey renamed it "Music Vale Seminary and Academy of Music" and finally "Music Vale Seminary and Normal Academy of Music."[104]

SALEM AND MUSIC VALE

The rural village of Salem, Connecticut (thirty-two miles from Hartford and thirteen miles from Norwich and New London), was Music Vale's home for forty-one years.[105] Although Salem might seem a remote location for a school, it was not as secluded as one would suppose. New London and Norwich, both on the Thames River, "were open to commerce brought on the high seas from exotic places," importing "silks and spices from the Orient, and treasured things from Europe."[106] The flourishing farming community, with its blacksmith shops, gristmills, and sawmills, proved to be beneficial to the school's location—a safe and peaceful environment away from larger towns. The seminary and the grounds appeared to be more homelike than a boarding school—an ambiance that readily ingratiated itself to parents and young women.[107]

The oldest building at Music Vale was likely Whittlesey's house. As the student body increased, it became necessary to add accommodations. In 1839 the school erected a two-story structure "with a steeply inclined roof, topped by one stout chimney." Further additions were constructed in 1845 (a building to the north) and 1849 (a building with a tower and a barn), and ten years later the concert hall was built. At least six cottages were used as practice rooms, each with an outside entrance so that the student and instructor would not be disturbed. Names were painted on each door—for example, "Arbor," "Cottage," "Retreat," or "Boudoir."[108]

It seems unlikely such a school would be found in a farming community. Yet Music Vale commanded a respect of its own and included a farm of approximately one hundred acres. Whittlesey managed the farm "in a scientific manner." The crops provided a variety of fruits and vegetables for the Music Vale family.[109]

In 1868 a horrific fire destroyed the building; fortunately no one was harmed.[110] Students helped to save various items, including silver pieces and seven pianos. The loss was estimated at fifteen thousand dollars, with only five thousand dollars recovered from insurance. Whittlesey spared no expense in immediately rebuilding at a cost of forty thousand dollars. He proudly displayed a golden harp weather vane on a large flagpole; two bronze lions guarded the entrance, and a bronze deer added to the beauty of the well-manicured grounds.[111] It was a decided improvement, with one hundred rooms—a pleasing structure for any institution or town (fig. 3.9).[112]

The elaborate concert hall, designed by a New York architect, had no equivalent in eastern Connecticut. Frescoes ornamented the walls and ceilings, decorative boxes stood on either side of the stage, and there was a small gallery at the rear. Ornate curtains added to the sophisticated design: one displayed the Arch of Titus, with a faint scene of the Tiber, steeples, and towers; the other was a replica of Music Vale. Concerts and staged productions made Music Vale a popular gathering place.[113]

Fig. 3.9. Music Vale Seminary, 1868. Courtesy of William Schultz, Salem Historical Society, Salem, Massachusetts.

Whittlesey was also involved in law and politics, serving as a member of the House of Representatives and the senate of Connecticut. Despite his demanding schedule at Music Vale, he took time to represent local farmers in the legislature and served as judge of probate.[114] Further, Whittlesey was recognized by contemporary distinguished musicians and teachers. Nathan Richardson, revered author of *The Modern School for the Piano-Forte*, had a high regard for Whittlesey and Music Vale and offered his services and use of his name as a means of support.[115]

In addition to numerous teaching responsibilities and directing the operations of Music Vale, Whittlesey found time to compose a considerable amount of music—piano, vocal, and opera. His music could be purchased at the seminary, Oliver Ditson's music store in Boston, and J. E. Gould and Company in New York.[116] Some of his compositions, including staged productions, were performed at Music Vale.[117]

Music Vale Seminary soon achieved distinction as a first-class music school, attracting visitors from nearby towns and from a distance, who came to witness some of the finest music-making in the United States during the mid-nineteenth century. Whittlesey was appalled at the unsatisfactory musical standard in the nation—"playing a little of everything, but nothing well"—and desired to graduate teachers who would help elevate the level of music teaching:[118] "We believe that a great deal of the value that has been placed upon Music, as a mere accomplishment, had been owing to the fact that it is made such, by so many who pursue it. It is not looked upon *as a science to be studied*, over which years may be spent with *pleasure and profit*, but as a mere amusement for an idle hour."[119] He was likely referring to the philosophy of music as taught at finishing schools. Contrary to the instruction received at these popular schools, Music Vale's intentions were "not to make merely superficial players . . . but thorough pianists, skilled alike in theory and practice."[120] This intense emphasis on music instruction was unheard of during the mid-1800s.

Whittlesey embraced the saying of famed English statesman William Pitt II, "If it be that I have done so much, it is that I have done one thing at a time," as the school's philosophy.[121] Initially Music Vale provided only piano instruction; voice was added by 1849, and harp, guitar, melodeon, and organ by 1855. Although Whittlesey only required students to study piano, he encouraged them to take advantage of other instruction offered at Music Vale, since it would be beneficial in obtaining employment.[122] The full name of the school at that time was "Music Vale Seminary and Normal Academy of Music."[123] The normal department comprised the "Piano Teachers' Graduating Course," which included thoroughbass and composition; other theory courses were added later.[124] The year the Connecticut State Board of Education authorized Whittlesey to confer a normal or "teaching" degree on graduates is unknown. Nevertheless it was a boon to its already high standing; for many years no other school enjoyed this distinction.[125] In 1854 Governor Henry Dutton praised Whittlesey for the excellent education offered at Music Vale: "I am passionately fond of Music, and believe that when properly taught it promotes refinement and morality. I feel proud that Connecticut can boast of so fine an institution. If you think my name will be of any use to you, it is at your service."[126] Testimonials came from other prominent citizens of Connecticut, validating the seminary's reputation. Governor William A. Buckingham provided timely praise after the Civil War:

Norwich, July 4th, 1865

From what I know of the principles upon which your Seminary is established, and of your character for adhering to those principles, I can commend it to public favor. If by reference to me I can be of any service it will give me great pleasure.[127]

When the Civil War began, Whittlesey installed a "Liberty Pole" near the highway; the Stars and Stripes displayed his support for the Union. He also housed a small brass cannon at Music Vale, fired whenever the North gained a victory. In addition, he formed an organization at the school known as the Ladies' Loyal Union League of Music Vale Seminary.[128] The members drew up a formal pledge and set of rules at its first meeting, on June 6, 1863, promising unwavering loyalty to the Union. Although Whittlesey's commitment stands to reason (his son-in-law John T. Maginnis, Eliza's husband, was killed in the conflict), the league was not a financial benefit to the seminary.[129]

Music Vale prospered until the Civil War. A depressed economy and Whittlesey's staunch support of the Union led to a substantial decrease in the number of students from the South and the West. Further, Mrs. Whittlesey, an integral member of the staff, died in 1865. With the devastation of the war and increased competition from other conservatories being established in large cities, it never regained the prestige it once enjoyed. Whittlesey's health declined, and his second daughter, Sarah (Mrs. George Pratt), assumed leadership. There is some discrepancy as to when the school permanently closed: 1876, 1878, or 1879.[130]

Conclusion

Examining the biographies of Pierce, Willard, Lyon, and Whittlesey, along with the histories of their respective schools, reveals the significance of these educators and institutions in the development of women's higher education. With the exception of Music Vale, these schools were founded by women who today would be classified as visionaries. Individually the contributions of the founders are momentous; collectively their work was a major force in women's education. Given that the Moravian Young Ladies' Seminary was founded fifty years prior to these other pioneering schools, and its reputation for prestigious music and academic curricula, it should be considered a cornerstone of women's education. Nor can Music Vale be overlooked in its importance in helping to establish music as an integral part of a young woman's education.

4

Seminary Structure

A Comparison

An examination of the personnel, student body, admission and retention, and organization of Litchfield, Troy, Mount Holyoke, and Music Vale reveals both similarities and differences. Each school became well recognized as an institution of women's higher education (in the case of Music Vale, a first-class music conservatory). However, diverse cultural environments had profound effects on government, the number of staff and faculty employed, and board and tuition.

Personnel

Founders of the better female seminaries realized the necessity of having a board of trustees (a board of visitors at Music Vale) in order to succeed. Many of the so-called finishing schools were business ventures, managed by proprietors seeking to profit. A board of trustees, however, had a different purpose. As Emma Willard explained, "A judicious board of trust, competent and desirous to promote its interests, would, in a female as in a male literary institution, be the corner-stone of its prosperity."[1] While Troy and Mount Holyoke were initially placed under boards of trustees, it is uncertain when the board of visitors became part of Music Vale's organization. In 1827, hoping to counter a decline in enrollment, Litchfield was incorporated as Litchfield Female Academy and placed under the jurisdiction of ten board members.[2] The boards that presided over Troy, Litchfield, Mount Holyoke, and Music Vale consisted of five to fourteen professional men (clergymen, businessmen, and attorneys), usually from the area of the school they administered.[3] As early as 1836, Troy's mayor and recorder began to appear regularly on the list as ex officio members. In addition the Troy board of trustees appointed a "Committee of Ladies," who periodically met with Willard on school concerns.[4] Perhaps the board decided such a committee was necessary to ensure that students' needs were being met.

STAFF

The number of personnel at each institution varied depending on its operating system, finances, and the availability of qualified employees. Litchfield and Music Vale began with a meager staff, Mount Holyoke opened with a slightly larger number, and that at Troy was even greater. Sarah Pierce served as administrator and sole teacher when Litchfield was established. Apparently Pierce's two older sisters, Anna and Susan, occasionally assisted her. By the early 1800s, a half-sister, Mary Pierce, served as an assistant and took charge in Sarah's absence. She continued in this capacity until 1814, when John P. Brace, Pierce's nephew, joined the staff as co-principal and teacher. Mary Pierce supervised the students who boarded with the Pierce sisters and served as the school's business manager.[5]

As with Litchfield in its early days, Music Vale depended on Orramel Whittlesey to serve as administrator and instructor. His wife acted as domestic supervisor and financial adviser. Originally she did not favor accommodating students in their home, having a "genteel horror of boarders," and thus denied many requests. Yet Mrs. Whittlesey became a mother-like figure to the "daughters" away from home and in return was admired by the pupils.[6] The position of vice principal was added sometime before 1858. Sarah Whittlesey, the second daughter, filled this position for several years.[7] Beginning in 1863, Eliza Whittlesey (Mrs. John T. Maginnis, the oldest daughter) likewise served in that capacity in addition to teaching. Six years later Whittlesey employed his youngest daughter, Karolyn, as second vice principal as well as teacher.[8]

Mount Holyoke and Troy operated under a board of trustees who had an avid interest in women's education and the government of the schools. Unlike Music Vale, Mount Holyoke opened after significant planning. Troy was initially founded in Middlebury, Vermont; later moved to Waterford, New York; and finally made its home in Troy.

When Mount Holyoke opened in 1837, its personnel consisted of the principal (Mary Lyon), an assistant principal (Eunice Caldwell), two teachers, three students serving as assistant pupils (teaching assistants), and a supervisor (Miss Peters) of the domestic department. Miss Peters stayed only a few months; rather than finding an outside replacement, Lyon chose two pupil assistants, "General Leaders," to co-supervise the work, especially the cooking.[9] Since one of Lyon's main purposes in founding Mount Holyoke was to provide education for middle-class women, she determined that the school would be conducted on a tight budget. Although the board of trustees gave Lyon permission to hire her own staff, she did so judiciously.[10] Lyon served as the principal of the seminary until her untimely death in 1849. Mary C. Whitman, who joined the faculty in 1839 and became an associate principal in 1842, accepted the principal's position but soon resigned because of failing health. At that time Mary W. Chapin, who had been on the faculty since 1843, assisted by an unnamed colleague, assumed the duties of acting principal. In 1852 the board appointed Chapin as principal, a position she retained for twelve years. Sophia D. Stoddard accepted the position of acting principal in 1865. It was common for the seminary to employ one or two associate principals, although some catalogs do not mention anyone filling this position.[11]

When Emma Willard moved her school to Troy, New York, she decided upon the personnel necessary for the seminary to operate efficiently. The faculty and staff consisted of a principal, vice principal, business manager, and physician, along with domestic superintendents, teachers, and assistant teachers. Dr. John Willard (Emma's husband) served as the business manager and school physician until his death in 1825, after which Emma assumed the responsibility of business manager in addition to her duties as principal.[12] Emma Willard served as principal from 1821 to 1838, except for 1830 when her sister, Almira Hart Lincoln, held this position during Willard's sabbatical in Europe.[13] Around 1829 Willard sought assistance in administering the school and engaged Lincoln as vice principal. In 1832 Lincoln was replaced by Nancy Hinsdale and Sarah L. Hudson.[14] In 1838 Willard relinquished her position as principal to her son, John, and his wife (Sarah L. Hudson, whom he had married in 1834).[15] Theodosia Hudson (sister of Sarah Hudson Willard) was hired in 1841 to assist Nancy Hinsdale, who continued as vice principal until 1851.[16]

INCREASE IN STAFF AND FACULTY

The number of staff and faculty increased at each institution in order to keep pace with rising enrollment and changes in curriculum. Litchfield and Music Vale continued to have the smallest faculties; Troy had the largest, although Mount Holyoke was close behind. The largest number of teachers at Litchfield, recorded in 1825, was five: Sarah Pierce and John P. Brace; Mrs. L. E. Brace, an assistant; drawing teacher Mary W. Peck; and music teacher George R. Herbert.[17] A paucity of documentation makes it difficult to determine when Whittlesey began to hire other teachers at Music Vale. Each of the Whittlesey daughters, Eliza, Sarah, Jennette ("Nettie"), and Karolyn ("Katie" or "Kate") served on the faculty at various times.[18] In 1851 Eliza was the only other instructor besides her father. Six years later, however, there were five teachers called "assistants" (apparently not students, as referred to at other institutions), and in 1869 (when Music Vale had its largest faculty) there were six teachers in addition to the principal and the first and second vice principals (see fig. 3.7 for a faculty photograph).[19]

During Lyon's tenure at Mount Holyoke (1837–1849), the number of teachers, including Lyon, ranged from four in 1837 to nineteen in 1844, with an average of thirteen to sixteen. Following Lyon's death in 1849, the number of teachers varied from sixteen to twenty in 1857 and increased to twenty-two or twenty-four between 1859 and 1865.[20] In 1828 Troy employed thirteen teachers and officers.[21] By 1847 there were eighteen teachers and two domestic instructors.[22] As of 1865 there were twenty-eight teachers, including two principals and one vice principal.[23]

In order to maintain high standards, the principals were selective in their choice of teachers. Although Lyon was a devout Christian and emphasized more religious training than was provided at Litchfield, Troy, or Music Vale, she did not require any specific religious affiliation of the faculty members other than that they should be Christians.[24] Likewise, Mount Holyoke employed only women as full-time teachers. Troy and Litchfield hired both men and women, while Whittlesey was the sole male teacher at Music Vale. Whittlesey required his teachers to have an advanced education; most had several years of teaching experience. Lyon and Willard preferred to hire teachers they had trained to teach the academic courses. When Willard moved her seminary to Troy, a number of teachers accompanied her, most of whom she had instructed, along with "accomplished" professors who taught the modern languages, painting, and music. At that time it would have been financially prohibitive to employ educated male professors to teach all subjects.[25] The two teachers employed during the first year of Mount Holyoke were graduates of Ipswich Female Seminary in Ipswich, Massachusetts; thereafter Lyon chose Mount Holyoke graduates as teachers. She selected only those who had been good students, dedicated to the seminary, capable, and eager to work.[26]

ASSISTANT TEACHERS

In order to meet the demand for teachers, Litchfield, Mount Holyoke, and Troy chose some of the best students to serve as "assistant teachers" in addition to attending their own classes.[27] In the early years of Litchfield, Pierce began to have some advanced students teach music, art, and needlework, courses in which she lacked proficiency.[28] Mount Holyoke appointed current students to serve as teaching assistants, who often taught such subjects as vocal music, drawing, Latin, and French.[29] Some years there were as many as four teaching assistants, while other years only one or two; in 1856 and 1862 there were none. Additional students were chosen as "Candidates for Teachers."[30]

Pupils at Music Vale who had done exceptional work and possessed leadership skills served as student officers: superior, premier, and monitress.[31] Twice a year the pupils nominated the superior and premier officers, subject to Whittlesey's endorsement. He selected those for the position of monitress.[32] To further signify this honor, the superior, premier, and monitresses wore special regalia.[33] The number of student officers apparently varied according to the number of teachers, size of the student body, and number of qualified students to fill these roles. In 1857, for example, in addition to six faculty, a superior, premier, and four monitresses were chosen, while in 1869 there were nine teachers but only three student officers: superior, premier, and monitress. It seems probable that having fewer student officers can be attributed to a decrease in the student body, undoubtedly a result of the Civil War. In 1857 the number of each was the same, but in 1863 and 1869 the number of students was one-third that of the faculty.[34]

TEACHERS' RESPONSIBILITIES

Teachers had demanding loads. In addition to academic teaching at Mount Holyoke, for instance, each teacher was required to perform extra duties such as hearing recitations, supervising the study and reading rooms, doing library and domestic work, monitoring hallways or the visiting room, teaching calisthenics, and helping to care for students in the sickroom. If capable of teaching drawing or singing, these were added to her load. The number of extra duties and hours varied weekly, ranging from 17 to 58 1/2 per week.[35] Perhaps the number of academic classes increased during the weeks her additional duties were reduced. Some teachers also had charge of a "section" of pupils and received an extra forty dollars in annual compensation.[36]

There was a large turnover among the faculty at Mount Holyoke. Marriage, health issues, and heavy workloads forced many to leave their positions temporarily or even permanently. Mary Q. Brown, who joined the faculty in 1850, wrote to her mother shortly after the school year had begun concerning the demands of her job: "I know my health will never hold out. No one that has never tried them, can tell anything at all about the duties of a teacher here. It is a *constant* wear & tear, no cessation whatever."[37] Apparently Brown did not return the following year, as her name is not listed in the catalog.

Student Body

Each institution attracted a diverse student body depending on its location, expenses, courses offered, and socioeconomic status. According to tradition, Litchfield opened in 1792 with 1 student; Music Vale had 2, Troy, 90, and Mount Holyoke, 116. The peak enrollment at Litchfield occurred in 1816 with 157 students, after which attendance began to decline.[38] Mount Holyoke experienced its highest enrollment in 1847 with 235 students chosen from over 500 applicants, while the largest enrollment at Troy occurred in 1853 with 414 students.[39] The student body continued to grow at Music Vale until the Civil War; the average number of students was 80, and some years there were as many as 100 pupils.[40] It was common for the schools to receive more applications than they could accept; often they had to put students' names on waiting lists. Mount Holyoke requested that students apply to the principal around the first of October preceding the beginning of the next school year. Students making later applications risked refusal for lack of room. The general character and educational background of each young woman, as well as the timing of her application, were taken into account; those denied for lack of room were given priority the next year.[41] By at least 1851 Music Vale applicants were advised to make written applications to the principal; they would be notified when a vacancy occurred.[42]

GEOGRAPHIC DIVERSITY

Only Mount Holyoke did not accept day scholars in addition to boarding students. One of the most remarkable features of Litchfield was the number of nonresident students. A majority of the students beyond Litchfield had associations with people in the town or in the state: many came because they could board with relatives or friends; others had a parent or relative who had attended the academy or Judge Tapping Reeve's law school; and some had brothers currently enrolled in the law school. Distinguished local names proved helpful in attracting daughters from other elite families. Because of the town's nationwide reputation, by 1802 only 11 percent of the student body was from Litchfield; 25 percent came from outside the state. Students came from Connecticut, New York, Georgia, Massachusetts, and the islands of West Indies. Eventually the school attracted young women from nearly every state in the Union as well as from Upper and Lower Canada, Ireland, and the West Indies.[43]

Like Litchfield, most of the students attending Music Vale came from outside Connecticut.[44] As Whittlesey's reputation spread beyond the local communities, Music Vale attracted young women from a wider geographical area, including the Carolinas, Kansas, Kentucky, Nova Scotia, and the West Indies. In its heyday, nearly one-half of the students were "genteel beauties from the south."[45] Although Troy drew pupils from every part of the nation, Canada, and the West Indies, a large number were often day students. Of the 222 students enrolled in 1831, for example, 103 were from Troy.[46] Young women attending Mount Holyoke came from across the nation, including the Sandwich Islands (Hawaii), American Indian reservations, and foreign countries (Canada, India, Turkey, Ceylon, China, Borneo, and Holland).[47] Most of the student body, however, came from rural New England and the state of New York; nearly one-half of the pupils were from Massachusetts.[48]

STUDENTS' AGES

The varied ages of the student body reflected the family's status. Those from upper-class homes tended to begin school at an earlier age and remained longer, and with less frequent periods of absence, than those of lesser means. Older students often came from less privileged homes, where limited assets allowed them to attend only brief summer sessions at town-supported schools. Many women among these students wanted to become teachers; some were already teaching in a town school. Because of their ages and experience, these pupils frequently served as assistant teachers while attending Litchfield.[49]

There does not appear to have been a specific age for admission to Litchfield or Music Vale, and no age requirement was in place at Troy until 1865. Unlike other women's seminaries and academies, Mount Holyoke's minimum admission age of sixteen was comparable to that of applicants to regional men's colleges.[50] Pupils could be as young as six or as old as their mid-twenties when they enrolled at Litchfield Academy; the majority were between thirteen and sixteen.[51] No documentation exists to indicate students' ages at Music Vale. Given the intensity of the program, it seems likely that the pupils would have been at least in their teens. Although Willard's *Plan for Improving Female Education* suggests students would not be ready to enter the seminary until about age fourteen, no age was specified in Troy catalogs until the 1865–1866 academic year, when the school required students to be at least seven years old. The average age was seventeen, though many older women enrolled, some of them young widows wanting to further their education.[52] Mary Lyon's objective was to educate mature young women; thus, Mount Holyoke reserved space for older pupils.[53] In 1845 a student in the junior class wrote to a friend that many of her classmates were between twenty and thirty but looked older. She doubted whether more than twenty were younger than seventeen.[54] By 1846 the preferred age limit for entrance was seventeen or eighteen.[55] Those entering the senior class in 1860 were required to be at least eighteen.[56] The senior class was intended for young women who could demonstrate exceptional emotional and mental maturity. In order to achieve educational benefits in this class, Mount Holyoke encouraged prospective pupils to postpone this part of their education if possible.[57]

GENDER AND CLASS

Litchfield was unique in that it accepted male students. Since records of male pupils were not kept until 1817, it is not possible to determine exactly how many attended. After that year twelve boys were enrolled. The number of male students peaked in the summer of 1822 with twenty-six; there were only two in the summer of 1828. There were never more than five males in one term from outside Litchfield. All of the male students who came from out of town either had a connection with someone in Litchfield or accompanied their sisters to the academy.[58]

Although Lyon founded Mount Holyoke specifically for women of the middle class, some students from the lower and upper classes did enroll. It appears that many of the students who attended Litchfield or Music Vale were from the upper-middle or upper class. While Troy catered to the upper class, it also accepted students from lower classes.[59] Leading families of the nation were eager to place their daughters under the tutelage of Emma Willard—a woman who had attained much fame.[60] The fathers of some of the students who attended Litchfield and Troy were judges, governors, lawyers, congressmen, ministers, physicians, or businessmen. Writing about the Troy student population, biographer Alma Lutz names daughters of several governors: Van Ness of Vermont, Cass of Michigan, Worthington of Ohio, and Skinner of Georgia, in addition to three nieces of Washington Irving (Effie, Catherine, and Sarah) and a niece of Mary Wollstonecraft.[61] Well-known names on enrollment charts at Litchfield included the Livingstons, the Gardiners, and the Delafields, all of whom can be traced back to the "long-established pre-Revolutionary English 'aristocratic' or 'manor' families of New York State."[62] Without the patronage and support of prominent and well-to-do families, it is unlikely that Pierce's school would have achieved its reputation and permanence as a foremost female institution.[63]

No information is available regarding the economic level of students at Music Vale. Given that daughters of many families in the United States during Music Vale's existence would have been fortunate to receive a higher education, it seems the school must have attracted students from the upper-middle or upper classes. Further, Whittlesey's aid in the students' preparation and initial admittance aligned with a higher class status. He made it as convenient as possible for students to arrive at Music Vale in a notice titled "Directions for THE JOURNEY" with specific travel instructions and promised a warm welcome.[64]

Unlike the other educators, Mary Lyon's primary goal was to establish an institution of higher learning for young women who, like herself, could not otherwise have afforded an education. The majority came from families who could pay only a modest sum for their daughters' education, and such schools as Troy Female Seminary likely would not have been considered. Lyon made special arrangements to accommodate those whose finances did not allow them to pay for board and tuition. More than any other institution, Mount Holyoke succeeded in providing a higher education for young women from families whose real estate was valued at no more than three thousand dollars.[65]

Admission and Retention

There was a significant variation in the admission and retention requirements at Music Vale, Troy, Litchfield, and Mount Holyoke. Music Vale appears to be the only institution to require an endorsement validating the student's character. Young women who were not acquainted with a current student or a member of the faculty needed to bring a letter of recommendation from a minister or leading citizen of their village as an introduction to Whittlesey.[66]

The length of the academic year was forty to forty-eight weeks.[67] Pupils were admitted at Troy, Litchfield, and Music Vale anytime during the year, while Mount Holyoke required students to be present at the beginning of the fall term.[68] Troy required its students to remain through the examination held at the close of each term, while Mount Holyoke expected them to stay through the academic year, including the public examination and anniversary exercises, unless prior arrangements had been made upon entrance.[69] No student was admitted to Music Vale for less than one term. Litchfield had no such requirement; the majority of students stayed only one or two semesters, although some stayed for two to four or more years.[70] Most of the pupils with the longest attendance were from the town and had enrolled at an early age. It was common for young women to transfer to other female schools. At least thirteen students enrolled at Troy after leaving Litchfield.[71]

Music Vale, Troy, and Mount Holyoke proposed programs with designated lengths of time for students to complete their education. Whittlesey maintained that students attending Music Vale could complete the course in one school year. Willard purported that the allotted time for a pupil to complete her education would be three years but could extend to four or more, depending on the number of electives the parents and guardians chose for their daughters or wards to pursue. However, if a student had previously studied any of the subjects offered at the school, she might enroll in a higher class, perhaps reducing graduation time by one or two years. Mary Lyon also constructed a three-year program, which was expanded to four years in 1860.[72] Lyon was aware that some who entered the junior class would not have the finances, time, or discipline to finish the program.[73] Given existing views on women's education, she faced opposition in retaining the one-year requirement.[74] She disliked the practice of a student moving from one school to another, even between schools with comparable academic standards.[75]

Mount Holyoke set a new standard for women's higher education, requiring entrance examinations and initiating a probationary period.[76] Every pupil had to pass comprehensive entrance examinations on all preparatory studies in order to be admitted into the junior class.[77] Students frequently had difficulty passing these examinations and were either forced to return home or placed in a remedial class until they could demonstrate proficiency.[78] In 1847 Emily Dickinson noted that "quite a number . . . left, on account of finding the examinations more difficult than they anticipated." She explained that Mary Lyon had increased the standard of the entrance examination to eliminate students who were not prepared to pursue a collegiate education. Dickinson continued: "You cannot imagine how trying they [the examinations] are, because if we cannot go through with them all in a specified time, we are sent home. . . . I am sure that I never would endure the suspense which I endured during those three days again for all the treasures of the world."[79] Candidates desiring admission to the middle or senior classes needed to pass examinations on all preparatory studies and on "as many branches of the regular course as shall be equivalent to a full preparation."[80] Each year Lyon admitted an average of twenty students for advanced standing either in the middle or senior classes. In addition, returning students were required to take examinations on their studies from the previous year. A probationary period at the beginning of the school year allowed seminary personnel to ascertain whether any students lacked discipline or maturity. Those deficient in either area were sent home for their own betterment as well as that of other students.[81]

DOMESTIC WORK

Unlike the other institutions, Mount Holyoke students performed domestic duties to reduce tuition and to promote a family atmosphere. Lyon argued that domestic work should not be mistaken for manual labor, which was then popular among contemporary schools, yet she faced strong opposition to her plan well before Mount Holyoke opened its doors. In a letter to Hannah White, dated August 1, 1834, Lyon wrote: "You know it has become very popular for our highest and best seminaries for males, to be moderate in the expenses. . . . But how different it is with regard to female seminaries. Even at the present time, almost the middle of the 19th century, do not many value our high female seminaries according to their expenses? Is it not popular, & rather gratifying to young ladies to attend expensive seminaries when perhaps their brothers would rather glory in being able to pursue their studies at a moderate expense?"[82] It was difficult for many to appreciate the value of higher education for women obtained at a reduced cost through housekeeping duties.

Mary Lyon concluded that domestic work would weed out problematic students: "The domestic work would prove a sieve, that would exclude from the school the refuse, the indolent, the fastidious, and the weakly, of whom you could never make much, and leave the finest of the wheat, the energetic, the benevolent, and those whose early training had been favorable to usefulness, from whom you might expect great things."[83] Lyon was as judicious regarding the students she admitted as the teachers she employed.

Rather than detract from education, the domestic requirement proved beneficial: it reduced the operating costs enough to allow students to live in campus housing instead of residing with local families, created additional exercise, improved students' health, and provided a tonic for homesickness and despondency.[84] Each student received an assignment with which she was familiar and worked from thirty to sixty minutes daily.[85] Lyon did not propose that students learn new domestic chores; she insisted that the home provided the best place for this, with the mother as the appropriate teacher. Lyon did not intend to replace a mother's responsibility in teaching her daughter domestic duties, thus removing any suspicion that education would make a woman unfit for her role in life.[86]

EXPENSES

Many parents financially sacrificed to send their daughters to Litchfield, Troy, Music Vale, or Mount Holyoke. Table 4.1 provides a comparison of

Table 4.1. Annual Expense Chart

Year	Litchfield	Troy	Mount Holyoke	Music Vale
1823	$180–$200	$200		
1835		$240		
1851		$200	$60	$180
1855		$200	$75	$200
1865		$300	$125	$300

the expense to attend each institution.[87] The minimum figure often covered only board and tuition. The earliest record at Litchfield is a bill addressed to Susan Masters in 1805, which covered twenty-one weeks' tuition ($7.00), school expenses ($.33), and entrance fee ($1.00). In 1819 the tuition fee was $6 per quarter (twelve weeks). By 1823 a student studying music and painting in addition to the regular course of study and boarding could expect to pay a minimum of $180 to $200.[88] Troy's cost was higher. In 1823, $200 covered only board and tuition in academic subjects. Because of inflation, Willard found it necessary in 1835 to raise the fee to $240, while five years later a reduction reflected an economic depression.[89] The cost of board and tuition remained the same from 1840 until 1863, when it increased to $280 per year. In 1865 the price increased by $20 per year, or $150 per term. "Extra" courses, such as music, painting, drawing, and languages, could significantly drive up the cost. For example, in 1865 a student enrolled in extra courses could pay as much as $500 per year.[90]

Although Orramel Whittlesey did not view Music Vale as a business venture and was not interested in making a profit, the cost of board and tuition there was comparable to that at Troy. Daughters of clergymen and missionaries received liberal discounts—one-fourth of the expenses. The same privileges were granted to widows and daughters of soldiers who died in the war. Whittlesey also encouraged students to remain the full school year by offering a substantial discount. In 1855, for example, the fee per quarter (eleven weeks) was $58; should the pupil remain all four quarters, the charge would be only $200, a savings of $32. In addition, there was no extra charge for instruction in voice, thoroughbass, counterpoint, composition, voice, guitar, harp, melodeon, organ lessons, or for instrument use.[91] By at least 1863, expenses increased by $50 per term (twenty weeks).[92]

Since Mary Lyon hailed from central New England, she was aware of the need for an institution for middle-class students in that area. To help reduce financial strain, she established Mount Holyoke in the vicinity to minimize travel expenses. She strove to help young women whose circumstances required them to be self-supporting, setting the board and tuition at two-thirds the cost of higher education at schools such as Ipswich and Troy. Initially the board of trustees set the fee at $64 per year. Against the board's recommendation, she made it more affordable by reducing the fee to $60 per year.[93] The cost of tuition remained the same for sixteen years; the seminary raised it to $68 per year in 1854. There was an increase each of the following two years and again in 1863; it began to rise annually thereafter.[94] Unlike Troy, Litchfield, or Music Vale, there was no additional fee for elective courses at Mount Holyoke.

Conclusion

An examination of the structure at Litchfield Female Academy, Troy and Mount Holyoke Female Seminaries, and Music Vale Seminary is telling on many levels. Though the institutions shared some similarities, the cultural context and goals for each school had a distinct effect on its government, personnel, and student body. The setting for Litchfield Academy, a town known for its professional and social status, created an environment that appreciated and supported women's higher education. This elitist group, along with the prestige of the law school, helped the academy to attract students from the upper levels of society. By the time Emma Willard moved her school to Troy, she had achieved an exalted reputation for her work in women's higher education. The support of city officials and the citizens of Troy enabled Willard to operate the institution envisioned in her plan, one that would provide an optimal education for women at the collegiate level.

Mary Lyon succeeded in managing Mount Holyoke on a reasonable budget that allowed women to obtain a higher education. Admission prerequisites and domestic duty requirements were a major distinction between Lyon's seminary and those at Litchfield and Troy. Music Vale, like Litchfield and Troy, appealed to women of the higher class. Further, it was unique in offering an intense one-year program that trained women to teach music on a professional level.

The cultural contexts and structures of these four institutions are crucial to understanding the academic and music education they provided. An examination of the curricula they offered reveals that music education at these schools was valued as more than a mere social accomplishment.

5

Curricula

Academic and Ornamental

The founding of Litchfield Female Academy, Troy and Mount Holyoke Female Seminaries, and Music Vale Seminary was revolutionary in providing women the opportunity to obtain a deeper and broader level of knowledge than had been taught at common and private schools focusing on rudimentary instruction or finishing schools aimed at making a woman marketable for marriage. Educational leaders were aware of the weaknesses in many schools, which offered too many subjects with superficial instruction.[1] Litchfield, Troy, and Mount Holyoke achieved renown for curricula that closely mirrored the education offered at men's colleges such as Brown, Dartmouth, Amherst, and Williams.[2] An examination of the academic and ornamental curricula at these female institutions illuminates both the value placed on a solid education within the acceptable realm for women and the distinctiveness of each school. Since the public examination exercises were a highlight at the close of the school year and testify to the high standards of each institution, including Music Vale, a comparison of these events affords another window on the educational privileges for women.

By the end of the eighteenth century, most young women still had little opportunity for an advanced education. Thus it was left for educators like Sarah Pierce, Emma Willard, and Mary Lyon to break new ground in the development of women's higher education. They maintained that women were men's intellectual equals and deserved an equivalent education, albeit within their accepted sphere.[3]

While Litchfield, Troy, and Mount Holyoke endeavored to provide women with a solid academic education, each school served a disparate purpose.

Pierce was adamant that students attending Litchfield should receive an education for genteel society as well as for a useful life. Willard contended that young women should be educated to "enter the teaching profession, a profession which she considered highly proper for young ladies and well-suited to their abilities."[4] Lyon's objective was to provide education for middle-class women, training them to be missionaries or teachers, and to perform domestic duties.

Level of Curricula

Students enrolling in these institutions would have been expected to demonstrate a prescribed academic proficiency obtained at town, common, or private schools or taught at home by a parent or other relative. Mount Holyoke appears to have been the only institution to require entrance examinations; students deficient in any subject were sent home or placed in remedial classes until they could pass the examination that granted admission into the junior class. When formulating the plans for Mount Holyoke, Mary Lyon determined to offer an education comparable to that of the sister schools: "The course of study, and standard of mental culture will be the same as that of . . . the Ipswich Female Seminary—or of the Troy Female Seminary—or of some other institution that has stood as long, and ranked as high as these seminaries."[5] Rather than offer a smattering of courses to appear impressive, Pierce, Willard, and Lyon labored intensively to develop their students' intellectual abilities.

Troy, Mount Holyoke, and Litchfield upheld high scholastic principles. According to Harriet Beecher Stowe, Pierce insisted that Litchfield not offer "trashy or sentimental" subjects typically found in female schools.[6] Lyon was aware that many students who attended Mount Holyoke could not afford to stay long enough to graduate and thus tried to impart the "key of knowledge," enabling them to continue their studies after leaving school.[7]

Organization of Curricula

The curriculum was divided into classes, such as junior, middle, and senior. Litchfield's program was divided into three "divisions" sometime after 1814 when Pierce's nephew, John P. Brace, joined the faculty as co-principal. By 1823 Troy's curriculum was organized into two classes, expanded to three in 1865. Lyon initially proposed a thorough and graded English (academic) course of studies to be completed in three years; in 1860 a fourth year was added to the program: junior, junior middle, senior middle, and senior.[8] Students were promoted to the next class depending on their progress rather than the length of time they spent at the seminary. It appears the course requirements for each class could be completed in one year at these institutions; however, no specific number of years was stipulated. The length of time a student remained in one class depended on her progress. Students often found it necessary to spend two years to complete the requirements for the junior class in order to prepare for upper-class subjects.[9]

Mary Lyon organized the Mount Holyoke curriculum so that students focused on two or three major subjects simultaneously for a series of six to ten weeks. The academic year was divided into four or five series. The first four weeks were allocated for review and examinations; the remaining thirty-six weeks were devoted to regular classes divided by subject. Apparently Litchfield and Troy operated under a less structured environment, allowing the students to study several subjects concurrently.

Mount Holyoke required its students to pursue each class in a prescribed order, regardless of whether they planned to graduate or to remain at school solely for one year.[10] It seems that Litchfield allowed students to choose the courses and order from those designated for their class level unless they intended to graduate, in which case they were expected to follow a set program. There does not appear to have been a fixed schedule of courses at Troy. Students attending Mount Holyoke had the option of taking additional courses, such as Latin, which could delay advancement to the next class.[11]

Academic Curricula

The academic curriculum referred to the "solid" or "English" subjects with "intellectual content" that had practical applications, such as English grammar, history, geography, and mathematics. Each institution introduced courses while retaining or deleting others to maintain a cutting-edge curriculum. It was common for institutions during this time to identify courses according to the textbook author's surname—for example, *Day's Algebra*.[12]

When Pierce founded Litchfield in 1792, she laid the groundwork for the female seminary movement that followed thirty years later. Although her knowledge was limited to the education she had received, she expanded the curriculum as broadly as she was able; it was left to Brace to take it to new heights, helping to set the school apart as an "outstanding female academy."[13]

An examination of the academic courses offered at Litchfield, Troy, and Mount Holyoke reveals the standard of curricula for women's higher education as established by Pierce, Willard, and Lyon. Compared to Troy and Mount Holyoke, the amount of information pales for Litchfield, making it difficult to determine the extent of its curriculum during the academy's forty-one-year history. Nevertheless, similarities and differences are apparent among the three institutions, including the introduction and deletion of courses, especially at Troy and Mount Holyoke.

ENGLISH AND LITERATURE

Given that students needed to be educated about how to hold intelligent conversations or write letters, Mount Holyoke, Troy, and Litchfield emphasized English grammar, reading, spelling, rhetoric, and composition.[14] Parsing (identifying and describing the grammatical parts of speech) was an important part of the students' English education at Litchfield. Brace and Pierce contended that it helped the students to conquer the difficulties of the English language, claiming that, along with spelling and vocabulary, it was beneficial "to exercise the faculties of the mind" and to develop "the nice habit of discrimination."[15] The first sentence of Milton's *Paradise Lost* (sixteen lines; no verb or subject until the sixth line) was frequently used as a parsing exercise. By 1847 parsing was one of the prerequisites to enter the junior class at Mount Holyoke;[16] undoubtedly the same would have been expected at Troy.

All three schools stressed writing, requiring the students to write weekly compositions. Litchfield students wrote "dissertations" of four to ten pages, while compositions by Mount Holyoke students frequently surpassed twenty pages. Some students at Mount Holyoke also wrote poetry that was periodically published in *The Casket*, a school magazine containing "literary jewels."[17] The length of compositions is not apparent at Troy; however, given the examples included in the examination reports, they would have been similar to those at Mount Holyoke.[18] Willard stressed neatness, requiring the girls to rewrite their compositions, copying them "carefully in their neatest handwriting."[19] The seminary included writing in every course when appropriate, along with such exercises as analyses and abstracts.[20] Testimonies found in annual examination reports demonstrate that some students excelled in composition.

Some courses remained part of the curricula, while others were offered for a moderate or short length of time. Rhetoric, for example, was taught at Mount Holyoke and Troy from the outset through 1865 and appears to have been a staple course at Litchfield. Penmanship was first available at Troy in 1849 and continued through 1864, and Mount Holyoke periodically paid a writing instructor to teach the "niceties of penmanship in an age which made much of this art."[21] Troy offered dictation from 1828 through 1834; Mount Holyoke did not introduce its Analysis of the English Language course until 1860.

Litchfield did not offer formal literature classes, but Pierce encouraged students to read a wide variety of novels and writings concerning women's education. She sought to acquaint her pupils with the literature of respected British authors such as Hannah Moore, Mary Wollstonecraft, Lord Lyttleton, and Sir Charles Grandison.[22] Milton's *Paradise Lost* was offered as early as 1838 at Mount Holyoke, although literature courses were not added until the 1840s: History of Literature (1843) and History of English Literature (1846).[23] Troy introduced English Literature in 1848; Shakespeare's dramas provided material for oral readings, practiced to perfection and read before an audience.[24] Given that elocution was part of the regular curriculum, these performances must have been a feast for the ears.[25] Unlike those attending Troy or Litchfield, students at Mount Holyoke had opportunities to participate in rousing debates on contemporary issues, such as matrimony versus celibacy and the equality of men's and women's intellectual abilities.[26]

Apparently neither Pierce nor Brace had taken courses in literature, which negated including it in the curriculum. However, Litchfield students performed plays written by Sarah Pierce, such as "Ruth," "The Two Cousins," and "Jephthah's Daughter," at the close of a school term, such performances being a tradition at that time in Puritan New England.[27] The plays must have been demanding, since no other studies or obligations were conducted during preparation or performances. Pierce left nothing to be desired, as Lyman Beecher confirmed: "A stage was erected, scenery was painted and hung in true theatre style, while all wardrobes of the community were ransacked for stage dresses."[28] The public was impressed by the excellent staging and acting.[29]

HISTORY AND GEOGRAPHY

Along with English grammar and composition, the study of history and geography remained part of the core curricula at Litchfield, Troy, and Mount Holyoke. Pierce underscored the importance of these subjects as venues for "educating the intellectual, the moral, the spiritual, the social and the artistic facets of her students."[30] Willard concurred with this philosophy, convinced that through studying historical events, students would be better prepared to make appropriate moral decisions for themselves and for their families.[31] Lyon also emphasized these subjects, given that she required "a good knowledge" of the history of the United States and modern geography as a prerequisite to enter the junior class at Mount Holyoke.[32]

Pierce and Willard soon became dissatisfied with the textbooks in print and resolved to write their own. Pierce published the first volume of *Sketches of Universal History Compiled from Several Authors for the Use of Schools* in 1811, followed by a second volume in 1816, a third in 1817, and a fourth in 1818.[33] Willard gained recognition for her *History of the United States or Republic of America* (1828) and *Universal History* (1837), as well as her collaborations with William Woodbridge—for example, *Woodbridge's and Willard's Geographies and Atlas*, published in 1822.[34]

From the outset students were educated in history and geography, from the ancient world through modern times. Willard, Pierce, and Lyon used history and geography as a means of expanding their curricula; for example, Litchfield offered study of the American Revolution by 1821 and various branches of natural history no later than 1827. Universal Geography was introduced at Troy in 1825, Geography of the Heavens in 1832, and Universal History in 1834. Chronography was introduced in 1849, two years before Willard received a medal at the World's Fair of London for her time maps, "Temple of Time," and *Chronographer of Ancient and English History*.[35] Astronography (astronomical geography) was added in 1855, perhaps because Willard had published *Astronography or Astronomical Geography, with the Use of the Globes* the previous year.[36] Mount Holyoke likewise presented specialized topics, such as studies of France, and Greece, Rome, and England in 1828; a Political Class course in 1837; and Political Economy in 1838.

MATHEMATICS

It appears that mathematics had a slow introduction at Litchfield compared to Mount Holyoke and Troy. No instruction in any mathematical subject is documented until the early 1800s when James Brace, Pierce's brother-in-law, taught ciphering (arithmetic).[37] Apparently students entering the first class at Troy could study basic arithmetic, since no level is stipulated.[38] Mount Holyoke, however, had strict arithmetic admission requirements from the start; students needed to demonstrate their knowledge of "Colburn's First Lessons and the *whole* of Adam's New Arithmetic, or what would be equivalent in Written Arithmetic" in order to enter the junior class.[39] The entrance examinations began with arithmetic, which many students dreaded; those who were deficient were sent home or enrolled in a remedial class until they could pass the examination.[40]

Emma Willard maintained that advanced mathematics was a definitive landmark of women's higher education and argued it would help train the mind so that women would be capable of solving their problems "on the basis of abstract truth." Further, she opined that since women were beings of feeling and impulse, the study of mathematics could aid a woman in reasoning and clear judgment.[41] Pierce and Brace also maintained that the study of mathematics would intensify women's intellectual capabilities and aid them in becoming independent.[42] Lyon likewise supported higher mathematics and continued to increase the admission requirements.[43]

After John Brace was employed in 1814, he raised the level of instruction to include advanced mathematics.[44] By 1821 students intending to graduate were required to complete "arithmetic through interest," and Brace taught algebra by 1827.[45] Mount Holyoke offered algebra and Euclid (geometry) from the beginning but delayed trigonometry until 1860. Troy, however, initially offered Elements of Geometry, added algebra two years later, and introduced trigonometry as early as 1848. The school continued to maintain a solid mathematics curriculum as evinced in the report of the 1858 examining committee: "The Committee were peculiarly gratified to have another additional proof to the many already in their possession, of the ability of the female mind to master the higher branches of the mixed Mathematics. It is ardently hoped, . . . that the time is not far distant when the pure Mathematics, also, in their differential and integral beauties will meet with a hearty welcome to the Troy Female Seminary, demonstrating to the world, that America, as well as the British Isles, can produce her Somervilles."[46] As the committee witnessed, women were capable of mastering higher mathematics, and Troy Female Seminary deserved praise for its instruction.

SCIENCE

The sciences did not become established in the curricula of schools and colleges until the 1820s and 1830s; thus, Litchfield gave little attention to this area until Brace joined the faculty in 1814.[47] Willard added the sciences at the suggestion of renowned scientist Amos B. Eaton (senior professor at the Rensselaer School, later known as Rensselaer Polytechnic Institute, in Troy), with whom she and her sister, Almira Lincoln, studied. Eaton assumed the responsibility for this department at Troy, perhaps giving the lectures for an additional fee, until women were qualified to offer instruction.[48] Natural Philosophy was the only science course available when Troy opened its doors in 1821. One year later students could pay an extra fee to attend lectures on botany and chemistry, but these were not included as individual courses in the tuition covering academic instruction until 1837.[49]

People in different areas of the country, especially the South, argued that science should not be part of women's education, claiming it was pointless and impossible for women to understand.[50] Nevertheless, Brace, Pierce,

Lyon, and Willard included it as an essential part of their curricula. Prior to Brace's departure from Litchfield in 1832, he was eager to broaden the sciences, offering courses in astronomy, botany, chemistry, entomology, mineralogy, and natural philosophy—areas in which Pierce had not been educated.[51] Lyon had a particular affinity for the sciences, having studied with Professor Eaton. Thus, it is not surprising that she heavily weighted the curriculum at Mount Holyoke with the sciences—astronomy, botany, chemistry, geology, natural philosophy, and physiology—from its inception in 1837.[52] Troy added geology and physiology in 1842 and astronomy in 1846 and introduced some sciences not taught at Mount Holyoke, such as Circulation of the Blood, 1846; and Hydrostatics (a branch of physics) and Optics (studies with light), 1850.

In addition to the courses, guest speakers periodically supplemented the instruction. On January 31, 1844, Professor Edward Hitchcock began a series of lectures for the entire Mount Holyoke student body on human anatomy and physiology, using a full-size mannequin that could be disassembled to display the different organs. The teachers then held discussions of his lectures in small groups. Physiology became regarded as one of the most exceptional courses offered at Mount Holyoke.[53] Troy likewise augmented the classes with noted scholars; for example, the 1843 catalog emphasizes the lectures as an added attraction: "Extensive Courses of Lectures are annually delivered by Professors, on Chemistry, Natural Philosophy, Geology, Botany, Astronomy, Physiology."[54] This seems unusual for women's higher education in the 1840s. According to historian Anne Firor Scott, the seminary was soon regarded as unique among the female seminaries for its science instruction.[55]

Philosophy and Religion

Courses on the difficult subject matter of philosophy and religion were not deemed appropriate for junior class (or first class) students. In the late eighteenth and early nineteenth centuries, only female institutions offering rigorous and advanced education included Moral Philosophy in their curricula. Litchfield did not introduce this subject until sometime after Brace became a faculty member.[56] It was initially included at Troy and Mount Holyoke and taught through at least 1865. American men's colleges made Moral Philosophy a requirement in the senior year, considering it "the capstone" of students' education; likewise Mount Holyoke and Troy reserved it for upper division classes.[57]

The study of philosophy was combined with psychology, as presented at Troy and Mount Holyoke. Such subjects, including Intellectual Philosophy, were taught at Mount Holyoke from 1837 to 1839 and then replaced by Mental

Philosophy for the middle or senior classes. Students of the second class at Troy studied Philosophy of the Mind, first offered in 1823.[58]

Given the dearth of documentation, it cannot be determined if Litchfield offered courses in philosophy other than Moral Philosophy, although it is certain that Pierce emphasized formal religious education, teaching sacred history and incorporating Christian doctrine in such subjects as history, geography, and the sciences whenever possible. Further, the Rev. Lyman Beecher taught the weekly religion course during the fourteen years (1810–1824) he lived in Litchfield.[59]

Emma Willard and Mary Lyon also wanted their students to be grounded in philosophy and religion. Lyon was a devout Puritan and emphasized religious training at the seminary. Willard likewise viewed religious education as a priority, although it was not given the same emphasis at Troy as at Mount Holyoke. Evidence of Christianity and Theology, both courses taught from the first year, remained part of the core curriculum for middle or senior class students at Mount Holyoke and for those of the second class at Troy. Ecclesiastical History and Analogy were taught from the outset and continued as part of the studies for the middle class at Mount Holyoke; Troy introduced Analogy for the second class in 1848, offering it until at least 1865.[60]

Thoroughness in philosophy and religion as taught at these schools undoubtedly equaled the instruction available at other institutions of higher education. A review of the 1861 examining committee's report at Troy reveals the serious attention given to Analogy, Theology, and Mental and Moral Science: "The power of original thought displayed by the graduating class, and the ready manner in which they met and answered objections, and responded to questions suddenly propounded by the committee would have done honor to the senior class in our highest colleges."[61] Although such reviews are not available for Litchfield and Mount Holyoke, the same could unquestionably be said of these schools given the emphasis placed on intellectual education.

Additional Subjects

All three institutions offered courses in aesthetics, identified by such titles as Elements of Criticism and Principles of Taste. Perhaps aesthetics was considered an appropriate subject for educated women who would have been expected to understand and appreciate beauty and degrees of the senses. Litchfield offered Taste and Elements by 1821; Troy introduced Elements of Criticism in 1823, and Mount Holyoke followed in 1838.

Logic, concerning thinking and reasoning, was undoubtedly recognized as an important subject for young women to study. Although various courses were frequently deleted or added, Logic was one that remained many years in the curricula at Troy, Litchfield, and Mount Holyoke.

While the academic curricula are similar in many respects at the three schools, some courses were offered at only one institution. Troy, for example, began teaching bookkeeping in 1848. Perhaps Troy's reputation as an industrial center influenced the seminary's curriculum; women needed instruction in accounting in order to help with their husbands' businesses. Students attending Mount Holyoke in 1838 and 1839 were offered instruction in Alexander Young's "Night Thoughts," a widely admired poem covering the topics of "life, death, loss, and immortality." Such a course reflects the emphasis placed on the brevity of life, a common concern at the time.

Foreign Languages

Troy offered instruction in more foreign languages than Mount Holyoke and Litchfield; Mount Holyoke taught French and Latin, whereas students at Litchfield had the option of studying French, Latin, and Greek. Troy, however, provided instruction in French, Italian, Latin, Spanish, and German.[62] Given that refined women should know how to speak a little French, it was common for it to be taught at schools offering a "finishing" education; thus, it is not surprising that Troy, Litchfield, and Mount Holyoke included this subject in their curricula. Initially Troy charged an extra fee, while it appears French was included in the tuition at the other two institutions.[63] Willard claimed that the study of languages was easier for young people to master; therefore, in 1833 she offered a reduced fee for French to parents and guardians who entered their daughters or wards in the seminary at a young age (unspecified) and would keep them at the school for an extended time.[64] She obtained a French teacher from Paris in order to ensure that the students would learn correct pronunciation. By 1848 the French teachers lived with the students to assist them with conversational French. In addition, history and rhetoric were taught in French, natural philosophy and botany were translated from English into French, and students also gave recitations in French.[65] Abigail Moore, Mary Lyon's niece, taught French for nine years at Mount Holyoke, and in 1843 a native French teacher, Edward Church of Northampton, Massachusetts, gave an additional twenty-four lessons in conversational French. After 1846, assistant pupils were largely responsible for teaching French.[66]

Since the Renaissance, Latin has been deemed the "traditional language of the learned scholar" and was thought to be especially useful in training the mind.[67] Brace occasionally taught Latin and Greek, but according to historian

Lynne Templeton Brickley, it is likely that only a few students took advantage of these classes. In 1846 Troy changed Latin from an elective to a required course for the first class. Initially Latin was optional at Mount Holyoke; however, the trustees and faculty highly recommended it to students for its mental discipline in preparation for advanced courses. Although they suspected that members of the community would disapprove, by 1845 it became a requirement. Latin began as an introductory course; within three years students were required to have a basic knowledge of the language upon entering the seminary. Mount Holyoke also introduced courses on such writers as Cicero, Virgil, and Cornelius Nepos or Sallust, emphasizing the importance of Latin.[68] See table 5.1. for a comparison of academic subjects taught at the schools.

Table. 5.1. A Comparison of Academic Subjects at the Schools

Title of Subject	LFA (1814)	LFA (1833)	TFS (1821)	TFS (1837)	MHFS (1837)	MHFS (1847)
Algebra				X	X	X
Analogy					X	X
Ancient and/or Modern History		X			X	
Ancient Geography				X	X	
Arithmetic	X		X	X		
Astronomy		X			X	X
Botany					X	X
Chemistry	X	X			X	X
Ecclesiastical History					X	X
Elements of Criticism/ Principles of Taste	X	X	X	X		
Elements of Moral Science				X		
Euclid					X	X
Evidences of Christianity				X	X	X
Geography	X	X	X	X		
Geology				X	X	
Geometry			X	X	X	
Grammar	X	X	X	X	X	X
History	X	X	X	X		X
Logic	X	X	X	X		X
Moral Philosophy	X	X	X	X		X
Natural Philosophy	X	X	X	X		X
Philosophy of the Mind			X	X		
Reading	X	X	X	X		
Rhetoric	X	X	X	X		X
Theology				X		
Trigonometry						X
Writing Compositions	X	X	X		X	

The dates in the table correspond to significant developments at the schools:
1814—John P. Brace joined the Litchfield faculty and expanded the curriculum
1833—Litchfield closed
1821—Troy Female Seminary was founded
1837—Mount Holyoke was founded, with a comparison of courses also offered at Troy
1847—Mount Holyoke's curriculum ten years later

Ornamental Curricula

Rather than focusing on academic subjects, finishing and private schools of the late eighteenth and early nineteenth centuries emphasized instruction in ornamental subjects—needlework, painting, drawing, instrumental and vocal music, and dancing—an education that would enable young women to enter genteel society and make them marketable for marriage.[69] Given that Pierce founded the Litchfield Female Academy in 1792, she realized the importance of including instruction in the ornamentals to attract students, especially considering the professional society of Litchfield. In addition, such offerings were financially profitable for the academy and could help graduates secure teaching positions. Nevertheless, it became challenging to balance the retention of ornamental subjects that were of practical value with an intense academic program. Pierce's attempt to combine ornamental and academic branches was a pioneering effort for future educators.[70]

There was a distinct difference in the number and type of so-called ornamental subjects offered at Litchfield, Troy, and Mount Holyoke. For example, Litchfield was the only institution to offer instruction in needlework. Since little documentation exists regarding students' work, it would seem that Pierce did not emphasize this branch. Limited ornamental options were available at Troy and even fewer at Mount Holyoke. Willard recommended as a necessary part of young women's education only the ornamental branches she considered important in forming their character: drawing and painting, elegant penmanship, the grace of motion (dancing), and music. She did not include needlework, since it was taught in the domestic department of study at the school or made an entrance requirement. Willard argued that needlework "affords little to assist in the formation of character" and is therefore a "waste of time."[71] She referred to instruction in ornamental subjects such as needlework as "the fripperies of filigree," claiming it should not be part of higher education.[72]

The number of ornamental subjects available at Mount Holyoke diminishes in comparison to Troy and Litchfield. The Mount Holyoke catalogs do not list a division between academic and ornamental courses, nor were extra fees charged for any ornamental course as they were at Litchfield and Troy. Since Lyon tried to reduce the tuition so that middle-class girls could attend, finances were available to hire teachers for academic subjects only. Students or teachers who had been previously trained provided instruction in any of the ornamental subjects offered, such as vocal music, calisthenics, and linear and perspective drawing. As mentioned in the previous chapter, Lyon contended that the home was the best place for students to receive instruction in needlework and the like and that mothers were the best teachers.

DRAWING AND PAINTING

Litchfield offered instruction in drawing, and Troy extended the training to include painting on velvet. Willard contested contemporary arguments concerning the appropriateness of young women's study of painting, since it often required an extensive amount of time to become proficient. She argued that the purpose of studying painting was not to make the students professionals but rather to cultivate their "refinement."[73]

DANCING AND CALISTHENICS

Willard, Lyon, and Pierce had controversial opinions regarding dancing. Although Willard and Pierce agreed it was the best form of instruction for the grace of motion, Willard restricted dancing to being a form of exercise and recreation, claiming it would promote physical and emotional health.[74] She included dancing as part of the regular schedule; the students danced for one hour in the evening after dinner as a form of relaxation and exercise.[75] It does not appear that dancing was taught at Litchfield. However, students could participate in a monthly evening ball at the school, dancing until midnight under Sarah Pierce's watchful eye.[76] Perhaps they had learned how to dance before entering the school. This form of social training was common at schools contemporary with Litchfield, since parents viewed such activities as opportunities for their daughters to be exposed to genteel society. Litchfield pupils were required to be at least sixteen years of age to attend a ball, unless they had their parents' permission. The academy invited the students from Judge Tapping Reeve's law school, who were honored to receive invitations and a list of eligible ladies.[77] In turn Litchfield students attended balls given by the law students in Deacon Buel's ballroom and those hosted by the citizens of Litchfield at the local tavern, public house, or the United States Hotel.[78]

Dancing was not taught at Mount Holyoke, where religious doctrine was strictly followed; rather, the students received instruction in calisthenics.[79] Letters and journal entries reveal that students enjoyed these exercises accompanied by music.[80] The practice sessions frequently turned into cotillion parties until a teacher happened to walk by the room. To avoid Lyon's wrath or, as some letters suggest, her "tak[ing] off their heads," the students quickly changed the dance steps to form the shape of a "Cross or Mountain Wreath."[81] By 1862 the seminary catalog had changed the term "calisthenics" to "gymnastics"; if there was any difference between the calisthenics and gymnastic exercises, it was not mentioned.[82]

While each class at Mount Holyoke had a set curriculum, all students received instruction in vocal music, calisthenics, reading, composition, and

Bible study throughout the year. Troy students likewise studied the Bible, English composition, elocution, gymnastics, dancing, drawing, and singing throughout their time at the seminary, whether or not they pursued any of the elective courses. It can also be assumed that students at Litchfield received training in specific subjects regardless of whether they were pursuing a diploma. For example, everyone participated in physical exercise, and each Saturday morning Pierce instructed the students in religion and morals.[83] This was definitely a challenging curriculum for women of the time; however, as Willard observed, such an education would only reveal their beauty.

Public Examinations and Graduation

Public examination exercises (also known as "exhibitions" or "anniversary exercises") were held semiannually at Troy and Litchfield and annually at Mount Holyoke and Music Vale.[84] Although students attending Music Vale were not examined in academic subjects, they endured strenuous examinations in music performance before a private committee.[85] Troy and Music Vale hosted concerts separately from the examinations. The examination schedule at Troy continued for six days, often beginning on Thursday and concluding the following Wednesday; no examinations were held on Sunday.

Examinations at Music Vale were normally held in June, but extant programs indicate they could have been scheduled in July or August.[86] The exercises were a highlight of the school year and drew large crowds that included parents, distinguished educators, and friends. Young men from different colleges attended the events at Mount Holyoke, and Litchfield attracted literary intelligentsia of the town.[87] The young ladies at Litchfield, Troy, Music Vale, and Mount Holyoke dressed in white, as was normal for special events.[88] Litchfield exhibitions were conducted at the academy or at the Litchfield County Courthouse; those at Troy, Music Vale, and Mount Holyoke were held on campus. Troy's hall hosting most of the examinations had a seating capacity of approximately six hundred; the walls displayed students' artwork—drawings in pencil and color as well as watercolor and oil paintings (fig. 5.1).[89] Litchfield students likewise exhibited their art and needlework, judged by leading women of the town.[90]

A poem by Troy student Lucretia Davidson describes the young women's anxiety over the upcoming examinations:

> One has a headache, one a cold
> One has a neck in flannel rolled;

Fig. 5.1. Examination Room, Troy Female Seminary. Courtesy of Emma Willard School Archives, Troy, New York.

Ask the complaint, and you are told,
Next week's Examination.

One frets and scolds, one laughs and cries,
Another hopes, despairs, and sighs;
Ask but the cause, and each replies,
Next week's Examination.

One bangs her books, then grasps them tight,
And studies morning, noon, and night,
As though she took some strange delight
In these Examinations.

The books are marked, defaced, and thumbed,
Their brains with midnight tasks benumbed;
Still all in one account is summed,
Next week's Examination.

Thus speed ye all, and may the smile
Of approbation crown your toil,
And Hope the anxious hours beguile
Before Examination.[91]

As the poem implies, students dreaded the grueling questioning; however, according to examining committee reports, students performed admirably and many times beyond the examiners' expectations.[92]

The examinations assessed pupils' knowledge gained during the term or year and served as confirmation that graduating students were worthy of their diplomas or certificates. To make the demanding process more comfortable, Willard had two students stand together before the examination board while each recited and received questions.[93] Willard chose educators, clergymen, and legislators not associated with the seminary to question the Troy students, whereas instructors responsible for teaching the subjects at Mount Holyoke served as that school's examiners.[94] Orramel Whittlesey obtained such renowned musicians as Nathan Richardson, Louis Ernst, Oliver Ditson, and John E. Gould as judges at Music Vale.[95] Musical performances and readings of student compositions were presented between oral examinations of academic subjects at Troy, Litchfield, and Mount Holyoke to help relieve tension and provide variety.[96] Mount Holyoke's exercises also included calisthenics. Willard, Pierce, Lyon, and Whittlesey had high standards; for example, if Litchfield students' work did not represent the school in its best light, Sarah Pierce canceled that portion of the exhibition. In 1825 Elizabeth Wolcott noted, "We had no exhibition in music this spring as the young ladies had not devoted their attention to it as much as usual."[97]

Each day at the close of the final session, Troy's young women sang a hymn expressing their gratitude to the Creator who gave them the ability to improve their minds. Their favorite hymn was one of Willard's:

O Thou, the First, the Last, the Best!
To Thee the grateful song we raise,
Convinced that all our works should be
Begun and ended with Thy praise.

It is from Thee the thought arose
When chants the nun or vestal train,
That praise is sweeter to thine ear,
When virgin voices hymn the strain.

Lord, bless to us this parting scene;
Sister to sister bids farewell;
They wait to bear us to our homes,
With tender parents there to dwell.

Oh, may we ever live to Thee!

Then, as we leave earth's care-worn road,
Angels shall wait to take our souls,
And bear them to our Father God.[98]

The annual examinations at Music Vale were likewise intense, consisting of music theory and piano exercises as well as instrumental and vocal performances. Although the students had practiced diligently and undoubtedly performed numerous times for the faculty and guests, the examination was still a challenge for some young ladies. S. T. Holbrook, member of the 1872 board of examiners, reported the following about the students' performances: "We are well aware that young ladies who are placed before their instruments to play difficult music in the presence of half a dozen gentlemen stationed there *for the very purpose of criticizing them*, are naturally somewhat embarrassed. Notwithstanding this, they played and sang with a steadiness, a firmness of finger and voice, a brilliancy of execution, and good taste rarely found among so many performers."[99] The report of arduous standards confirms the excellent instruction provided to Music Vale students and the dedication of the students and faculty.

According to the Music Vale catalog, a successful graduate in 1857 would have demonstrated competence in:

1. Running easily and readily all the scales, both major and minor, including the chromatic;

2. Passing through, and then carefully reviewing, *Richardson's Modern School for the Piano;*[100]

3. Transposing with the greatest rapidity, from one key to another, every scale in use, whether major or minor, either orally or upon the blackboard;

4. A thorough knowledge of the rules of fingering;

5. A thorough knowledge of the technical language of Music, composed of two thousand German, French, Italian, Spanish, English and Latin words, together with technical musical phrases and signs, etc. etc.;

6. A thorough knowledge of the formation of tetrachords, elucidating and showing the order of flats and sharps, as they arise;

7. A graceful and easy position at the Piano;

8. A knowledge of the rudiments, theory and practice of Thorough Bass— sufficient to read and play from a figured bass any ordinary composition, without the aid of a teacher, and a knowledge of the rules of figuring—so as to [be] able, without assistance, in all cases, to figure any bass when it has been omitted;

9. An ability to count in perfect time, and to play to that count;

10. The ability to procede to the learning and execution of the finest compositions, in a graceful, pleasing and elegant style—every principal having been in the course of study, both practically and theoretically elucidated and settled in such a manner as to be at the perfect command of the pupil. In short, they had "learned how to learn," and to communicate to others the knowledge they possessed.[101]

The requirements testify to thorough instruction and serious commitment of the students.

In 1857 performances were interspersed between theory examinations, providing a change of pace for the students and examiners. By 1863 the format changed: the theory examinations occurred after the performances.[102]

PRIZES, CERTIFICATES, AND DIPLOMAS

Students who fulfilled the requirements received diplomas, prizes, or certificates. Litchfield awarded prizes to those who had excelled in their studies; for example, the notice of the semiannual exhibition in the *Litchfield County Post*, April 24, 1828, includes the names of seven students who received prizes.[103] Students who completed a partial course of study at Troy were granted a certificate. Troy achieved renown throughout the nation as an institution of women's higher education; a certificate with Emma Willard's signature served as a ticket to nearly any appropriate employment.[104]

Many women could not remain at school long enough to complete the prescribed course for financial, health, or other reasons; thus, graduating classes were not large in comparison to the student body. Each institution maintained stringent requirements for graduation. For example, by 1821 Litchfield denied candidate status to students who wished to obtain a diploma or the "last honors" if any course had been omitted from her studies. Additional requirements included having earned a designated number of credit marks for "academic work, attendance, and proper behavior, to have received no major punishments, and to have written three months' worth of a journal or eight dissertations." Further, the successful candidate would have correctly answered eight-ninths of the questions in all the subjects required for graduation as covered in the "general Exams."[105]

Litchfield began awarding diplomas by 1816, while Troy waited until 1843. Qualified students at Mount Holyoke received diplomas in 1838, the first year after the school's opening.[106] Historian Lynne Brickley notes that for the years 1816 to 1832 there were only thirty-five graduates at Litchfield; however, records exist for only ten of more than thirty terms during this time.[107]

According to historian Mary J. Mason Fairbanks, although Troy had a thriving student body, most of the young women received part of their education elsewhere; only a few completed the full course of study and were granted a diploma.[108] By 1861 there were sixty-six graduates at Mount Holyoke, the largest graduating class to that date in the school's history.[109] Mount Holyoke graduates received diplomas signed by both the principal and the secretary of the board of trustees.[110] The certificate, designed by Mrs. Hitchcock, cited Psalm 144:14: "That our daughters may be as corner stones, polished after the similitude of a palace."[111]

Given the lack of documentation regarding Music Vale, it cannot be determined when the school began awarding diplomas. Nevertheless, students who were in residence for four quarters of twelve weeks each and successfully passed the examinations were granted diplomas by the board.[112] An average number of twenty students remained through the year and graduated. During the 1857–1858 school year, however, forty-five of the fifty students were awarded diplomas. Following graduation the examining committee, distinguished guests, friends, and relatives were treated to the "Young Ladies' Annual Concert" at 7:00 or 8:00 P.M.[113] In 1863 the concert consisted of two melodramatic operas, *Ralvo* and *Canawahoo*, along with charades, which were "both amusing and instructive": "Isle of the Syrens," "Invisible Chorus," "Address of the Queen," "March of the Amazons," "Song of the Pirates," and others.[114] By 1869 there was an admission charge of one dollar.[115]

Conclusion

The academic and ornamental curricula offered at Troy, Litchfield, and Mount Holyoke and the music training at Music Vale place these schools as pioneering institutions that helped establish the standards for women's higher education. In plowing new ground, they served as models for other academies and seminaries in their formative stages. Emma Willard, Sarah Pierce, Mary Lyon, and Orramel Whittlesey were convinced that women were as intelligent as men and deserved a comparable education. They recognized the importance of providing an education that enabled women to think for themselves, make wise decisions, and broaden their sphere, thus preparing them for genteel society as educated women capable of teaching their children or, if necessary, supporting themselves or their families as teachers or governesses.

Understanding the depth and breadth of the curricula provides insight into the foundation for women's education beyond the superficial finishing and private schools and the common and district elementary levels. While these four schools were independent institutions in their own right, they shared the same educational philosophy in affording women a higher education. An examination of music education in the next chapter reveals that music was elevated to an art with intrinsic value.

6

Music Education for a Young Lady

Music played a crucial role in the education young women received at such respected academies and seminaries as Litchfield, Troy, Mount Holyoke, and Music Vale. The founders of these institutions of higher learning agreed that their establishments should not resemble finishing schools where students could learn to play a few simple pieces on the parlor piano and sing pleasing tunes. To compete with these schools, however, music needed to be part of the curriculum. Willard emphasized the importance of music instruction in the 1835 school catalog by informing Troy citizens that she would lower fees for both French and music to those who enrolled their daughters at a young age if they remained for a long (unspecified) period of time.[1] Willard's views coincided with those in an article published the same year in *American Ladies' Magazine*: "The education of a young lady now-a-days, can hardly be considered provided for, unless she have the advantage of learning music."[2] Pierce concurred with this philosophy, claiming that "playing on an instrument or occasionally singing is a very desirable acquisition in any woman" privileged to have the time and means to develop her skills.[3]

Unlike Music Vale, Litchfield, Troy, and Mount Holyoke did not concentrate solely on music education, yet the founders of these institutions deemed music on a par with academic subjects. A comparison of the music programs, importance of music within the curricula and school activities, number and gender of faculty, employment of student assistants, fees for lessons and instrument use, courses and instruments offered, and performance opportunities at each of these institutions reveals similarities as well as differences.

Music Teachers

Teachers at these institutions were either trained faculty or qualified student assistants. Since Sarah Pierce was not proficient in music and likely could not find qualified teachers in the early years of Litchfield Female Academy, she employed students as teaching assistants.[4] By 1825 the school had hired a music teacher. Student assistants served as music teachers at Mount Holyoke until 1862; one student filled this position annually.[5] Many of the student assistants at Mount Holyoke retained the position during their three-year enrollment.[6] Some students, however, served as music teachers for only one or two years, depending upon the length of time they attended the seminary. Having to direct four choirs made this a demanding responsibility. Apparently teachers and other pupils who had some musical background assisted the student selected to be in charge. For example, in 1845, according to the "Candidates for Teachers" chart, ten pupils aided Harriet Hawes (student music teacher).[7] The weekly schedule for faculty member Miss Thurston from November 18, 1846, through March 10, 1847, indicates that her assignment included twenty-six hours assisting Hawes with the singing class.[8] Perhaps Mary Lyon decided it was less expensive to have a student serve as the music instructor, since she determined to reduce the cost for middle-class women.[9]

After Lyon's death in 1849, Mount Holyoke continued the practice of hiring student assistants as music instructors until 1862, when the administration created a faculty position and employed accomplished pianist and vocalist Eliza Wilder.[10] Although the school had already achieved a reputation for its high standard of vocal instruction, Wilder raised the bar. In 1865 Mount Holyoke had only two pianos; Wilder threatened to leave unless the board of trustees purchased new instruments and music. As a result the board bought two new pianos and allocated money solely for musical instruction.[11]

The number of music instructors and student assistants varied. Litchfield hired one music teacher in any given year: George R. Herbert in 1825, Maretta Kimberly in 1828, and Emily Hart in 1830.[12] In 1814 there were four student assistants but only one in 1815.[13] Unlike Mount Holyoke and Litchfield, Troy and Music Vale employed only trained music instructors. Music lessons were offered at Troy from the beginning; evidently some of the academic teachers also taught piano and guitar. Since faculty names were not listed with the subjects they taught until the 1848 catalog, it is difficult to determine the number of music teachers from 1821 through 1847.[14] Afterward the seminary employed as many as nine music instructors. Troy did not use student assistants, but Music Vale often had several student officers: assistants, one superior, one premier, and occasionally four monitresses.[15] Music Vale began with one teacher and reached a peak of nine in 1869.[16]

Most of the music teachers were women. Troy, however, over time hired several men while Litchfield employed only one male music teacher. Likewise Orramel Whittlesey was the sole male instructor at Music Vale. It seems unusual that he would not have hired men, given his connections with some of the leading names in music. Further, he was no stranger to the local Salem community and the surrounding area, having achieved renown as a performer and teacher. The *Weekly Democrat* applauded Whittlesey's teaching:

> MUSIC VALE SEMINARY, SALEM, CONN.—We invite the attention of our readers to the Report of the Board of Examiners, on the Annual Examination of Music Vale Seminary, at *Salem, Conn.*, June 17th and 18th, published in our columns to-day. It is not necessary for us to allude to the high standing to which the successful and popular Principal, Hon. O. WHITTLESEY, has brought this institution. It is one of the most successful and substantial institutions of the country. . . . The system adhered to at this Institution, we deem to be the only one that can be successful, viz:—of applying the energies of the pupil to one thing at a time, and only one. Mr. WHITTLESEY graduates some of the best musicians and composers to be found in this or any other country.[17]

Music Vale was becoming nationally recognized as a first-rate music school. Further, Whittlesey's brothers were well-respected piano builders, thus providing another association for Whittlesey with the outside world.[18]

Mount Holyoke invited several male guest lecturers on various subjects, though rarely for music. Mary Lyon was in contact with Lowell Mason concerning music instruction, but it was not until 1857 that he fulfilled a long-standing promise and presented a lecture at the school.[19] The seminary continued its practice of employing female music teachers when Miss Almeda N. Tirrell joined the faculty in 1866, replacing Eliza Wilder.[20]

Troy Female Seminary employed a diverse music faculty. Beginning in 1848 the catalog included five music instructors: one man and four women.[21] During some years there was an equal number of men and women; at other times one gender dominated, such as 1861, when there were five men and one woman.[22] The seminary garnered a high reputation for its music instruction. Reports from committees that examined students in academic subjects repeatedly commend the music faculty; for example, in 1850: "The corps of teachers in this department combine a rare amount of musical talent, and their skills and devotion to their profession, are manifested in the proficiency of their pupils, who seem to have imbibed, in a high degree, the state of excellence of their instructors."[23] Each year the anniversary exercises at the close of the school year included a musical program showcasing the talented instructors and students. In 1855 the examining committee again responded with a glowing account: "The teachers and professors of this branch have evidently been selected with discrimination; and they have done honor to the judgment that chose them."[24] The seminary apparently upheld the same high standards for music instructors as those for academic subjects.

Faculty Composers

Several faculty members at Troy were composers, as were Orramel Whittlesey and his oldest daughter, Eliza, at Music Vale.[25] Troy's music programs include works by music teachers: Gustave Blessner, Faustina Hodges, John C. Andrews, Kjell Volmar Barnekov, and Matthieu Philippi.[26] Blessner received numerous accolades for his compositions. In 1847 the examining committee congratulated "the friends of the Institution" for hiring such an "accomplished" professor as Gustave Blessner, "whose whole soul seems enraptured with his science." He "evinces not less skill in the composition than in the execution of Music."[27] Blessner was head of Troy's music department from 1848 to 1850 and composed solo works for piano and voice, along with such ensemble pieces as "Daguerre," for piano, harp, and violin. His compositions appeared regularly on the programs from 1847 through 1850.[28]

Kjell Volmar Barnekov emigrated from Sweden to Boston in 1842 and taught piano, guitar, and organ at Troy from 1855 to 1860. His name does not appear as often on extant programs as do those of Blessner, Hodges, or Philippi; nevertheless, Barnekov's "Fantaisie for piano" was performed at the seminary on February 20, 1857. His name was misspelled as "Barnekoy" on the program and on the title page of his "Valse à La Fantasie," published in 1844. While his was not a household name, Barnekov must have been an excellent musician and teacher, since it was unusual for the seminary to employ foreigners.

Faustina Hasse Hodges was a member of Troy's music faculty from 1849 to 1852. She wrote works for piano, sacred songs, and approximately twenty-five "drawing-room" songs.[29] Several programs given by the students and faculty include her compositions, such as the vocal works "Maiden Fair" (duet), "The Holy Dead" (trio), and "Speed Away" (quartet), and "Variations—on an Air of Pleyel," for solo piano.[30]

Matthieu Philippi, head of the music department from 1851 to 1853 and again from 1859 to 1866, composed and arranged instrumental and vocal works. His pieces, such as those for piano ensemble (eight or twelve hands) and vocal works—for example, "Forest Song" (glee), "Our Country," from *Lombardi* (chorus), "Nights of Music" (trio), and "[La] Serenade" (quintet)— regularly appeared on programs during the first three years he was at Troy.[31]

Orramel Whittlesey's compositions likewise figured frequently on Music Vale programs. None of Eliza Whittlesey's pieces appear on any programs, but the 1851 brochure advertising the school includes two of her compositions under "New Music": the second edition of "Why Weep for the Dead" and the forthcoming publication of "We Meet Again."[32] Several of Orramel's compositions are also advertised in the "New Music" section: "Dying Soldier of Buena Vista," 5th ed.; "Farewell to My Home," 6th ed.; "Warrior's Rest," 4th ed.; "Salem Quick Step," 4th ed.; "Wild Roses," 6th ed.; "American Eagle," 6th ed.; and the forthcoming publication of "Harp of the Wild Wind."[33] Whittlesey's compositions must have been popular, given the various editions and repeated performances. Twelve years later, for example, several of the pieces mentioned above were performed on the "Twenty-Fourth Annual Examination Program" in 1873.[34] "Welcome to Music Vale" was a school favorite and often served as the opening number on programs for over thirty years.[35] Whittlesey composed both the music and the text.

"Music Vale Seminary Quick Step" frequently followed the "Welcome"; thereafter the program had no set order. Whittlesey may have attempted to describe the flurry of activity abounding at Music Vale—the "Quick Step's" eight-measure staccato introduction is repeated, followed by a march, *dolce con gusto*, in ABA form. The sixteenth- and thirty-second-note octaves, chords, and melodic notes and sixteenth-note rests, in addition to the melodic and accompanimental leaps, may be meant to portray the excitement of the event.[36] Unlike Troy, Music Vale offered composition lessons. Therefore, it seems possible that missing programs contained pieces by students or other faculty.

Music Fees

Unlike Mount Holyoke, which did not offer individual lessons, Litchfield and Troy charged extra fees for private music instruction, thus considerably increasing tuition.[37] In 1823 the fee for piano instruction was the same at Litchfield and Troy. Students at Litchfield received five lessons per week, but the number of lessons given each week at Troy is unknown. By 1826 Catharine Bronk was paying fifteen dollars for two summer quarters of piano lessons at Litchfield.[38] Perhaps there was a reduction in the fee for summer lessons.

In 1825 Troy reduced the lesson fee by one dollar per quarter. Three years later Emma Willard was forced to increase the fee to fifteen dollars when she obtained "at a high salary, a first rate professor of music."[39] Students who preferred to continue with their current teacher could do so for the lower fee of eleven dollars per quarter. Troy's fee for piano lessons remained fifteen dollars per quarter until 1864, when it was raised to forty dollars per term (twenty dollars per quarter). One year later the fee was reduced to thirty-four dollars per term.[40] The price for the lessons was included in the general tuition at Music Vale.[41] Litchfield, Troy, and Music Vale also charged four dollars per quarter for use of the piano; however, by 1855 Music Vale eliminated this fee. Students attending Mount Holyoke who desired access to a piano incurred no extra charge.[42]

Music Instruction

The amount of music instruction varied at the four schools. Class singing was offered at no extra charge. Piano, the chief instrument, was taught at all schools save Mount Holyoke. Music Vale and Troy added instruction in other instruments as the student body increased. Students at Music Vale could also study melodeon, harp, guitar, organ, and voice. By 1843 organ lessons became an elective at Troy for fifteen dollars per quarter. Beginning in 1848 Gustave Blessner is listed as a violin instructor for three consecutive years.[43] Troy also offered private lessons in guitar, harp, voice, and organ. Although some students at Music Vale and Troy took advantage of the instruction offered for other instruments, piano remained the most popular choice (see table 6.1).

Students attending Music Vale were devoted to music study, as exemplified in a young woman's admonition to interested candidates:

—[Music Vale] is a place where young ladies are assembled to learn music, combined with common sense, and not to flirt with young gents, no such place as that, and I advise all those who wish to carry on that sort of business, to keep from here; . . . Now, the fact of my being here, shows that I have given up childish things, such as flirting, *etcetera*, and have my mind fixed intently on music. I can assure you it is no fool's play, as some imagine, to produce a combination of sounds. It is work, and not easy either. In the first place, we hold to the old maxim, "early to bed and early to rise," taking for granted that "wealth and wisdom" must necessarily follow. We don't doze away all our pleasant mornings (though we wish we could,) but endeavor to redeem the character of our sex, regain the name given to our grandmothers, who did not make their appearance at the hour of ten, with languid looks,

Table 6.1. Musical Instruments/Vocal
Instruction Offered at the Seminaries

Instrument	LFA	TFS	MHFS	MVS
Guitar		X		X
Harp		X		X
Melodeon		X		X
Organ		X		X
Piano	X	X		X
Violin		X		
Voice (private)		X		X
Voice class	X	X	X	X

showing the effect of the party of the previous evening. . . . As I have said, we drop all adorables, fix our imaginations on the more solid science of music; this is our only theme.[44]

The regimented schedule and work ethic at Music Vale supported the philosophy of higher education rather than the finishing school mentality.

Piano

Before founding Mount Holyoke Female Seminary, Mary Lyon had contact with Lowell Mason while she was employed at Ipswich Female Seminary. In a letter dated November 20, 1832, Mason advised her to "promote universal vocal music" but defer offering instruction in instrumental music.[45] She carried out his advice at Mount Holyoke and did not encourage students to pursue instrumental music, because "it interferes so much with the solid branches." Lyon was not, however, opposed to students who chose otherwise, claiming, "those who do [practice], make good progress."[46] According to the 1844–1846 school catalogs, private lessons were offered by special request; no additional fee was mentioned. Perhaps a teacher was available during these few years. Apparently one or more piano students accompanied the choirs, work that would have required a trained pianist.

Shortly after the seminary opened, Deacon Daniel Stafford (a member of the board of trustees) gave the school a piano. Many students were pleased and interest in piano study increased; Stafford purchased two additional instruments in 1842.[47] Periodically the school purchased a new piano; for example, in March 1857 Sarah A. Start noted in a journal letter that "a fine new piano arrived."[48]

Though Mount Holyoke catalogs did not include piano instruction in the curriculum, the school occasionally received letters of inquiry regarding music lessons. Jeremiah Wilcox requested in 1844 that his daughter continue piano lessons while attending Mount Holyoke: "Harriet is going through a course of Music Lessons on the Piano Forte and would be pleased to pursue it in the seminary if she can be accommodated with a teacher."[49] That same year E. A. Cahoon also inquired about piano lessons, expressing concern because his daughter planned to be an instructor: "[I would] be pleased to communicate the facilities for acquiring a knowledge of music on the Piano. As the latter is a matter, in this instance, of more particular importance, since she is already considerably advanced in the science, and wishes to acquaint herself sufficiently to teach that branch, will you give information on this point more in detail than is found in the Catalogue."[50] It seems that some parents felt their daughters were qualified to teach and hoped doing so would offset their educational expenses.[51]

Mount Holyoke catalogs never mention a fee for piano use, but according to student Abby Allen, in 1842 those desiring to practice paid a fee for instrument use. This undoubtedly made it difficult for some students to continue practicing, as Allen indicated in a letter to her father: "I fear I shall lose all I have ever known about playing. No one can use the piano *at* all without paying quite a sum ($6 or 8 I believe). Those who pay that sum have the use of it an hour a day. My lesson in Algebra is recited in the room adjoining that containing the piano, where a young lady practices the same hour; and you will not doubt, dear Father, that it requires all of my power of abstraction to shut my ears to the music, and attend to my lesson."[52] Practice could also have been a distraction for students trying to study.

Piano was the only instrument available for private study at Litchfield, and initially at Troy and Music Vale as well. Instruction was offered at Litchfield by the early 1800s. The number of entries in student diaries and journals regarding music study infers that numerous students elected to study piano.[53] In addition, the April 1828 report of the "Semi-Annual Exhibition," published in the *Litchfield County Post*, affirms that pupils took advantage of music lessons: "The exhibition of music was good, and gave evidence of much improvement in this polite branch of education."[54] Performances were normal occurrences at such events, giving students an opportunity to display their progress.

"Music lessons" (meaning piano instruction, since no other private lessons were offered) were given throughout the day, Monday through Saturday. Mary Ann Bacon, for example, noted in her diary that she rose at 4:30 A.M. in order to be ready for a music lesson one hour later. Lucy Sheldon recorded in her journal that lesson days or times varied: Tuesday afternoon,

Wednesday, or Saturday.[55] Along with full schedules, the few available pianos were in heavy demand, making lesson and practice times difficult to arrange. Catherine Cebra Webb, a student during the 1815–1816 school year, reported, "I went into the back parlor of Miss Pierce's *residence*, to take my lesson on the piano."[56] Perhaps no piano was available at the school during her lesson time. Some fortunate students had their instruments shipped to the school. As noted in her diary, Mary Ann Bacon experienced great pleasure when her piano arrived: "I Neglected my Gurnal [journal] Ever Since I received my Piano Forte the 9 of October."[57] Lucy Sheldon, too, obtained her own piano, made by George Astor.[58]

Piano was the preferred instrument at Troy, although instruction on other instruments was available. In 1835 the seminary housed fourteen pianos, which were "in almost constant requisition."[59] As the student body increased, the school found it necessary to purchase additional instruments; by 1854 there were eighteen pianos. According to the 1836 "School Rules," young women normally practiced one hour per day (the "Rules" do not specify if the students practiced five or six days per week).[60]

Orramel Whittlesey initially founded Music Vale around 1835 primarily for piano instruction. He practiced the philosophy of "doing one thing at a time," meaning solely studying music. By 1863 Music Vale had thirty-nine pianos, which were in constant use.[61] The seminary offered a rigorous one-year course. Students at Music Vale received careful instruction under the teachers' eagle eyes. Daily (except Sunday) supervised practice sessions left little room for acquiring bad habits, evident in the annual public examination: "The accuracy of the recitation in Theory, the correct and elegant fingering, and above all the perfect time observed in the playing, were eminently noticeable and pleasing."[62] Use of the metronome at Music Vale was strictly adhered to, as indicated in the "Thirty-First" (1869–1870) catalog: "we consider its [the metronome's] use absolutely necessary. . . . We must first have perfect time, which is the foundation of all that is good in Music."[63] Students who fulfilled the proposed requirements received a nationally recognized diploma.

Music Vale Seminary was not for the faint of heart, as an advertisement for the school testifies: "We claim for our graduates a perfect development of the hand. Faults in practice are never allowed at Music Vale, and only such pupils are sought, as are willing to follow our directions constantly and in every particular."[64] S. T. Holbrook, member of the examining board for the anniversary exercises on June 13, 1872, noted the students' exceptional training: "The playing of the pupils was uniformly excellent, and this was noticeable in all who took part, from those least advanced to the most skill-ful. It gave evidence of faithful practice and of careful supervision on the part of the teachers. As a rule, the fingering was firm, delicate and elastic, showing that special pains had been taken with this branch of study."[65] The disciplined teaching at Music Vale produced competent pianists.

Voice

The amount and level of music instruction offered at each school is reveal-ing in its own right. At first it might appear that Mount Holyoke students received a less structured music education than those at Litchfield and es-pecially at Troy and Music Vale. While Mount Holyoke did not encourage instrumental music, it emphasized vocal music and kept pace with recent publications. Because of her musical deficiencies, Mary Lyon gave special attention to vocal training with graded classes and specific instructions for the school choir. On November 9, 1843, Lyon lectured the students on the topic of "talents." She followed this with a lecture stressing "the importance of cultivating singing by daily practice." One student noted that "she hoped we w'd [would] all learn to *sing & write well*. And in all our pursuits not to ne-glect the collateral means of improvement."[66] As a letter from Mount Holyoke student Sarah Burnham confirms, there were three regular graded choirs and a sacred music choir: "The music teacher came this term and the classes in music have been formed. There is a choir for sacred music who sing half an hour before tea three days in the week (all who wish to) and besides this, three other regular choirs: the first, second, and third choirs. . . . They sing an hour on Wedns. and Saturdays."[67] Perhaps the choir levels corresponded to the three class levels at the seminary: junior, middle, and senior.[68]

Authors of music books used at Mount Holyoke had different opinions regarding the question of whether everyone had the ability to sing. George J. Webb and Lowell Mason proposed that all voices, except those with natural talent, are "more or less defective, and require a regular process of cultiva-tion to polish and perfect them." They did, however, qualify that statement, claiming there are some people with "natural defects" that are impossible to correct. These include such voices as those with "an absolute want of just-ness of intonation; an habitual production of the extreme nasal and guttural tones, from the nose or throat; [and] a short and painful respiration." Con-versely, there are others whose voices have "artificial defects"—"bad habits" that modify the normal sound of the voice by directing "the sound to the nose or throat," altering the voice by "forcing or straining," or distorting the "natural position of the mouth"—all acquired from a lack of training.[69] However, Thomas Hastings and William B. Bradbury contended that everyone is trainable: "to be able to sing in tune is always an acquired faculty." Thus the need to sing scales and intervals. "Every voice is found to need tuning; and some of the more obstinate ones demand an amount of practice far greater than the pupil has time and patience to bestow."[70] Apparently Mary Lyon believed the students who attended Mount Holyoke either had natural talent or were teachable, since all of them received vocal training.

Unveiling the vocal music studied at Mount Holyoke is a complex task. The school catalogs include titles of music books the seminary asked students to bring if they owned them. New titles frequently appeared, testifying that Mount Holyoke kept abreast of current publications. Thus it is safe to assume the choirs used these music books for vocal training and performed many of the songs. Further, some of the musical numbers on the programs at the close of the school year appear in these books.[71]

The books usually contain music scores along with the texts except for *The Psalms, Hymns, and Spiritual Songs* and the *Village Hymns*, which provide only the texts.[72] Some books consist of either sacred or secular music, while others have both. Given Mount Holyoke's emphasis on religious instruction, it is not surprising that some books were solely devoted to sacred music.

It was common for music books to include an introductory section on the rudiments of music. *The Odeon*, *The Key-Stone Collection*, and *The Jubilee* contain sections on vocal production, examples, exercises to accompany and reinforce the concept being taught, and vocalises.[73] Instruction covered such topics as position of the head, body, and mouth; breathing (sometimes referred to as "respiration"); voice equalization; articulation (such as vowel and consonant elements, speaking tones, open and closed vowel sounds, and positions of the mouth while singing each element); ornamentation; voice registers; and blending the registers. A. N. Johnson discussed "Musical Expression" (mechanical and emotional) in *The Key-Stone Collection*: the former refers to expressions given in the score; the latter exemplifies singing from the heart—a natural and spontaneous form of expression.[74]

While Litchfield students did not have the advantage of private vocal training, they had the opportunity to receive instruction during "singing meetings" held on Wednesday and Sunday evenings at the school or local church. Sarah Pierce was not musical, so she hired singing masters to teach this art to the students. These meetings appear to be much like the singing schools taught by musicians of the New England Singing School. There is no indication that students were required to attend the "singing meetings"; from numerous entries in diaries and journals, however, it seems that most students gladly accepted the offer or studied on their own. Charlotte Sheldon, for example, noted in her diary that she had "Learn't one or two verses in a song" and on another day "Partly learned the words to a song."[75] Both entries were on days other than those appointed for singing meetings.

During the first one hundred years after colonists settled in the New World, little encouragement was proffered for music-making outside of the church. Sarah Pierce, undoubtedly influenced by Puritan views regarding the vanities of music, did not fail to emphasize her preference for sacred music:

> The passions of mankind, however, have very much debased and profaned this art, which like others, was originally sacred and intended to chant the praises of the Almighty. many songs are couched in such indelicate language and, convey such a train of luscious ideas, as are only calculated to soil the purity of a youthful mind. i should therefore recommend, (if I may so express myself,) rather the sacred than the profane, of this study, indeed church music is in itself more delightful than any other, what can be superior to some passages of Judas Maccabaeus or the Messiah there is not, perhaps an higher among the melancholy pleasures than a funeral dirge.[76]

Pierce's preference for sacred music may also have reflected many parents' views regarding the influence of secular music on their daughters.

Students attending Troy Female Seminary had the privilege of receiving voice lessons, in addition to class instruction in singing, at no extra charge.[77] By 1829 private lessons taught by Mr. Powell were offered at eleven dollars per quarter.[78] A majority of the music teachers gave voice lessons as well as instruction on one or more instruments, testifying to the number of students studying voice. In 1849, for example, there were six music teachers, five of whom taught voice; some also gave lessons in piano, harp, or guitar. The number and type of vocal works performed, according to existing programs, indicate that voice training was highly regarded.

Given the popularity of music books, such as those used at Mount Holyoke, it seems likely that Troy would have used the same or similar books for teaching class singing. The concerts given at the seminary often included operatic arias, airs, choruses, ballads, glees, and songs by such composers as Gaetano Donizetti, Vincenzo Bellini, Franz Joseph Haydn, and Daniel-François-Esprit Auber, in addition to Blessner and Philippi, who taught at the school.[79] Solos, duets, trios, quartets, and choruses were included in performances. For example, on February 19, 1850, the school presented a duet and chorus from *Norma* to conclude the first part of the program. Five years later, on

June 26, 1855, the chorus performed "Joy, Joy," from Michael William Balfe's *Gipsy's Warning* as the opening number; a sextet from Donizetti's *Lucia di Lammermoor* for two sopranos, two tenors, and two basses concluded the program.[80]

Music Vale initially concentrated on piano instruction. Although it appears that class singing was available, private vocal instruction was not offered until at least 1849.[81] Both piano and voice students received superior training.[82] The seminary followed the Italian school of instruction. Perhaps they used the Luigi Lablache method referred to in George F. Root's *The Academy Vocalist*.[83]

Music Courses

Apart from singing classes, Music Vale Seminary was the only school to offer course instruction. Students had classes in harmony, thoroughbass, counterpoint, fugue, notation, and composition on Tuesday and Thursday evenings and were required to spend two hours daily in private study. An article in *Gleaner of the Vale*, the school newspaper, detailed the education offered at the seminary: "The instructions are of the most thorough and scientific character, enabling the pupil not only to read the most difficult music, but to write it according to the strict rules of the art of musical composition."[84] This comprehensive music education was completely different from what was taught at the finishing schools.

Troy and Mount Holyoke offered less instruction in music theory than did Music Vale. Some of the music books used at Mount Holyoke contained music theory, but specific classes were not offered outside scheduled rehearsals. According to the 1843 catalog, every student at Troy was taught the science of music. Possibly the teachers included theory in singing classes, since it is not mentioned as a separate course. It is plausible that students pursuing piano also studied music theory, which was usually included in piano method books of the time. In addition, Augustus Backus, member of the Troy music faculty from 1834 to 1842, compiled a textbook, *History, Theory, and Analysis of Music: Designed for the Music Department of the Troy Female Seminary*, published in 1839, that was used at the school. The title of this book is somewhat misleading, since it contains little music history scholarship. A large part of the book is devoted to music theory, including a short history and numerous exercises (for example, harmonic, consonant, and dissonant intervals, chords and inversions, and modulation). Backus must have had piano students in mind when he compiled this book, since it includes instructions for fingering and hand position and a list of rules on deportment during piano lessons.[85] It also contains brief histories of several instruments: pianoforte, organ, harp, guitar, and violin (including information on some of the main composers writing for each instrument) and the countries where they were then popular (such as the organ in Holland, the Low Countries, Germany, and England); descriptions of various musical genres; a discussion regarding the importance of expression in music-making; advice to parents concerning pianoforte study; and instructions on tuning.[86]

Music Performances

Performances were part of the music training at the four schools. Musical entertainments or concerts were held at various times during the academic year. In 1862, after Eliza Wilder joined the Mount Holyoke faculty as music instructor, advanced students began presenting musical entertainments every two weeks.[87]

Troy likewise hosted various performances during the school year, usually given by students and instructors. Programs were divided into two parts, although occasionally they were extended with a third section. Overtures, sinfonias, or choral works often served as bookends for each part. A musical potpourri comprised the remainder of the program—solos, duets, or trios. Piano and vocal solos and duets were common; other instruments, such as the harp, violin, flute, violoncello, and guitar, provided welcome variety. A male professor would have played the violin, violoncello, and flute parts, since, except for three years when violin lessons were available, Troy did not offer instruction on these instruments. Occasionally a larger work, such as a cantata, was included; on February 9, 1854, for example, Andreas Jakob Romberg's *The Transient and Eternal* closed part one of the program.

Concerts were open to the public; tickets were rarely sold. An exception was a concert given by the teachers and pupils (date unknown) to raise money for gas fixtures in the "Concert Room." The tickets, costing fifty cents, could be obtained at music and bookstores, presumably in Troy. The program, undoubtedly used as an advertisement, included admission time: "Doors open at 7 o'clock; Concert to commence at 8." The school likely anticipated a large attendance.[88]

Music Vale students had more opportunities for performances than did those at the other schools. Since the seminary trained young women to perform as well as teach, performance was an important part of their education. Every Friday evening the students gave free concerts.[89] Visitors came from far and near to witness some of the finest music-making in the area.[90] Although the students performed on a regular basis, some apparently struggled with performance anxiety:

> When the word is given to the Superior, "Call the next," our name is called instantly; thump—thump, go our hearts, and, "Oh! I never can" rises to our lips, but we choke it back with a brave "I will!" We reach the piano, get seated, our music adjusted, and then "commence!" We try, but for some reason our wits leave us, (and you know we generally have a superabundance of those,) we re-adjust our music, move the lamp, still the notes remain as before—seen only in the distance, finally, somehow (I'm sure I don't know how,) the piece is finished.[91]

Such a reaction was undoubtedly common especially among new students; thus, the concerts were organized to help remedy their lack of self-confidence. They were not, however, expected to perform until their pieces were meticulously learned:

> The pupils are obliged to perform before the whole school, and in presence of such visitors as may be there, pieces that they have previously learned and learned so thoroughly that there can be no possibility of failure unless from a lack of confidence in playing before a large company, and which lack of confidence this discipline is intended to overcome. The pupils by this practice gain an ease and self-possession that they could not acquire in any other way. They learn the art of executing the most difficult pieces in public, and more than all are taught the great lesson of SELF-RELIANCE.[92]

As would be expected, Music Vale had excellent results with this type of training. Students once plagued with performance anxiety displayed self-confidence to the satisfaction of the seminary and board of examiners.

Performances given close to, or during, the public examination exercises were highlights of the concerts held at the conclusion of the school year and often drew large crowds. Vocal and piano performances punctuated the academic sessions at Mount Holyoke when teachers orally examined the students. The program for July 23, 1861, does not include titles of the pieces and names of the performers.[93] Nonetheless, handwritten notations help determine the type of performance and number of performers. Most of the program consisted of vocal music; some pieces were scored for a few voices or the school choirs, and others invited audience participation. The piano solos testify to the talent Mount Holyoke attracted, though it did not offer private instruction.

Visitors often commended the students for their performance skills. One of these visitors was William Gardiner Hammond, a student attending Amherst school for men in Amherst, Massachusetts, who visited Mount Holyoke with his father in 1847 to witness the examinations: "Then music from the piano, and singing: very fair. Then five compositions [readings]: very good, indeed, though rather for style than ideas: even in the style it was often easy to detect traces of some popular author. Then more music, and the performance closed."[94] As Hammond testifies, music was an important part of the examination programs.

Guests attending the exhibitions at Music Vale were treated to a musical feast:

> The exhibitions at this Seminary have been very interesting for years past. The young ladies, a fairy band, are seen upon the stage in striking and picturesque groups, their happy faces beaming with hope and ambition while stirring strains from the piano float through the hall. Or one gifted with keen sensibility, sweeps the strings of the harp or guitar, eliciting tones, that ravish the ear with melody.
>
> And thus through the hours set apart for the exercises, the entertainment ever varying through song and solo, duett, and trio, until the hospitable mansion of the Principal, receives the crowd of pupils, friends and guests.[95]

Along with the concerts held throughout the year, the musical performances during the exhibition affirmed the professional training offered at Music Vale.

Musical performances added variety to the demanding academic examinations at Troy Seminary. Although the examining committee did not grade the students on their performances, they repeatedly commended them, as exemplified in the report from 1850: "The fatigues of a protracted examination were relieved at intervals by music, both vocal and instrumental, performed by the young ladies, assisted sometimes by their teachers, and such music, in strains from solemn to gay, whether in solo, duet, or chorus, we venture to say, can be found in but few institutions of the kind in the land. In point of excellence and variety, it was such as would have done credit to a musical Academy where that science only is taught."[96] Such a critique testifies to the high level of training offered at Troy.

One evening during the six days of examinations (often Tuesday), the students and teachers usually gave a concert similar to those given during the school year. The examining committee praised the brilliant performances of the concert of June 26, 1855: "By invitation of the Principal . . . the Hall was filled with an appreciative audience to listen to a vocal and instrumental Concert

given by the teachers and pupils of the Institution." The performances undoubtedly met or even surpassed the expectations of the audience: "Every one who
had an ear to distinguish articulate sounds and a soul behind it must have
been greatly pleased. It were difficult to decide which was the more remarkable,—the taste with which the selections were made, or the skill with which
they were executed."[97] The program presented that evening, under the direction of Professor E. Thorbecke, head of the music department from 1854 to
1858, represented a typical concert at Troy Seminary. Seventeen compositions
for piano, vocal solo, and ensemble comprised the program; choral or smaller
ensemble numbers framed parts one and two. Except for Mozart's "Magic Flute
Overture," arranged for piano duet, all of the compositions were nineteenth-
century works. The examining committee's report alludes to the professional
quality of the performances: "Prof. Thorbecke performed with graceful facility
a fine specimen of severely classic composition; Mdme Stephani appeared to
have every variety of the scale under her control, and made rare sport of what
demands labored effort in others; Miss Bayeau gave forth her sweet tones with
a gracefulness in perfect harmony with the beautiful repose of her expression;
the gentlemen rendered their parts effectively; the choruses lacked neither in
force nor in precision; and, as a whole, the effort was entirely successful."[98] It
was common for performers' names to be omitted from the programs. Possibly
the invited audience knew the music faculty and the students, or the head of
the music department may have announced the performers' names.

While music examinations were not part of the anniversary exercises held
at Litchfield, Troy, or Mount Holyoke, students at Music Vale endured theory
examinations in addition to performing before the examining board. The
annual examinations lasted a full day. By 1871 the programs consisted of
three parts with fourteen to twenty-four performances—musical numbers,
exercises, and recitations—each with musical numbers taking the lead.[99]
Given that piano was the chief instrument studied at Music Vale, it is not
surprising that piano solos, duets, trios, quartets, or piano with harp, organ,
or guitar made up most of the program. A student performing a piano solo
usually played an etude or a scale, likely to warm up, prior to the solo. S. T.
Holbrook, writing on behalf of the examining board in 1872, applauded the
piano performances:

> The piano forte selections on the programme were progressive in difficulty and
> brilliancy, and the concluding part was fairly a "grand concert." In this part
> several pieces were quite noticeable: "Fair Fingers," played with brilliancy by
> Miss Ella Chamberlin; a transcription of "The Last Rose of Summer" for the

left hand, by Miss Ora Maginnis; a "Fantaisie Briliante," "Oberon," by Miss Nettie Baker; "Finale from Lucia," well executed by Miss Grace Bancroft; "Sonata, No. 2," [by] Mozart, played with grace and delicacy by Miss Eva Pratt; "Saltarello," by S. B. Mills, rendered by Miss Sallie Fuller in dashing style, which gives good promise for the future; Thalberg's "Home Sweet Home," finely executed by Miss Lula Merwin, and encored. A piano forte duet and quartette were also played with excellent precision. . . .

The board of examiners would add to the above that the exercises were, in all respects superior to any preceding anniversary that they have attended at this institution.[100]

Since Whittlesey founded Music Vale with the intention of offering piano instruction, as observed in Holbrook's report, it was the primary focus at this institution. The program included compositions for voice (solo, duet, trio, or quartet), although it does not appear the examining board graded performances other than piano.

Guest Performances

Students had various opportunities to hear musical performances. Occasionally guest artists gave concerts in the area, as when the Hutchinson family came to South Hadley.[101] Although the family had given a Mount Holyoke student a complimentary ticket and Mary Lyon did not think it best to allow students to attend the program, the family "serenaded the seminary after their performance" on their own accord. Lyon evidently had a change of heart and invited the Hutchinson family to give a one-hour concert at the seminary the following day.[102]

Students attending Litchfield Female Academy also had the privilege of hearing musical performances.[103] Charlotte Sheldon, for example, noted in her diary on May 20, 1796: "Heard Mrs. Beardsley [and] Miss Polly Tod play on the Forte Piano." On February 7, 1803, Lucy Sheldon (Charlotte's half-sister) reported in her journal: "In the afternoon attended school, wrote and heard Miss Leavitt play on the piano[;] thinks she plays very handsomely."[104] Since the academy did not have boarding accommodations, students from a distance stayed with families in the town. Entries in their diaries are not always clear whether the events happened at school or after the student returned to her boarding home. On June 16, 1796, Charlotte Sheldon wrote in her diary, "Heard some very good music" and included "after I got home" in the entry for which she added "flute [and] violin."[105] Some students, like Miss

Sheldon, were fortunate to live with families who promoted musicians. Eliza Ogden likewise enjoyed hearing music at the home where she boarded. She commented in her journal: "In the evening Miss Denison and Miss Landon called at our house and spent the evening. We had a number of very good songs sung by Miss Landon."[106] The students must have enjoyed hearing the teachers and perhaps members of the community or other guests perform.

Troy Seminary offered various opportunities for students to hear professional performances given by their instructors as well as by guest artists, as indicated in the 1848 catalog: "In addition to the instructions and performance of our own skillful teachers, the pupils have frequent opportunities of hearing the best Artists at concerts given in the Institution. The musical taste is thus cultivated, and a standard of excellence presented for imitation."[107] The trustees of the Troy fire department appointed a committee to organize a concert to support the charitable fund. Some of the music faculty at Troy along with other musicians "generously offered their services for the occasion."[108] Committee chairman Joseph C. Taylor recommended the concert: "The Committee refer with pleasure to the well known ability of the performers, and also to the Programme for the evening; and confidently anticipate that the entertainment will be one of the most brilliant Musical Festivals of the Season."[109] As Taylor inferred, the music teachers were highly regarded.

On May 14, 1850, Gustave Blessner gave a farewell concert assisted by eight musicians: Miss J. A. Andrews, Miss F. H. Hodges, Miss Miller, Miss Thompson, Miss E. Kinnicutt, Mr. Jno. C. Andrews, Mr. E. P. Jones, with Mrs. Blessner as accompanist.[110] The concert was held at Apollo Hall in Troy rather than the seminary, perhaps because the school was not large enough to accommodate the crowd. Tickets cost fifty cents and could be purchased at music stores or at the door the evening of the concert. The concert began at 8:00, but the doors opened one hour earlier. Blessner composed six of the twelve pieces performed.[111]

Music Use in Seminary Life

Students at Litchfield and Mount Holyoke exercised to musical accompaniment. It is possible this was also the case at Troy and Music Vale, but no documentation confirms the practice. Young women at Litchfield moved in uniform step to flute and "flageolet" accompaniment as they daily made their way under the trees lining North Street. The scene made a vivid impression on E. D. Mansfield, a visitor to the town: "The beauty of nature, the loveliness of the season, the sudden appearance of this school of girls, all united to strike and charm the mind of a young man, " who had never witnessed such a parade.[112]

Students attending Mount Holyoke participated in three levels of calisthenics to musical accompaniment. Mary Lyon's response to a student who apparently had inquired regarding the prospect of pursuing calisthenics in order to be qualified to teach testifies to the importance placed on this branch of education: "The classes in calisthenics are so arranged that you can practise three times a day with classes in different parts of the course. I hope you will make your plan to stay as long as will be necessary in view of our teachers to become a superior teacher in this branch."[113] Calisthenics was emphasized as part of seminary lifestyle to ensure ample physical activity.

The *Calisthenics Exercises* manual used at Mount Holyoke includes titles of songs to be used with various exercises, including "Lightly Row" and "What Fairy Like Music."[114] The rhythms of the songs matched those of the exercises; for example, the "double spring" was used with "Lightly Row": "Skip twice with the right foot, springing on the left at the same time; then twice with the left, springing on the right."[115] "What Fairy Like Music" was used with the "triple spring": "Extend the right foot in front, resting on the toe; carry it to the side; then resume the standing position, springing on the left foot with each change of the right. Repeat the same, with the left foot springing on the right."[116] Such exercises not only provided healthful benefits but taught the students rhythmic movement and graceful motions.

Music also played a decided role during special occasions at Troy, such as General Lafayette's visit to the seminary. The students graciously welcomed Lafayette with a song, "My Own Sunny France," which Emma Willard composed for the event:

And art thou, then, dear hero, come?
And do our eyes behold the man,
Who nerved his arm and bared his breast
For us, ere yet our life began?
For us and for our native land,
Thy youthful valor dared the war;
And now, in winter of thine age,
Thou'st come, and left thy loved ones far.
Then deep and dear thy welcome be,
Nor think thy daughters far from thee,
Columbia's daughters, lo! We bend,
And claim to call thee father, friend.

> But was't our country's rights alone
> Impelled Fayette to Freedom's van?
> No, 'twas the love of human kind—
> It was the sacred cause of man;
> It was benevolence sublime,
> Like that which sways the eternal mind!
> And, benefactor of the world,
> He shed his blood for all mankind.
> Then deep and dear thy welcome be,
> Nor think thy daughters far from thee.
> Daughters of human kind we bend,
> And claim to call thee father, friend.[117]

Willard's text, set to music by faculty member John C. Andrews, emphasized the honor of having such a distinguished guest.[118]

Church Music

Students also heard music performed at church, though it did not necessarily represent what they were accustomed to at home. Litchfield student Eliza Ogden must have been accustomed to fine church music. She observed with interest the difficulty the choir director experienced one evening before the bishop delivered his sermon: "The chorister had a great deal of trouble to get the young ladies put in the singers seat and a great deal of trouble to make them sing well."[119] It appears these choir members had not been properly trained.

Anne Walker, a student from Mount Holyoke, for instance, was critical of the South Hadley church:

> A good house, a good minister, but deliver me from the music. I will give a description in the words of another for they are very appropriate. It is very Mason like in one respect that is in numbers for there are over fifty [instruments], small and big. They have six violins, three bass viols, besides a whole brass band. The chorister rising gives three taps with his fiddle bow then the rest rise, then he commences [the musical tone] *do*, then they all take the pitch and sing; such time you never heard, the chorister always commences each line before the rest and then they follow and catch up with him. It is impossible to attempt to describe it, it must be heard to have any idea of it.[120]

This seems to represent a merging of two practices: the old way of lining out and Lowell Mason's scientific arrangements.

Apparently the singing in church did not improve, at least in the students' minds. Six years later Lydia French wrote to her sister concerning the difficulty she had in maintaining proper respect: "Imagine the front pews . . . filled with far sighted teachers who think it a crime to smile in church, and a choir, with a chorister who, when he wishes them to rise, flings up his arms as though he were driving a flock of sheep when the *fiddle* begins to squeak, the other instruments to groan, etc. and you will have some idea of my horror . . . and trying in vain to keep my face straight."[121] It must have been difficult for these students to adapt to a different form of choral performance.

Conclusion

Music was emphasized at Litchfield, Troy, Mount Holyoke, and Music Vale seminaries as an important part of female education and as an art in its own right. While differences are evident in the curricula, number of personnel, fees, instruments, and music-making within and outside the institutions, music was highly regarded for its potential health and intellectual benefits as well as refining the sentiments of young ladies. The level of music education offered at these schools enabled the students to study and perform the instrumental and vocal repertoire discussed in chapters 7 and 8.

7

Instrumental Music at the Seminaries

Although it was not socially acceptable for American women of the eighteenth and early nineteenth centuries to enjoy public music careers (for example, touring virtuosos or theater musicians), educators in such seminaries as Litchfield, Troy, Music Vale, and Mount Holyoke posited that women should fully develop their musical talents. An investigation of these institutions sheds light on the music young women were performing at the time. Women's repertoires went beyond a few simple tunes suitable for the church or parlor, often corresponding to music heard in the concert hall and on the recital stage in Europe. Extant programs for Mount Holyoke, Music Vale, and Troy seminaries; newspaper articles; music books used at Music Vale and Mount Holyoke; student diaries from Litchfield; and music books belonging to Lucy Sheldon (a student at Litchfield; see chapter 6) offer a wealth of information concerning the repertoire studied and performed at these schools.[1]

Music Vale focused solely on music instruction, and students' repertoires maintained a professional level. Founder Orramel Whittlesey stressed that the seminary's philosophy was unlike that practiced at other boarding schools: "Music is something distinct from all other parts of a young lady's education. To teach it there is not needed an intimate acquaintance with Botany or Chemistry, or with any other of the multifarious studies which young ladies are taught at boarding schools." He argued that the goal of Music Vale's program was "not to make merely superficial players, . . . but thorough pianists, skilled alike in theory and practice." An account in a local newspaper verifies the seminary's professional status: "[Whittlesey] graduates some of the most thorough accomplished artists in the country and his institution stands in the very first rank."[2] After Music Vale's founding around 1835, it soon became recognized as a renowned music school.

The repertoire studied at Troy largely rivals that at Music Vale.[3] Emma Willard, however, viewed music as an intellectual subject and encouraged the young women to achieve their utmost potential. The 1848 examining committee praised the music faculty, saying that based on "a pretty extensive observation elsewhere, [we] believe [they] are unsurpassed, if not unequalled in any other school in this country."[4] Four years later the committee attested that music instruction received as much emphasis as any academic subject: "Both the ornamental and solid branches of female education receive their appropriate share of attention. Indeed, there seems to be no deficiency with respect to tuition, discipline and liberal culture in any department of study."[5] The committee recognized the importance given to music instruction.

Compared to the music studied at Music Vale and Troy, Litchfield appears to have been somewhat restricted in its choice of composers, genres, and level of difficulty. Lucy Sheldon's music books mirror the philosophy set forth at the academy, where young women were exposed to and participated in the upscale social culture of Litchfield beyond the realm of activities at the other schools under discussion. Further, through the interaction of the distinguished Judge Tapping Reeve's law school for men, also in Litchfield, "many of Miss Pierce's young ladies found their future husbands."[6] Although the students received a higher education, the lifestyle at the academy suggests that it stressed the importance of preparing the young women to enter society. (See chapters 4 and 5 for a discussion of the education offered at Litchfield.)

The music studied at Mount Holyoke differed significantly from that of the other institutions. While the seminary valued vocal music over instrumental, it also emphasized choral music rather than private instruction.[7] Founder Mary Lyon strongly argued for the cultivation of vocal music; however, she purposely established Mount Holyoke so that middle-class women could attend. Most of the students needed to provide their own financial support or to help with family income. Like Troy's graduates, those who completed the required curriculum at Mount Holyoke were prepared to enter the teaching profession. Undoubtedly few of the students would have been able to afford private piano instruction, and even fewer would have owned a piano; thus piano was not offered.[8] The vocal music books used at Mount Holyoke contained many pieces requiring piano accompaniment, some quite difficult. Since a few public examination exercise programs specify the vocal numbers performed, it is likely that Mount Holyoke attracted students who were capable of playing the accompaniments.

Troy and Music Vale achieved distinction for their music instruction: Litchfield and Mount Holyoke were not far behind. The level of the literature, genres, and composers testifies that women were encouraged to study and perform a challenging repertoire of both lesser- and well-known composers. None of the music was scored for orchestra, which complies with the instruments considered appropriate for women to study.

Musical Entertainments

Various musical events provided opportunities for the students to display their talents. A musical entertainment occurring during the course of the annual public examinations served as a highlight of the year before the summer break.[9] In 1858 the examining committee liberally applauded Troy Female Seminary's music teachers and students: "The Committee would express their highest gratification at the success with which music is taught in the institution. Seldom have they listened to better singing, or witnessed more accomplished performances on the piano and harp. These exercises did much to relieve the labors of the examination. The *Concert* on Tuesday evening, would not have appeared out of place in an Academy of Music."[10] Such commendations confirm Troy's reputation for musical excellence.

Annual examination exercises at Music Vale and Troy included a variety of musical performances. Given that Music Vale was devoted to music instruction, it is logical that the program would be considerably longer. By 1869 the performances were divided according to instrument: piano, voice, cabinet organ, or guitar.[11] Since piano was the most popular instrument studied at Music Vale, the majority of the programs consisted of piano performances—solo, duet, trio, quartet, and sextet—followed by a significantly smaller number of vocal, organ, and guitar pieces. Unlike the printed programs at Troy, those at Music Vale included the names of the performers and composers.

Young women at Music Vale presented a concert the evening after examinations. By 1869 one dollar was charged for admission, as announced on the program.[12] Two years later this was reduced to fifty cents; possibly financial issues affected the nation's economy. The differences between the programs at Music Vale and Troy illustrate the philosophies of the two schools. Whittlesey established Music Vale to train young women as pianists and teachers. Although voice was added later, except for operas given at the school, the students seem not to have performed large choral numbers. Willard, however, intended Troy Female Seminary as a school to train educators. Though music instruction was as rigorous at Troy as at Music Vale, Troy apparently deemed ensemble participation, especially choral, to be an important part of the students' education. Litchfield and Mount Holyoke differed from Troy and Music Vale by including musical performances during the examination exercises rather than hosting separate concerts.[13] Litchfield also received approbation for its painstaking instruction. An account recorded in April 1828, in the *Litchfield County Post*, gave evidence that the exercises did not fail to please a "crowded and highly delighted audience." The musical performances far surpassed those heard at the finishing schools: "The compositions and the music, previously prepared, were . . . of a character suited to the occasion, exciting nothing like trifling and levity, yet so good as highly to interest and engage the attention of the audience." Students arduously prepared to present musical performances that "gave evidence of much improvement in this polite branch of education." Those who were privileged to attend admired the students' progress: "Upon the whole, all the services of the evening gave pleasing evidence that there has been no falling off, either on the part of the instructors or the pupils, connected with this valuable school; and we believe that no previous exhibition ever gave greater satisfaction to the friends of female education."[14] Like Music Vale, Mount Holyoke, and Troy, Litchfield continued to receive recognition for its excellent education.

In addition to the programs held during the examination exercises, each school presented musical entertainments, concerts, or recitals (all terms apparently synonymous) within the academic year. Music Vale's Friday evening recitals were open to the public and attracted local guests. Once a month the school hosted an event that brought visitors from far and wide, traveling in summer carriages and sleighs in the winter over hard-packed snowy roads. Anyone making the trip was treated to a memorable event, observing "ingenious things, full of naivete, but withal played with such perfection under that rigorous daily drill, as regards exact tempo, phrasing and note accuracy, that it could not help drawing exclamations of praise and delight from those who came to these concerts and to the annual examinations. And of course, the pianos were kept always in excellent tune!"[15] A new student who arrived during a concert noted that "the pupils were called in regular succession to the Piano. There was no hesitation, all moved easily, and many gracefully."[16] As Whittlesey projected, these events proved to be a boon to the students' training.[17]

Troy presented musical entertainments two or three times a semester. It was common for these programs to consist of a musical potpourri, such as the one on February 1, 1853 (fig. 7.1).[18] Performers' names are not given; members of Troy's faculty participated in student programs, since the heading on the

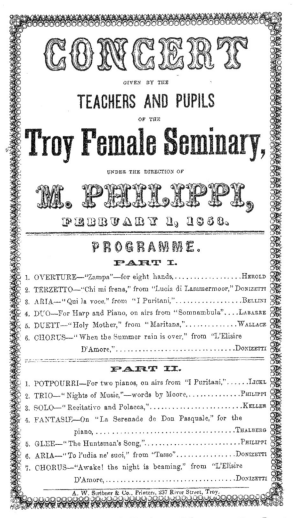

Fig. 7.1. Concert Program, Troy Female Seminary, February 1, 1853. Courtesy of Emma Willard School Archives, Emma Willard School, Troy, New York.

printed program read "Concert Given by Teachers and Pupils of the Troy Female Seminary." Usually the programs were divided into two parts; each opened and closed with an instrumental or vocal ensemble; then solo, duet, trio, and larger chamber works randomly followed. Compositions by current faculty members frequently graced the programs (for example, Matthieu Philippi), along with works by such popular contemporary composers as Louis Joseph Ferdinand Hérold, Donizetti, Bellini, and Sigismond Thalberg.

Beginning in 1862, when Mount Holyoke hired its first music teacher, musical entertainments were held approximately every two weeks. Music-making was a significant part of Litchfield's culturally rich environment, though not necessarily with the same types of musical entertainments as those given at other schools. For instance, it was common for dramatic performances to include some vocal music, and students frequently played chamber music in the evening, either at the home in which they boarded or at the Pierces' home. Although no printed programs survive, it seems likely that the school would have had regular public musical entertainments, given the town's social climate, as well as events connected with Reeve's law school.[19]

Music for Piano

The solo and ensemble piano music studied at the four schools indicates that students performed repertoires comparable to works by such contemporary professional musicians as Chopin, Henri Herz, Liszt, Thalberg, and Clara Schumann. Music Vale offered the most extensive piano program, with Troy close behind. According to the literature found in Lucy Sheldon's music books and students' diaries, Litchfield's piano training seems less intense than that offered at Music Vale or Troy. However, Sheldon's books do provide diverse and up-to-date publications for the serious piano student, including battle pieces, waltzes, sonatas, marches, sets of variations, and transcriptions. If the 1869 annual examination exercise program from Mount Holyoke can be taken as representative of the piano music performed at this seminary, it is safe to assume that in spite of the absence of regular instruction, students who continued their piano study after enrolling played repertoires similar to those heard at Troy and Music Vale.[20] The literature studied and programmed at Litchfield and Mount Holyoke reflects the level of students these schools attracted, though neither made music study a central focus of the curriculum.

Much of the repertoire at these schools would have been considered popular music at the time—"polkas, rondos, schottisches, quick steps, [and] variations."[21] Music Vale's 1857 catalog assures parents and prospective students that "the most approved and fashionable Music [is] furnished, if desired, at the lowest cash prices."[22] The schools kept pace with current publications, as testified on the program for Music Vale's twenty-fifth anniversary, June 22 and 23, 1864: Joseph Ascher's arrangement of "Grand Capriccio de Concert" from *La Traviata*; Louis Moreau Gottschalk's "Caprice Espagnol"; Johann Baptist Cramer's duet arrangement of a selection from Giacomo Meyerbeer's *Les Huguenots*; "Fantasie on Scottish Airs" arranged for six hands by Carl Czerny;

a sextet on Mozart's *The Marriage of Figaro*, and a sextet on the Overture to Daniel-François-Esprit Auber's *Fra Diavolo*, also arranged by Czerny.[23]

Although solo literature was the most popular, piano students at Music Vale, Troy, and Litchfield frequently performed chamber music. Performances for piano ensemble (four, six, eight, or twelve hands) or piano with other instruments (flute, violin, cello, harp, or guitar) were favored at Music Vale and Troy. Piano ensemble repertoires included marches, waltzes, themes and variations, and character pieces (for example, caprice and galop). There is no evidence that students at Litchfield or Mount Holyoke played piano ensemble repertoires, but Music Vale students often played arrangements for four, six, eight, or twelve hands. For instance, the annual examination program at Music Vale on June 24, 1869, includes ten piano ensemble pieces: three for two pianos, eight hands ("Sonnambula" by Christian Traugott Brunner; "Battle March of the Priests—Athalia" by August Horn, and Albert Berg's "March de Concert"). The last two pieces on the program were for two pianos, twelve hands ("Paddy Carey" and "Tancredi" by Czerny). There were also twelve vocal, seven cabinet organ, and four guitar performances, in addition to theoretical exercises. An anonymous new student who arrived at Music Vale during a concert described the setting in an article published in the school newspaper, *Gleaner of the Vale*: "We entered the concert room. Some of the pupils were playing a Quartette for eight hands upon two Pianos. This was new to me, and I was puzzled to know how they could keep such perfect and exact time with the Pianos so far separated. The effect upon entering the concert rooms was very pleasing."[24] This exemplifies the careful training of Music Vale students.

Troy students likewise frequently performed piano ensemble literature, especially for four and eight hands; works for twelve hands were rare. Nonetheless, no program includes as many ensemble compositions as those at Music Vale. The "Concert Given by the Teachers and Pupils of the Troy Female Seminary, under the Direction of M. Philippi, July 22d, 1851," for example, included three piano ensemble pieces: Gioachino Rossini's "Overture to *Guillaume Tell*" for eight hands; "Echo—Waltzes," for eight hands by Philippi; "Sounds from the Heart," waltzes for twelve hands, also by Philippi; plus two piano solos. This program was the final concert of the academic year during the six-day examination period.[25]

Over 120 composers are represented in the students' repertoires, many now little known and rarely performed on recitals. The majority of the composers are from the Romantic period, a few represent the Classical era, but Handel is the only one from the Baroque.[26] Except for a limited number of American composers, such as Louis Moreau Gottschalk and Charles Grobe, most are of European descent—German, French, Bohemian, Irish, British, or Austrian. Music Vale students performed works composed by the largest number of composers, followed by Troy, then Litchfield, and finally Mount Holyoke.[27] Several of the names found at Music Vale, such as Theodore Oesten, Henri Herz, Sigismond Thalberg, William Vincent Wallace, Beethoven, and Mozart, also appear at Troy.[28] Lucy Sheldon's books seldom include composers' names, but James Hewitt and Ignaz Pleyel are prominent. None of the names in her books appear on programs at Music Vale, Troy, or Mount Holyoke.[29] Until 1869 the programs from Mount Holyoke did not include composers' names. Along with the shortage of programs, it is difficult to form a concrete impression of the repertoire performed.

Student pianists at all four schools performed intermediate to advanced literature. While it was common for these schools, save Mount Holyoke, to offer instruction at all levels, Troy and Music Vale showcased their advanced students. Some of the piano pieces in Lucy Sheldon's music books represent early intermediate literature; others require more expertise, although none are as technically or musically challenging as those performed at Music Vale or Troy.[30] Litchfield music students were serious, for example, rising at 4:00 A.M. to have their music lessons. As was customary in the early 1800s, much of the music in Sheldon's books is in manuscript; only book 3 contains printed music.

Collectively the piano literature provides a wide representation of standard nineteenth-century repertoire, such as character pieces, transcriptions, sets of variations, battle pieces, dances, etudes, marches, and sonatas. No fugues or sonatinas are included. A comparison of the repertoires at the four schools reveals that students attending Music Vale performed the largest variety of music in popular nineteenth-century genres, with those at Troy close behind. Lucy Sheldon's books exhibit some of the preferred genres in the late eighteenth and early nineteenth centuries; the march and the waltz were the two favorite genres for solo piano. The marches, along with a set of variations on "Yankee Doodle," battle pieces, and vocal pieces with political themes, lend a patriotic flavor to her books. Some genres are found only on Music Vale programs—etude, impromptu, and mazurka—while hymn, allemande, and gavotte appear only at Litchfield, and the concertante at Troy.[31] The repertoire at Music Vale and Troy corresponds closely to that of the Moravian Young Ladies' Seminary in Bethlehem, Pennsylvania, affirming that Troy and Music Vale offered some of the finest opportunities for piano study for young women in the northern United States.[32]

BATTLE PIECES

Battle pieces for piano were fashionable in the late eighteenth century and through much of the nineteenth. One of the most popular, Franz Koczwara's "The Battle of Prague for the Piano Forte," is included in Lucy Sheldon's third book and was also performed at Music Vale. Sections of the piece represent various stages of the battle, beginning with a slow march followed by such events as "Word of Command," "Trumpet Call," "The Attack," "Attack with Swords," "Cries of the Wounded," and "Trumpet of Victory." Battle pieces were difficult to perform. J. Bunker Clark describes the agility required:

> Many kinds of special keyboard techniques depict drums, guns, bullets, swords, galloping horses, and the confusion of battle. In Koczwara's *Battle of Prague*, the Prussians attack, with the right hand, the left-hand Imperialists (represented by an Alberti bass). Prussian cannons are fired by crossing the right hand over the left for isolated low notes. Rapid descending scales in the treble represent "flying bullets," and sword attacks are rolled chords in the right hand accompanied by "horses galloping" (triplet Alberti bass). Heavy cannonfire is depicted by rapid rising scales in the left hand and general rifle fire in the right.[33]

It must have been as much a treat for the audience to observe the performance as to hear it.

Secondary descriptions—for example, "Horses galloping," "Light Dragoons advancing," and "Cannons"—help the pianist to vividly portray the battle's progress. A rendition of "God Save the King" followed by a "Turkish March" quickstep precede the finale, which concludes with "Go to Bed Home." One wonders whether someone held up placards or spoke the captions in the score. Since no text was sung, might some actions have been pantomimed? These questions remain unanswered.[34] No composer for "The Battle of Prague" is given in Sheldon's music book; however, Franz Koczwara's name is normally associated with this title.[35] While battle pieces were not among the more popular works at the time, a copy of "The Battle of the Nile" also appears in Sheldon's book 4; the "Battle March" from *Athalia* was performed at Music Vale.

CHARACTER PIECES

Character pieces with descriptive titles comprise some of the most popular compositions studied and performed at Music Vale. Numerous composers are represented, including Franz Abt, Franz von Suppé, Anton Rubinstein, Sigismond Thalberg, Louis Moreau Gottschalk, Theodore Oesten, William

V. Wallace, and Johann Baptist Cramer. Many of the titles suggest programmatic content, such as "Poet and Peasant" by von Suppé; Abt's "The Chime of Silvery Sabbath Bells"; "Fairy Fingers," op. 26 by S. B. Mills; Sydney Smith's "La Harpe Eolienne"; "Les Belles de l'Amérique" by Gustave Blessner; "Jefferson's Whim"; and "The Opera Neel."[36] Other character pieces had generic titles, such as Anton Rubinstein's "Melodie in F." Occasionally more than one work bore the same title: both Harry Harris and J[acob] A[lfred] Getze wrote pieces titled "Banjo" that were performed at Music Vale.

Gottschalk's name appears several times on Music Vale programs. On March 14, 1854, Whittlesey, together with teachers and students, attended a performance by Gottschalk in Norwich, Connecticut (thirteen miles from Salem). Gottschalk's impression of Whittlesey is noteworthy:

> Professor Whittlesy introduced himself to me. He is a singular personage who deserves to be described to you. Small, fat, a large bust, short and crooked legs, heavy black eyebrows, from beneath which appears a roll of oily, ruddy flesh. The professor in a basso-profundo voice informed me that he has been the founder, director, headmaster, professor, and proprietor for forty years of a normal college of music for young girls who intend to teach. "All pretty, sir, never less than fourteen or more than twenty years of age. In good health—and I have the satisfaction of being able to say that during the forty years that I have been the head of Music Vale" (the name which he has given to his colony, situated in the idle of a picturesque and lonely valley) *"there has not been one death.* The principals have come with me today to go to your concert. But I desire particularly to introduce you to my pupils. I only teach theory, and I make them work it out by practicing on three harps, which cost me eight hundred dollars, the first in 1825; and I have besides twenty-five pianos, but they are a little old" (judging from the harps which are from 1825). Every time the professor gets up he looks as if about to take wings to fly away. I gave him seats for himself and his school. After the concert he came and grasped my hand warmly; "never, no never, have I heard anything so touching." His enthusiasm knew no bounds; he embraced me, and I am convinced from making acquaintance with his breath of what I had already suspected—that is to say, the worthy professor of Music Vale is a much greater amateur of whiskey than of music; and after having been introduced to his pupils, I discovered that Apollo has less to do at the seminary than his mother.[37]

Whittlesey had a high regard for Gottschalk and undoubtedly encouraged the students to study his music. "The Last Hope" and "La Gallina" are examples of character pieces performed at Music Vale. "The Last Hope," written for solo piano, became Gottschalk's signature piece and the most favored nineteenth-century American published piano composition.[38] It came to be regarded as "one of America's best-known melodies" and "as a 'Religious Meditation.'" The piano duet "La Gallina" ("The Hen") begins "with an attractive Cuban dance" and "slides into some bold dissonances" creating a descriptive ensemble work.[39]

George W. Warren's "La Fête des Fées," op. 13, a dramatic character piece for an advanced player, was performed by Miss F. Palmer at Music Vale's thirtieth annual examination on June 24, 1869. The cadenza passage, replete with octaves and thirds performed at a presto tempo, and the improvisatory and arpeggiated flourishes that follow exemplify the technical skills required throughout the piece and testify to Music Vale's demanding standards (ex. 7.1).[40]

Arrangements of popular tunes, such as "Home Sweet Home," were fashionable character pieces. Sigismond Thalberg arranged this piece for both piano solo and duet; James M. Wehli arranged and performed it for left hand alone. All of these compositions were performed at Music Vale. Some of the character pieces are of moderate difficulty while others reflect the professional level. Both Thalberg's solo and Wehli's arrangements represent the virtuosic level of repertoire studied at Music Vale. Thalberg's brilliant keyboard ability is evident in his solo arrangement. Even at an adagio tempo, the pianist encounters difficulty in bringing out the embedded melody within the thirty-second-note figures, frequently requiring the left hand to cross over the right. The technical complexity increases with sixty-fourth-note scalar passages in the right hand above the thirty-second-note arpeggios (ex. 7.2).[41] Wehli's arrangement, which became his signature piece, is no less virtuosic, abounding with scalar and arpeggiated passages.[42] The main difference between Thalberg's and Wehli's arrangements is Wehli's scalar and arpeggiated thirty-second-note octaves and thirds in the accompaniment (ex. 7.3).[43] Both pieces provide challenges for the advanced student.

MARCHES

Marches are prominent in Lucy Sheldon's books and at Music Vale. Several were performed at Troy, though to a lesser extent than the other two schools. Marches are represented as piano solos in Sheldon's four books. Most titles reflect an association with a person or place, the former including "The Duke of Lord's March," "Governor Femer's March," "Buonaparte's Grand March," and "The New President's March"; those associated with a place include "London March," "Paris March," "The Edinburgh Volunteers Grand March," and "Swiss Guards March."

Only three of the marches cited on Troy's extant programs include a name or place: "Grand Amazon March," "Florida March," and "Montezuma—Grand

Ex. 7.1. George W. Warren, "La Fête des Fées," op. 13, mm. 46–61. Courtesy of New York State Library, Albany, New York.

Heroic March, dedicated to Maj. Gen. Wool," all by Gustave Blessner. *Lee and Walker's Musical Almanac for 1869, for the Use of Seminaries, Professors of Music, and the Musical Public* includes "Florida March" among the compositions, "New and selected. All are choice and useful pieces, by the best Authors."[44] "Florida March" appears on a program at Troy dated April 26,

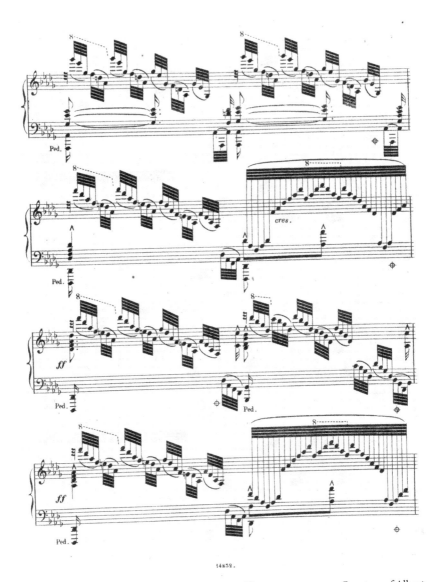

Ex. 7.2. Sigismond Thalberg, "Home! Sweet Home!," op. 72, mm. 37–41. Courtesy of Albert and Shirley Small Special Collections Library, University of Virginia.

Ex. 7.3. James M. Wehli, "Home Sweet Home, for the Pianoforte, Transcribed for the Left Hand Only," mm. 73–81. Courtesy of Albert and Shirley Small Special Collections Library, University of Virginia.

1849, but without indicating solo or duet. Given that it was included in *Lee and Walker's Musical Almanac* as a new four-hand arrangement, it must have remained popular, since Blessner arranged it for piano duet.

Marches performed at Music Vale included those of Felix Mendelssohn, Louis Streabbog, Jean-Baptiste Duvernoy, Gottschalk, Albert Berg, Ferdinand Ries, and Franz Lachner, and others arranged by Zungmann and Ascher.[45] Several marches had a celebratory flare, such as Mendelssohn's "Wedding March"; "Gran Marche Solennelle" by Gottschalk; "Grand March Triomphale" by Ries; and Berg's "Marche de Concert." Others favor a military theme, for example, Streabbog's "Le Défilé—March Militaire," and Zungmann's arrangement of Beethoven's "Türkischner Marsch," op. 143. It was common for marches to be arranged for piano duet or two pianos, eight hands, such as Mendelssohn's "Wedding March" (four hands) and Ascher's "Concordantia. Andante et Allegro Marziale" (eight hands). Ascher's arrangement appeared on two consecutive anniversary exercise programs at Music Vale: June 29, 1871, and June 13, 1872. It was the penultimate piece in 1871 and the final number one year later. The prominent place given to Ascher's march on these two programs confirms that it was a crowd pleaser.

ETUDES

The etude is one of the few genres that appeared solely at Music Vale. Technical study was an important part of the students' foundation; teachers carefully guided the correct position of the fingers and the hands. Students studied and performed etudes by such composers as H[ermann] Berens, Friedrich Burgmüller, Oscar Comettant, Cramer, Czerny, Duvernoy, Louis Köhler, Louis Plaidy, and Sydney Smith. Miss M. L. Brooks performed "Gabrielle: Etude d'Expression pour Piano" by Comettant on the thirtieth annual examination program. This concert etude for the advanced student is no less challenging than many Chopin studies. The two-against-three pattern is complicated by repeated octaves in the right hand and the repetitive octave and melodic figure in the left hand, performed *con eleganzia*. A graceful yet virtuosic pianistic agility is necessary to give a *molto eleganzia e aporosamente* performance (ex. 7.4).[46]

RONDOS

The rondo does not seem to have been as popular as some other genres; however, it was studied and performed at both Troy and Music Vale. Rondos performed at Music Vale were for piano solo, while C. M. von Weber's "Grand Rondo Brillant" for four hands is the only one appearing on Troy programs. Two of those performed at Music Vale, both by Wilhelm Iucho, are

Ex. 7.4. Oscar Comettant, "Gabrielle: Etude d'Expression pour Piano," mm. 45–57. Courtesy of the Library of Congress.

technical studies in rondo form. The "Third Calisthenic Rondo," for example—an intermediate-level piece similar to an etude—focuses on an Alberti bass, chords, and octaves in the accompaniment.[47] Other rondo composers represented include Franz Abt, Beethoven, and Jules Egghard. Abt's "Golden Chimes" is classified as a rondoletto.

TRANSCRIPTIONS

Transcriptions comprise some of the most favored nineteenth-century repertoire. Such contemporary composers as Thalberg, Herz, Oesten, Cramer, Czerny, Brinley Richards, Rudolphe Kreutzer, Wilhelm Kuhe, and Maurice Strakosch frequently transcribed operatic airs, arias, and overtures for solo or ensemble performance or used the borrowed melody as a theme for a pianistic genre. Pieces such as Kuhe's "Grand Fantaisie" on *Il Trovatore* and "Fantaisie" on *Tannhäuser* were performed at Music Vale; Thalberg's "Fantasia" on Meyerbeer's *Les Huguenots* and "Fantasia" on a "Serenade and Minuet" from *Don Giovanni*, and Strakosch's "Fantasie on Airs from *Lucia di Lammermoor*" were programmed at Troy.

"The Celebrated Overture to *Lodoïska*" by Kreutzer, in Lucy Sheldon's book 3, an example of an early transcription, displays a classical style with a repeated right-hand accompanimental figure and left-hand bass melody played in octaves (ex. 7.5).[48] While there are few dynamic markings, the intensity of the music is indicative of Kreutzer's intended mood.

Overtures transcribed for solo, four, six, or eight hands were frequently performed at Troy. Arrangements for six or eight hands repeatedly served as opening numbers on musical programs, such as Auber's "Overture to *Masaniello* for Eight Hands, Performed on Two Pianos," for Professor Gustave Blessner's farewell concert on May 14, 1850. This must have been a favored piece, since it often appears as the initial number on several of Troy's student/faculty programs. Transcriptions of Auber's overtures were featured at Troy; other performances include *Fra Diavolo*, *Le Cheval de Bronze*, and *Le Domino Noir*. Overtures by Saverio Mercandante, Mozart, Carl Maria von Weber, Czerny, and Hérold likewise appear on programs.

Students at Music Vale often performed transcriptions, but the overture was not as popular as it was at Troy. Beethoven's overture to *Fidelio*, arranged for piano duet, for example, appeared on the June 29, 1871, program at Music Vale, sandwiched between two pieces for cabinet organ: "Die Ehre Gottes; aus der Natur" by Beethoven, and Schubert's "Twenty-Third Psalm" (arranged for three performers). A transcription of Hérold's overture to *Zampa* was the only overture programmed at both Troy and Music Vale. Czerny's sextet arrangement of the overtures to *Fra Diavolo* and *The Marriage of Figaro* were performed at Music Vale; his eight-hand transcription of the overture to *Guillaume Tell* was programmed at Troy. Given that Czerny's transcriptions were prevalent during the nineteenth century, it seems likely that more of his arrangements would have been studied at both schools. Again, a dearth of programs prevents a definitive conclusion.

Printed for HEWITT & RAUSCH

Ex. 7.5. Rudolphe Kreutzer, "The Celebrated Overture to *Lodoïska*," mm. 81–111. Lucy Sheldon's Music Book 3. Courtesy of the Collection of the Litchfield Historical Society, Litchfield, Connecticut.

Various other transcriptions were part of the standard repertoire at Music Vale, including Albert Berg's arrangement of "Grand Duo de Concert" from *I Puritani* for two pianos. Ascher's arrangement of "Andante—Sur le Final de la *Lucia di Lammermoor*" and James Bellak's arrangement of "Buds from Opera—*Ernani*" are for solo piano. Theodore Mœlling's piano duet arrangement (of a selection from) *Un Ballo in Maschera* was performed on June 29, 1871, and August 14, 1873. He must have been an admired composer, since *Lee and Walker's Musical Almanac* from 1869 includes Mœlling's work in the section "New and selected. All are choice and useful pieces, by the best Authors."[49] Rather than operatic transcriptions, Brinley Richards's solo piano arrangements are apparently based on contemporary popular songs, such as "Cottage by the Sea" by J. R. Thomas. Richards's transcription includes an introduction comparable to that for a vocal performance. The arrangement provides directions to aid the pianist in rendering an expressive interpretation.[50]

THEMES AND VARIATIONS

The nineteenth century was a heyday for sets of themes and variations. Such composers as Herz, Franz Hünten, Thalberg, William V. Wallace, and Faustina Hodges found a ready market for their works. Well-known melodies, including "The Last Rose of Summer," "Home, Sweet Home," "Annie Laurie," "O, Dear! What Can the Matter Be," and "My Lodging Is on the Cold Ground" (also known as "Believe Me if All Those Endearing Young Charms"), served as fodder for sets of variations. Likewise, composers used operatic themes— for example, Herz's "Grandes Variations for Four Hands on a Favorite March from *Guillaume Tell*," performed at Troy, and I. Moscheles's and Felix Mendelssohn's arrangement of "Variations Brillantes. Sur la Marche Bohemienne," performed at Music Vale.

Charles Grobe's arrangement of "Smile On: Brilliant Variations on Wallace's Beautiful Melody, 'Katie Strang,'" follows the form often used in sets of themes and variations: introduction, theme, a number of variations (here, three), and a finale. Although this piece was performed at Music Vale as a duet, I have been able to locate only the solo piano version. It does not present the bravura difficulties of some repertoire at Music Vale; however, Grobe employs a variety of pianistic skills for the advancing pianist. The triplet figuration and the octave and chord leaps in variation 2 present a challenge to perform this movement *Più mosso e brillante*.[51] Henri Herz's arrangement of "The Last Rose of Summer," op. 159, with an "Introduction and Brilliant Variations for the Piano Forte, as Performed in All His Concerts in the United

States," was also performed at Music Vale. It features a dramatic introduction and concludes with a *brillante* cadenza passage.[52]

Variations seem to have been most performed at Music Vale and Troy. Lucy Sheldon's book 3, however, includes a copy of "Pleyel's Favorite German Hymn" with four variations. This is the only sacred piece I have found in all the schools' piano repertoires. Apparently after the three verses were sung, the pianist would play the variations. The third variation is the most difficult, with demanding passagework in the right hand.[53]

It is unusual to find the same set of variations at more than one school. An exception is the set based on the theme "Lee Rigg" in Lucy Sheldon's music books 1 and 2 and programmed at Music Vale in 1873. This must have been a popular piece, appearing as early as 1818 and again fifty-five years later. Furthermore, since it occurs twice in Lucy's book, it must have been worth a second look.

DANCES

Dances (allemande, polka, mazurka, galop, gavotte, saltarello, quadrille, tarantella, and waltz) were fashionable nineteenth-century piano literature. The allemande and gavotte are represented only at Litchfield, the former in "Lady Barton's Allemande," in Sheldon's book 1, and "Allemande," in book 4. No composer is given for either dance. Handel's Gavotte in D major is also in book 1. It seems that Troy and Music Vale were more concerned than Litchfield with providing the most up-to-date repertoire for students. Since the allemande was in vogue during the Baroque and Classical periods, this may explain why it was not part of the students' repertoires at Troy or Music Vale. The galop and polka appear on programs at Music Vale and Troy, although the mazurka and saltarello were performed only at Music Vale. The saltarello remained popular throughout the nineteenth century. The cover of the "Saltarello" by S. B. Mills (fig. 7.2) portrays the sprightly character of this dance, abounding in pyrotechnics performed at a presto tempo (ex. 7.6).[54]

The quadrille (also called cotillion) was a popular ballroom dance during the nineteenth century. Cotillion parties were a favored recreation at Litchfield. Although dancing was not allowed at Mount Holyoke, calisthenic exercises often resembled dance steps. The quadrille normally includes five diverse parts: *Le pantalon, L' été, La poule, La pastourelle,* and a "Finale." *La pastourelle* was frequently replaced with *La Trénis,* as seen in Gustave Blessner's *Les Echos de l'Europe.* He composed this "brillante" quadrille in 1848 and dedicated it to Emma Willard, who had taken an extensive trip to Europe eighteen years earlier. Blessner also included a waltz and trio

Fig. 7.2. S. B. Mills, "Saltarello," op. 26, title page. Courtesy of Albert and Shirley Small Special Collections Library, University of Virginia.

titled *Olympia*, to be played after the "Finale." His arrangement for two pianos, eight hands was performed during a concert at Troy seminary on November 30, 1848.

The waltz was the most favored dance, appearing several times in Sheldon's music books and on programs at Troy and Music Vale. Frequently the waltz was programmed at Troy as an ensemble piece, such as Matthieu Philippi's waltzes for six, eight, or twelve hands. Wilhelm Neuland's "Gallenberg Waltz, with Variations" for piano and guitar was the sole piece including guitar on the June 26, 1855, program. Although students at Music Vale played waltzes as ensemble works (for example, Joseph A. Fowler's "Rosemary Waltzes" for eight hands), most of the performances were for solo piano.

"The Celebrated One Finger'd Sliding Waltz," in Sheldon's book 1, is a late intermediate piece employing the glissando technique. Apparently the term

Ex. 7.6. S. B. Mills, "Saltarello," op. 26, mm. 149–187. Courtesy of Albert and Shirley Small Special Collections Library, University of Virginia.

"glissando" was not used at that time; rather the students were directed to play the "sliding" passages with the index finger (ex. 7.7).[55] The sliding technique appears again in "Clementi's Favorite Waltz" (Sheldon's book 4), where it is reserved for a few passages instead of the entire treble part. "Sliding" is written over the glissando notes.[56]

Ex. 7.7. "The Celebrated One Finger'd Sliding Waltz," mm. 1–18. Courtesy of Albert and Shirley Small Special Collections Library, University of Virginia.

SONATAS

Sonatas are less represented than other genres. A single example is found in Lucy Sheldon's books, and none appear on existing programs at Troy and Music Vale until the early 1870s. Valentino Nicolai's Sonata No. 1 is included in Sheldon's book 3. This piece exemplifies the classical style—Alberti bass accompaniment with a technically demanding right-hand melody; thirds and octaves in the first movement performed at an allegro tempo, followed by a second movement rondeau. The level of difficulty affirms Lucy Sheldon's pianistic skills. Her penciled fingerings indicate that she gave it serious attention. The program for the anniversary exercises held on June 13, 1872, at Music Vale includes a performance of Mozart's Sonatas Nos. 2 and 3, op. 6; and Beethoven's "Moonlight Sonata" one year later. The "Moonlight Sonata" also appears on a Soirée Musicale program at Troy on May 13, 1872, and Beethoven's Sonata No. 12 was performed at Mount Holyoke Seminary on July 12, 1869, for the thirty-second anniversary of the public examination exercises. Although these schools maintained high musical and, except for Music Vale, academic standards, their repertoires reflected currently fashionable works. Sonatas may have been too academic to be considered popular. Thus the inclusion of sonatas in the early 1870s speaks to a decided change in what was considered appropriate repertoire.

Ensemble Music

The study and performance of ensemble music enriched the students' training and provided a welcome diversity to the programs. Although there is not a large volume of this literature, extant programs include enough pieces to confirm it as an important part of their music curriculum. Music Vale and Troy programmed repertoire for various combinations of instruments, such as piano with harp, violin, guitar, or cabinet organ; two guitars; harp and guitar; piano, violin, and cello; and piano, flute, violin, and cello. Gustave Blessner's farewell concert included two pieces scored for an unusual ensemble: "Les Belles de l'Amérique"—classified as "New Quadrilles"—"two Pianos, Harp, Violoncello, etc., with Solos for Cornet à Piston and Violin," and "The Empire State Quick Step." The latter piece served as the program finale, performed by the same instruments, save the solo violin.

The most popular ensemble at Troy was piano and harp, while at Music Vale it was piano and guitar, although students did perform pieces arranged for piano and harp or organ. None of Troy's or Music Vale's students studied wind or string instruments, with the exception of violin at Troy from 1847 to 1850.[57] The addition of string instruments (apparently one or more faculty members also played the viola) made it possible for Troy to include more diverse combinations of chamber performances than any other school. A Beethoven sinfonia scored for piano, flute, violin, and cello is included on the February 9, 1854, program, and on June 27 three performers (piano, violin, and cello) presented the second movement of Beethoven's Trio in G Major, op. 1, no. 2.

Collectively the ensemble music is entirely secular and includes nineteenth-century composers and arrangers, mostly European, who are either obscure (for example, Neuland, Spinaleo, and Holland[58]) or canonized (such as Chopin, Schubert, Beethoven, and Mendelssohn). The majority of the pieces are arrangements of other composers' works, such as galops or operatic airs and arias. A few examples are originals, such as Blessner's "Daguerre" for piano, harp, and violin and Whittlesey's "Music Vale Seminary Quickstep" for piano and harp.

Most of the compositions are classical; others can be described as popular music, such as F. Barclay Halévy's "Bright Star of Hope," a Romance from *L'Eclair*. Popular pieces often have descriptive titles or suggest programmatic intent, like "Spanish Fandango" with variations, composed for two guitars, or Neuland's "Buona Notte" for guitar and piano. Classical compositions can be categorized into various genres: airs, variations, serenades, dances (polka, galop, quadrille, quickstep, and waltz with variations), marches, concertantes, sinfonie, and sonatas. Titles frequently infer a genre, such as Schubert's "La Serenade," arranged for organ and piano, while some indicate instrumentation, for example, Chopin's "Duet, Organ and Piano," op. 32, and Philippe-Jacques Meyer's "Harp and Piano."

Dances appear among the most stylish ensemble pieces at Troy and Music Vale. Arrangements of Charles-François Gounod's "Storm Bird Galop" for guitar and piano must have been well liked by Music Vale students and professors: Spinaleo's duet setting was performed at the annual examination program in 1871, and Holland's duet arrangement appeared on programs the following two years. "Gallenberg Waltz," with variations by Neuland, for guitar and piano, performed at Troy in 1855, combines two genres. It is unusual for a waltz to serve as a theme for variations; normally the chosen theme is a popular melody or operatic selection.

Although both Music Vale and Troy offered harp instruction, operatic arrangements for harp and piano are found solely at Troy. Duos or duets by Théodore Labarre, Auber, and Robert Nicolas-Charles Bochsa are scattered over extant programs. Labarre's name appears more frequently as arranger of both duos and duets, such as a duet from *Fra Diavolo* and a duo from *Guillaume Tell*, while Bochsa's "Airs from *Lucia*" must have pleased the audience, since it was performed on the concerts of May 13 and July 22, 1851. Both Bochsa and Labarre arranged a duo from *La Sonnambula*, and Auber and Labarre each arranged a duo from *Le Cheval de Bronze*.

The organ was one of the least favored instruments for ensemble music. Music Vale was the only seminary to program pieces composed for organ and piano or harp, though Troy also offered organ instruction.[59] Blessner's "Commencement March," for organ, piano, and three performers (presumably piano four hands), appeared on the thirty-second annual examination program at Music Vale on June 29, 1871. Although the program was held at the close of the school year, and the march's title suggests this piece would have been used as the students filed in for commencement, it was the eighteenth of twenty selections on part two of the program. It preceded a class recitation on "Nomenclature," followed by the school chorus performing "Our Harp and Banner" as the final number. The program continued with part three, which included sixteen performances. "Commencement March" was not used as might be expected.

Guitar, Organ, Harp, and Violin

In addition to piano and voice, Troy and Music Vale offered instruction in guitar, organ, and harp. Although it was acceptable for women to play these instruments, the number of pieces programmed confirms that students studied mostly piano or voice. Troy's offering of violin was unusual, since American society was hesitant to consider it an appropriate instrument for women to play.

As early as 1846 students at Troy could pursue organ for an extra fee, though no organ solos appear on a program. Since the seminary continued to offer organ, there must have been lesson requests. Further, given the level of music students Troy attracted, as exemplified in piano, vocal, harp, guitar, and violin repertoire, it seems likely there would have been organ students capable of public performance.

Music Vale Seminary held Sunday church services. Organ students likely played during the service, though no documentation exists to either support or negate this argument. Several pieces for cabinet organ appear on existing programs, with the exception of 1863, and more organ solos were included in 1869 than for other years. Of the fifty-eight pieces on the program, seven for organ were grouped together under the heading "Cabinet Organ." After 1869 the number of organ solos diminished significantly; they were interspersed in the programs. Collectively the pieces are sacred compositions composed or arranged as hymns, solos, trios, quartettes, sentences, or motets. Representative examples include the following hymns: George William Warren's "Rock of Ages" and T. Wood's "Nearer My God to Thee"; solo, "Die Ehre Gottes aus der Natur" by Beethoven; trio, Schubert's "Twenty-Third Psalm"; quartette, "Father, Wilt Thou Guard and Guide Us" by Howard Malcolm Dow; sentence, "Cast Thy Burden on the Lord" by W.B.B.;[60] and motet, Felix Mendelssohn's "Come Unto Me." The composers or arrangers, such as Warren, Wilhelm Müller, Dow, and [O. R.] Brown, are mostly obscure today. Such hymns as those mentioned above were undoubtedly arrangements for organ, since Thomas Hastings composed "Rock of Ages" and Lowell Mason wrote "Nearer My God to Thee."

Violin performances, either solo, accompanying, or part of an ensemble, added variety to Troy's programs. Apparently few students took advantage of violin instruction while Blessner was employed at Troy, as only a small number of violin solos or violin with piano accompaniment works are scattered over the extant programs from 1847 through 1850. The literature appearing on the programs—sonata, concertante, and variations—attests to the ability of students studying violin. Representative composers include Felix Mendelssohn, Ole (Bornemann) Bull, Gustave Blessner, Charles De Bériot, and Charles Lafont. Ole Bull's "Variations Fantastique" for solo violin was programmed on April 27, 1848. Two years later Blessner's composition under the same title appeared on the program. Blessner performed the work at his farewell concert on May 14, 1850, as well as "Duet Concertant" by Henri Herz (piano) and Charles Lafont (violin), accompanied by his wife, probably "Grand Duo Concertante sur 'Niobe,' op. 110."

Some programs, in addition to those during Blessner's time at the school, also included violin performances, such the one for March 23, 1838, that included a piece scored for harp, piano, and violin by Bochsa, Herz, and La Port.[61] Further, more than one program in 1854 includes pieces composed for violin with other instruments, such as an unspecified sonata by Mendelssohn on February 9, 1854. This suggests that either Troy attracted students who studied violin before coming to the seminary or a faculty member was proficient on the instrument.[62] Some vocal works also called for violin accompaniment.[63]

Guitar pieces likewise constitute a small number of performances on the programs at Music Vale and Troy; none are present at Litchfield or Mount

Holyoke. Many works appear to be popular songs of the day composed by now obscure composers. Examples of solo compositions include "Over the River" by Johann Melchior Molter, "Softly O'er the Rippling Waters" by Winslow L. Hayden, and "Spanish Retreat" by Antonio de Auguera. The latter piece was the sole example on extant Troy programs.

Conclusion

The emphasis given to music instruction at Troy, Litchfield, and Mount Holyoke reveals the importance of music education in their curricula. Although the music programs at each institution differed in many respects, Emma Willard, Sarah Pierce, Mary Lyon, and Orramel Whittlesey contended that music study deserved to be taken as seriously as any academic subject. Individually each of these institutions garnered and maintained a valued reputation for its music training. The entertainments occurring at various points during the academic year testify to the enrichment that students received from music instruction.

For most students piano was the favored instrument. Opportunities for instruction in such instruments as organ, harp, and guitar at Music Vale and Troy, and violin for a brief time at Troy, provided an additional level of musical training. Though Mary Lyon initially chose to focus on vocal music, Mount Holyoke attracted students who had previously studied piano and were interested in furthering their talent. An examination of the piano repertoires at these four schools reveals that students had opportunities to study and perform popular musical works. While it appears that Music Vale and Troy offered a broader and perhaps more professional level of instruction, Litchfield and Mount Holyoke maintained high standards in their own right.

8

Singing Ladies

Vocal Repertoire at the Seminaries

Since all students could participate in singing, vocal music was extensively incorporated into the curriculum and activities at Litchfield, Troy, Mount Holyoke, and Music Vale. Although Sarah Pierce was not proficient in music, she engaged a singing master and encouraged Litchfield students to participate in singing schools.[1] Mary Lyon likewise had not received vocal training but, realizing the intellectual and physical advantages of singing, insisted that Mount Holyoke students have the opportunity to receive instruction, albeit in a chorus. Given limited funds, student assistants provided instruction until 1862, when Eliza Wilder was hired. Troy and Music Vale, however, offered a higher level of instruction: the support of city officials and residents of Troy enabled Emma Willard to employ professionally trained teachers, and the growing number of students at Music Vale led Orramel Whittlesey to include voice lessons. No "model" vocal curriculum, however, existed among the female seminaries.

An examination of the repertoires found in journal and diary entries, music books, concert programs, and school advertisements sheds light on how they were tailored to each school, offering a window onto the popular vocal literature from the late eighteenth through the mid-nineteenth century. Students sang sacred and secular music, though the repertoire at Mount Holyoke initially comprised sacred literature. By 1840 students had begun to sing secular pieces, but sacred music remained an essential part of their repertoire; nine of the thirteen vocal performances during the examination exercises on July 20, 1863, were sacred works.

Ballads and popular patriotic, war, and art songs constituted the secular repertoire at Music Vale. School programs do not differentiate between genres, since the lines are often blurred; rather, they are noted as "songs" on the programs. Solo "songs" represent the favored type of vocal literature, as presented on the program for July 8, 1863. Secular vocal repertoire at Music Vale featured choruses or moderately easy ballads and popular songs. As was common in the nineteenth century, programs included a variety of sacred and secular music—songs, ballads, glees, cantatas, oratorio and operatic arias, and choruses. There does not seem to be a common theme, though texts concerning nature or love are more prevalent than those on other topics.

Composers and Genres

Over forty European, British, and American composers are represented among the works performed at Music Vale. Whittlesey, who became recognized for his compositional talents in addition to those of pianist and teacher, began composing vocal music by 1849.[2] His vocal oeuvre consists of ballads; popular, patriotic, and war songs; and operas. The songs range from solo voice up to four parts for female chorus. Several of Whittlesey's vocal works refer to the seminary, such as "Welcome to Music Vale," the opening number on several anniversary examination exercise programs. Other examples include "A Great Big House" and "Our Harp and Banner," in which Whittlesey attempts to portray the harp-shaped weather vane in front of the school. According to historian Frances Hall Johnson, "Harp of the Wild Wind," published in 1851, was Whittlesey's most popular piece.[3] Her claim corresponds to the number of performances recorded on the few surviving annual examination programs: 1863, 1871, and 1872. No other vocal piece was repeated two years in succession.[4] A Music Vale brochure includes an advertisement reading, "This piece being of the descriptive character, is designed to represent the effect of a storm upon the Æolian, or 'Harp of the Wild Wind'"; the "effect produced upon its trembling strings by the fury of the storm, is to cause them to *discourse more eloquent* music."[5] The fury of the storm at sea, vividly depicted on the title page, is portrayed in the music (fig. 8.1).[6] The dramatic vocal line, with octave leaps and repeated sixteenth notes supported by an equally picturesque piano accompaniment replete with octaves and tremolos, requires the skill of both a trained singer and pianist (ex. 8.1).[7] Whittlesey dedicated this song to his oldest daughter, Eliza Tully Whittlesey.

Fig. 8.1. Orramel Whittlesey, "Harp of the Wild Wind," title page. Courtesy of William L. Clements Library, University of Michigan.

Ex. 8.1. Orramel Whittlesey, "Harp of the Wild Wind," mm. 29–45. Courtesy of William L. Clements Library, University of Michigan.

Few Americans besides Whittlesey can be identified in the solo literature at Music Vale. The 1851 brochure for the "Salem Normal Academy of Music" advertises two songs by daughter Eliza: the second edition of "Why Weep for the Dead," then in press, and "We Meet Again," projected to be available by September 1 that year.[8] Other Americans whose songs were played at Music Vale include Chas. F. Thompson, whose ballad "Who Will Care for Mother Now?," published in 1863, appeared the same year on a Music Vale program, and [Luther Orlando] Emerson's "Flower Girl" was performed on June 24, 1869.

Like Music Vale, over forty composers can be identified in the Troy repertoire: parlor songs by British and American composers, and Italian, French, and German art songs and operatic repertoire. Composers' names appeared on more than one program, but compositions were rarely repeated. Nineteenth-century composers are in the majority; Haydn, Mozart, and Beethoven represent the Classical period; there is no evidence of Baroque or Renaissance composers. Some names are still well known today—Daniel-François-Esprit Auber, Henry Bishop, Felix Mendelssohn, Rossini, and Verdi; however, many are obscure—Michael Curschmann, Vincenzo Gabussi, Charles Glover and his brother Stephen, James Gasper Maeder, and Thomas Moore. In addition, compositions by faculty members John C. Andrews, Gustave Blessner, Faustina Hodges, and Matthieu Philippi were programmed, especially during their tenures.

Composers' names are often omitted in Lucy Sheldon's music books, which represent the vocal literature studied at Litchfield. European composers include James Hewitt, James Hook, Joseph Mazzinghi, Ignaz Pleyel, and Theodore Smith. Various songs indicate foreign influence in lieu of the composer's name—for example, "My Heart's in the Highlands"; "Scots, What Have We Wallace Bled!"; "The Contented Cottage"; "Roselin Castle"; "Denmark"; and "A Canadian Boat Song." "Bonnie Doon" and "Benny Charley" are favorite Scottish songs.

Students and faculty at Troy frequently performed in concerts, although their names are rarely given. Genre or number of performers often precede composition titles, followed by the composer's name—for example, "Cavatina—Jo l'udia, . . . Donizetti," or "Trio—The Alp Horn . . . F. H. Hodges."[9] Likewise, Troy students had the privilege of attending faculty recitals. The vocal performance by Jane A. Andrews (daughter of John C. Andrews), graduate of the seminary and member of the faculty from 1843 to 1847, was a highlight of Gustave Blessner's farewell concert on May 14, 1850, given by music faculty members and guest performers. Andrews, applauded for her acclaimed talent, sang three solos: "Jennie with Her Bonnie Blue E'e" by John C. Andrews; "Farewell to the Alps," a Tyrolese ballad by Blessner;[10] and L. Kücken's "We Met by Chance," noted on the program as a "New Song."

Sacred Music

References to church services and singing schools in students' diaries at Litchfield, in addition to several sacred pieces in Lucy Sheldon's music books—including "Psalm CV," "God Bless You Ye Sweet" (children's hymn), "Our Lord Is Risen from the Dead" (Easter and a recital piece), "A Portuguese Hymn for Christmas Day," and "Pleyel's Favorite German Hymn"—verify that religious music was a staple of the vocal repertoire.[11] Most of the pieces are written for unison or solo singing; "Psalm CV" is an exception, scored for SAB with organ accompaniment. All of these works are in manuscript save "Pleyel's Favorite German Hymn."

Village Hymns for Social Worship and *The Psalms, Hymns, and Spiritual Songs* served as the first music books for choral instruction at Mount Holyoke; both include texts but no music. As compiler, the Reverend Asahel Nettleton explained, the songs in *Village Hymns* were beneficial for young Christians, thus appropriate for Mount Holyoke, where religious instruction was emphasized.[12]

The Psalms, Hymns, and Spiritual Songs contains 474 "hymns of high character," suitable for all "special occasions." According to the Reverend Isaac Watts, expression was necessary to perform the hymns and psalms appropriately: "The best psalm may be sung to the best tune, and every note, in the several parts, be sounded with the utmost exactness, and yet the performance have little interest or effect. That performance of psalmody, and that only, is entitled to be called good, in which the movement, quantity, and tone of voice, are well adapted to the general subject, and so varied as justly to express the different thoughts, sentiments, and passions."[13] The edition contains Samuel Worcester's instructions for singing with expression; symbols were included with the hymn and psalm text indicating how the passages should be sung (ex. 8.2).[14] The meter and tune names are given with each psalm, hymn, and song; biblical passages referenced at the top of each hymn or psalm serve as a source of inspiration.[15] Mount Holyoke continued to use *Village Hymns* and *The Psalms, Hymns, and Spiritual Songs* until 1859, when *The Sabbath Hymn Book* and *The Sabbath Bell* replaced them.[16]

By 1840 the seminary added *The Boston Academy*—a compilation of psalms, hymns, anthems, motets, sentences, chants, and selections from

HYMN 66. C. M. *York.* [*]
Joys of Saints. Neh. ix, 10.

1 JOY is a fruit that will not grow,
   In nature's barren soil ;
e All we can boast, till Christ we know,
   Is vanity and toil.

—2 But where the Lord has planted grace,
   And made his glories known ;—
o There fruits of heavenly joy and peace,
   Are found—and there alone.

e 3 A bleeding Saviour seen by faith,
 — A sense of pard'ning love,—
o A hope that triumphs over death,
o   Gives joys like those above.

·—4 To take a glimpse within the vail,
   To know that God is mine—
o Are springs of joy that never fail,
   Unspeakable, divine !

—5 These are the joys which satisfy,
   And sanctify the mind ;
o Which make the spirit mount on high,
   And leave the world behind.   **NEWTON.**

Ex. 8.2. Hymn 66, "Joy of Saints," Isaac Watts, *The Psalms, Hymns, and Spiritual Songs.* Courtesy of Special Collections, Princeton Theological Seminary Library.

masses and other sacred works by such composers as Handel, Joseph and Michael Haydn, Mozart, Beethoven, William Billings, and Lowell Mason— a decided advancement over the earlier books.[17] Most of the pieces are in four-part (SATB) hymn arrangement with the melody in the tenor: one part to each staff, and text printed under one line, with additional verses often printed at the side or under a different vocal line.

Four years later *Carmina Sacra*, compiled by Lowell Mason, replaced *The Boston Academy*.[18] Along with "a choice selection of the old standard tunes" considered essential for singing books, the collection included numerous motets and anthems not previously published, some "adapted to English words" for the first time, and a wider variety of chants than normally found in similar collections.[19]

The school choirs possibly sang repertoires derived from *Carmina Sacra* for special occasions, such as the annual examination exercises held on July 31, 1845. A review appeared in the *Springfield Daily Republican*, the local newspaper in Springfield, Massachusetts.[20] An anonymous reporter referred to the event as a "Female College Commencement," commenting that it was "one of exceeding great interest to all visiters." Performances by a large choir that preceded duets and solos, all accompanied by piano, were well received: "We think we never listened to better or sweeter vocal music; some of the voices were exquisitely sweet, rich and powerful. It was gratifying to witness such perfection in this delightful art—one which has heretofore received too little attention in our schools and seminaries."[21] Such testimony adds credence to the music training offered, though students served as instructors.

Mount Holyoke continued to keep pace with current publications, adding or discontinuing the use of music books. In 1850 *The Anthem Dulcimer*, edited by I. B. Woodbury, replaced *Carmina Sacra*. The collection comprises "New Tunes, Chants, Anthems, Motets, etc.," composed by "the Best Foreign and American Composers." [22] As with *Carmina Sacra*, nearly all works are written for SATB. Six years later Mount Holyoke began using A. N. Johnson's *The Key-Stone Collection of Church Music*, signifying another improvement in repertoire. Along with "A Complete Collection of Hymn Tunes, Anthems, Psalms, Chants, etc.," it includes a detailed analysis of the physiological system and instructions for training choirs.[23] As a bonus, Johnson added a copy of his cantata *The Morning of Freedom*.

Another benchmark occurred when Eliza Wilder joined the faculty, confirmed by the repertoire performed during the examination exercise on July 20, 1863. While not demanding, the performance of Robert Topliff's "Ruth and Naomi"—a recitative and air—attests to the vocal training then offered at the seminary.[24] That same year Mount Holyoke began using *The Jubilee*,[25] which served as a source for two of the choral selections: William B. Bradbury's "Blessed Are the Peacemakers" and "The Lord Is Nigh" (composer unidentified).

In 1866 the *Springfield Daily Republican* printed a review of the concert given during the examination exercises, which included choruses from Handel's *Messiah*. The reporter noted improvement in the repertoire and performance and praised Miss Wilder's conducting and vocal abilities:

The crowning glory of the week was the concert by the young ladies on Wednesday evening. Two hundred female voices swelling those grand choruses of the oratorio of the Messiah; carrying every part except the base; and all with rare harmony and power; rendering the finer passages with an appreciation which famous societies might envy; led by a lady worthy to stand beside the best conductors of the country; all this afforded the rarest feast to the genuine lover of music. There was, indeed, something to criticise in an occasional lack of decision and power on the opening notes, and in a want of perfect harmony in the minor passages; but the effect of the whole was elevating, soul-stirring, and the concert won most hearty approbation, which was happily expressed in behalf of the audience by a neat little speech from Rev Dr Kirk of Boston. The program also included an instrumental duet from Norma, arranged for two pianos, played by the Misses Davis of Pittsfield; and the song "Hear Our Prayer," exquisitely rendered by Miss Wilder, assisted by Misses French and Gordon. The concert should have been given in a larger room, as for instance the village church or the gymnasium. No singers could do themselves justice, and no music could have its best effect in the stifling air and under the low ceiling of Seminary Hall.[26]

As this testimony confirms, Mount Holyoke continued to raise the bar in vocal training.

According to Troy programs (1838–1872), sacred vocal literature was performed less frequently than secular compositions.[27] Felix Mendelssohn's works, which appeared more often than those of any other composers, included "If with All Your Hearts," an aria from the oratorio *Elijah*; "I Waited for the Lord" (trio) and an unspecified duet and chorus, all from the cantata "A Hymn of Praise"; "O Praise the Lord," a trio with chorus; and "How Lovely Are the Messengers," a chorus from the oratorio *St. Paul*. Other examples include an aria and chorus from Giovanni Tadolini's "Ave Regina," "The Heavens Are Telling" (chorus) from Haydn's *The Creation*, and Faustina Hodges's "The Holy Dead" (trio). Hodges's composition was performed on May 13, 1851, while she was employed at the seminary. Selections from Mozart's "Benedictus" appeared on two concerts: a quartet (SATB) and chorus on February 20, 1857, and a solo and chorus four months later, on June 23.

In 1830 Emma Willard took a leave of absence as principal of Troy Female Seminary and, accompanied by her son, embarked on an extensive European tour. Her perilous voyage across the Atlantic undoubtedly provided the inspiration for the lyrics of "Rock'd in the Cradle of the Deep":

Rock'd in the cradle of the deep
I lay me down in peace to sleep;
Secure I rest upon the wave
For thou oh! Lord, hast power to save.
I know thou wilt not slight my call,
For thou dost mark the sparrow's fall!

And calm and peaceful is my sleep
Rock'd in the cradle of the deep.
And calm and peaceful is my sleep
Rock'd in the cradle of the deep.

And such the trust that still were mine
Tho' stormy winds swept o'er the brine
Or through the tempest's fiery breath
Roused me from sleep to wreck and death!
In ocean cave still safe with thee,
The germ of immortality;

And calm and peaceful is my sleep
Rock'd in the cradle of the deep.
And calm and peaceful is my sleep
Rock'd in the cradle of the deep.[28]

Joseph Knight set the text for solo soprano with piano accompaniment. It was published by 1840 and presented in a student concert on April 26, 1849.[29] The accompaniment depicts a rocking cradle with alternating intervals such as thirds and sixths or octaves. Changing dynamics in the vocal line and the accompaniment also lend a picturesque touch: pianissimo is used with "calm and peaceful is my sleep" and fortissimo with "tempest's fiery breath . . . to wreck and death." Knight adds drama with a fermata on the word "death."

Some concerts at Troy included performances of larger works, such as Andreas Jakob Romberg's *The Transient and Eternal*. This dramatic work (for soprano, tenor, and bass solos; soprano duet; tenor and bass duet; trio and recitatives for soprano, alto, and tenor; and four choruses, two as bookends) provided a climactic end to part 1 of the program for February 9, 1854.[30] Nearly five months later, on June 27, Sigismund Ritter von Neukomm's cantata *The Easter Morning* for SATB and chorus, served as the sole piece for part 2 of the program.[31]

Only a few sacred vocal works appear on extant Music Vale programs, though several sacred pieces arranged for cabinet organ were included. Further, the seminary had Sunday services, and students undoubtedly sang hymns. Three examples represent the type of sacred vocal repertoire performed at concerts: Hans Michael Schletterer's SSA arrangement of "Ave Maria," "Consider the Lilies" (solo) by Robert Topliff, and Emma Willard's "Rock'd in the Cradle of the Deep."[32]

Patriotic Music

Music programs offered during the Civil War at Mount Holyoke and Music Vale exemplify the schools' support of the Union Army. Most of the vocal compositions on the July 8, 1863, Music Vale program focused on a patriotic or war theme.[33] There are no examples of patriotic or war songs on existing programs after the war's end. Whittlesey composed several songs reflecting his patriotism, such as "American Eagle" and "The Dying Soldier of Buena Vista."[34] He dedicated the latter to Charles J. M. McCurdy, lieutenant governor of Connecticut; Colonel Henry Petrikin penned the text. The title page portrays a dying soldier with the war raging in the background. Whittlesey's pianistic skills are evident in this descriptive piece: a march-like introduction with repeated chords in the right hand; tremolo sections; and an interlude, with the left hand playing chords while crossing over the right-hand bass melody, builds from piano to fortissimo.

The program beginning July 23, 1861, at Mount Holyoke includes "The Star Spangled Banner," "Red, White, and Blue," and "Never Forget the Dear Ones." Two years later the students performed patriotic works: "[unreadable] America" and "Our Native Land," and one young woman read a poem titled "Dirge for a Soldier."[35]

Secular Music

The secular vocal numbers found in Lucy Sheldon's music books and referred to in student diaries, plays given at the school, and historical documentation of Litchfield Academy—folk and popular songs, incidental music, ballads, airs, and sonnets—all accommodated the fashionable social climate of Litchfield. Singing schools, private parties, and public gatherings, in addition to academy events, provided opportunities for students to engage in various cultural activities.

Vocal pieces in Sheldon's books 1, 2, and 4 are in manuscript, while most songs in book 3 are printed; nearly all are scored for unison or solo voice; duets are rare.[36] The majority of the folk or popular songs for amateur voices are strophic: two to six verses. "There's No Luck about the House," for example, features an octave-range melody with simple bass-line accompaniment.[37] Some songs, such as "He Sleeps in Yonder Dewy Grave," while still within the capability of an untrained singer, have a slightly wider range with occasional grace notes or trills to ornament the melody. An Alberti bass or comparable level of accompaniment is common, though easier and more advanced piano parts are evident.

"A Winter's Evening" by Dr. George K. Jackson is a song beyond the amateur level. Such descriptive phrases as "Fall of Snow" and "Blast of Wind" printed above the staff are reminiscent of the descriptions used in Franz Koczwara's "The Battle of Prague," evoking the character of a programmatic work. "A Winter's Evening" begins in recitative style; periodic fermatas and "Espressivo" sections aid the singer in rendering a sensitive performance.[38]

The words "A Favorite New Song" are printed under the titles of several compositions in Sheldon's book 3—such as Thomas Thompson's "Orphan Bess and the Beggar Girl" and "Sadi the Moor" by James Hewitt—indicating that they were current publications.[39] Many songs are comparable in difficulty to those in Sheldon's other books. Piano is the favored accompanying instrument; occasionally harp can substitute. Some songs include an optional part for German flute, such as "The Wounded Hussar" and "The Poor Village Boy." Clarinet, guitar, and violin are also mentioned as optional instruments or to be used when a piano was unavailable.[40]

In 1840 Mount Holyoke began using *The Odeon* and *The Social Choir*.[41] *The Odeon*, compiled by George J. Webb and Lowell Mason, contains popular tunes for amateur choirs, such as "Home, Sweet Home"; "The Minute Gun at Sea" by Matthew P. King; and "Araby's Daughter" by G. Kiallmark. "Hail Columbia" and "America" are representative of the book's patriotic songs.[42] Various composers and tune sources are represented; occasionally the composer's name is not given or is replaced with a generic title, such as "Irish Melody."[43] The arrangements for unison, or two to four voices, comfortably fit within the tessitura for each part, are easy to moderately difficult, and run usually two to four pages. Some accompaniments are provided; other songs were apparently performed a cappella.

The Social Choir, edited by George Kingsley, is a collection of accompanied choral arrangements by composers including Rossini, Bellini, Weber, Auber, Hérold, Meyerbeer, and Kingsley.[44] Songs, airs, operatic excerpts, and miscellaneous pieces (for example, a Scottish melody, a round, and glees) are scored for unison or for two, three, or four voices.[45] Some works feature tempo changes and rhythmic and harmonic diversity that would be suitable for one of the upper-level choirs at Mount Holyoke. Kingsley selected the poetry "with particular reference to moral sentiment," undoubtedly aware of parents' concerns regarding improper texts.[46] The Reverend Edward W. Hooker addressed this issue in 1843, advising fathers and daughters to avoid purchasing pieces with poetry imbued "to absolute insipidity, with the declarations or sighings and groanings of love. Such music belongs, with nine tenths of the novels of our day, in one vast pile, with torches applied on all sides of it."[47] Mary Lyon undoubtedly exercised such judgment in choosing music for her students.

Along with sacred music books, Mount Holyoke continued to provide new secular publications. In 1860 the seminary began using *The Festival Glee Book* by George F. Root and William B. Bradbury.[48] Several works from this book were performed during the 1861 public examination exercises—for example, "The Crystal Stream," "The Convent Bells," and "While All Is Hushed," all sung by two choirs.[49]

Parlor Songs

Nineteenth-century parlor songs—classified as ballads or popular songs—printed in songbooks and periodicals or as individual pieces of sheet music, became regarded as "music for the millions."[50] Parlor songs were composed for solo, duet, trio, quartet, ensemble (five or six performers), or choral performance. Ballads represent one of the most popular types of nineteenth-century parlor song for solo voice and were often performed at Troy between 1838 and 1857. Given the sentiments portrayed in the texts, they provided an excellent repertoire for teaching expression. Whittlesey emphasized the importance of expression in performance at Music Vale: "Great care is taken to lay a sure foundation for good *Expression*, which is the very life, essence, and soul of music, the polish and finish of all that is excellent, and without which any performance, either vocal or instrumental is mere trash, and not worthy of the name of music."[51] As music historian Nicholas Tawa observed, "The most important objective of the ballad singer . . . was to arouse emotions."[52] While parlor songs were largely suitable for amateur singers, most repertoires performed at Troy and Music Vale exemplified a higher level; many of those at Mount Holyoke and Litchfield are designed for voices with less training.

Lucy Sheldon's book 3 includes several ballads, signifying their popularity at Litchfield: "The Welch Harper," "The Maid of Lodi," and "The Beggar Girl," classified as "favorite ballads," and "Willy's Rare and Willy's Fair," a Scottish ballad by James Hook, made popular by "Mrs. [Mary Ann] Wrighten at Vauxhall."[53] These ballads require a singer with moderate training; for example, "The Maid of Lodi," an Italian ballad, features an angular vocal melody with leaps of an octave or a tenth and periodic ornamentation, with little support from the piano.

Parlor songs accounted for most vocal performances on Troy's earliest extant program, March 23, 1838. Sydney Nelson's "The Winds Are Up—The Stars Are Out" is written for two treble voices, with ornamentation (trills, grace notes, and turns) in both parts. The accompaniment, more challenging than what is found in most parlor song literature, requires a skilled pianist to play legato and staccato thirds, scale passages, arpeggiated chords, and repeated notes at a *Poco allegretto con anima* tempo.[54]

"True Love Can Ne'er Forget" depicts the sentiments of a blind Irishman. Samuel Lover, Esq., a native of Ireland, wrote the words and music hoping to obtain assistance from his compatriots.[55] The epigraph must have served as a source of inspiration: "It is related of Carolan, the Irish bard, that after his loss of sight, and the lapse of twenty years, he recognised his first love by the touch of her hand."[56] Lover obviously included the subtitle, collection, and artist—"A Favorite Ballad from the *Songs of the Legends and Traditions of Ireland* sung by Madame Caradori-Allan"—on the title page in order to aid sales.[57] The date of publication is uncertain; it was performed during the December 16, 1847, concert.[58] A short refrain serves as a bookend, encasing the verses with variations, ending with a postlude. The simple accompaniment allows the audience to focus on the singer and the text.

Canzonets such as "Lay of the Sylph" ("Sono il Silfo"), a strophic song by Maria Caterina Rosalbina Caradori-Allan, also fall within the category of parlor songs. While the simplicity of many nineteenth-century parlor songs makes them appealing to an amateur singer, this *canzonetta* (forty-eight measures with the introduction and second verse) has a range of C^1 to F^2, wide leaps (sixths and octaves), melodic ornamentation, and sixteenth-note scale passages, all reminiscent of operatic writing. It was performed during an undated benefit concert given by the music faculty and students, along with several other parlor songs, operatic selections, and instrumental numbers.

Charles Glover's "The Flower Queen," a through-composed ballad for two treble voices, each within the range of an octave, was performed on June 24, 1847.[59] The difficulty of this work lies in the tertian harmony. Stephen Glover's "What Are the Wild Waves Saying?," scored for tenor and soprano or alto with guitar accompaniment, was performed on June 29, 1849. Although the concert included faculty members as performers, the tenor part may have been sung by a female, as all of the voice teachers that year were women.

Themes of loyalty to loved ones and friends frequently served as material for texts, such as "The Old English Gentleman," a popular English ballad performed at Troy.[60] No composer's name is given on the program or music; rather, "As sung by Mr. H. Russell" is printed on the title page.[61] This simple

THE OLD ENGLISH GENTLEMAN

A POPULAR ENGLISH BALLAD,

As sung by

MR. H. RUSSELL.

New York. Published at ATWILLS MUSIC SALOON 201 Broadway.

Fig. 8.2. "The Old English Gentleman," title page. Courtesy of Lester S. Levy Collection of Sheet Music, Sheridan Libraries, Johns Hopkins University.

strophic song with five verses gives a quaint description of "The Old English Gentleman" depicted on the title page and uses a tune that "is an adaptation of an air already old in the eighteenth century [fig. 8.2]."[62]

Subjects concerning love and sorrow were frequently used for ballads, such as George Linley's "Why Do I Weep for Thee?," set by British composer William V. Wallace. The mood of the ballad—that of grieving over a departed lover—is portrayed in a strophic song with a short refrain. It was sung at a concert on July 13, 1852, possibly by a beginning student. This ballad became popular during the Civil War, which seems suitable given the second verse:

Once, ah! what joy to share
With thee the noontide hour;
Then, not for a grief nor care
Had canker'd the heart's young flow'r.
The sun seems not to shed
A radiance o'er me now,
Save mem'ry, all seems dead,
Since lost, since lost art thou.[63]

Three of Gustave Blessner's ballads appear on programs of 1849–1850 when he served as head of Troy's music department—"Farewell to the Alps," a Tyrolese ballad, and "Nanny's Mammy" and "I Have Got the Blues," both comic ballads. "Farewell to the Alps" was published in 1849 and performed on June 29. Another performance occurred almost one year later (May 14, 1850), when Jane A. Andrews sang this ballad during a faculty concert. Although the form is simple—typical of a ballad with verse and refrain—Blessner allows for vocal display with short flourishes and numerous dynamic markings, specifically diminuendos. "Nanny's Mammy" was the penultimate number on the 1850 faculty concert. The vocalist's name is not specified, but the text is included. The guests were unquestionably entertained by the humor.[64]

I

A spinster of uncertain age,
But somewhere past the middle stage,
Who thought herself extremely sage,
Thus to the giddy Nanny;
Her fair adopted daughter said,
Your inexperience much I dread,
So listen to your Mammy!

II

Your youth forbids that you should know,
This world is all a fleeting show;
Ah! Listen, don't be laughing so,
For I have proved it, Nanny!
For love, and health, and youth have wings,
And men are such deceitful things!
So listen to your Mammy.

III

I'm sorry one so wise to grieve,
I've listened but I can't believe,
That dear delighted men deceive,
They do not frighten Nanny!
In wealth no danger I can see,
And flirting is as sweet to me,
As once it was to Mammy!

Mammy is warning young Nanny about men's wiles, but the daughter remains unconvinced. The singer would need to reflect the daughter's response in the third verse.

John C. Andrews, a member of Troy's music faculty from 1841 to 1847, composed numerous songs, many of them ballads—for example, "Somebody's Coming, but I'll Not Tell Who";[65] "O Love Is Like the Rose, Rosalie"; and "He Tells Me He Loves Me, or Aileen Mavourneen." Typical of a nineteenth-century parlor song, "O Love Is Like the Rose, Rosalie," has a romantic text, simple melody, narrow range (E–F♯), with simple accompaniment. Andrews inserted an "*ad lib.*" for the singer and pianist, encouraging them to make the most of the *con affectuso* style of the song.[66] Given that his daughter had achieved popularity for her vocal ability, Andrews frequently included her name on title pages—"Sung with Great Applause by Miss Jane A. Andrews"— as a marketing ploy.

Frederick N. Crouch's ballad "Kathleen Mavourneen," with words by Mrs. Crawford, was, according to Tawa, the most popular British parlor song of considerable difficulty. Crouch used numerous dynamic markings in the vocal line and piano prelude, interludes, and postlude. Chromaticism, modulations, and wide vocal leaps (such as an octave or an eleventh), and lack of recurring phrase patterns make this song challenging for a first-year student.[67] Further, the piano accompaniment requires such skills as playing consecutive thirds in the right hand and chords in both hands simultaneously.[68]

In contrast to Troy, Music Vale seldom included songs classified as ballads on programs or documented in other primary source materials. Whittlesey's "Take Care!" is an example of a ballad with three verses by Professor Henry Wadsworth Longfellow, advising one not to trust a woman who will fool you with her "witching eyes and bonny brown hair." Whittlesey dedicated this song to one of his students, Emily T. Shaurman. The tessitura is a comfortable soprano range (D¹–F²), with an easy to moderate piano accompaniment. Leaps of an octave or a tenth on the words "Take care" present the greatest challenge. Nathan James Sporle's ballad "The Star of Glengary" was performed on the thirty-second annual examination program, June 29, 1871.[69] This love song requires the ability of a performer trained to sing with expression, as exemplified in its periodic ornamentation, vocal flourishes (the second verse includes a miniature cadenza-like passage), fermatas, and rallentandos at the ends of verses.

Art Songs

In addition to parlor songs, voice students at Troy performed art songs—air, recitative and polacca, theme and variations, and waltz—scored for solo, duet, trio, and quartet, frequently exhibiting extended melodic lines, complex musical structures, richer harmonic material, and more complicated accompaniments than found in many parlor songs. Ornamented melodies and protracted melismatic passages, much like those in operatic arias, are common and can "obscure the sense of the words."[70] Though Faustina Hodges and Matthieu Philippi composed art songs, most of those performed were written by Europeans.

Karl Anton Florian Eckert's "Swiss Song," performed by Jenny Lind and Henriette Sontag, contains both German and English texts.[71] Since the title was printed in English, it can be assumed the soloist at Troy sang it in that language on February 9, 1854. The challenging vocal line with melodic ornamentation, arpeggios, trills, and repeated leaps—noticeable in the concluding "la, la, la" section—are meant to showcase the trained singer (ex. 8.3).[72]

Lucy Hansen's performance of "Swiss Boy" (May 13, 1872), a theme and variations for soprano voice by Johann Peter Pixis, is the sole representation of this genre on extant programs at Troy. Seven measures before the end of the piano introduction, the voice enters with a repeated pattern on the vowels "A–I." Pixis set the theme syllabically with few leaps. He wrote both a simplified voice part in English translation and an arduous version in German. As noted in the score, famed Italian soprano Madame Caradori-Allan sang the advanced version of the variations, which may account for its performance at Troy.[73]

"L'Estasi" by Luigi Arditi is the only "Valse Brillante" in the vocal repertoire. The triple-meter waltz pattern sets the mood for the piece. Tempo and key changes, and leaps of a sixth, seventh, or octave, contribute to the song's difficulty. May 13, 1872, the first extant program at Troy to include performers' names, lists student Abbie McNary as the performer of "L'Estasi." Nicola de Giosa's "I Tamburelli I Campanelli" (translated as "Now Sounds the Tambourine"), presented on the same concert, is a challenging work with melismatic passages, changes in tempo, and chromatic lines. The accompaniment

Ex. 8.3. Karl Anton Florian Eckert, "The Celebrated Swiss Song," mm. 46–56. Courtesy of Sibley Music Library, Eastman School of Music, University of Rochester.

likewise calls for a trained pianist capable of performing octave leaps, double thirds, and tremolos at an *Allegro giusto* tempo.

Although trios were not as prevalent as solos at Troy, they appear to be as favored as duets, adding variety to the concerts and providing additional opportunities for ensemble performances. Programs from 1849 include vocal trios by the Jenny Lind Club, possibly an auditioned ensemble. Given the intensity placed on vocal instruction, it seems likely that other vocal clubs existed; no others are mentioned, nor does this club appear on other programs. It is unusual that neither titles nor composers are provided for the club's performances; such information is rarely omitted.[74]

Trios by Faustina Hodges and Matthieu Philippi were performed at the seminary while they were faculty members. Hodges adds variety to the strophic structure of "The Alp Horn" with repeated vocables for the refrain, possibly to imitate the echoes of an alp horn (ex. 8.4).[75] This work was the sole trio performed on June 20, 1850, while "O'er the Alps," another trio by Hodges, was presented on an undated benefit concert.[76] Philippi's "Nights of Music," with text by Irish poet Thomas Moore, was programmed on two concerts within nearly five months: February 1 and June 28, 1853.

Other composers of vocal trios include Fabio Campana, Friedrich Curschmann, J. E. Gleffer, and William V. Wallace. The concert of February 20, 1857, included a performance of Curschmann's trio "Addio," for soprano, alto, and tenor. Although young women sang tenor parts, the program indicates that a male faculty member participated in the performance. Gleffer's "Music Comes with Various Power," performed on July 13, 1857—the penultimate day of the annual examinations at the close of the school year—was the only trio on that event's program. Campana composed "Madre del Sommo Amore" for soprano, tenor, and contralto or bass.[77] In addition to emphasizing the tenor part (including an opening solo and short cadenza near the end), Campana showcases each voice with short solo passages and melodic flourishes that tend to obscure the text. This challenging *terzettino* served as the dramatic opening number on May 13, 1872.

Quartets provided opportunities for young women to participate in four-part harmony.[78] Quartet literature seemed to be favored during the 1850s, featuring such composers as Faustina Hodges, Julius Koethen, Felix Mendelssohn, and Wilhelm Müller. Male music faculty sang tenor and bass whenever the pieces required four parts, as in Mendelssohn's "The First Day of Spring" and "On the Sea," performed on December 21, 1855.

Vincenzo Gabussi's "La Calabrese," a solo art song, was performed during Music Vale's annual examination on June 23, 1857. This French song for soprano and contralto (although sung by two sopranos) must have delighted the audience with its demanding vocal agility and artistic expression; vocable sections in each part separately and simultaneously contribute to its whimsical mood. The report of the examining committee expresses its admiration: "the Concert of Pupils and Teachers on Tuesday evening, was uncommonly brilliant, displaying very fine voices and a high degree of cultivation in this

Ex. 8.4. Faustina Hasse Hodges, "The Alp Horn," mm. 11–24. Courtesy of Albert and Shirley Small Special Collections Library, University of Virginia.

direction."[79] The committee was undoubtedly pleased to hear such progressive performances.

Beginning in 1869, nature becomes a common theme in vocal literature performed at the schools—for example, "Swallow's Farewell" by Friedrich Wilhelm Kücken, "When the Pale Moon Arose Last Night" by Mary Ann Virginia Gabriel, "The Nightingale's Trill" by Wilhelm Ganz, and Orramel

Whittlesey's "Harp of the Wild Wind." The vocal agility and expressive singing required to render a sensitive performance of "Nightingale's Trill" is comparable to that of "Harp of the Wild Wind." "The Nightingale's Trill" reflects the level of vocal training available at Music Vale. The audience must have been impressed to hear a young woman surmount the difficulties of this art song at the annual examination on June 29, 1871. Trills, some extending fifteen beats and terminating with a fermata, optional brief cadenzas, and multiple dynamic changes performed rubato require the skill of an advanced singer. Mademoiselle Parepa popularized this song in a performance with the Bateman Concert Company at the 1866 inauguration of Steinway and Sons' new music hall in New York.[80]

John Demar's "Hunting Tower or When Ye Gang Awa, Jamie" requires a different type of expression. The performer sings in Scottish dialect as she portrays two characters: Jeanie and Jamie. This twelve-stanza dialogue fits comfortably within the soprano range (E♭–E♭¹). The prevalent rhythm of dotted eighth and sixteenth notes suits the text and adds a lively character.

Duets, trios, quartets, and choruses added variety to Music Vale's programs, though they were not performed as often as piano ensemble literature. As with solo repertoire, there is little duplication of ensembles; the majority of the pieces are of European origin. Duets began to appear on the extant programs by 1869. The examination exercise program that year includes four duets, but only one singer's name is provided for each performance. Perhaps an unnamed teacher sang with the students. All duets on this program were sung in English, including "Thou Art So Near and Yet So Far" by German composer Johann Friedrich Reichardt.

Examples of other duets include "L'Amicizia" by Faustina Hodges, Franz Schubert's "Serenade," and Robert Schumann's "Schön Blümelein." Some duets were performed by four singers, apparently doubling the parts, such as Vincenzo Gabussi's "I Pescateri," performed by Misses Fuller, Baker, Elden, and Goodwin on June 13, 1872.

According to existing programs, trios and quartets were not as common as duets. Examples of trios include "Still ist nur die Welle" by W. A. Mozart,[81] "Das Veilchen" by Karl Friedrich Curschmann, "Maidens' Spring Song" by Ferdinand Gumbert, and Fabio Campana's "Quando Fice Genere." Quartet performances consisted of four to seven singers, some parts obviously doubled. For instance, British composer Henry Smart's "Down in the Dewy Dell" was performed by seven singers. Some quartets, however, were performed by four voices, such as Fabio Campana's "Barcarola" and a selection from Robert Schumann's *Paradise and the Peri*, op. 50.[82]

Programs from Troy and Music Vale reveal that most of the songs were in English or English translation; however, some were sung in the original language. Auber's "El Jaleo de Xeres," translated as "The Evening Dance," is an example of an air performed at Troy on June 24, 1847.[83] The words "Spanish Song" preceded the title on the program, indicating that it was performed in the original language. This pleasing air with melodic ornamentation, melismatic passages, and a cadenza performed *Allegro brillante* is suitable for a trained singer. "Je suis la Bajadere," arranged by Robert Nicolas-Charles Bochsa, and "Tu Sandunga," for example, were performed on February 19, 1850.[84] "Je suis la Bajadere," with its operatic flourishes, along with repetitive "tra la" passages, was most certainly a crowd pleaser. Although both French and English texts are given, it can be assumed it was performed in French, according to the title on the program. "Tu Sandunga," translated as "What Enchantment," a Spanish song by Signor Blanco, was made popular by contralto Rosina Pico.[85]

Songs in foreign languages were apparently performed in English at Music Vale until 1871, since the translated titles, such as "Orange Girl" ("La Naraniera") by Friedrich Wilhelm Kücken and "Swiss Song" by Karl Anton Florian Eckert, are found on the program. In 1871 the annual examination exercise program included two German songs: Franz Abt's "Ich Bin Der Klein Postillon" and Kücken's "Gut Nacht, Far Wol."[86] One year later French was added with "Comme à vingt ans" by Emile Durand.

CHORUSES

Choruses often closed the first and second halves of Troy's program; some were from operas or oratorios, such as the "Wedding Chorus" from Bellini's *La Sonnambula* or "The Heavens are Telling" from Haydn's *The Creation*. Others were self-contained works—for example, "Dearest Mae: A Celebrated Ethiopian Song," which closed the program on February 19, 1850. Although no review of the performance exists, it surely piqued the audience's interest to hear young women attending an elite female institution in upstate New York singing the vernacular language of this comic minstrel song made popular by the Harmoneons:

> Now Niggers listen to me, a story I'll relate;
> It happen'd in de vally, In de Old Carlina state;
> Way down in de meadow, 'twas dare I mow'd de hay;
> I always work de harder, when I think ob lubly Mae
>
>> Oh! dearest Mae,
>> You'r lubly as de day;
>> Your eyes so bright

Dey shine at night
When the moon am gwane away!

2

Old Massa gib me a Holiday an' say he'd gib me more,
I tank'd him bery kindly an' shoved my boat from shore;
So down de river I glides along wid my heart so light and free,
To de cottage ob my lubly Mae I'd long'd so much to see.

    Oh! dearest Mae, etc.

3

On the banks of de river whar de trees dey hang so low,
De coon among thar branches play, while de mink he keeps below;
Oh! dar is de spot an Mae she looks so neat,
Her eyes dey sparkle like de stars, her lips are red as beet.

    Oh! dearest Mae, etc.

4

Benead de shady old oak tree, we sat for many an hour,
Happy as de Bussard bird dat flies about de flower;
But oh dear Mae I leff her she cried when boff we parted,
I bid sweet Mae a long farwell and back to Massa started.

    Oh! dearest Mae, etc.[87]

This performance seems unusual, given that it is the only example of a minstrel song to appear on existing programs.

Two of Whittlesey's choruses, "Welcome to Music Vale" and "Our Harp and Banner," provided an opportunity for all students to participate. Some choruses, however, were performed with only four or five voices. On the 1873 program, for example, four students sang "The Spanish Tamborine Girl" and five performed "Les Glaneuses" by Antoine-Louis Clapisson, Wilhelm Richard Wagner's "Song of the Spinning Maidens," and "Blance de Provence" by Luigi Cherubini.

GLEES

From 1838 through 1855, glees by such composers as Thomas Atwood, Reginald Spofforth, Samuel Lover, and Henry Bishop added diversity to Troy's programs. Atwood scored "Hark! The Curfew" for two treble voices (notated as "1st" and "2d voice") and basso. Spofforth's "Hail! Smiling Morn" requires four parts: SATB. This spritely piece showcases the close harmony of the four parts. The alternation of unison and disparate rhythm among the parts provides diversity; for example, the soprano voice in the B section sustains the melody while the remaining parts sing an echo before all voices join in unison rhythm.[88] Five programs include glees composed by faculty: "The Last Rose of Summer" harmonized by Gustave Blessner and Matthieu Philippi's "Forest Song" and "The Huntsman's Song."

Operas

Two of the vocal numbers in Sheldon's book 3 are from operas, suggesting that Litchfield students had access to music from dramatic productions, although there is no indication that students gave operatic performances. "When Pensive I Thought on My Love" comes from *The Grand Dramatic Romance of Blue Beard, or Female Curiosity* by Michael Kelly and George Colman; "Paul and Mary" is from the opera *Paul and Virginia*.[89]

By 1861, operatic selections were occasionally sung on the programs during Mount Holyoke's examination exercises. For example, during the exercises commencing July 23, 1861, the "4 o'clock choir" sang "These Moments of Pleasure," a chorus from Donizetti's opera *L' elisir d' amore*, arranged for *The Festival Glee Book*. The ability to instruct and direct fellow students in singing this level of repertoire speaks well for Fanny M. Hidden, a student in the middle class from Candia, New Hampshire, who served as music teacher that year. It seems likely the chorus was performed in English; nevertheless, its performance represents significant progress in literature performed at Mount Holyoke since its founding.

Entire operas were not performed at Troy, yet an investigation of the repertoire reveals that operatic numbers—solos, duets, trios, quartets, and choruses—accounted for the majority of the vocal literature on the programs.[90] Such well-known composers as Bellini, Donizetti, Rossini, and Verdi are often represented, while Auber, Hérold, and Meyerbeer are less so.

Opera arias and ballads were frequently performed—most titles are in the original language; few were translated into English. Occasionally the title was replaced with the genre, such as a "cavatina" from *L'elisir d'amore*. Perhaps the audience was familiar with the cavatina, making it unnecessary to include the title. Cavatinas appear to be the most popular type of solo; examples include "Ecco ridente [in cielo]" from Rossini's *Il Barbiere di Siviglia*," and "Glöcklein im Thale" from Carl Maria von Weber's *Euryanthe*. Usually no accompaniment is mentioned, though the performance of "Glöcklein im Thale," on June 27, 1854, was accompanied by piano, flute, violin, and cello.[91]

William Michael Rooke's "To the Vine Feast" from *Amilie* is suitable for an intermediate student. The lighthearted text, including vocables along with short melismas and octave leaps, makes this an entertaining piece.[92] Other representative arias include "Qui la voce [sua soave]" from *I Puritani*, "O luce di quest' anima" from Donizetti's *Linda di Chamounix*, and "Non più mesta" by Rossini. Mrs. Anna Bishop had performed "The Banks of the Guadalquiver" from Louis Henry Lavenu's *Loretta, a Tale of Seville* during an Operatic Entertainment at Boston's Howard Athenaeum on August 25, 1847, along with Donizetti's *Linda di Chamounix*.[93] Lavenu's ballad was first published in New York in 1847 and performed at the Troy seminary on December 16 that year.

Operatic duets were performed less frequently than solos though more often than trios or quartets.[94] As with solos, duets were sung in the original language or in translation. Donizetti's were the most popular—for example, "On to the Field of Glory" from *Belisario*, "Torna mia" from *Don Pasquale*, and "Sul la Tomba" from *Lucia di Lammermoor*.[95] Max Maretzek's arrangement of Donizetti's "The Celebrated Rondo Finale" from *Linda di Chamounix* is scored for two sopranos. Unison voices periodically break into two parts singing sixteenth-note triplets, trills, and thirty-second-note flourishes. The vocal agility required to perform this dramatic duet attests to the seminary's professional instruction. The duet was performed on June 25, 1853, as the penultimate number on the program.

"Chi mi frena" from *Lucia di Lammermoor* was performed as a trio on February 1, 1853, while a faculty member (Madame Holbrooke) and three students (Misses Nason, McNary, and Bacon) performed the quartet "Good Night" from Friedrich von Flotow's *Martha* on May 13, 1872. Since this piece is scored for SATB, two of the singers must have sung the tenor and bass an octave higher.

Opera choruses were common fare on Troy concerts; male faculty likely sang the tenor and bass parts. Part 1 of the concert given on November 30, 1848, for example, concluded with the "Wedding Chorus" from *La Sonnambula*, while the finale to the second half was an untitled chorus from Auber's *Masaniello* [*La muette de Portici*]. The program for May 13, 1851, was divided into three parts, each concluding with a chorus: "Pour Out" from Meyerbeer's *Robert le Diable*; "Our Country" from Verdi's *I Lombardi*, arranged by Matthieu Philippi, then head of the music department; and "O Hail Us" from Verdi's *Ernani*. Philippi's arrangement of "Our Country" must have been well received, since it was repeated as the program finale on July 22 that same year. "Happy and Light" from Michael William Balfe's *Bohemian Girl* was likewise performed on at least two different occasions: a finale to the first half of the concert, June 29, 1849, and to conclude the second half of an undated benefit concert. Examples of other choruses include "When Daylight's Going" and "Phantom Chorus" from *La Sonnambula*, "Hail to Thee Liberty" from *Semiramide*, and "Gently Fall the Dews" from *Il Giuramento*.

Some choruses were scored for soloist and chorus. Occasionally the title was not provided, such as a cavatina and chorus from Rossini's *Semiramide* performed on June 20, 1850, and an aria and chorus from Bellini's *Beatrice di Tenda* performed on February 20, 1857. "Rest, Spirit, Rest" from William Michael Rooke's *Amilie, or The Love Test*, performed on November 30, 1848, opens with the chorus, followed by a soprano solo, and concludes with the chorus supporting the soloist.[96]

Music Vale was the only school to produce operas. Whittlesey composed dramatic works "based on important events of his own times," such as *Ralvo, the Pirate of the Gulf*—an opera for the students to perform not only as a "source of pleasure" but also "of practical use, on account of the discipline we have received in composition, elocution, and particularly in regard to expression."[97] As was common in his melodramatic works, this opera "contained many pretty, catchy airs and was full of melody."[98] Apparently a brass band from Colchester, a nearby town, served as the orchestra. The performances drew large crowds and received enthusiastic reviews in local newspapers: "Prominent persons gathered from far distant places to attend the spectacular performances and to talk for months afterwards of the amazing lighting and sound effects. Real thunder crashed when stage hands rolled iron balls across white oak boards in the wings and lightning flashed from lighted blasting powder strung out on tin plate."[99] This opera must have been well liked, since it was frequently produced for the annual concert. *Canawahoo, or The Perils of the Wilderness*, an opera "written by the Pupils and inmates of the Vale," was first produced in 1864 to conclude the annual examination; admission charge was one dollar.[100] It must have been well received, as it was repeated the following year. Rehearsals and productions were likely a source of pleasure and relief from the rigorous schedule.

Plays

Sarah Pierce wrote plays for student performance that were often presented at the end of the school year for parents, citizens of the town, and other guests. Pierce invited young men from Judge Tapping Reeve's law school to participate in productions requiring male characters. She included lyrics or song titles in some plays, such as *Ruth* and *Jephthah's Daughter*, both biblical subjects.[101] In the first of these, Rebecca, the mother of Boaz, has come to the field where Ruth and other young women are gleaning grain: "I thought I heard a soft, melodious voice, warbling sweet music as I passed this way. It would much delight me would you sing again." Ruth responds, "Alas! My voice so long attun'd to woe, but ill accords with harmony. But my poor talents are ever at command, when worth invites, or friendship sues." She then sings the following stanzas (no title is given):

Tho' tender and young, my fortune is gone,
My husband I've lost to increase my sad moan.
A gleaner alas! to the fields I must go,
To ask of the swains some relief from our woe.
My story would soften the heart of a churl,
O pity a hapless girl.

2ND.

The blessings of plenty press your basket and store
Then distribute those gifts to the stranger and poor;
Your friends too smile 'round you, but I to my cost,
Now reckon them o'er by the tears for their loss.
My story etc.

3RD.

Tho' a wanderer from my country I roam,
From the blessings of plenty, and the pleasures of home,
Yet Naomi's fond love would repay all my care,
Could I chase from her mind the mists of despair.
Her story etc.

4TH.

Then steel not your bosoms against my sad tale
But think on my years; they will surely prevail—
My tears kindly dry, and O may you ne'er know,
The horrors of want, or the heart ache of woe.
Our sorrows etc.

Later in the play it appears Ruth is singing another song, although her name is not mentioned. The first line of the first stanza addresses "Sons of Judah."

The first act of *Jephthah's Daughter* begins with Jephthah's daughter, Elizabeth, singing the Irish song "Silent O Moyle." Act 2, scene 1 opens with Elizabeth and several young women singing stanzas 2 and 3 of a paraphrase of the hymn "Guide Me Oh Thou Great Jehovah"; Pierce dedicated it to the young men who had serenaded students outside their windows after they retired. Act 2 concludes with "Strike the Cymbal," but no lyrics, author, or composer are named. It seems likely, though, that the author is Vincenzo Pucitta, as he set this text around 1816–1817. The play concludes with a procession accompanied by unidentified "solemn music." Undoubtedly law students sang the male parts in such songs as "Strike the Cymbal," composed for treble (or tenor) soloist and SAB chorus.[102]

Conclusion

A comparison of the vocal repertoires studied and performed at the four schools under study reveals more parallels between Music Vale and Troy than between these schools and Litchfield or Mount Holyoke. European and American composers, both lesser and well known, are represented in both vocal and piano repertoires. Names of composers rather than titles of their works appear at more than one institution. The lack of professional instruction at Mount Holyoke and Litchfield explains the disparity in literature. Collectively the repertoires of these two schools includes sacred and secular pieces composed or arranged for solo, duet, trio, quartet, sextet, and chorus. Genres range from simple folk tunes and anthems to operettas and operas. Though male students were not usually present,[103] part songs and choruses written for SATB were not excluded from the literature. Bass parts could have been sung one or two octaves higher or performed by male faculty. Low altos could have sung the tenor parts, or, if needed, these parts could have been transposed an octave higher. It appears that the vocal repertoire at Troy encompassed a wider variety than that at Music Vale; missing programs for Music Vale could explain the difference.

Singing was a significant part of students' lives at Litchfield, Troy, Mount Holyoke, and Music Vale. Sarah Pierce, Emma Willard, Mary Lyon, and Orramel Whittlesey encouraged their students to develop their talents to the fullest. Although all of the schools valued Christian training and required the students to attend church services, where they had the opportunity to sing hymns, Mount Holyoke gave more emphasis to sacred music than did the other schools. The hymn book was regarded as important as any textbook at Mount Holyoke. I have not found documents from Litchfield, Troy, or Music Vale requesting that students bring specific hymn books; perhaps these schools supplied them.

Personnel and resources at Litchfield and Mount Holyoke were lacking in comparison to those available at Troy and Music Vale; nevertheless, students were exposed to various types of sacred and secular vocal literature. Litchfield students had the opportunity to attend singing schools and church services where choral music was performed and to participate in plays that included musical performances. For twenty-five years talented students at Mount Holyoke continued to raise the level of music instruction, requiring the seminary to purchase new hymn or secular music books. When Miss Eliza Wilder joined the faculty in 1862, she introduced a more demanding vocal repertoire than what was used prior to her tenure.

Troy and Music Vale were rivals with respect to the level and genres of music studied and performed. Both schools excelled in offering some of the finest instruction available to young women in the United States at that time. Students sang popular and art song repertoires that were comparable to the literature performed by professional singers. Troy, however, took a back seat to Music Vale with regard to operatic productions.

The educational philosophy at each institution becomes clear when one examines the emphasis on vocal instruction and the literature that students studied and performed. Given the social climate at Litchfield, including the renowned law school, the academy students received an education that prepared them to enter refined society. While Mount Holyoke students were of lesser means, Mary Lyon wanted them to learn to sing for their physical, emotional, and spiritual well-being. Emma Willard was adamant that students at Troy receive professional vocal training equal to the level of instruction in academic subjects. Initially Music Vale did not include vocal instruction. As the school expanded and was professionally recognized, Orramel Whittlesey became aware that proper vocal training was a vital part of the young ladies' education. Although the schools did not prepare their students for concert careers, they supported the philosophy that learning to sing properly was a critical part of women's education in preparation for their roles in society.

Afterword

Educators and proponents of women's higher education in the late eighteenth and early nineteenth centuries supported the founding fathers' philosophy that as a new nation, America demanded a literate citizenry. Such activists as Sarah Pierce, Emma Willard, Catharine Beecher, Zilpah Grant, and Mary Lyon argued that both women and men needed to be educated in order to produce a learned public. They endorsed the philosophy "When you educate a woman, you educate an entire family," implemented at the Moravian Young Ladies' Seminary, Bethlehem, Pennsylvania, founded in 1742.[1] Like the Moravians, Pierce, Willard, and Lyon insisted that women were as intelligent as men and deserved an equivalent education.[2]

Rather than establishing fashionable schools where young women would obtain an education that focused on fripperies and made them marketable for marriage, these educators advocated a liberal arts education that prepared young women to make laudable contributions to the home and society. Without such training, women were "deprived of intellectual pursuits and pleasure" that would enable them to have a proper influence on their sons and daughters.[3] While education for men was liberally supported, instruction for young women had been "left to the individual exertions of a private preceptress, whose health is worn out in the service of others, and to whom a bare subsistence is scarcely allotted as a reward for a useful life of industry and talent."[4] Those who received a fashionable education had no greater advantage than those of lesser means:

> Shut out from intellectual enjoyments and their minds deprived of wholesome food, is it any wonder that their mental and social powers were frit-

tered away upon unworthy objects? that they fell into foolish and extravagant views? that they became the devotees of fashion and the slavish worshippers of dress, finery, and show? What else was left to them? And yet, without a tithe of the elevating influences that man enjoyed, and in spite of those faults that circumstances wove around her sex, woman contrived to keep ahead of him in refinement, in purity, in sobriety, and in all of those virtues that most adorn human nature. . . . Is it not the least that we can do, to bring her out of this unwilling and enforced bondage to frivolity and ignorance?[5]

Such was the state of education for most women in the United States when Pierce, Willard, and Lyon began their innovative work.

The founding of academies and seminaries that offered a liberal arts education ushered in a new era in the history of women's education. Litchfield Female Academy (as a precursor) and Troy and Mount Holyoke Female Seminaries laid the foundations for the "female seminary movement" that spread across the nation between 1830 and 1860. An author writing in the *New York Mirror* in 1832 argued, "How important, then, are these seminaries, and how deserving of notice and encouragement. How much it is the duty of every one, and more especially of the public press, to foster them, and make them what they should be—the nursery of the virtues."[6] If the new republic was to survive and advance as a nation in its own right, women needed to be properly educated to fulfill their responsibilities.

Music instruction became a vital part of the liberal arts education offered at the seminaries and academies. Instead of offering instruction in music as an accomplishment, as taught at the fashionable schools, Litchfield Female Academy, Troy and Mount Holyoke Female Seminaries, and Music Vale Seminary viewed music education as an academic subject with physical, mental, and emotional benefits. Students who had the privilege of attending these schools were encouraged to develop their talents to the fullest. Further, young women who enrolled at Troy and Music Vale had the opportunity to receive instruction from some of the finest professionally trained teachers available in the United States.

These schools were important institutions in laying the groundwork for women's education as we know it today. While much has been accomplished in the history of women's education, more research needs to be done with regard to the influence of these schools and later developments in music instruction. For example, what influence, if any, did these schools have on the founding of later music departments in colleges, universities, or conservatories? What were the graduates' careers? How do the music instruction and repertoires studied and performed at such schools as Troy and Music Vale compare with that of the music departments and music schools established in the later nineteenth century? Was there any difference between music education in women's and men's institutions? An investigation of the work of Emma Willard, Sarah Pierce, Mary Lyon, and Orramel Whittlesey is vital in understanding the history of American institutions for women that offered musical training as part of a liberal arts education.

Notes

Abbreviations

CLHS   Collection of the Litchfield Historical Society, Litchfield, Connecticut.
EWSA   Emma Willard School Archives (Troy Female Seminary), Emma Willard School, Troy, New York.
MHCASC   Mount Holyoke College Archives and Special Collections, South Hadley, Massachusetts.
MVSA   Music Vale Seminary Archives, Salem, Connecticut.

Introduction

1. The terms "seminary" and "academy" were often reciprocal, although the term "academies" was more common in the Early Republic and "seminaries" in the antebellum period. Margaret A. Nash, *Women's Education in the United States, 1780–1840* (New York: Palgrave Macmillan, 2005), 6. During the late eighteenth and early nineteenth centuries, schools for women were commonly referred to as "seminaries" or "academies," while "college" was reserved for institutions of higher education for men.

2. Charles Hamm, *Music in the New World* (New York: W. W. Norton, 1983); Gilbert Chase, *America's Music: From the Pilgrims to the Present*, rev. 3rd ed. (Urbana: University of Illinois Press, 1992); Richard Crawford, *America's Musical Life: A History* (New York: W. W. Norton, 2001).

3. This particularly applies to music scholarship. Seminaries and academies have rarely been discussed in detail by music historians. However, a wealth of research on women's education in general has been conducted and published for several decades. Thomas Woody's *A History of Women's Education in the United States*, 2 vols. (New York: Science Press, 1929), for example, remains a respected source.

4. Michael L. Mark and Charles L. Gary, *A History of American Music Education* (New York: Rowman and Littlefield Education, 2007). The authors include three paragraphs on "The Academy," but no mention is made of the seminary or of music as part of the curriculum. They credit Benjamin Franklin with the founding of the academy as a new type of institution (116–17).

5. James A. Keene focuses on Burlington Female Seminary and Essex and Barre Academies, all in Vermont. He briefly mentions Emma Willard's work in Vermont (although he does not include the name of her school). *A History of Music Education in the United States*, 2nd ed. (Centennial, CO: Glenbridge Publishing, 2009), 156–62. I recently became aware of, but have not read, Jennifer E. P. Campbell's dissertation, "Music Education at the Troy Female Seminary: 1817–1904" (PhD diss., University of Mississippi, 2016).

6. Mary Kelley, *Learning to Stand and Speak: Women, Education, and Public Life in America's Republic* (Chapel Hill: University of North Carolina Press, 2006).

7. Nash confirms that the better female schools were not initially open to women of color: "Virtually all of the students in institutions of higher education in the 1820s and 1830s were white and either middle or upper class." *Women's Education*, 13.

8. For example, Arthur Loesser argues, "Only a very restricted number of people, in the United States as elsewhere, conceived of music as a fine art or as an object of absorbed scrutiny. To most it was an easy pleasure, an entertainment that would defeat its purpose if it required a serious effort of attention." *Men, Women, and Pianos: A Social History* (New York: Simon and Schuster, 1954), 503. While this seems to be the attitude promoted at the finishing schools, I contend that it did not concur with the philosophy of music as studied at the seminaries and academies offering a strong liberal arts education. As we will see later, the level of instruction provided at Music Vale Seminary in Salem, Connecticut, far exceeded this mentality.

9. Linda K. Kerber, *Women of the Republic: Intellect and Ideology in Revolutionary America* (Chapel Hill: University of North Carolina Press, 1980), 189.

10. Ibid.

11. Nash, *Women's Education*, 2.

12. Elaine Kendall, *Peculiar Institutions: An Informal History of the Seven Sister Colleges* (New York: G. P. Putnam's Sons, 1976), 9.

13. John Lord, *The Life of Emma Willard* (New York: D. Appleton, 1873), 58. According to Nancy Iannucci, librarian and archivist at Emma Willard School, Lord's book is a primary source, since it contains the only existing record of some of Willard's letters and material from her diaries. Email to author, July 29, 2008.

14. Kendall, *Peculiar Institutions*, 9; David Boers, *History of American Education Primer* (New York: Peter Lang Publishing, 2007), 10, 11; Lord, *Life of Emma Willard*, 52. See Woody, *History of Women's Education*, 1:144–45, for examples of schools opened to girls during hours when boys were not present.

15. Lord, *Life of Emma Willard*, 53–54.

16. Ibid., 54.

17. According to some scholars, the female seminary movement began as early as 1790. Mary Kelley maintains that "between 1790 and 1830, 182 academies and at least 14 seminaries were established exclusively for women in the North and the South." Kelley does not refer to this development in the history of women's education as the "female seminary movement," although the type of school to which she is referring fits this description. Kelley, *Learning to Stand and Speak*, 67. Margaret Nash, however, claims that historians often consider the institutions founded by Emma Willard and Mary Lyon as "dramatically different from other schools of their time, and credited their founders with inaugurating new types of education for women." Nash, *Women's Education*, 3. In addition, Kendall defends Willard's school as a new venture in women's education, stating that it was "the first to draw public and private support for women's education." Kendall, *Peculiar Institutions*, 9. Thus, I have chosen to use the establishment of Troy Female Seminary in 1821 by Emma Willard as initiating the female seminary movement.

18. See chapter 3 for a discussion of Willard's plan and its far-reaching influence.

19. Mary Kelley confirms that Litchfield Female Academy was "one of the nation's most prominent academies." *Learning to Stand and Speak*, 3.

20. Barbara Miller Solomon, *In the Company of Educated Women* (New Haven, CT: Yale University Press, 1985), 3, 4.

21. Frances B. Cogan, *All-American Girl: The Ideal of Real Womanhood in Mid-Nineteenth-Century America* (Athens: University of Georgia Press, 1989), 74–75.

22. Alma Lutz, *Emma Willard: Daughter of Democracy* (Boston: Houghton Mifflin, 1929), 106.

Chapter 1. Philosophies of Women's Education in the United States

1. Willystine Goodsell, *Pioneers of Women's Education in the United States: Emma Willard, Catherine Beecher, and Mary Lyon* (New York: AMS Press, 1970; repr. of the 1931 edition), 1, 2 (citations refer to the AMS Press edition); Gerda Lerner, *The Woman in American History* (Menlo Park, CA: Addison-Wesley, 1971), 9.

2. Lerner, *Woman in American History*, 9.

3. Goodsell, *Pioneers of Women's Education*, 2, 3; Ann D. Gordon and Mari Jo Buhle, "Sex and Class in Colonial and Nineteenth-Century America," in *Liberating Women's History: Theoretical and Critical Essays*, ed. Berenice A. Carroll (Urbana: University of Illinois Press, 1976), 284. The word "sphere" is commonly used to describe women's "domain" during this time period. To maintain the contemporary terminology, I have retained "sphere" when referring to women's area of responsibility.

4. Goodsell, *Pioneers of Women's Education*, 2, 3; Barbara Miller Solomon, *In the Company of Educated Women: A History of Women and Higher Education in America* (New Haven, CT: Yale University Press, 1985), 3. George Winthrop, governor of Massachusetts, expressed the then popular opinion when he advised women to restrict

their knowledge to that appropriate for household skills and to avoid inquiring into subject matter suitable only for men who have greater intellectual skills than women. Lerner, *Woman in American History*, 12. Mistress Hopkins, wife of the governor of Hartford Colony, was belittled for her educational pursuits. Winthrop's comments in his journal of 1645 regarding Mistress Hopkins concurred with the majority of views concerning the education of women: "[It had caused her to fall] into a sad infirmity, the loss of her understanding and reason . . . by occasion of her giving herself wholly to reading and writing, and had written many books. . . . For if she had attended her household affairs, and such things as belonged to women, and had not gone out of her way and calling to meddle in such things as are proper for men, whose minds are stronger, etc., she had kept her wits, and might have improved them usefully and honorably in the place God had set her." Goodsell, *Pioneers of Women's Education*, 3–4. For nearly two hundred years, the tale of Mistress Hopkins served as a warning against women's education. It provided material for countless sermons admonishing young women of the dangers that would befall them should they pursue such immorality. Ibid., 4.

5. Elaine Kendall, *Peculiar Institutions: An Informal History of the Seven Sister Colleges* (New York: G. P. Putnam's Sons, 1976), 12.

6. Solomon, *In the Company of Educated Women*, 3.

7. Thomas Woody, *A History of Women's Education in the United States* (New York: Science Press, 1929), 1:138; Solomon, *In the Company of Educated Women*, 3; Goodsell, *Pioneers of Women's Education*, 4–5.

8. Woody, *History of Women's Education*, 138.

9. Barbara Solomon notes that by the mid-eighteenth century, women were active in nearly every religious organization. Further, she comments, "Increasingly it appeared men who were not ministers left religion along with domestic duties to women." *In the Company of Educated Women*, 4.

10. Ellen Carol DuBois and Lynn Dumenil, *Through Women's Eyes: An American History with Documents*, 2nd ed. (Boston: Bedford/St. Martin's, 2009), 1:147.

11. Ibid.; Solomon, *In the Company of Educated Women*, 4.

12. Solomon, *In the Company of Educated Women*, 3, 4, 5; Margaret A. Nash, *Women's Education in the United States: 1780–1840* (New York: Palgrave Macmillan, 2005), 18.

13. Nash, *Women's Education*, 18.

14. Linda Grant DePauw and Conover Hunt, with the assistance of Miriam Schneir, *Remember the Ladies: Women in America, 1750–1815* (New York: Viking Press, 1976), 101.

15. Solomon, *In the Company of Educated Women*, 6.

16. Lynne Templeton Brickley, "Sarah Pierce's Litchfield Female Academy, 1792–1833" (EdD diss., Harvard University, 1985), 3 (hereafter, "Sarah Pierce's LFA").

17. During the eighteenth and nineteenth centuries, "seminary" was a generic term used for a male or female institution offering instruction in several branches

of learning that prepared students for future employment. Some schools, such as the Ursuline Convent and the Moravian Young Ladies' Seminary, would also have included religious training. Benigna Zinzendorf, founder of the Moravian Young Ladies' Seminary, a woman ahead of her time, was the daughter of Count Nicholas Louis von Zinzendorf, the first leader of the renewed Moravian Church in Germany and instrumental in establishing the Moravian Church in America (Bethlehem, Pennsylvania) in 1741. Jewel A. Smith, "Music, Women, and Pianos: The Moravian Young Ladies' Seminary in Antebellum Bethlehem, Pennsylvania (1815–1860)" (PhD diss., University of Cincinnati, 2003), 36, 44, 67.

18. Goodsell, *Pioneers of Women's Education*, 7–8; Woody, *History of Women's Education*, 1:108; Merle Curti, *The Social Ideas of American Educators, with New Chapter on the Last Twenty-Five Years* (Paterson, NJ: Pageant Books, 1959), 170–71, 174–75; DePauw, Hunt, and Schneir, *Remember the Ladies*, 98, 101.

19. Solomon, *In the Company of Educated Women*, 5–6.

20. DePauw, Hunt, and Schneir, *Remember the Ladies*, 109.

21. Louise Schutz Boas, *Women's Education Begins: The Rise of the Women's Colleges* (New York: Arno Press, 1971), 51.

22. "Progress of Female Education," *American Journal, and Annals of Education and Instruction* 1, no. 7 (1830): 421, ProQuest. The author argues that girls were never taught arithmetic.

23. Senex [Rev. William Woodbridge], "Female Education in the Last Century," *American Annals of Education* 1, no. 11 (1831): 522, ProQuest.

24. Curti, *Social Ideas of American Educators*, 170–71. See note 4 above regarding Governor Winthrop.

25. Solomon, *In the Company of Educated Women*, 7.

26. Ibid., 7, 11.

27. Kendall, *Peculiar Institutions*, 12.

28. DuBois and Dumenil, *Through Women's Eyes*, 174.

29. Lerner, *Woman in American History*, 31.

30. Curti, *Social Ideas of American Educators*, 170–71.

31. Ibid., 174–75.

32. These included such subjects as mathematics, natural sciences, history, geography, classics, and calisthenics as well as more unusual courses, such as chirography, uranography, mythology, and mezzotint. Ibid., 175.

33. Ibid.

34. DuBois and Dumenil, *Through Women's Eyes*, 146, 187.

35. Nancy F. Cott, *The Bonds of Womanhood: Women's Sphere in New England, 1780–1835* (New Haven, CT: Yale University Press, 1978), 109–10.

36. Sophia, "Article 2—No Title," *Evening Fire-side; or, Literary Miscellany* 1, no. 17 (1805): 5–6, ProQuest.

37. Rush was a physician and a leading citizen of Philadelphia, member of the Continental Congress, signer of the Declaration of Independence, and member of

the American Philosophical Society and of the original board of directors of the Philadelphia Academy for Young Ladies. Cott, *Bonds of Womanhood*, 104–6.

38. Benjamin Rush, *Thoughts upon Female Education, Accommodated to the Present State of Society, Manners, and Government in the United States of America. Addressed to the Visitors of the Young Ladies' Academy in Philadelphia, 28 July 1787, at the Close of the Quarterly Examination* (Philadelphia: Prichard and Hall, 1787), 110–11, Gale.

39. Ibid.

40. Ibid.

41. Ibid.

42. Abigail Adams to John Adams, August 14, 1776, in *Adams Family Correspondence*, ed. L. H. Butterfield (Cambridge, MA: Belknap Press, 1963), 2:94.

43. Abigail Adams, *Letters of Mrs. Adams, the Wife of John Adams* (Boston: C. C. Little and J. Brown, 1840), 446–47, Gale.

44. Boas, *Woman's Education Begins*, 55.

45. Cott, *Bonds of Womanhood*, 106.

46. Lerner, *Woman in American History*, 40.

47. Ruth Perry, *The Celebrated Mary Astell: An Early English Feminist* (Chicago: University of Chicago Press, 1986), xi.

48. Mary Astell, *A Serious Proposal to the Ladies, for the Advancement of Their True and Greatest Interest. In Two Parts. By a Lover of Her Sex* (London, 1697 [1701]. Eighteenth Century Collections Online, 47–48, Gale.

49. Linda K. Kerber, *Women of the Republic: Intellect and Ideology in Revolutionary America* (Chapel Hill: University of North Carolina Press, 1980), 222, 224.

50. Ibid., 189, 206.

51. Ibid., 206–7.

52. Kendall, *Peculiar Institutions*, 9; Jewel A. Smith, *Music, Women, and Pianos in Antebellum Bethlehem, Pennsylvania: The Moravian Young Ladies' Seminary* (Bethlehem, PA: Lehigh University Press, 2008), 35–37; Goodsell, *Pioneers of Women's Education*, 9–10; Cott, *Bonds of Womanhood*, 115. After emigrating from Britain, Susanna Rowson achieved fame as a stage actress and as the author of *Charlotte Temple*, America's first best-selling novel. Cott, *Bonds of Womanhood*, 115.

53. Brickley, "Sarah Pierce's LFA," 1.

54. George Emerson was a distant cousin of Ralph Waldo Emerson. The relationship between George and Joseph is not clear. "Emerson Family Correspondence, 1827–1957," A45, Emerson Unit 2, https://find.minlib.net/iii/encore/record/C__Rb2189123?lang=eng.

55. DeWitt Clinton, "1819. January. Legislature, Forty-Second Session: Opening Speech," *State of New York: Messages from the Governors Comprising Executive Communications to the Legislature and Other Papers Relating to Legislation from the Organization of the First Colonial Assembly in 1683 to and Including the Year 1906. With Notes*, ed. Charles Z. Lincoln (Albany, NY: J. B. Lyon, 1909), 2:972.

56. "An Address of Female Education, delivered in Portsmouth, New Hampshire, October 26, 1827," *American Journal of Education* 3, no. 1 (1828): 52, ProQuest; Cott, *Bonds of Womanhood*, 119.

57. Woody, *History of Women's Education*, 1:317, 328.

58. Curti, *Social Ideas of American Educators*, 176–77.

59. According to Arthur C. Cole, "Emerson was the apostle of a rigid mental discipline, without distinction as to sex." *A Hundred Years of Mount Holyoke College: The Evolution of an Educational Ideal* (New Haven, CT: Yale University Press, 1940), 6.

60. Henry Barnard, ed., *Educational Biography, Pt. 1. Teachers and Educators*. Vol. 1. *United States: Memoirs of Teachers, Educators, and Promoters and Benefactors of Education, Literature, and Science*, 2nd ed. (New York: F. C. Brownell, 1859), 337–38. The name of the school for girls was not given.

61. Cott, *Bonds of Womanhood*, 120–22; Curti, *Social Ideas of American Educators*, 177.

62. See chapter 3 for a discussion of Sarah Pierce, Emma Willard, and Mary Lyon. Almira Phelps is mentioned in chapter 2.

63. Solomon, *In the Company of Educated Women*, 17, 18.

64. See chapter 3 for a discussion of Willard's plan. Kendall, *Peculiar Institutions*, 9; Curti, *Social Ideas of American Educators*, 170; Kerber, *Women of the Republic*, 226.

65. Nancy Woloch, comp., *Early American Women: A Documentary History, 1600–1900*, 2nd rev. ed. (Boston: McGraw-Hill, 2002), 141.

66. Ibid., 141, 142.

67. Alexis de Tocqueville, *Democracy in America*, trans. Henry Reeve, with original preface and notes by John C. Spencer, 4th ed. (New York: J. and H. G. Langley, 1841), 2:225.

68. DuBois and Dumenil, *Through Women's Eyes*, 188.

69. Woloch, *Early American Women*, 141, 142, 143.

70. Barbara Welter expounds on the phrase "cult of true womanhood" in her article "The Cult of True Womanhood: 1820–1860," *American Quarterly* 18 (1966): 151–74.

71. Gordon and Buhle, "Sex and Class," 284.

72. Kendall, *Peculiar Institutions*, 24.

73. Sarah J. Hale, *Manners, or, Happy Homes and Good Society* (Boston: J. E. Tilton, 1868; New York: Arno Press, 1972), verso (citations refer to the Arno Press edition).

74. Mary P. Ryan, *Womanhood in America: From Colonial Times to the Present*, 3rd ed. (New York: Franklin Watts, 1983), 118.

75. Solomon, *In the Company of Educated Women*, 15–16; Ryan, *Womanhood in America*, 127; Cott, *Bonds of Womanhood*, 118; Boas, *Woman's Education Begins*, 62; DuBois and Dumenil, *Through Women's Eyes*, 189, 191.

76. Unfortunately this did not transpire. The female seminaries, with the exception of Mount Holyoke, catered to women of the upper class; see chapter 3.

77. Cott, *Bonds of Womanhood*, 121.

78. Marion Lansing, ed., *Mary Lyon through Her Letters* (Boston: Books, 1937), 134.

79. DuBois and Dumenil, *Through Women's Eyes*, 147.

80. Goodsell, *Pioneers of Women's Education*, 8–9; Brickley, "Sarah Pierce's LFA," 3, 4; Solomon, *In the Company of Educated Women*, 15; Cott, *Bonds of Womanhood*, 118.

Chapter 2. Beyond an Accomplishment: A Philosophy of Music Education

1. H. Wiley Hitchcock, *Music in the United States: A Historical Introduction*, with a final chapter by Kyle Gann, 4th ed. (Upper Saddle River, NJ: Prentice Hall, 2000), 57.

2. Thomas Woody, *A History of Women's Education in the United States* (New York: Science Press, 1929), 1:110–111.

3. Judith Tick, *American Women Composers before 1870* (Ann Arbor, MI: UMI Research Press, 1983; repr., Rochester, NY: University of Rochester Press, 1995), 13, 15 (citations refer to the University of Rochester Press edition).

4. The words "academy" and "seminary" were used interchangeably during the late eighteenth and nineteenth centuries. Hereafter I will not make this distinction with regard to Litchfield Female Academy.

5. Ipse Vidi, "Musical Talent" *American Annals of Education* 1, no. 11 (1831): 518, ProQuest.

6. "The Beauties of Music," *Ladies' Garland and Family Wreath Embracing Tales, Sketches, Incidents, History, Poetry, Music* 1, no. 4 (1837): 62, ProQuest.

7. Edward W. Hooker, "Music as a Part of Female Education," *Musical Reporter* 9 (September 1841): 5, ProQuest; repr. *Music as a Part of Female Education* (Boston: T. R. Marvin, 1843), 3 (citations refer to the T. R. Marvin edition).

8. Ibid., 5–6.

9. Tick, *American Women Composers*, 17.

10. "Ladies Department: The Use and Abuse of Music," *Western Christian Advocate* 7, no. 27 (1840): 108, ProQuest.

11. John Lord, *The Life of Emma Willard* (New York: D. Appleton, 1873), 73.

12. Quoted in Edward Hitchcock, comp., *The Power of Christian Benevolence Illustrated in the Life and Labors of Mary Lyon*, new edition (New York: American Tract Society, 1858), 95–96.

13. Lowell Mason to Mary Lyon, November 20, 1832, MHCASC, Mary Lyon Collection, series A, "Correspondence, 1818–1849," http://clio.fivecolleges.edu/mhc/lyon/a.

14. According to R. Allen Lott, Herz toured the United States from 1846 to 1850; Thalberg from 1856 to 1858. Their music was well known in the United States before their arrival. *From Paris to Peoria: How European Piano Virtuosos Brought Classical Music to the American Heartland* (New York: Oxford University Press, 2003), 56, 116.

Possibly a town band or orchestra or a second piano performed the orchestral part of the concerti.

15. Hooker, *Music, as a Part of Female Education*, 4.

16. Ibid.

17. Mrs. Sarah D. (Locke) Stow, *History of Mount Holyoke Seminary, South Hadley, Mass. during its First Half Century, 1837–1877* (South Hadley: MA: Mount Holyoke Seminary, 1887), 103–104.

18. Benjamin Rush, *Thoughts upon Female Education, Accommodated to the Present State of Society, Manners, and Government in the United States of America. Addressed to the Visitors of the Young Ladies' Academy in Philadelphia, 28 July 1787, at the Close of the Quarterly Examination* (Philadelphia: Prichard and Hall, 1787), 10–11, Gale; Dr. [Benjamin] Rush, "Use of Vocal Music," *The Euterpeiad; An Album of Music, Poetry, and Prose* 1, no. 2 (1830): 9, ProQuest.

19. [William] Alcott, "Female Education: Young Woman's Guide," *Musical Reporter* 5 (May 1841): 218, ProQuest.

20. "Music in Common Schools," *Boston Musical Visitor* 3, no. 4 (1842): 52, ProQuest.

21. Mary J. Mason Fairbanks, ed. *Emma Willard and Her Pupils or Fifty Years of Troy Female Seminary: 1822–1872* (New York: Mrs. Russell Sage, 1898), 11.

22. L[ydia] H[oward] Sigourney, *Letters to Young Ladies*, 3rd ed. (New York: Harper and Bros., 1837), 111.

23. "Beauties of Music," 62.

24. Alcott, "Female Education," 218.

25. Mrs. L. G. Abell, *Woman in Her Various Relations: Containing Practical Rules for American Females* (New York: R. T. Young, 1853), 33–34.

26. Rush, *Thoughts upon Female Education*, 10; William C. Woodbridge, "On Vocal Music as a Branch of Common Education," *American Annals of Education* 3, no. 5 (1833): 205–6, ProQuest. For information on how interest in music education and the family continued into the Victorian era, see Ruth A. Solie, "'Girling' at the Parlor Piano," chapter 3 in *Music in Other Words: Victorian Conversations* (Berkley: University of California Press, 2004).

27. George W. Burnap, *Lectures on the Sphere and Duties of Woman and Other Subjects* (Baltimore: John Murphy, 1841), 148–49.

28. Frances B. Cogan, *All-American Girl: The Ideal of Real Womanhood in Mid-Nineteenth-Century America* (Athens: University of Georgia Press, 1989), 63, 73. See chapter 2, "Education and Real Womanhood," in Cogan's book for a detailed discussion of the pros and cons regarding women's education in mid-nineteenth-century America.

29. T. Mechanic and A. W. Farmer, "Music in Common Schools: Number Two," *Boston Musical Gazette; A Semimonthly Journal, Devoted to the Science of Music* 1, no. 9 (1838): 68, ProQuest.

30. W[illiam] Nixon, "A Guide to Instruction on the Pianoforte," *American Musical Journal* 1, no. 12 (1835): 283, ProQuest. Nixon's *A Guide to Instruction on the Pianoforte: Designed for the Use of Both Parents and Pupils; in a Series of Short Essays, Dedicated to the Young Ladies of the Musical Seminary* was published by Josiah Drake in Cincinnati, 1834. For more information on Nixon, see William Osborne, *Music in Ohio* (Kent, OH: Kent State University Press, 2004), 43, 93, 208, and Robert C. Vitz, *The Queen and the Arts: Cultural Life in Nineteenth-Century Cincinnati* (Kent, OH: Kent State University Press, 1989), 13, 75.

31. Mechanic and Farmer, "Music in Common Schools," 68. The author explained the level of memorization required: all of the characters and symbols of notation and rhythm and the sound of each note. In addition, the student was usually required to memorize the texts of vocal pieces.

32. Susan Rowson, *Mentoria* (Philadelphia, 1794), 2:65, quoted in Tick, *American Women Composers*, 20.

33. "Thoughts on Music," *American Annals of Education* (February 1837): 82, ProQuest.

34. In order to ensure that students at Troy Female Seminary received an education comparable to that offered at Middlebury College for men, Emma Willard introduced an examination period at the end of each term and obtained a committee consisting of men in prestigious positions. For example, professors at West Point and Columbia College and the president of the University of Vermont examined the students in their academic studies. See chapter 5 for more information on these committees. *Catalogue of the Officers and Pupils of the Troy Female Seminary, for the Academic Year, Commencing September 9, 1863, and Ending June 29, 1864, Together with the Conditions of Admittance, etc.* (Troy, NY: Daily Whig Presses, 1864), 19, folder "Troy Female Seminary Catalogues, 1855" (hereafter, "TFS Catalogues and year" box), "Troy Female Seminary Catalogues, 1820–1895" (all of the catalogs are housed in this box), EWSA. When Emma Willard's son and his wife replaced Willard as principal in 1838, they continued this practice, thus the reason for the plural form of "Principal" in the quote.

35. Almira Phelps, *The Female Student; or Lectures to Young Ladies on Female Education. For the Use of Mothers, Teachers, and Pupils* (New York: Leavitt, Lord, 1836), 376.

36. "Advantages of Musical Instruction," *Musical Visitor* 2, no. 8 (1841): 58, ProQuest.

37. T. Mechanic and A. W. Farmer, "Miscellaneous: Music in Common Schools: Number Three," *Boston Musical Gazette; A Semimonthly Journal, Devoted to the Science of Music* 1, no. 10 (1838): 75, ProQuest.

38. "Music as a Branch of Common Education," *American Annals of Education* 1, no. 6 (1831): 272.

39. Mechanic and Farmer, "Miscellaneous: Music in Common Schools," 74.

40. "Vocal Music," *The Euterpeiad: An Album of Music, Poetry, and Prose* 2, no. 1 (1831): 5, ProQuest.

41. "On Cultivation of Taste," *Ladies' Garland and Family Wreath Embracing Tales, Sketches, Incidents, History, Poetry, Music, etc.* 1, no. 1 (1837): a12, ProQuest.

42. *Catalog of the Officers and Pupils of the Troy Female Seminary, for the Academic Year, Commencing September 10, 1856, and Ending June 24, 1857, Together with the Conditions of Admittance, etc.* (Troy, NY: A. W. Scribner, 1857), 26, folder "TFS Catalogues, 1857," EWSA.

43. Phelps, *Female Student*, 375; "Music, as a Branch of Common Education," *American Annals of Education* 1, no. 2 (1831): 67, ProQuest.

44. Phelps, *Female Student*, 376.

45. Woodbridge, "On Vocal Music," 205.

46. Hooker, "Music as a Part of Female Education," 5.

47. Amicus, "The Influence of a Musical Education," *The Family Minstrel: A Musical and Literary Journal* 1, no. 22 (1835): 170–71, ProQuest.

48. T. S. Arthur, *Advice to Young Ladies on Their Duties and Conduct in Life* (Boston: Phillips and Sampson, 1848), 27.

49. "Suggestions to Parents on Female Education: Accomplishments," *American Journal of Education* 3, no. 5 (1828): 278, ProQuest.

50. Arthur, *Advice to Young Ladies*, 56.

51. For example, this was a viable rationale for many parents and guardians who sent their daughters or wards to the Moravian Young Ladies' Seminary in Bethlehem, Pennsylvania. Mrs. C. R. Clarke, for example, emphatically stated that her niece must become a music teacher, and thus it was important that she not only play well but also have a thorough understanding of the rudiments of music. In inquiring about admission for his sister, Dr. C. S. Smith claimed that she would need to obtain work as a governess or a family teacher in the South; in order to do so, she must be well trained in music. C. R. Clarke to Sylvester Wolle, September 1, 1859, folder "Ci–l," box "Fem. Sem., Wolle Corr.: C–F"; Dr. C. S. Smith to Sylvester Wolle, August 5, 1859, folder "Sm," box "Fem. Sem., Wolle Corr.: R–U," Moravian Archives, Bethlehem, Pennsylvania.

52. Daniel Wright to Miss Lyon, September 10, 1844, MHCASC, Mary Lyon Collection, series A: Correspondence, 1818–1849, http://clio.fivecolleges.edu/mhc/lyon/a.

53. Mary Lyon to Susannah Fitch, September 17, 1848, MHCASC, Mary Lyon Collection, series A, "Correspondence, 1818–1849," http://clio.fivecolleges.edu/mhc/lyon/a.

54. T. S. Arthur, "The Young Music Teacher," *Arthur's Ladies' Magazine of Elegant Literature and the Fine Arts*, October 1844, 191–96, ProQuest.

55. Woodbridge, "On Vocal Music," 207.

56. "Suggestions to Parents," 277, 278.

57. Hooker, *Music as a Part of Female Education*, 7.

58. Rush, *Thoughts upon Female Education*, 15–17.

59. Hooker, *Music as a Part of Female Education*, 8–9.

60. Gail Hamilton, *Gala-Days* (Boston: Ticknor and Fields, 1863), 276, 285–86. Mary Abigail Dodge (1833–1896) used the pseudonym "Gail Hamilton." She graduated from Ipswich Female Seminary in 1850 and remained there as a teacher for four years. Thereafter she taught at Hartford Female Seminary for one year before leaving to accept a position at Hartford High School, Hartford, Connecticut. *History's Women: The Unsung Heroines*, http://www.historyswomen.com/thearts/MaryAbigailDodge .html.

61. Sarah J. Hale, *Manners, or Happy Homes and Good Society All the Year Round* (Boston: J. E. Tilton, 1868; repr., New York: Arno Press, 1972), 177 (citations refer to the Arno Press edition).

62. Hooker, *Music as a Part of Female Education*, 8.

63. Phelps, *Female Student*, 366–68.

Chapter 3. The Dawn of a New Era in Women's Education

1. A survey of the literature on the history of women's education in America reveals that this school was the earliest to offer higher education for women. See, for example, Thomas Woody, *A History of Women's Education in the United States*, 2 vols. (New York: Science Press, 1929). Also see my dissertation, "Music, Women, and Pianos: The Moravian Young Ladies' Seminary in Antebellum Bethlehem, Pennsylvania (1815–1860)" (University of Cincinnati, 2003), or my book *Music, Women, and Pianos in Antebellum Bethlehem, Pennsylvania: The Moravian Young Ladies' Seminary* (Bethlehem, PA: Lehigh University Press, 2008).

2. Anne Firor Scott, *Making the Invisible Woman Visible* (Urbana: University of Illinois Press, 1984), 39–40.

3. Elizabeth Williams Anthony Dexter, *Career Women of America, 1776–1840* (Francestown, NH: M. Jones, [1950]), 20.

4. Lynne Templeton Brickley notes that Pierce's older brother, John, "was said to have been an accomplished man in English & French tongues & the dead languages," and her younger brother, James, was "noted for a classical education & refined taste in literature." "Sarah Pierce's Litchfield Female Academy, 1792–1833" (EdD diss., Harvard University, 1985), 13 (hereafter, "Sarah Pierce's LFA").

5. Ibid., 13, 21.

6. Brickley does not refer to any schools by name, but it can be assumed that these were private female academies in existence for a few years, since they were not endowed.

7. After the war John Pierce had a romantic relationship with Ann Bard, daughter of Dr. John Bard, an eminent physician in New York City. Thus, his associations with prominent families in New York undoubtedly influenced his choice of schools for his sisters. He was eager for his sisters to assume the family financial responsibility

so that he could marry Bard. In addition, having his sisters establish a school for the daughters of esteemed families could further his own aspirations in New York. Brickley, "Sarah Pierce's LFA," 22, 23.

8. Ibid., 14–16, 18, 20–25, 34–36.

9. Emily Noyes Vanderpoel, comp., and Elizabeth C. Barney Buel, ed., *Chronicles of a Pioneer School from 1792 to 1833 Being the History of Miss Sarah Pierce and Her Litchfield School* (Cambridge, MA: University Press, 1903), 8.

10. Brickley, "Sarah Pierce's LFA," 10, 13; Catherine Fennelly, "Sarah Pierce" in *Notable American Women, 1607–1950: A Biographical Dictionary*, ed. Edward T. James, Janet Wilson James, and Paul S. Boyer (Cambridge, MA: Belknap Press, 1971), 3:67.

11. For example, those of the cabinet, the senate, and the bench, such as John Caldwell Calhoun, John Middleton Clayton, George Mason, Levi Woodbury, Abraham Oakey Hall, and William Henry Ashley. Vanderpoel, *Chronicles of a Pioneer School*, 7; Brickley, "Sarah Pierce's LFA," 38.

12. Brickley, "Sarah Pierce's LFA," 39; Vanderpoel, *Chronicles of a Pioneer School*, 8.

13. Brickley, "Sarah Pierce's LFA," 49–50.

14. Emily Noyes Vanderpoel corresponded with Perkins while acquiring material for *Chronicles of a Pioneer School*. Brickley, "Sarah Pierce's LFA," 50; J. Deming Perkins to Emily Noyes Vanderpoel, March 3, 1897, Emily Noyes Vanderpoel Collection, Litchfield Female Academy Collection, Collection of the Litchfield Historical Society, Litchfield, Connecticut.

15. According to Brickley, Judge Tapping Reeve was Sarah Pierce's main supporter in founding her school in Litchfield. His pledge headed the list at forty dollars; eight others pledged twenty dollars each, five promised fifteen dollars, ten for ten dollars, and two for five dollars. Five of the subscribers were some of Litchfield's wealthiest taxpayers. Eleven of the group were college graduates, a high percentage when only a few men in Connecticut had attended college. The list continues to be distinguished, including men in national, state, and local political offices, who proved to be crucial to the academy's development and success. Most of these supporters had children or relatives who attended the school. Brickley, "Sarah Pierce's LFA," 37, 46, 47–48.

16. Ibid., 48.

17. Ibid., 49.

18. Ibid., 5.

19. See chapter 5 for a discussion of the public exhibitions and chapters 6–8 for an examination of Pierce's involvement in the music taught and performed at Litchfield Female Academy.

20. Emma Hart Willard, folder "Troy Female Seminary—Photographs and Photographic Copies," box "MSS#6, Middlebury Academy, Waterford Academy, Troy Female Seminary, Records, Articles, Pictures," EWSA. All of the primary source material from the Emma Willard School is housed in this archive unless otherwise noted.

21. Scott, *Making the Invisible Woman Visible*, 38.

22. Alma Lutz, *Emma Willard: Daughter of Democracy* (Boston: Houghton Mifflin, 1929), 1, 12–15, 22–23, 25–27, 33–35.

23. John Lord, *The Life of Emma Willard* (New York: D. Appleton, 1873), 34. According to Scott, Lord lectured at Willard's school and gained access to primary sources such as her letters and diaries, which have since been lost. *Making the Invisible Woman Visible*, 44. Also see Lord, *Life of Emma Willard*, 139.

24. Lutz, *Emma Willard*, 44.

25. Sarah Josepha Buell Hale, "Willard, Emma," in *Woman's Record; or Sketches of All Distinguished Women from the Creation to A.D. 1868. Arranged in Four Eras. With Selections from Authoresses of Each Era*, 3rd ed. revised with additions (New York: Harper and Brothers, 1870), 816, Gale.

26. Frederick Myron Colby contends that with this idea Willard initiated what became known as the "normal school." "Emma Hart Willard and Her Work," *Potter's American Monthly* 13, no. 96 (1879): 438, ProQuest.

27. Ibid.

28. Natalie A. Naylor, "Emma Hart Willard," *Women Educators in the United States, 1820–1903: A Bio-bibliographical Sourcebook*, ed. Maxine Schwartz Seller (Westport, CT: Greenwood Press, 1994), 527.

29. "Emma Willard," *Journal of Education* 27, no. 6 (February 9, 1893): 1–2.

30. Colleen McDannell, *The Christian Home in Victorian America, 1840–1900* (Bloomington: Indiana University Press, 1986), 132.

31. Lord, *Life of Emma Willard*, 47.

32. Ibid., 51–52. Willard's plan is given in its entirety in ibid., 56–84.

33. Lutz, *Emma Willard*, 56.

34. Emma Willard, "Mrs. Willard on Female Education: An Address to the Public; Particularly to the Members of the Legislature of New York, Proposing a Plan for Female Education 'Defects in the Present Mode of Female Education, and Their Causes' of the Principles by Which Education Should Be Regulated; Sketch of a Female Seminary Benefits of Female Seminaries," *American Ladies' Magazine; Containing Original Tales, Essays, Literary and Historical Sketches, Poetry, Criticism, Music, and a Great Variety of Matter Connected with Many Subjects of Importance and Interest* 7, no. 4 (1834): 165, ProQuest.

35. Lord, *Life of Emma Willard*, 59.

36. Ibid., 82.

37. Ibid., 59–60.

38. Quoted in ibid., 61.

39. I have been unable to find further information regarding Dr. Merrill.

40. Quoted in Lutz, *Emma Willard*, 60.

41. Ibid.

42. Edward A. Fitzpatrick, *The Educational Views and Influence of DeWitt Clinton* (New York: Teachers College, Columbia University, 1911; repr., New York: Arno Press, 1969), 52 (citations refer to the Arno Press edition).

43. Lutz, *Emma Willard*, 67. In 1837 Willard received a letter from British phrenologist George Combe (1788–1858) applauding her and Troy Female Seminary. He had published Willard's plan in his *Phrenological Journal*. His letter stated: "Your school is so extensive, and the influence on women on the state of society is, in my opinion, so important that I regard you as the most powerful individual at present acting on the condition of the American people of the next generation. . . . You may never live to see the good you are doing, but you may see it by faith." Quoted in Lutz, *Emma Willard*, 193.

44. Willard finally received word that the legislature had passed an act granting a charter to the "Waterford Academy for Young Ladies." Lutz claims this was the "first legislative measure recognizing woman's right to higher education." In addition to granting the charter, the legislature voted to include Waterford in the list of schools that were to receive a share of the literary fund provided by the state. Previously this had been reserved for boys' schools. Lutz, *Emma Willard*, 65.

45. Lord, *Life of Emma Willard*, 49; Lutz, *Emma Willard*, 64, 76; Mary J. [Mason] Fairbanks, ed., *Emma Willard and Her Pupils, or Fifty Years of Troy Female Seminary: 1822–1872* (New York: Mrs. Russell Sage, 1898), 13.

46. Lutz, *Emma Willard*, 64–65.

47. Quoted in Henry Fowler, "Educational Services of Mrs. Emma Willard," in *Memoirs of Teachers, Educators, and Promoters and Benefactors of Education, Literature, and Science*, ed. Henry Barnard, 2nd ed. (New York: F. C. Brownell, 1859), 145.

48. Lord, *Emma Willard*, 91.

49. Dexter, *Career Women of America*, 22.

50. Lutz, *Emma Willard*, 68.

51. Ibid., 81.

52. Ibid., 83–84; Louise Schutz Boas, *Women's Education Begins: The Rise of Women's Colleges* (New York: Arno Press, 1971), 100.

53. Lutz, *Emma Willard*, 83.

54. Ibid., 84–85; Lord, *Life of Emma Willard*, 95.

55. Fowler, "Educational Services of Emma Willard," 156; Lord, *Life of Emma Willard*, 93; Lutz, *Emma Willard*, 88, 113, 115. For a description of the campus, see *Catalogue of the Officers and Pupils of the Troy Female Seminary, for the Academic Year, Commencing September 19, 1849, and Ending July 24, 1850; Together with the Conditions of Admittance, etc.* (Troy, NY: John F. Prescott, 1850), 20, folder "TFS Catalogue 1849," box "Troy Female Seminary Catalogues 1820–1895," EWSA.

56. Lutz, *Emma Willard*, 102–6, 115, 135–37.

57. Scott, *Making the Invisible Woman Visible*, 45.

58. Scott claims that Willard's pedagogy, unlike that of contemporary men's colleges, stressed critical thinking. Further, she argues, "While even Harvard still depended upon the deadly daily recitation as its chief pedagogical tool, [Willard] introduced the Pestalozzian dialogue and assured her pupils that until they had learned a subject well enough to teach it, they could not consider that they had mastered it." Ibid., 86n10. Johann Heinrich Pestalozzi (1746–1827) was a renowned Swiss educator

who taught by object lessons using the objects themselves to develop the powers of observing and reasoning.

59. Ibid., 47.

60. See chapters 6–8 for a discussion of Willard's participation in music instruction and performances at Troy Female Seminary.

61. [Rev. Dr.] Edward Hitchcock, comp. *The Power of Christian Benevolence Illustrated in the Life and Labors of Mary Lyon*, new edition (New York: American Tract Society, 1858), 13–15, 20; Willystine Goodsell, *Pioneers of Women's Education in the United States: Emma Willard, Catharine Beecher, and Mary Lyon* (New York: AMS Press, 1970; repr. of the 1931 edition), 229 (citations refer to the AMS Press edition).

62. Hitchcock, *Power of Christian Benevolence*, 20.

63. Sydney R. MacLean, "Lyon, Mary," in *Notable American Women, 1607–1950: A Biographical Dictionary*, ed. Edward T. James, Janet Wilson James, and Paul S. Boyer (Cambridge, MA: Belknap Press, 1971), 2:443–44; Hitchcock, *Power of Christian Benevolence*, 20–24.

64. Hitchcock, *Power of Christian Benevolence*, 24.

65. Ibid., 25, 26, 28.

66. Amos B. Eaton was known as a "lawyer apostle of laboratory science and Senior Professor of the Rensselaer School" (now Rensselaer Polytechnic Institute). MacLean, "Lyon, Mary," 444. Three years later, Lyon studied again with Eaton in Troy, New York, where she also had contact with Emma Willard. Marion Lansing, ed., *Mary Lyon through Her Letters* (Boston: Books, 1937), 56.

67. Woody, *History of Women's Education*, 1:357.

68. Hitchcock, *Power of Christian Benevolence*, 29.

69. Goodsell, *Pioneers of Women's Education*, 233–34.

70. Hitchcock, *Power of Christian Benevolence*, 37, 40; Woody, *History of Women's Education*, 1:358; Sarah D. (Locke) Stow, *History of Mount Holyoke Seminary, South Hadley, Mass. during Its First Half Century, 1837–1887* (South Hadley, MA: Mount Holyoke Female Seminary, 1887), 29.

71. Zilpah Grant (1794–1874), a leading voice in women's higher education, is best known for her association with Mary Lyon. She served as the principal of Ipswich Female Seminary from 1828 to 1839. "The Historic Ipswich Female Seminary," *Historic Ipswich*, https://storiesfromipswich.org/2014/04/03/ipswich-female-seminary.

72. L[inda] T[hayer] Guilford, comp., *The Use of a Life: Memorials of Mrs. Z. P. Grant Banister* (NY: American Tract Society, [1885]), 54; Gail Hamilton, "An American Queen," *North American Review (1821–1940)* 143, no. 359 (1886): 335, ProQuest.

73. Stow, *History of Mount Holyoke Seminary*, 30.

74. Hitchcock, *Power of Christian Benevolence*, 73, 77, 80–81; Goodsell, *Pioneers of Women's Education*, 234; Stow, *History of Mount Holyoke Seminary*, 30.

75. Hitchcock, *Power of Christian Benevolence*, 90, 94.

76. Stow, *History of Mount Holyoke Seminary*, 33–34.

77. Quoted in ibid., 34. Lyon wished to see the expenses for a student at Ipswich reduced by one-third to one-half.

78. Hitchcock, *Power of Christian Benevolence*, 97; Barbara Miller Solomon, *In the Company of Educated Women* (New Haven, CT: Yale University Press, 1985), 20.

79. Quoted in Hitchcock, *Power of Christian Benevolence*, 98–99.

80. Lansing, *Mary Lyon through Her Letters*, 118–19.

81. Quoted in Fidelia Fisk, *Reflections of Mary Lyon, with Selections from Her Instructions to the Pupils in Mt. Holyoke Female Seminary* (Boston: American Tract Society, 1866; repr. Los Olivos, CA: Olive Press Publications, 1995), 91–92 (citations refer to the Olive Press Publications edition). Fisk graduated from Mount Holyoke in 1842 and became a member of the faculty the following year. She used students' notes from Mary Lyon's lectures in the early years of Mount Holyoke as source material for much of this monograph but did not include documentation.

82. Goodsell, *Pioneers of Women's Education*, 237.

83. Dexter, *Career Women of America*, 26.

84. Boas, *Woman's Education Begins*, 34.

85. The committee consisted of the Reverend Daniel Dana, D.D., Newburyport; the Reverend Theophilus Packard, D.D., Shelburne; the Reverend Edward Hitchcock, professor at Amherst College; the Reverend Joseph B. Felt, Hamilton; George W. Heard, Esq., Ipswich; General Asa Howland, Conway; and David Choate, Esq., Essex. Stow, *History of Mount Holyoke Seminary*, 39–40.

86. Ipswich pupils contributed $269; a previous student then employed as a teacher in the South sent $400; Ipswich ladies donated $475; and the remaining amount was given by women in adjacent towns—all prior to the decided location and school's name. Lyon continually referred to these gifts as "the corner-stone of the institution." Historians concur that "it was the first attempt for advancing the education of woman by public benevolence and was a thorough committal to the object." Stow, *History of Mount Holyoke Seminary*, 40–41. Through her pursuits Mary Lyon was breaking new ground for middle-class women.

87. The Reverend Roswell Hawks was president of the board of trustees of Mount Holyoke Female Seminary for many years. He was subsequently active in establishing the Lake Erie Seminary at Painesville, Ohio, which is considered "one of the earliest offshoots from the Holyoke stock." *Historical Sketch of Mount Holyoke Seminary* (Springfield, MA: Clark W. Bryan, 1878), 10.

88. This seems unusual behavior for a woman at this time. Stow, *History of Mount Holyoke Seminary*, 39; Goodsell, *Pioneers of Women's Education*, 239–40; *Historical Sketch of Mount Holyoke Seminary*, 9–10; Fisk, *Reflections of Mary Lyon*, 95.

89. Quoted in Fisk, *Recollections of Mary Lyon*, 95.

90. Boas, *Woman's Education Begins*, 36.

91. Stow, *History of Mount Holyoke Seminary*, 41.

92. Quoted in ibid.

93. Professor Emerson was a brother of Rev. Joseph Emerson, Lyon's teacher at Byfield Seminary. Stow does not include the former Emerson's given name. Quoted in ibid., 42–43.

94. Ibid., 40; *Historical Sketch of Mount Holyoke*, 9; Goodsell, *Pioneers of Women's Education*, 241.

95. Quoted in Stow, *History of Mount Holyoke Seminary*, 40; Mount Holyoke Seminary Building, 1846, Physical Plant Collection, folder 8, Buildings, series 5, drawings, and prints, box 9, shelf location: LD7094.6, MHCASC. This is a print of an original drawing taken from the autograph album of Mary Jane Guild. The name of the original artist is unavailable. "Mount Holyoke Female Seminary" was changed to "Mount Holyoke College" in 1888.

96. According to Jean Ashburn Keeney, several accounts "with varying degrees of certainty" refer to Music Vale as the first school in the nation solely founded for music. "Orramel Wittlesey, Lyricist and Teacher, Set Standards," *Norwich Bulletin* (Norwich, CT), July 18, 1976. Unless otherwise noted, all primary source material is housed in the Music Vale Archives, Salem, Connecticut (MVSA). Nearly all of this material is housed in unmarked folders and boxes.

97. Vera Lear Grann, "Salem, Conn., Boy Who Built His Own Piano Opened Nation's First Music Normal School," *Hartford Daily Times*, May 26, 1928. Orramel's father spent half of his time preaching in New York City. Many eminent clergymen visited his home during the time he spent in Salem, thus giving it the name "Methodist Tavern." Frances Hall Johnson, *Music Vale Seminary, 1835–1876* (New Haven, CT: Yale University Press, 1934), 9.

98. Donald A. Fraser, "Historical Addresses Given for Music Vale's Centenary," *New London Evening Day* (New London, CT), October 30, 1939, MVSA.

99. "Anniversary of Music Vale Seminary Celebrated by Salem," *Norwich Bulletin* (Norwich, CT), October 30, 1939, MVSA.

100. Johnson, *Music Vale Seminary*, 9–11; "First U. S. Music School Disappeared from State Almost without Trace," *New Haven Register* (New Haven, CT), September 5, 1948, MVSA.

101. Grann, "Salem, Conn., Boy."

102. Ibid. Florence Whittlesey Thompson, "Music Vale," *Connecticut Quarterly* 3, no. 1 (1897): 20, MVSA. To further complicate the issue, Whittlesey gave private lessons to students in Salem and the neighboring communities before the night the two young women arrived.

103. *Music Vale Seminary: 1835–1876*, by Frances Hall Johnson, long regarded as the first published secondary source on Music Vale, gives 1835 as the year when the school was founded. *Music Vale Seminary*, 1. Connecticut senator Donald A. Fraser, reporting on the "Historical Addresses Given for Music Vale's Centenary," October 30, 1939, writes that the school was officially established in 1839. This undoubtedly refers to the first "school year" when Whittlesey introduced public examinations, which usually took place in July. Sarah Augusta Shoner, writing in a biography of

"Karolyn Bradford Whittlesey," reports that according to her father, it was likely he did not consider Music Vale founded until enough students were enrolled to call it a school and ascribe a name. "The Story of Karolyn Bradford Whittlesey and Her Family," part 3, "Karolyn Bradford Whittlesey: 1843–1928" (n.p., n.d.), 8, MVSA. Hereafter, this source, including part 4, will be referred to as "KBW."

104. Ibid.; Johnson, *Music Vale Seminary*, 11.

105. Salem was originally called "New Salem," after Salem, Massachusetts. It was incorporated as a town in 1819. Johnson, *Music Vale Seminary*, 2.

106. Shoner, "KBW," part 3, 27.

107. "Miner's Rural American," in *Board of Examiners*, MVSA; Grann, "Salem, Conn., Boy."

108. Oscar F. Hewitt, "Fun at a Female Seminary," in "Mrs. Celvy Morgan's Scrapbook" (typed manuscript taken from *Hartford Times* (Hartford, CT), n.d., 15; Music Vale with Practice Rooms, from "First and Second Music Vale," in *New London Evening Day* (New London, CT), October 30, 1839, MVSA.

109. Shoner, "KBW," part 3, 24.

110. There appears to be some controversy regarding the date of the fire. All sources I have seen give the year as 1868, except Sarah Augusta Shoner's biography of Karolyn Bradford Whittlesey (KBW). Shoner gives the date of the fire as January 21, 1869. Shoner, "KBW," part 3, 74. According to niece Minnie Whittlesey (daughter of Orramel's brother Henry), the citizens of Colchester, Connecticut, were going to give a benefit concert to help the school after the fire. Minnie to Dear Cousin [Ora], January 29, 1868, quoted in ibid., 76–77. I have not seen any other reference to confirm this claim; however, it supports the date of the fire as 1868. Perhaps Shoner's date of "1869" is a typographical error.

111. "Harp of the Wild Wind" is the title of one of Whittlesey's songs (see chapter 8 for a discussion of this piece). The lions were moved to Moss Wood Cemetery in Salem, Connecticut, Orramel and Charlotte Whittlesey's burial place. Perhaps the lions were moved when the school was closed, or possibly after the second fire in 1897. Ibid., 13, 76.

112. Music Vale Seminary, 1868, in "First and Second Music Vale," in *New London Evening Day* (New London, CT), October 30, 1839, MVSA. The style of the building commanded a respect that was imitated in the surrounding towns. According to Miss Maginnis (Whittlesey's great-granddaughter), the seminary had a toilette room, which was likely the first in Salem; her father noted that it was a "great luxury." The room had several toilets, with dividing walls, much like modern buildings. It drew attention from people near and far. "Local Music Vale Seminary," in "Mrs. Celvy Morgan's Scrapbook," 4; Donald A. Fraser, "Historical Address Given for Music Vale's Centenary," *New London Evening Day* (New London, CT), October 30, 1939, MVSA; Shoner, "KBW," part 3, 8, 27.

113. Shoner, "KBW," part 3, 37; Frederick P. Latimer, "In the Midst of Straggledom," MVSA.

114. John Maginnis, *New York Times*, December 1895, quoted in Shoner, "KBW," part 3, 28; Charles J. M'Curdy and Henry M. Waite, "Statement," quoted in "Salem Normal Academy of Music" [1851], MVSA.

115. *Thirty-First Annual Circular of Music Vale Seminary and Normal Academy of Music, 1869–70*, 10, MVSA.

116. "Salem Normal Academy of Music" [1851], MVSA.

117. See chapters 6, 7, and 8 for more information on Whittlesey's music.

118. "Notes from the Thirty-First Annual Circular of Music Vale Seminary and Normal Academy of Music, Salem: 1869–70," quoted in Shoner, "KBW," part 4, 12.

119. Quoted in Shoner, "KBW," part 3, 18.

120. Quoted in ibid.

121. "Music Vale Seminary," from "Ballou's Pictorial Drawing Room Companion," July 11, 1857, in *Board of Examiners*, MVSA; Grann, "Salem, Conn., Boy." Pitt's motto appeared on every document associated with Music Vale. Shoner, "KBW," part 3, 14.

122. "Notes from the Thirty-First Annual Circular," quoted in Shoner, "KBW," part 4, 16.

123. "Music Vale Seminary and Normal Academy of Music," in *Gleaner of the Vale* (February 1855), MVSA. The *Gleaner of the Vale* was the school newspaper.

124. Thompson, "Music Vale," 20.

125. "Notes from the Thirty-First Annual Circular," quoted in Shoner, "KBW," part 3, 16.

126. Henry Dutton, Governor of the State of Connecticut, to O. Whittlesey, Esq., August 25, 1854, quoted in *Board of Examiners*, MVSA.

127. Quoted in Johnson, *Music Vale Seminary*, 12.

128. Shoner, "KBW," part 3, 1.

129. Eliza was Whittlesey's oldest daughter. See chapter 4 for more information on her.

130. "Anniversary of Music Vale Seminary Celebrated by Salem," *Norwich Bulletin* (Norwich, CT), October 30, 1939; John Cleary, "Salem Music Vale Seminary"; Shoner, "KBW," part 3, 76. Most sources I have seen give 1876 as the date for Music Vale's closing. Frances Hall Johnson claims Mrs. Pratt (Sarah) closed the school shortly after her father died on September 9, 1876. *Music Vale Seminary*, 21. Shoner, however, reports that Whittlesey closed the school in 1873, and after his death in 1876 Sarah and Karolyn reopened it for two or three years, "but the struggle was too great." "KBW," part 3, 87. A second fire on March 16, 1897, completely destroyed the buildings. Johnson, *Music Vale Seminary*, 22.

Chapter 4. Seminary Structure: A Comparison

1. Quoted in John Lord, *The Life of Emma Willard* (New York: D. Appleton, 1873), 68.

2. Theodore and Nancy Sizer, Sally Schwager, Lynne Templeton Brickley, and Glee Krueger, *To Ornament Their Minds: Sarah Pierce's Litchfield Female Academy,*

1792–1833, ed. Catherine Keene Fields and Lisa C. Kightlinger (Litchfield, CT: Litchfield Historical Society, 1993), 68.

3. For example, the board of visitors at Music Vale was comprised of five or six professional men, but several of them lived out of state. Five members are listed in the 1857 catalog: His Honor Lt. Gov. Grien Kendrick, Waterbury, Connecticut; the Reverend E. R. Warren (also president of the examining committee), East Greenwich, Rhode Island; Hon. Ira Harris, Albany, New York; the Reverend J. B. Woodward, Middle Hadam, Connecticut; and the Reverend William Davison, Winthrop, Connecticut. *Catalogue of Music Vale and Normal Academy of Music for 1857–8*, 5; *Gleaner of the Vale* 2, no. 1 (1859), MVSA. All of the primary source material is housed in the MVSA. Nearly all of the material is housed in unmarked folders and boxes.

4. *Catalogue of the Officers and Pupils of the Troy Female Seminary, for the Academic Year, Commencing September 21, 1836, and Ending August 9, 1837. Together with the Conditions of Admittance, etc.* (n.p.), 4, folder "TFS Catalogue 1837," box "Troy Female Seminary Catalogues: 1820–1895," EWSA. All of the catalogs are in the same box unless otherwise noted. Alma Lutz, *Emma Willard: Daughter of Democracy* (Boston: Houghton Mifflin, 1929), 84.

5. Lynne Templeton Brickley, "Sarah Pierce's Litchfield Female Academy, 1792–1833" (EdD diss., Harvard University, 1985), 122–24 (hereafter, "Sarah Pierce's LFA").

6. "First U.S. Music School Disappeared from State Almost without Trace, *New Haven Register* (New Haven, CT), September 5, 1948; Vera Lear Grann, "Salem, Conn., Boy Who Built His Own Piano Opened Nation's First Music Normal School," *Hartford Daily Times*, May 26, 1928; Mrs. Darwin S. Moore, "Music Vale Seminary—Salem, Conn." (n.p., n.d.), 3, MVSA.

7. Sarah Augusta Shoner, "The Story of Karolyn Bradford Whittlesey and Her Family," part 3, in "Karolyn Bradford Whittlesey: 1843–1928," 54, unpublished notebook. Hereafter this source, including part 4, will be referred to as "KBW." The dates when Sarah served as vice principal are not given. On the 1859 "Music Vale Seminary & Normal Academy of Music" prospectus, Sarah's title is "First Assistant," the equivalent of vice principal. See note 18 below for additional information on Sarah.

8. "Music Vale Seminary. Twenty-Fifth Year" [1863]; *Thirty-First Annual Circular of Music Vale Seminary and Normal Academy of Music, 1869–70*, 2. Karolyn Bradford Whittlesey later settled in Topeka, Kansas, where she was highly regarded as a teacher of piano and harp. Helen B. Bodman [Mrs. John Morgan Bodman], "Music Vale Seminary, Salem, CT," 2, MVSA.

9. *First Annual Catalogue of the Officers and Members of the Mount Holyoke Female Seminary, South Hadley, Mass., 1837–8* (n.p.), 2, MHCASC. All of the annual catalogs are housed in the College Archives and are available at http://clio.fivecolleges.edu/mhc/catalogs; Arthur C. Cole, *A Hundred Years of Mount Holyoke College: The Evolution of an Educational Ideal* (New Haven, CT: Yale University Press, 1940), 42–43.

10. Apparently Mary Lyon did not intend to hire any men to assist with the upkeep of the seminary. However, she found it necessary to engage a young man (sixteen or

seventeen years old), the son of a local widow, who received his board and education as remuneration for performing various chores. Harriet Hollister to Ann Maria, December 25, 1837, "Harriet Hollister's Papers"; Mary Lyon to Rev. Mr. Theron Baldwin, July 12, 1838, folder 11: 1838, MHCASC, Mary Lyon Collection, Series A: Correspondence, 1818–1849, http://clio.fivecolleges.edu/mhc/lyon/a. Over the years several men were employed to manage the building and grounds.

11. Mrs. Sarah D. (Locke) Stow, *History of Mount Holyoke Seminary, South Hadley, Mass. during Its First Half Century, 1837–1887* (South Hadley, MA: Mount Holyoke Female Seminary, 1887), 91, 110; Elizabeth Alden Green, *Mary Lyon and Mount Holyoke: Opening the Gates* (Hanover, NH: University Press of New England, 1979), 230, 236; Cole, *Hundred Years of Mount Holyoke*, 129, 130, 131; *Annual Catalogues of the Officers and Members of the Mount Holyoke Female Seminary, 1837–65*. In the 1850 and 1851 catalogs, however, Chapin's name heads the list of teachers, with no indication that she served as principal. Possibly she was considered the one in charge but did not have the full responsibility of principal.

12. Lutz, *Emma Willard*, 111, 112.

13. Ibid., 128.

14. Sarah Hudson entered Emma Willard's seminary in Waterford, New York, in 1820 at eleven years of age. Soon afterward her mother moved to Troy, and Sarah and her sister attended another school until Willard moved her seminary there in 1821. Sarah rapidly advanced in her studies and became a teacher at the Troy Female Seminary at the age of sixteen. At twenty-one, during Willard's sabbatical, she became the second vice principal, under Almira Hart Lincoln. Mary J. Mason Fairbanks, ed., *Emma Willard and Her Pupils or Fifty Years of Troy Female Seminary: 1822–1872* (New York: Mrs. Russell Sage, 1898), 27.

15. Lutz, *Emma Willard*, 199, 204.

16. *Catalogue of the Officers and Pupils of the Troy Female Seminary for the Academic Year, Commencing September 15, 1841, and Ending August 3, 1842. Together with the Conditions of Admittance, etc.* (Troy, NY: N. Tuttle, 1842), 5, folder "TFS Catalogue 1842"; *Catalogue of the Officers and Pupils of the Troy Female Seminary for the Academic Year, Commencing September 18, 1850, and Ending July 23, 1851. Together with the Conditions of Admittance, etc.* (Troy, NY: Johnson and Davis, 1851), 4, folder "TFS Catalogue 1851."

17. During the fourteen years the Reverend Lyman Beecher lived in Litchfield (1801–1815), he taught the weekly religion course and was in charge of student prayer groups. Pierce also engaged instructors in dancing, singing, French, and ciphering. "Sarah Pierce's LFA," 122–24; Emily Vanderpoel, comp. and Elizabeth C. Barney Buel, ed., *Chronicles of a Pioneer School from 1792 to 1833 Being the History of Miss Sarah Pierce and Her Litchfield School* (Cambridge, MA: University Press, 1903), 420. According to *Webster's Dictionary*, ciphering involved "the Arabic system of numerical notation."

18. Whittlesey instructed all of his daughters. The youngest, Karolyn, reported that he began giving her lessons when she was three. No doubt the three older girls also

started music lessons when they were young. As young ladies they became known as "the four accomplished Whittlesey daughters, all proficient in the science of music." Shoner, "KBW," part 3, 9. Eliza Tully Whittlesey graduated from Music Vale in 1845, at nearly nineteen years of age. She soon moved to New York to work and to further her piano study. There is apparently a discrepancy in the date given for her marriage (December 18, 1851), since her name is listed in the 1851 catalog for Music Vale. At the time of her marriage, Eliza was still living in New York. In 1852 she opened a school in New London, Connecticut, known as the "Normal Institute and Classical Seminary," which offered academic subjects along with music. One wonders why Eliza started her own school rather than remaining at Music Vale to help her father. It seems possible that her father would have been offended, but no indication of that is given. Her school flourished until the Civil War. Her husband, John, answered the call for volunteers in 1862 and was killed two years later. Eliza closed her school and returned to New York. Sometime later she moved back to Music Vale with her two small daughters (Ora Maconda and Annie Elsie) and taught again at her father's school. Shoner, "KBW," part 3, 44, 47, 48, 49, 51.

Whittlesey supported academic education. He contended that "he would rather have a sick child (physically) than a sick fool." Quoted in Shoner, "KBW," part 3, 56. All of Whittlesey's daughters attended the Salem village school. In addition to musical training under her father, Sarah attended Troy Female Seminary in Troy, New York, from 1834 to 1836, and Providence Conference Seminary, East Greenwich, Rhode Island (exact dates not available; however, it can be ascertained she was a student there in 1850). Sarah, age twenty-five, married George Pratt on July 31, 1858. He also attended Providence Conference Seminary. Pratt furthered his education at Yale, graduating in 1857. He practiced law in Norwich, Connecticut, from 1860 until his death in 1875, following which Sarah returned to Music Vale. Shoner, "KBW," part 3, 54–55, 56, 57; *Catalogue of the Members of Troy Female Seminary Commencing March 5, 1834, and Ending February 18, 1835. Together with the Conditions of Admittance, etc.* (n.p., n.d.), 10, folder "TFS Catalogues 1835"; *Catalogue of the Members of Troy Female Seminary Commencing March 4, 1835, and Ending February 17, 1836. Together with the Conditions of Admittance, etc.* (n.p., n.d.), 9, folder "TFS Catalogues 1836," EWSA. Jennette was a talented vocalist, "the singer of the family." At age twenty she married William Henry Maginnis, brother to Eliza's husband. Shoner, "KBW," part 3, 60.

19. Although Music Vale Seminary continued until at least 1876, documentation is not available beyond 1869 to determine whether the number of faculty increased or decreased.

20. The numbers include the principal and associate principal (if the catalog listed both positions), since it is likely they would also have taught classes. Occasionally the school invited guest lecturers to enhance the curriculum. The Rev. Dr. Edward Hitchcock (board member of Mount Holyoke and president of Amherst College for men) lectured on geology, galvanism, and anatomy and physiology. Professor Ebenezer S. Snell (a renowned scientist from Amherst College) delivered lectures on architecture,

chemistry, natural history, and natural philosophy (contemporary with physics), and Professors Paul A. Chadbourne and Edward Lasell, both from Williams College, gave the standard lectures on chemistry. Cole, *Hundred Years of Mount Holyoke*, 63, 141, 156, 355n70; Anne Carey Edmonds, *A Memory Book: Mount Holyoke College, 1837–1987* (South Hadley, MA: Mount Holyoke College, 1988), 39; Green, *Mary Lyon and Mount Holyoke*, 239–40.

21. *Catalogue of the Members of Troy Female Seminary, for the Academic Year, Commencing September 17, 1828, and Ending August 5, 1829. Together with the Conditions of Admittance, etc.* (n.p., n.d.), 2, folder "TFS Catalogue (Waterford) Semi-bound 1820–35," EWSA. The catalogs do not specify officers' duties.

22. *Catalogue of the Members of Troy Female Seminary, for the Academic Year, Commencing March 3, 1847, and Ending February 16, 1848. Together with the Conditions of Admittance, etc.* (Troy, NY: Prescott and Wilson, 1848), 3, folder "TFS Catalogue 1848," EWSA. Lord lectured at the seminary during the 1830s and claimed it employed a larger faculty than most colleges. Lord, *Life of Emma Willard*, 139.

23. Mrs. John H. Willard and Theodosia Hudson taught classes in addition to their administrative duties. *Catalogue of the Officers and Pupils of the Troy Female Seminary, for the Academic Year, Commencing September 13, 1865, Ending June 27, 1866. Together with the Conditions of Admittance, etc.* (Troy, NY: A. W. Scribner, 1866), 4–6, folder "TFS Catalogue 1866," EWSA.

24. Stow, *History of Mount Holyoke Seminary*, 110. Given that Litchfield, Troy, and Mount Holyoke also stressed religious training, it can be assumed that the faculty at the three other institutions were likewise Christians. No documentation exists, however, to verify this claim.

25. Lord, *Life of Emma Willard*, 95–96; Lutz, *Emma Willard*, 86; Anne Firor Scott, *Making the Invisible Woman Visible* (Urbana: University of Illinois Press, 1984), 46.

26. Green, *Mary Lyon and Mount Holyoke*, 230.

27. The 1828 catalog lists three students (Almira S. Lee, Jane S. Jones, and Abby A. Dean) as "Assistant Teachers." *Catalogue of the Members of Troy Female Seminary, for the Academic Year, Commencing September 17, 1828, and Ending August 5, 1829,* 2. Given that Willard recognized the need for well-trained teachers not only for her school but for the nation as a whole, it can be assumed that this practice continued, though I have not found students listed in this capacity in any catalog after 1830.

28. Annabella Shedden, Jane Shedden, Caroline Tracy, and Louisa Wait were music mistresses; Betsy and Almira Colins, Flora Catlin, and Mary Wallace were art mistresses, and Idea Strong, Catharine Beecher, Julia Ann Shepard, and Julia Henrietta Jones were general assistants. Brickley, "Sarah Pierce's LFA," 122.

29. In 1839, for instance, Frances M. Wood taught vocal music and Maria K. Whitney taught drawing. *Third Annual Catalogue of the Officers and Members of the Mount Holyoke Female Seminary. South Hadley, Mass., 1839–40* (n.p., n.d.), 2. Evidently each one received a small stipend, since Miss Amelia F. Dickinson, a student in the senior class, is listed on the 1843–1844 payroll as receiving sixty dollars for teaching sing-

ing. Mary Lyon Collection, series B: "Writings and Documents," "Notebook: Record of Expenses of the Seminary, 1843–4," folder 2: [1840]–1845, MHCASC, http://clio .fivecolleges.edu/mhc/lyon/b/5mhs. The list of salaries also includes fourteen dollars paid to "assistant pupils"; however, no other students are listed in the catalog for this year. Perhaps "assistant pupils" could refer to other students, such as "Candidates for Teachers," who taught only a few hours per week.

30. "Candidates for Teachers," facsimile, Mary Lyon Collection, series B: "Writings and Documents," sub-series 5: Writings from Mount Holyoke Seminary, [1833?]–1848, folder 3: 1845–1848 and undated, MHCASC, http://clio.fivecolleges.edu/mhc/lyon/b/5mhs. All students on this list were in the senior class. It appears that an "X" preceding students' names indicates those chosen as teaching assistants. For example, Caroline Avery is listed in the 1845 catalog as one of the assistant pupils who taught vocal music. *Eighth Annual Catalogue of the Mount Holyoke Female Seminary, in South Hadley, Mass. 1844–45* (Amherst, MA: J. S. & C. Adams, 1845), 3.

31. A student writing in the *Gleaner of the Vale*, 2, no. 1 (1873), the school newspaper, defined the role of the "superior": "[She] is a young lady who, for her diligence, studiousness, and lady-like deportment has been appointed to fill that important office. She is associated with the Principal, as well as the officers and teachers in the instruction and government of the institution. She has certain duties to perform, among which is the allotment of hours [practice schedule]." "Louise and I: Or the Way I Came Here," in *Gleaner of the Vale* 2, no. 1 (1873). This article was reprinted in the January 1, 1874, issue of *Gleaner of the Vale* 2, no. 2, MVSA.

32. "Salem Normal Academy of Music" [1851], MVSA.

33. Grann, "Salem, Conn., Boy," mentions only the superior, premier, and first and second monitress wearing the regalia.

34. "Music Vale Seminary, Twenty-Fifth Year" [1863]; *Thirty-First Annual Circular of Music Vale Seminary and Normal Academy of Music, 1869–70*, 2, MVSA.

35. Weekly Schedule for Miss Susan L. Tolman. End of week November 18, 1846–End of week March 25, 1847, Mary Lyon Collection, series B: "Writings and Documents," folder 3: 1845–1848 and undated, Notebook "Candidates for Teachers," 8, MHCASC, http://clio.fivecolleges.edu/mhc/lyon/b/5mhs. Her extra duties included hearing recitations, supervising study periods, monitoring hallways, teaching composition classes, washing, helping in the sickroom, keeping order, teaching a Bible lesson, monitoring the visiting room, and meeting with her section.

36. The assistant principals initially organized the student body into two divisions, "North" and "South," and oversaw the arrangement. Each division was then separated into either three large or five small sections, under "section teachers." Cole, *Hundred Years of Mount Holyoke*, 385n26; Susan Tolman, October 1, 1846, Journal Letter 13: September 30, 1846–August 6, 1847; "Book of Duties 1842–1846," 36, 37. Origins and Governance Collection, MHCASC; Stow, *Mount Holyoke Seminary*, 109. Tolman reported that the divisions were then called "First" and "Second" rather than "North" and "South."

37. Mary Q. Brown to her mother, October 10, 1850, "Mary Q. Brown's Papers." Mary Quincy Brown Papers, MHCASC; emphasis in the original.

38. Brickley, "Sarah Pierce's LFA," 52–54. There appears to be a disagreement concerning the peak enrollment number and year. Sizer et al. claim the enrollment reached 162 in 1819. *To Ornament Their Minds*, 67. The enrollments often exceeded those of contemporary male academies. For instance, in 1822 the highest number of graduates recorded from any male college in the United States was 135. Brickley, "Sarah Pierce's LFA," 55.

39. Green, *Mary Lyon and Mount Holyoke*, 219; *Catalogue of the Officers and Pupils, of the Troy Female Seminary, for the Academic Year, Commencing September 8, 1852, and Ending June 29, 1853*, 20, folder "TFS Catalogue 1853," EWSA.

40. Shoner, "KBW," part 3, 23; Jean Ashburn Keeney, "Orramel Wittlesey [*sic*], Lyricist and Teacher," *Norwich Bulletin* (Norwich, CT), July 18, 1976; Frederick P. Latimer, "In the Midst of Straggledom"; "Salem Normal Academy of Music" [1851], MVSA.

41. *Seventh Annual Catalogue of the Mount Holyoke Female Seminary, in South Hadley, Mass., 1843–44* (Amherst, MA: J. S. & C. Adams, 1844), 15.

42. Shoner, "KBW," part 3, 14.

43. Vanderpoel, *Chronicles of a Pioneer School*, 334; Brickley, "Sarah Pierce's LFA," 58–59, 60, 80; Emily Noyes Vanderpoel, comp., *More Chronicles of a Pioneer School from 1792 to 1833 Being Added History on the Litchfield Female Academy Kept by Miss Sarah Pierce and Her Nephew, John Pierce Brace* (Cambridge, MA: University Press, 1927), 7.

44. For example, in 1851 there were twenty-eight boarders, nine of whom were from Connecticut. "Salem Normal Academy of Music" [1851], MVSA.

45. Oscar F. Hewitt, "Fun at a Female Seminary," in "Mrs. Celvy Morgan's Scrapbook" (typed manuscript taken from *Hartford Times* [Hartford, CT], n.d., 15), MVSA. This must speak to the family's class status. It can be expected that only daughters from the upper-middle and upper classes would have had the money to attend a music conservatory.

46. *Catalogue of the Members of Troy Female Seminary, for the Academic Year, Commencing September 15th, 1830, and Ending August 3d, 1831. Together with the Conditions of Admittance, etc.* (n.p., n.d.), 3–7, folder "TFS Catalogue (Waterford) Semi-bound 1820-35," EWSA.

47. It seems likely that many of the foreign students were daughters of missionary families, since Mount Holyoke supported missions and trained missionaries.

48. *Annual Catalogues of Mount Holyoke Female Seminary, 1837–65*; David F. Allmendinger Jr., "Mount Holyoke Students Encounter the Need for Life-Planning, 1837–1850," *History of Education Quarterly* 19, no. 1 (1979): 31, doi: 10.2307/367808.

49. Brickley, "Sarah Pierce's LFA," 83–84.

50. Allmendinger, "Mount Holyoke Students," 37.

51. Brickley, "Sarah Pierce's LFA," 81; Vanderpoel, *Chronicles of a Pioneer School*, 297. At age twenty-three, Mary Chester, who attended Litchfield, thought she had waited too long and was not sufficiently prepared to enroll in the academy. After meeting one of her classmates, however, she was reassured that her age and background were not a hindrance. Mary addressed this issue in a letter to her family: "I shall not complain again that I am too old to go to school; for one of our boarders is said to be twenty-eight years old and besides that, which might be discouraging to a person in any Study; she has just commenced the study of English Grammar." Mary Chester to "Dear Brother Edwin," May 28, 1819, quoted in Vanderpoel, *Chronicles of a Pioneer School*, 191.

52. Emma Willard, *An Address to the Public; Particularly to the Members of the Legislature of New York, Proposing a Plan for Improving Female Education*, 75, quoted in Lord, *Life of Emma Willard*. Willard's entire plan is quoted in *Life of Emma Willard*, 56–84; *Catalogue of the Officers and Pupils of the Troy Female Seminary, for the Academic Year, Commencing September 13, 1865, Ending June 27, 1866*, 40, folder "TFS Catalogue 1866," EWSA. The catalog includes a "Course of Study" for students beginning at age seven and concluding with graduation at age nineteen. Ibid., 40–41; Lutz, *Emma Willard*, 95–96.

53. Cole, *Hundred Years of Mount Holyoke*, 33; *Annual Catalogues of Mount Holyoke Female Seminary*, 1837–38, 1846–47. This age range was equivalent to that of men's colleges in the North. Allmendinger, "Mount Holyoke Students," 37.

54. Green, *Mary Lyon and Mount Holyoke*, 222.

55. *Tenth Annual Catalogue of Mount Holyoke Female Seminary, in South Hadley, Mass., 1846–47* (Amherst, MA: J. S. & C. Adams, 1847), 11.

56. *Twenty-Fifth Annual Catalogue of Mount Holyoke Female Seminary, in South Hadley, Mass., 1861–62* (Springfield, MA: Samuel Bowles, 1862), 17.

57. *Twelfth Annual Catalogue of Mount Holyoke Female Seminary, in South Hadley, Mass., 1848–49* (Amherst, MA: J. S. & C. Adams, 1849), 13.

58. Brickley, "Sarah Pierce's LFA," 103.

59. Willard received many letters from less fortunate students asking to be admitted to the institution. Some young ladies struggled and saved enough to attend one term, while others requested admission on the credit plan. In the fourteen months prior to her resignation, Willard received five hundred such applications. The system had become so popular across the nation that "the simple certificate of scholarship, signed 'Emma Willard' served as a passport to almost any desirable situation." This was a testimony to Emma Willard and Troy Female Seminary, though the school was not incorporated or endowed. The admission of a large number of nonpaying students was a financial burden for the school. These students created additional expenses for teachers, rooms, and supplies. Fowler, "Educational Services of Emma Willard," 155.

60. Fairbanks, *Emma Willard and Her Pupils*, 15.

61. Lutz, *Emma Willard*, 96. Fairbanks, *Emma Willard and Her Pupils*, contains biographical information on students who attended the seminary between 1822 and 1872.

62. Brickley, "Sarah Pierce's LFA," 65. Undoubtedly many of the families, such as the Gardiners, had hired help. After attending the academy for a few days, Sarah D. Gardiner was surprised to find her roommate making the bed. Upon hearing that the students were expected to keep their rooms orderly, she remembered, "'Why didn't you tell me?' 'Because,' replied her true companion, who was an older student, 'I know that you were not accustomed to it!'" Sarah D. Gardiner to [Emily Noyes Vanderpoel], December 20, 1896, series 4, sub-series 1, folder 16, CLHS.

63. Brickley, "Sarah Pierce's LFA," 73.

64. "Directions for THE JOURNEY," in *Gleaner of the Vale* 2, no. 1 (1859), MVSA.

65. In 1850, for example, families whose property was valued at approximately five thousand dollars earned the minimum income needed to offer full support for a son in college. Over half of the students then attending Mount Holyoke Seminary came from families whose real estate was appraised at three thousand dollars or less. For more documentation on the social classes of about one-half of the student body between 1837 and 1859, see Allmendinger, "Mount Holyoke Students," 27–46.

66. *Thirty-First Annual Circular of Music Vale Seminary and Normal Academy of Music, 1869–70*, 14, MVSA.

67. In 1851 the school year at Music Vale consisted of four twelve-week quarters. The quarters were reduced to eleven weeks in 1855. In 1863 the school year comprised two terms, each of twenty-two weeks. The year was extended to three terms in 1869: one of twenty weeks and two of sixteen weeks. Pupils who stayed for the year were permitted to take four weeks' vacation whenever they chose but not before the end of the first quarter or term. According to the prospectus for 1851, only fifty students had stayed for four quarters. "Our Object," in "Salem Normal Academy of Music," [1851]; "Terms of Board and Instruction" [1863]; "Music Vale Seminary and Normal Academy of Music," *Gleaner of the Vale* (February 1855); "Terms of Board and Instruction: From and after August 1st, 1857," in *Board of Examiners*; Margaret W. Hilliard Stacy, "Music Vale Seminary, Salem, Once Was Great Institution; Turned Out Many Graduates"; "Expenses," in *Thirty-First Annual Circular of Music Vale Seminary and Normal Academy of Music, 1869–70*, 11, all in MVSA. No dates are given in the primary sources to indicate when the quarters/terms started or ended. Thus, since Music Vale was continually in session, perhaps private lessons were always available, but classes were held during the "academic" quarters or terms.

Litchfield divided the academic year into two terms: winter and summer. The winter term began around the end of November and concluded the middle of April. A four-to-six-week vacation followed, and then the summer term commenced and continued until late October. Attendance was greater in the summer term than in the winter because of difficult travel conditions. Brickley, "Sarah Pierce's LFA," 104.

The academic year at Troy comprised forty-four weeks: two terms of twenty-two weeks divided into two quarters per term. A two-week vacation occurred after the first term, and a six-week vacation followed the second. Apparently the school year was initially divided into three terms, since the brochure dated August 20, 1823, reads, "The academic year will hereafter be divided into two terms of twenty-two weeks each." *Troy Female Seminary [Catalogue]* (n.p., August 20, 1823), folder "Troy Female Seminary Promotional Materials," box "MSS#6 Middlebury Academy, Waterford Academy, Troy Female Seminary: Records, Articles, Pictures," EWSA. Fowler claims that Willard divided the year into two terms after her husband died, but according to the brochure, this occurred two years earlier. Fowler, "Educational Services of Emma Willard," 151–52.

Mount Holyoke divided the academic year into three terms (forty weeks total) and twelve weeks of vacation. The first and second terms were each ten to sixteen weeks, while the third term was ten to fourteen weeks. It was customary for the school to include a two-week vacation after both the first and second terms. A longer vacation of seven to ten weeks occurred after the third term. The number of weeks in each term varied over the years. Until 1844 there was a brief vacation period between the first two terms; only those students who lived nearby were allowed to go home. *Annual Catalogues of Mount Holyoke Female Seminary, 1837–65.*

68. *First Annual Catalogue of the Office and Members of the Mount Holyoke Female Seminary, 1837–8,* 10.

69. *Catalogue of the Members of Troy Female Seminary, for the Academic Year, Commencing September 17, 1828, and Ending August 5, 1829,* 8; *Second Annual Catalogue of Mount Holyoke Female Seminary, 1838–9,* 11. In some situations Lyon allowed an early dismissal: a family crisis, marriage, an impending teaching position, or violation of the school rules. Occasionally she admitted a student during the middle of the year to offset the decrease in enrollment caused by mandated withdrawals. Such admissions were usually friends of current students who would assist them in adjusting to the seminary lifestyle. Green, *Mary Lyon and Mount Holyoke,* 223, 224.

70. In 1855 one term at Music Vale consisted of eleven weeks. Eight years later the term was increased to twenty-two weeks. "Terms of Instruction," in *Gleaner of the Vale* (1855), MVSA; "Terms of Board and Instruction" [1863]; Brickley, "Sarah Pierce's LFA," 96.

71. Brickley, "Sarah Pierce's LFA," 99.

72. Mary Lyon's goal was to raise academic standards and extend the program: "[She] has determined to . . . press all the classes so much, that none but good scholars can complete the course in three years. She would like to require four years, but the trustees are afraid to venture it yet." Lucy T. Lyon, April 8, 1846, Journal Letter 11: April 8-May 5, 1846. In the fall of 1860, the program was increased to four years. However, the seminary expected many students to come prepared to enter the second year. *Twenty-Fifth Annual Catalogue of Mount Holyoke Female Seminary, 1861–62,* 18.

73. For instance, during the first thirteen years 1,397 students entered the seminary, but only 346 graduated. Allmendinger, "Mount Holyoke Students," 29.

74. Green, *Mary Lyon and Mount Holyoke,* 223.

75. Cole, *Hundred Years of Mount Holyoke*, 363n149.

76. Ibid., 38.

77. The preparatory studies consisted of English grammar, modern geography, history of the United States, arithmetic, and Watts on the mind. (The subjects often were identified by the author of the textbook the seminary used. In this case, "Watts" would have referred to Isaac Watts, the hymn writer, and the subject would likely have been mental philosophy.) By 1846 students were required to know Latin grammar and be able to read Latin. Over the years some courses were added, while others were dropped. *Annual Catalogues of Mount Holyoke Female Seminary, 1837–65.*

78. The first examination, arithmetic, was dreaded by many students, as Elizabeth M. Gordon recalled in 1845: "I should like to throw my arithmetic an hundred miles out of sight." Elizabeth M. Gordon to Eliza Hayden, October 16, 1845, "Elizabeth M. Gordon's Papers," MHCASC.

79. Emily Dickinson to [Miss] Abiah P. Root, November 6, 1847. Quoted in Cole, *Hundred Years of Mount Holyoke*, 67. This indicates not only the proficiency expected of incoming students but also the level of education offered at Mount Holyoke.

80. *Ninth Annual Catalogue of Mount Holyoke Female Seminary, in South Hadley, Mass., 1845–46* (Amherst, MA: J. S. & Adams, 1846), 12. Starting in the 1847–1848 academic year, there does not appear to have been an examination for advanced standing. Rather, the seminary offered a concentrated review of all the studies in which the candidate was expected to demonstrate competence. It is unlikely that any student would be advanced beyond the junior class. Students who had progressed well into the junior class but had not completed enough work to receive advanced standing were permitted to proceed in studies of the middle class as their time allowed. *Twelfth Annual Catalogue of Mount Holyoke Female Seminary, 1848–49*, 12. Ten years later students requesting advanced standing were required to take a condensed review in addition to passing an examination. *Twenty-Second Annual Catalogue of Mount Holyoke Female Seminary, in South Hadley, Mass., 1858–59* (Northampton, MA: Bridgman & Childs, 1859), 11.

81. Green, *Mary Lyon and Mount Holyoke*, 229; *Third Annual Catalogue of Mount Holyoke Female Seminary, 1839–40*, 9, 12.

82. Mary Lyon to Hannah White, August 1, 1834, Mount Holyoke College Archives, Mary Lyon Collection, Series A: Correspondence, 1818–1849, Letters by Lyon, 1818–1849, folder 5: 1834, Aug.–Dec., http://clio.fivecolleges.edu/mhc/lyon/a/1/ff5/340801/transcript/01.htm.

83. Quoted in Edward Hitchcock, comp. *The Power of Christian Benevolence Illustrated in the Life and Labors of Mary Lyon*, new edition (New York: American Tract Society, 1858), 198.

84. Stow, *History of Mount Holyoke*, 36; Hitchcock, *Power of Christian Benevolence*, 197; *Third Annual Catalogue of Mount Holyoke Female Seminary, 1839–40*, 11. It was common for students to express amusement about their assignments. Louisa M.

Torrey (mother of William H. Taft) commented: "With regard to the domestic work I do not find it as much of a hindrance as I expected. Everything is arranged with so much system that a great deal of work is performed in a little time. It would do your heart good to go into the domestic hall and see how conveniently everything is arranged. . . . My work at present is moulding bread. I mould about ten loves a day." Louisa M. Torrey to her mother, April [?], 1844, quoted in Cole, *Hundred Years of Mount Holyoke*, 88.

85. The time varied depending on the task. In 1848, for example, cleaning the floors and woodwork could be accomplished in thirty minutes, while baking required forty-five minutes and sewing, one hour. Cole, *Hundred Years of Mount Holyoke*, 88.

86. *First Annual Mount Holyoke Female Seminary Catalogue, 1837–38*, 11; Stow, *History of Mount Holyoke Seminary*, 36.

87. This chart shows the figures for boarding students. Obviously there would have been a reduction in expense for non-boarding students. Since such documentation does not exist for Litchfield or Music Vale, and Mount Holyoke did not admit resident students, I will focus on the expense for boarders.

88. Brickley, "Sarah Pierce's LFA," 117, 118.

89. *Catalogue of the Officers and Pupils of the Troy Female Seminary, February 1840* (n.p., n.d.), 3, folder "TFS Catalogue 1840," EWSA.

90. *Catalogue of the Officers and Pupils of the Troy Female Seminary for the Academic Year Commencing September 9, 1863, and Ending June 29, 1864. Together with the Conditions of Admittance, etc.* (Troy, NY: Daily Whig, 1864), 30, folder "TFS Catalogue 1864"; *Catalogue of the Officers and Pupils of the Troy Female Seminary, for the Academic Year, Commencing September 13, 1865, Ending June 27, 1866*, 36, EWSA.

91. In 1851 there was a fee of four dollars per quarter for use of the piano; this fee was eliminated by 1855. That same year Whittlesey offered free harp and guitar lessons to pupils who stayed at the school longer than one year. Perhaps he was in need of teachers or wanted to persuade the young ladies to become proficient on these instruments as well. "Salem Normal Academy of Music" [1851]; "Music Vale Seminary and Normal Academy of Music" (1855), MVSA.

92. "Salem Normal Academy of Music" [1851]; "Terms of Instruction," "Music Vale Seminary and Normal Academy of Music" (1855); "Terms of Board and Instruction" found on copy of "Resolution and Pledge of the Loyal League, of the Women of Salem" (June 1863); *Thirty-First Annual Circular of Music Vale Seminary, 1869–70*, 13–14, all in MVSA.

93. Allmendinger, "Mount Holyoke Students," 33. Expenses at Mount Holyoke were comparable to those at Amherst, the least costly men's college (which included lights but not board) at the time. Ibid.; *First Annual Catalogue of the Officers and Members of the Mount Holyoke Female Seminary, South Hadley, Mass. 1837–8*, 11.

94. *Annual Catalogues of the Officers and Members of the Mount Holyoke Female Seminary, 1854–65*.

Chapter 5. Curricula: Academic and Ornamental

1. Arthur C. Cole, *A Hundred Years of Mount Holyoke College: The Evolution of an Educational Ideal* (New Haven, CT: Yale University Press, 1940), 64.

2. Historian Anne Firor Scott claims that in addition to an equivalent curriculum, Emma Willard employed better pedagogical methods than men's colleges. *Making the Invisible Woman Visible* (Urbana: University of Illinois Press, 1984), 47. Biographer John Lord contends that regardless of the name given to Willard's school, "in all essential respects it was a college." *The Life of Emma Willard* (New York: D. Appleton, 1873), 51.

3. Lord, *Life of Emma Willard*, 96.

4. Ibid. Alma Lutz claims that Troy Female Seminary could be considered the forerunner of the normal school. Willard, however, argued that hers was the first normal school, claiming that Troy sent two hundred teachers "to every part of the country" before any were trained as such in public normal schools in the United States. She maintained that her school, which began in Middlebury, Vermont, in 1814, "had the honor of being the first normal school in the United States." Quoted in Lutz, *Emma Willard: Daughter of Democracy* (Boston: Houghton Mifflin, 1929), 97.

5. Quoted in Cole, *Hundred Years of Mount Holyoke*, 11.

6. Quoted in Barbara M. Cross, ed., *The Autobiography of Lyman Beecher* (Cambridge, MA: Harvard University Press, 1961), 1:399.

7. Mrs. Sarah D. (Locke) Stow, *History of Mount Holyoke Seminary, South Hadley, Mass. during Its First Half Century, 1837–1887* (South Hadley, MA: Mount Holyoke Female Seminary, 1887), 105.

8. Mary Lyon's goal was to raise the academic standards and extend the program: "[She] has determined to . . . press all the classes so much, that none but good scholars can complete the course in three years. She would like to require four years, but the trustees are afraid to venture it yet." Lucy T. Lyon, April 8, 1846, Journal Letter 11: April 8-May 5, 1846, MHCASC, http://clio.fivecolleges.edu/mhc/journal_letters/toc.htm.

9. *Fifth Annual Catalogue of the Officers and Members of the Mount Holyoke Female Seminary, South Hadley, Mass., 1841–2* (n.p., n.d.), 11, MHCASC. All of the annual catalogs used in this chapter are housed in the College Archives and are available online at http://clio.fivecolleges.edu/mhc/catalogs. The requirement for advancing to the next class is stated in the Mount Holyoke catalog, and it can be assumed that it was the same for students attending Troy and Litchfield, given the depth of their academic programs.

10. Mary Lyon made an exception to this rule for older students who could only stay one year, did not have previous opportunity to make significant progress in the English studies, or planned to finish their education during the year. *Twelfth Annual Catalogue of the Mount Holyoke Female Seminary, in South Hadley, Mass., 1848–9* (Amherst, MA: J. S. & C. Adams, 1849), 12. This exemption was not extended to

students of the "younger class," however. The seminary contended that if younger students could not delay the last year of their education for several years, their time would be spent more profitably at another institution. Ibid.

11. *First Annual Catalogue of the Officers and Members of the Mount Holyoke Female Seminary, South Hadley, Mass., 1837–8* (n.p., n.d.), 8, 9.

12. *Catalogue of the Members of Troy Female Seminary, for the Academic Year, Commencing September 16, 1829, and Ending August 4, 1830. Together with the Conditions of Admittance, etc.* (n.p., n.d.), 8, folder "TFS Catalogue (Waterford) Semi-bound 1820-35," box "Troy Female Seminary Catalogues 1820–1895," EWSA. All of the catalogs are in the same box. This was undoubtedly Jeremiah Day, *An Introduction to Algebra, Being the First Part of a Course of Mathematics, Adapted to the Method of Instruction in the American Colleges,* 5th ed. (New Haven, CT: Hezekiah Howe, 1829).

13. Lynne Templeton Brickley, "Sarah Pierce's Litchfield Female Academy, 1792–1833" (EdD diss., Harvard University, 1985), 123 (hereafter, "Sarah Pierce's LFA").

14. Mount Holyoke allowed little room for spelling errors; students who misspelled three words were required to enroll in a spelling class. Cole, *Hundred Years of Mount Holyoke,* 58.

15. Theodore and Nancy Sizer, Sally Schwager, Lynne Templeton Brickley, Glee Grueger, *To Ornament Their Minds* (Litchfield, CT: Litchfield Historical Society, 1993), 43.

16. *Eleventh Annual Catalogue of the Mount Holyoke Female Seminary, in South Hadley, Mass., 1847–8* (Amherst, MA: M. S. & C. Adams), 1848), 11.

17. Cole, *Hundred Years of Mount Holyoke,* 60. Poems about death and farewell were common fare. Ibid.

18. "Report of the Committee of Examination," in *Catalogue of the Officers and Pupils of the Troy Female Seminary, for the Academic Year, Commencing September 20, 1848, and Ending July 25, 1849. Together with the Conditions of Admittance, etc.* (Troy, NY: J. C. Kneeland, 1849), 24–32, folder "TFS Catalogue 1849."

19. Lutz, *Emma Willard,* 182.

20. *Catalogue of the Officers and Pupils of the Troy Female Seminary, for the Academic Year, Commencing September 15, 1847, and Ending July 26, 1848. Together with the Conditions of Admittance, etc.* (Troy, NY: Prescott and Wilson, 1848), 18, folder "TFS Catalogue 1848."

21. Cole, *Hundred Years of Mount Holyoke,* 58.

22. See Sizer et al., *To Ornament Their Minds,* 45, for a list of articles.

23. Many students found the study of *Paradise Lost* to be a "feast of reason & a flow of soul." Cole, *Hundred Years of Mount Holyoke,* 56.

24. Lutz, *Emma Willard,* 182.

25. Elocution is defined as the study of speaking with expression. John D. Philbrick, a member of the examining committee in 1855, praised the teaching of English literature at Troy:

Still no performance witnessed by me, afforded so much pleasure as the examination in English literature, . . . because it was the first time I had found this important branch of popular education properly attended to in any institution of learning. In the course of study pursued in this Seminary it occupies the place which it deserves, and while the pupils are properly instructed in mathematics and the sciences, they are not left in ignorance of the treasures of thought which are contained in the productions of the great masters of the English tongue. Nor are they taught merely the names of the writers and their works. They are put upon such a course of training as is calculated to inspire a love for good reading, by enabling them to understand and appreciate what is beautiful in thought and expression.

As Philbrick reiterates, the students received thorough instruction in analysis of the literature. "Report," in *Catalogue of the Officers and Pupils of the Troy Female Seminary, for the Academic Year, Commencing September 13, 1854, and Ending June 27, 1855. Together with the Conditions of Admittance, etc.* (Troy, NY: A. W. Scribner, 1855), 28, folder "TFS Catalogue 1855." For more information on the art of elocution, see Marion Wilson Kimber, *The Elocutionists: Women, Music, and the Spoken Word* (Urbana: University of Illinois Press, 2017).

26. Cole, *Hundred Years of Mount Holyoke*, 60.

27. Emily Noyes Vanderpoel, comp., *More Chronicles of a Pioneer School from 1792 to 1833 Being Added History on the Litchfield Female Academy Kept by Miss Sarah Pierce and Her Nephew, John Pierce Brace* (Cambridge, MA: University Press, 1927), 180.

28. Cross, *Autobiography of Lyman Beecher*, 1:226–28.

29. Emily Vanderpoel, comp., and Elizabeth C. Barney Buel, ed., *Chronicles of a Pioneer School from 1792 to 1833 Being the History of Miss Sarah Pierce and Her Litchfield School* (Cambridge, MA: University Press, 1903), 34. The students from Judge Tapping Reeve's law school attempted to either compete or return the favor, since they also wrote and acted in plays. No record, however, exists of these performances. Ibid. See chapter 8 for further discussion of the plays.

30. Sizer et al., *To Ornament Their Minds*, 46.

31. Lutz, *Emma Willard*, 125.

32. *First Annual Catalogue of the Officers and Members of the Mount Holyoke Female Seminary, 1837–8*, 8.

33. Brickley, "Sarah Pierce's LFA," 258.

34. Thomas Woody, *A History of Women's Education in the United States*, vol. 1 (New York: Science Press, 1929), 347n42.

35. Ibid., 346. Willard received a letter from Daniel Webster endorsing one of her books: "I cannot better express my sense of the value of your history of the United States than by saying I keep it near me as a book of reference, accurate in facts and dates." Quoted in Lutz, *Emma Willard*, 126.

36. Emma Willard, *Astronography or Astronomical Geography, with the Use of the Globes* (Troy, NY: Merriam Moore, 1854).

37. Brickley, "Sarah Pierce's LFA," 271.

38. "Troy Female Seminary," April 18, 1821, folder "Troy Female Seminary—Advertisements," box "MSS#6, Middlebury Academy, Waterford Academy, Troy Female Seminary, Records, Articles, Pictures," EWSA.

39. *First Annual Catalogue of the Officers and Members of the Mount Holyoke Female Seminary, 1837-8*, 5; Elizabeth Alden Green, *Mary Lyon and Mount Holyoke: Opening the Gates* (Hanover, NH: University Press of New England, 1979), 184; Warren Colburn, *Intellectual Arithmetic upon the Inductive Method of Instruction* (Bellows-Falls, VT, 1829); Daniel Adams, *Adam's New Arithmetic; Arithmetic, in Which the Principles of Operating by Numbers Are Analytically Explained and Synthetically Applied* (Keene, NH: J. Prentiss, 1827).

40. Cole, *Hundred Years of Mount Holyoke College*, 67; *First Annual Catalogue of the Officers and Members of the Mount Holyoke Female Seminary, 1837-8*, 8.

41. Henry Fowler, "Educational Services of Mrs. Emma Willard," in *Memoirs of Teachers, Educators, and Promoters and Benefactors of Education, Literature, and Science*, ed. Henry Barnard, 2nd ed. (New York: F. C. Brownell, 1859), 146; Lutz, *Emma Willard*, 181–82.

42. Brickley, "Sarah Pierce's LFA," 272.

43. The requirements for 1847 seem more demanding compared with those ten years earlier: "a readiness in Mental Arithmetic, (such as Colburn's First Lessons,) that is, an ability to give a correct answer to the questions as they are read by the teacher, and to give an account of all the steps of the mental process,—also a good knowledge of common Arithmetic, including all the more difficult rules. In the examination of Arithmetic, a list of questions taken from different authors is used. It is recommended that candidates for admission go through two or three different authors, so as thus to gain more mathematical discipline, and be better prepared for examination. Adams' New Arithmetic and Greenleaf's are particularly recommended." *Eleventh Annual Catalogue of the Mount Holyoke Female Seminary, 1847-8*, 11. Such intensity explains why some students could not stand the pressure and returned home. Cole, *Hundred Years of Mount Holyoke*, 67.

44. Brickley, "Sarah Pierce's LFA," 271. In his journal, Brace mentions having finished "quadratic equations" and makes a comment regarding their difficulty. He acknowledged he had never studied them before, since they were not taught at Williams College ("John P. Brace—Private Journal, Vol. 2, 1815"), quoted in Vanderpoel, *More Chronicles of a Pioneer School*, 116. Undoubtedly he was preparing to teach this level of mathematics at Litchfield.

45. "Arithmetic through Interest" might have indicated the level of mathematics required at the academy. Obviously many students had difficulty with this subject, as expressed in a letter from Charlotte Dering of Sag Harbor, Long Island, New York, to her family in 1825: "Fortunately I have long since finished the course of Arithmetic which is the great torment of most of the young ladies, especially Miss Gardiner who has been here two years and a half and I fear will not get through without very great exertion." Quoted in Sizer et al., *To Ornament Their Minds*, 37–38.

46. "Report" in *Catalogue of the Officers and Pupils of the Troy Female Seminary, for the Academic Year, Commencing September 9, 1857, and Ending June 30, 1858. Together with the Conditions of Admittance, etc.* (Troy, NY: A. W. Scribner, 1858), 35, folder "TFS Catalogue 1858."

47. Brickley, "Sarah Pierce's LFA," 275, 284.

48. *Catalogues of the Officers and Pupils of the Troy Female Seminary, 1821–1837*; Lutz, *Emma Willard*, 110. In 1824 Almira Hart Lincoln, then a widow with two children, joined the seminary staff. According to historian Anne Firor Scott, Eaton and Lincoln may have been the first teachers in the United States to allow their students to conduct their own scientific experiments. With Eaton's assistance, Lincoln wrote the botany text used in her class. It became a best seller and was used in colleges and schools for upward of fifty years. Willard's and Lincoln's textbooks received wide recognition and were used in both boys' and girls' schools. Furthermore, they were translated and used in European schools. Scott, *Making the Invisible Woman Visible*, 46; Louise Schutz Boas, *Woman's Education Begins; The Rise of Women's Colleges* (New York: Arno Press, 1971), 197.

49. "Natural Philosophy" is defined as natural science, particularly physical science. Historian Lynne Templeton Brickley notes that until the early 1800s, Natural Philosophy was the sole scientific course offered in American colleges. "Sarah Pierce's LFA," 275.

50. Cole, *Hundred Years of Mount Holyoke College*, 61.

51. Brickley, "Sarah Pierce's LFA," 284.

52. Cole, *Hundred Years of Mount Holyoke College*, 61; *Second Annual Catalogue of the Officers and Members of the Mount Holyoke Female Seminary, South Hadley, Mass., 1838–9* (n.p.), 8. Lyon had been privileged to attend Eaton's lecture at Amherst College and sometime afterward spent a summer in Troy studying science with him. Biographer Alma Lutz does not include dates for these events but notes that they occurred around the time Willard had contact with Eaton. *Emma Willard*, 110.

53. Cole, *Hundred Years of Mount Holyoke*, 61.

54. *Catalogue of the Officers and Pupils of the Troy Female Seminary, for the Academic Year Commencing Sept. 21, 1842, and Ending August 9, 1843. Together with the Conditions of Admittance, etc.* (Troy, NY: N. Tuttle, 1843), 15, folder "TFS Catalogue 1843."

55. Scott, *Making the Invisible Woman Visible*, 46.

56. Brickley, "Sarah Pierce's LFA," 296, 298.

57. *Catalogues of the Officers and Pupils of the Troy Female Seminary, 1821–1865; Annual Catalogues of the Officers and Members of the Mount Holyoke Female Seminary, 1837–1865*; Brickley, "Sarah Pierce's LFA," 295.

58. *Annual Catalogues of the Officers and Members of the Mount Holyoke Female Seminary, 1837–1865; Catalogues of the Officers and Pupils of the Troy Female Seminary, 1823–1865.*

59. Brickley, "Sarah Pierce's LFA," 124, 310.

60. *Annual Catalogues of the Officers and Members of the Mount Holyoke Female Seminary, 1837–1865; Catalogues of the Officers and Pupils of the Troy Female Seminary, 1823–1865.*

61. "Report," in *Catalogue of the Officers and Pupils of the Troy Female Seminary, for the Academic Year, Commencing September 12, 1860, and Ending June 26, 1861. Together with the Conditions of Admittance, etc.* (Troy, NY: A. W. Scribner, 1861), 22, folder "TFS Catalogue 1861."

62. Troy introduced French in 1823; Latin, 1825; Spanish, 1828; Italian, 1838; and German in 1843.

63. *Catalogues of the Officers and Pupils of the Troy Female Seminary, 1821–1832*; Brickley, "Sarah Pierce's LFA," 162; Cole, *Hundred Years of Mount Holyoke*, 57.

64. Two years later Willard offered this deduction for music as well as French, under the same conditions. There is no indication as to the number of years designated as "extended time," possibly long enough to graduate.

65. *Catalogue of the Officers and Pupils of the Troy Female Seminary, for the Academic Year, Commencing September 15, 1847, and Ending July 26, 1848*, 18; "TROY FEMALE SEMINARY: Method of Government Studies pursued Examination Domestic Training—Manners, Morals, and Health General Remarks," *American Ladies' Magazine; Containing Original Tales, Essays, Literary & Historical Sketches, Poetry, Criticism, Music, and a Great Variety of Matter Connected with Many Subjects of Importance and Interest* 8, no. 12 (1835): 700, ProQuest.

66. Eleanor Kevney, a young woman of French origin from New York who had received all of her previous education in French schools, was one of the assistant pupils. She entered the junior class in 1850 and taught French that year. Cole, *Hundred Years of Mount Holyoke*, 57; *Fourteenth Annual Catalogue of the Mount Holyoke Female Seminary, in South Hadley, Mass., 1850–51* (Springfield, MA: H. S. Taylor, 1851), 4, 9. Gertrude de Bruyn Kops, from Holland, entered the junior class the following year and also taught French. *Fifteenth Annual Catalogue of the Mount Holyoke Female Seminary, in South Hadley, Mass., 1851–52* (Springfield, MA: H. S. Taylor, 1852), 4, 9. It is not clear how long or to what extent Litchfield offered French.

67. Brickley, "Sarah Pierce's LFA," 301.

68. No documentation exists to provide an explanation for some of the community members' disapproval of Latin; perhaps it was because of its association with Catholicism. Given that a majority of the senior class had some knowledge of the language, the seminary officials deemed it more acceptable than previously. Stow, *Mount Holyoke Seminary*, 148; *Ninth Annual Catalogue of the Mount Holyoke Female Seminary, in South Hadley, Mass., 1845–46* (Amherst, MA: J. S. & C. Adams, 1846), 10; *Annual Catalogues of the Mount Holyoke Female Seminary, 1860–1865*.

69. For example, schools such as those of Mrs. Lydia Royce and the Misses Patten in Hartford, Miss Polly Balch's in Newport, and the Misses Saunders and Beach's in Dorchester, Connecticut. Brickley, "Sarah Pierce's LFA," 172.

70. Ibid., 162.

71. Lord, *Life of Emma Willard*, 72.

72. Cole, *Hundred Years of Mount Holyoke*, 64.

73. Lord, *Life of Emma Willard*, 73.

74. Ibid., 72–73.

75. Lutz, *Emma Willard*, 89.

76. "Notes Collected for Mrs. Asa Gray" (great niece of Sarah Pierce) from Lucy Beach [née Sheldon], series 4, sub-series 1, folders 18–20, CHLS. Vanderpoel includes the definition of a ball as "in those days, what would be called now a small dancing party, where 'Society' meant all one's acquaintances, or rather friends." *Chronicles of a Pioneer School*, 322.

77. Sizer et al., *To Ornament Their Minds*, 63.

78. Vanderpoel, *Chronicles of a Pioneer School*, 35, 322, 334.

79. "Book of Duties 1842–1846," 46, Origins and Governance Collection, MHCASC.

80. See chapter 6 for a discussion of calisthenics as a part of the students' music instruction.

81. Cole, *Hundred Years of Mount Holyoke*, 58.

82. *Twenty-Sixth Annual Catalogue of the Mount Holyoke Female Seminary, in South Hadley, Mass., 1862–63* (Springfield, MA: Samuel Bowles, 1863), 21. Anniversary exercises held at the close of the academic year included the performance of calisthenics. Religious critics attending the exercises in the early years of the school's history often equated the performances with dancing. The Reverend Lyman Beecher, who gave the address at the 1843 Anniversary Exercise, commented on the calisthenics presentation, "That must be orthodox dancing!" Quoted in Cole, *Hundred Years of Mount Holyoke*, 58.

83. Brickley, "Sarah Pierce's LFA," 310.

84. It cannot be ascertained when Litchfield started conducting the examinations, but given the reputation of the academy, it seems likely it would have occurred during the early history of the school. Troy and Mount Holyoke had such examinations from the beginning, while the first one at Music Vale occurred in 1839.

85. See chapter 6 for a discussion of the examinations at Music Vale. It appears Music Vale was the only institution to examine the students in music. Further, I have no evidence that ornamental arts at the other institutions were graded.

86. S. T. Holbrook, member of the board of examiners in 1872, reported on behalf of the board, "We would speak in the highest terms of commendation of all who took part in the exercises this afternoon, especially of the graduating class, whose diplomas we signed with unalloyed pleasure." "Music Vale Seminary," *Gleaner of the Vale* 2, no. 1 (1873), MVSA.

87. *Annual Catalogue of the Officers and Members of the Mount Holyoke Female Seminary, 1839–1865*; Cole, *Hundred Years of Mount Holyoke*, 46, 67, 68. "Harriet Wadsworth (Mrs. Kilbourn)—Her Reminiscences," quoted in Vanderpoel, *Chronicles of a Pioneer School*, 286; Cross, *Autobiography of Lyman Beecher*, 1:399.

88. Although no surviving Music Vale documents state that students were required to wear white dresses, it is apparent from letters to and from parents that the young ladies would need white dresses for special occasions. A. D. Beauchamp noted the scene as he approached Music Vale the day of the anniversary: "there were the young ladies of the Seminary, with the glow of health upon their happy faces and their tiny hats sit jauntily as they patroled the walk prior to the ordeal

which they were soon [to] pass." "Music Vale Seminary," in "Mrs. Celvy Morgan's Scrapbook," 12, MVSA.

89. Examination Room, folder "Troy Female Seminary—Photographs and Photographic Copies," box "MSS #6, Middlebury Academy, Waterford Academy, Troy Female Seminary; Records, Articles, Pictures." The report from the examining committee in 1855 commended the artwork, claiming it was of professional quality and would have been appropriate in a "select gallery." *Catalogue of the Officers and Pupils of the Troy Female Seminary, 1854–1855*, 30. It is unknown if students' artwork at Mount Holyoke was exhibited during the examinations.

90. Sarah Pierce wanted the students' work to receive an unbiased judgment. Inviting these women to be involved also provided a means of advertisement. Brickley, "Sarah Pierce's LFA," 187.

91. Mary J. Mason Fairbanks, *Emma Willard and Her Pupils or Fifty Years of Troy Female Seminary: 1822–1872* (New York: Mrs. Russell Sage, 1898), 58.

92. Reports began appearing in the 1848 seminary catalog.

93. Lutz, *Emma Willard*, 183–84.

94. It seems likely that the teachers examined the Litchfield students, since no one else is mentioned.

95. Frances Hall Johnson, *Music Vale Seminary: 1835–1876* (New Haven, CT: Yale University Press, 1934), 12; *Board of Examiners*, MVSA.

96. Harriet Beecher Stowe became known for her compositions at the age of twelve. She recalls the exhibition that year (1823): "I remember well the scene at that exhibition, to me so eventful. The hall was crowded with all the literati of Litchfield. Before them all our compositions were read aloud. When mine was read I noticed that father, who was sitting on high by Mr. Brace, brightened and looked interested, and at the close I heard him ask, 'Who wrote that composition?' '*Your daughter, sir!*' was the answer. It was the proudest moment of my life. There was no mistaking father's face when he was pleased, and to have interested him was past all juvenile triumphs." Cross, *Autobiography of Lyman Beecher*, 1:99.

97. Elizabeth Wolcott to John P. Jackson, April 27, 1825, "Alice Wolcott Collection, Litchfield Historical Society," quoted in Brickley, "Sarah Pierce's LFA," 188.

98. Hymn by Emma Willard, quoted in Lutz, *Emma Willard*, 185–86.

99. Holbrook, "Music Vale Seminary."

100. Nathan Richardson, *The Modern School for the Piano-Forte: Composed and Compiled from the Works of the Most Eminent Modern and Classical Authors and Teachers, Comprising a Complete Course of Instruction, Based Upon a New Principle, Progressive in Its Character, with Anatomical Illustrations of the Hands, Thoroughly Explained, Showing the Use of Their Muscles and Tendons in Playing the Piano* (Boston: O. Ditson, 1856).

101. *Catalogue of Music Vale and Normal Academy of Music for 1857–8*, in Sarah Augusta Shoner, "The Story of Karolyn Bradford Whittlesey and Her Family," in "Karolyn Bradford Whittlesey: 1843–1928," 54, unpublished notebook part 3, 54, MVSA. Hereafter this source will be referred to as "KBW."

102. Program: "Music Vale Seminary, Twenty-Fourth Annual Examination, July 8th, 1863," MVSA.

103. "Notice of Semi-Annual Exhibition. 'Female Academy,'" April 28, 1828, Litchfield County Post, quoted in Vanderpoel, *Chronicles of a Pioneer School*, 270-71.

104. *Catalogue of the Officers and Pupils of the Troy Female Seminary, for the Academic Year Commencing March 2, 1842, and Ending February 22, 1843. Together with the Conditions of Admittance, etc.* (Troy, NY: N. Tuttle, 1843), 15, folder "TFS Catalogue 1843"; Henry Fowler, "Educational Services of Mrs. Emma Willard," 155.

105. Sizer et al., *To Ornament Their Minds*, 38.

106. Brickley, "Sarah Pierce's LFA," 127; Fairbanks, *Emma Willard and Her Pupils*, 4–5; Edward Hitchcock, comp., *The Power of Christian Benevolence Illustrated in the Life and Labors of Mary Lyon*, new edition (New York: American Tract Society, 1858), 206–8.

107. Brickley, "Sarah Pierce's LFA," 129; Vanderpoel, *More Chronicles of a Pioneer School*, 8. According to the notice of the semiannual exhibition printed in the *Litchfield County Post* on April 24, 1828, there were two graduates that year. "Notice of Semi-Annual Exhibition. 'Female Academy.'"

108. Fairbanks, *Emma Willard and Her Pupils*, 4–5.

109. "Mount Holyoke Female Seminary," *Pittsfield Sun* (Pittsfield, MA), August 1, 1861.

110. Cole, *Hundred Years of Mount Holyoke*, 45, 100.

111. Ibid., 45, 350n70. Mrs. Hitchcock was the wife of board member Rev. Edward Hitchcock.

112. "Music Vale Seminary Diploma," MVSA.

113. There is no evidence that Litchfield or Mount Holyoke included concerts along with the examinations. Troy students and teachers frequently gave an evening concert during the examination week similar to those given at various times during the school year; however, none of them included staged productions like those at Music Vale. See chapter 6 for a discussion of these concerts.

114. Concert announcement on the back of the Twenty-Fourth Annual Examination program, July 8, 1863, MVSA.

115. "Music Vale Seminary. Thirtieth Annual Examination, June 24th, 1869." In 1871 the admission was reduced to fifty cents. "Music Vale Seminary. Thirty-Second Annual Examination. June, Twenty-Ninth, 1871," MVSA.

Chapter 6. Music Education for a Young Lady

1. *Catalogue of the Members of the Troy Female Seminary, for the Academic Year, Commencing September 16, 1835, and Ending August 3, 1836. Together with the Conditions of Admittance, etc.* (n.p., n.d.), 12, folder "TFS Catalogue 1836," box "Troy Female Seminary Catalogues 1820–1895," EWSA.

2. "TROY FEMALE SEMINARY: Method of Government Studies Pursued Examination Domestic Training—Manners, Morals and Health General Remarks,"

American Ladies' Magazine; Containing Original Tales, Essays, Literary & Historical Sketches, Poetry, Criticism, Music, and a Great Variety of Matter Connected with Many Subjects of Importance and Interest 8, no. 12 (1835): 704, ProQuest.

3. Emily Noyes Vanderpoel, comp., *Chronicles of a Pioneer School from 1792 to 1833 Being the History of Miss Sarah Pierce and Her Litchfield School*, ed. Elizabeth C. Barney Buel (Cambridge, MA: University Press, 1903), 73.

4. According to her nephew, John Pierce Brace, her assistant beginning in 1814, Sarah Pierce had no musical talent: "It is strange that Aunt Sarah has such an ear for rhythm in poetry, and writes tragedy blank verse so well, when she has no ear for music, and says she cannot distinguish one tune from another except as they vary in loudness." Given Pierce's creative ability, Brace must have been surprised that she was not musically gifted. Emily Noyes Vanderpoel, comp., *More Chronicles of a Pioneer School from 1792 to 1833 Being Added History on the Litchfield Academy Kept by Miss Sarah Pierce and Her Nephew, John Pierce Brace* (Cambridge, MA: University Press, 1927), 158.

5. No music teacher is listed in the catalog for 1837, but according to the 1915 issue of *The Llamarada* (Mount Holyoke College yearbook), music was offered from the beginning. The music teacher had numerous responsibilities; thus, it seems more than one instructor would have been required. *The Llamarada* (South Hadley, MA: Mount Holyoke College, 1915).

6. All of the Mount Holyoke catalogs are housed in MHCASC; they are also available online in the Mount Holyoke College Library Digital Collections: "Catalogs, Registers and Directories, Annual Catalogs only, 1837–1900," http://clio.fivecolleges .edu/mhc/catalogs.

7. There is no indication whether this was a daily, weekly, or monthly schedule, nor the length of time it was in place. The total number of students' hours was $21^1/2$.

8. Weekly schedule for Miss Thurston, November 18, 1846–March 10, 1847, facsimile, Mary Lyon Collection, series B: "Writings and Documents," sub-series 5: "Writings from Mount Holyoke Seminary," [1833?]–1848, folder 3: 1845–1848 and undated, MHCASC, http://clio.fivecolleges.edu/mhc/lyon/b/5mhs.

9. No doubt she gave the student a reduction in tuition, but no documentation supports this claim.

10. Arthur C. Cole, *A Hundred Years of Mount Holyoke College: The Evolution of an Educational Ideal* (New Haven, CT: Yale University Press, 1940), 143–44.

11. Journal entry of Mary A. Evans, November 15, 1864, quoted in ibid., 144.

12. *Catalogue of the Litchfield Female School, for the Year Ending November 1st 1825*, CLHS; *Catalogue of the Litchfield Female Academy* (1828), Misc. L. file, quoted in Lynne Templeton Brickley, "Sarah Pierce's Litchfield Female Academy, 1792–1833" (hereafter, "Sarah Pierce's LFA"), (PhD diss., Harvard University, 1985), 123; *Catalogue of the Litchfield Academy, 1830*, CLHS.

13. Though the student body at Litchfield did include some young men, I have found none who taught music.

14. I have obtained names of some music teachers appearing before that date through sources other than the catalogs.

15. There appears to have been only one superior and one premier, but the number of monitresses varied. Frequently there was only one monitress, but in 1857 there were four. *Catalogue of Music Vale and Normal Academy of Music for 1857–8*, 5. Catalog is quoted in Sarah Augusta Shoner, "Karolyn Bradford Whittlesey: 1843–1928," unpublished notebook (hereafter, "KBW"), part 4, 1-16, MVSA.

16. *Thirty-First Annual Circular of Music Vale Seminary and Normal Academy of Music, Salem, New London County, Connecticut, 1869–70* (n.p., n.d.), 2, MVSA.

17. *Weekly Democrat* (n.p., n.d.) in *Board of Examiners*, MVSA.

18. Frances Hall Johnson, *Music Vale Seminary: 1835–1876* (New Haven, CT: Yale University Press, 1934), 10.

19. Cole, *Hundred Years of Mount Holyoke*, 143.

20. *Thirtieth Annual Catalogue of the Mount Holyoke Female Seminary in South Hadley, Massachusetts* (Northampton, MA: Bridgman and Childs, 1867), 5, MHCASC.

21. *Catalogue of the Officers and Pupils of the Troy Female Seminary for the Academic Year, Commencing September 15, 1847, and Ending July 26, 1848. Together with the Conditions of Admittance, etc.* (Troy, NY: Prescott and Wilson, 1848), 4, folder "TFS Catalogue 1848," EWSA.

22. *Catalogue of the Officers and Pupils of the Troy Female Seminary, for the Academic Year, Commencing September 12, 1860, and Ending June 26, 1861. Together with the Conditions of Admittance, etc.* (Troy, NY: A. W. Scribner, 1861), 6, folder "TFS Catalogue 1861," EWSA.

23. *Catalogue of the Officers and Pupils of the Troy Female Seminary, for the Academic Year, Commencing September 19, 1849, and Ending July 24, 1850. Together with the Conditions of Admittance, etc.* (Troy, NY: John F. Prescott, 1850), 27, folder "TFS Catalogue 1850," EWSA.

24. *Catalogue of the Officers and Pupils of the Troy Female Seminary, for the Academic Year, Commencing September 13, 1854, and Ending June 27, 1855. Together with the Conditions of Admittance, etc.* (Troy, NY: A. W. Scribner, 1855), 29, folder "TFS Catalogue 1855," EWSA.

25. See chapter 8 for information on Eliza Whittlesey's compositions.

26. For information on vocal compositions by John C. Andrews, see chapter 8.

27. *Troy Daily Budget* (Troy, New York), August 11, 1847, EWSA.

28. The concert given on June 20, 1850, includes three of his pieces: "Les Belles de l'Amérique—Quadrilles," "Ma premiere Reverie" (for solo piano), and a comic ballad titled "I Have Got the Blues."

29. *The Grove Dictionary of American Music*, 2nd ed., s.v. "Hodges, Faustina Hasse."

30. See chapter 8 for more information on vocal compositions by Hodges.

31. Given the popularity of Philippi's compositions during his first tenure at Troy, it seems likely that his pieces would have been as well received during his second

tenure, but no programs exist to provide verification. See chapter 8 for additional information on Philippi's vocal works.

32. "Salem Normal Academy of Music" [1851], MVSA. It is possible that all of Whittlesey's daughters composed, but no documentation exists to provide confirmation. In the October 1855 issue of *The Northern Farmer*, T. B. Minor relates his visit to Music Vale. He applauds the performances and notes, "Some very excellent music has also been composed by one of his daughters." Sarah Augusta Shoner mentions in her notebook that this could have referred to Eliza. "KBW," part 3, 20.

33. "Salem Normal Academy of Music" [1851], MVSA.

34. These included "Farewell to My Home," "Warrior's Rest" (titled "Rest Warrior" on the program), and "Harp of the Wild Wind," in addition to "Take Care!"—another of Whittlesey's songs. "Music Vale Seminary, Twenty-Fourth Annual Examination, July 8th, 1863," MVSA. Whittlesey's music was published by Oliver Ditson, in Boston, and other publishers in New York. Shoner, "KBW," part 3, 40.

35. There is no documentation providing the date for Whittlesey's "Welcome to Music Vale." It appeared as the first work on the performances for June 29, 1871; June 13, 1872; and August 14, 1873, suggesting it commonly served as the opening piece. "Music Vale Seminary. Thirty-Second Annual Examination. June 29, 1871"; "Music Vale Seminary. Anniversary Exercises. Thirty-Third Year. Thursday, June 13, 1872"; "Music Vale Seminary. Anniversary Exercises. Thirty-Fifth Year. Thursday, August 14, 1873," all in MVSA.

36. Orramel Whittlesey, "Music Vale Seminary Quickstep," mm. 26–40 (New York: Horace Waters, 1855), in Lester S. Levy Collection of Sheet Music, Sheridan Libraries, Johns Hopkins University, Baltimore, Maryland, http://levysheetmusic.mse.jhu.edu .proxy.libraries.uc.edu/collection/044/092.

37. For example, in 1823 the tuition at Litchfield was $5 or $6 per quarter, but the fee for piano lessons was $12. Brickley, "Sarah Pierce's LFA," 167. That same year Troy's fees were similar to Litchfield's: tuition was $6 per quarter and piano lessons were $12, with a $2 fee for piano use. Emma Willard allowed a reduction if students paid by the term rather than the quarter. In 1823 tuition was $11 per term, while piano lessons were $22, and instrument rental was $3.67. If a student elected to study drawing, painting, or dancing, or to attend lectures in history, philosophy, or the sciences, she incurred an extra charge. "Troy Female Seminary," folder "Troy Female Seminary Promotional Materials"; box "MSS #6, Middlebury Academy, Waterford Academy, Troy Female Seminary, Records, Articles, and Pictures," EWSA. Along with the high cost of music instruction, students needed to purchase their own music. Catharine Bronk, a student at Litchfield, paid $2.50 for sheet music in 1826. Brickley, "Sarah Pierce's LFA," 167.

38. Brickley, "Sarah Pierce's LFA," 167.

39. *Catalogue of the Members of Troy Female Seminary, for the Academic Year, Commencing September 17, 1828, and Ending August 5, 1829. Together with the Conditions of Admittance, etc.* (n.p., n.d.), 8, EWSA.

40. Perhaps the fee fluctuated due to the Civil War.

41. See chapter 4 for a discussion of the fees charged at Music Vale.

42. "Music Vale Seminary and Normal Academy of Music" (1855), MVSA; *Second Annual Catalogue of the Mount Holyoke Female Seminary, in South Hadley, Mass. 1838–39* (n.p., n.d.), 9, MHCASC.

43. Blessner was on the faculty from 1847 to 1850, but the 1847 catalog does not include the subjects or instruments the faculty taught. Since the 1848 catalog lists Blessner as a violin teacher, it is possible that he also offered violin instruction in 1847. Although his name is given as a violin teacher, the instrument was not listed in the catalog as a possible elective until 1866.

44. CHICK, "Music Vale," *Gleaner of the Vale*, 2, no. 2 (1874), MVSA.

45. Lowell Mason to Mary Lyon, November 20, 1832, Lowell Mason, folder, LD 1082.25 1837, Papers, MHCASC. Arthur C. Cole claims that private piano and voice lessons were only offered after Eliza Wilder joined the faculty in 1862. *Hundred Years of Mount Holyoke College*, 144. No mention is made, however, of private instruction in the seminary catalogs with the exception of 1844–1846.

46. Mary Lyon to Frances L. Green, May 9, 1844, folder 16, 1843, 1844, Mary Lyon Collection (MHCASC), series A. Correspondence, 1818–1849, http://clio.fivecolleges .edu/mhc/lyon/a (all of the letters from and to Mary Lyon are available in series A at this website). Apparently Eliza P. Knight, who attended the seminary from 1841 to 1844, was an example of such a student based on Lyon's response to the Reverend Mr. Lyman regarding his inquiry for a music teacher: "I can now recommend a young lady [Eliza P. Knight], whom you can probably obtain who has practiced music about a year, and by a little continued attention to the subject, . . . [will] probably be able to teach well." Mary Lyon to Rev. Mr. Lyman, January 30, 1846, MHCASC.

47. Repairs and shipping cost $55.75 each. Daniel Stafford to Mary Lyon, December 10, 1842, MHCASC. Also cited in Cole, *Hundred Years of Mount Holyoke College*, 57.

48. Journal letter of Sarah A. Start, March [?], 1857, quoted in Cole, *Hundred Years of Mount Holyoke College*, 370n28.

49. Jeremiah Wilcox to Miss Lyon, July 16, 1844, MHCASC.

50. E. A. Cahoon to Miss Lyon, August 15, 1844, MHCASC.

51. In 1847, for example, Rev. Mr. Thurston asked whether his daughter, who was qualified to teach music, might receive employment. Mary Lyon could not give a favorable response: "I think we shall have no occasion to employ her in teaching music at present." Mary Lyon to Rev. Mr. Thurston, March 29, 1847, MHCASC.

52. Abby Allen to "My dear Father," October 26, 1842, folder Abby Allen, file LD 7096.6 X1845, MHCASC. The information Allen gives concerning the fee to use the piano does not agree with that in the catalogs. According to the catalogs, the students could use the piano for one hour daily, but no fee was mentioned.

53. Examples of entries in diaries and journals are as follows: "took a lesson in music returned to Mr. Adams pricked off 2 or three tunes," "Journal of Mary Ann

Bacon," July 1, 1802, series 2, folder 102, Litchfield Female Academy, CLHS; "Came to school, took a music lesson," "Journal of Lucy Sheldon," February 19, 1803, series 2, folder 4, CLHS.

54. "Notice of Semi-Annual Exhibition. Female Academy," *Litchfield County Post*, April 24, 1828, quoted in Vanderpoel, *Chronicles of a Pioneer School*, 271.

55. "Journal of Mary Ann Bacon," July 21, 1802; "Journal of Lucy Sheldon," series 2, folder 4, January 4, 1803, CLHS.

56. "Diary of Catherine Cebra Webb, 1815–1816," quoted in Vanderpoel, *Chronicles of a Pioneer School*, 149.

57. September 14, 1802, "Journal of Mary Ann Bacon," quoted in Vanderpoel, *Chronicles of a Pioneer School*, 71. Either the date printed for the journal entry is inaccurate, or Miss Bacon seriously neglected writing in her journal, since it precedes the date Bacon received her piano—October 9.

58. Sheldon's piano "was probably bought of his brother John Jacob Astor. . . . It is made in two parts, the body of the instrument fitting on the top of a light separate frame with four slender legs." "Journal of Lucy Sheldon," Winter 1893, series 2, folder 4, CLHS. Students seldom had their own instruments. Undoubtedly many families could not afford them. George Astor (1752–1813) was a piano builder in London. John Jacob Astor (1763–1848) moved to the United States; he marketed his brother's instruments made in England.

59. "TROY FEMALE SEMINARY," 704.

60. "School Rules," folder "Transcript of School Rules—TFS 1836"; box "MSS#6, Middlebury Academy, Waterford Academy, Troy Female Seminary, Records, Articles, Pictures," 5, EWSA.

61. Papers of Aunt Eliza's (n.p., n.d.), MVSA.

62. H. M. Sherman, "Music Vale Seminary," *Gleaner of the Vale* [2, no. 1, January 1873], MVSA.

63. *Thirty-First Annual Circular of Music Vale Seminary and Normal Academy of Music*, 5.

64. "Continuous Study," *Gleaner of the Vale* (1874), MVSA.

65. S. T. Holbrook, "Music Vale Seminary," *Gleaner of the Vale* 2, no. 1 [1873], MVSA.

66. Quoted in Cole, *Hundred Years of Mount Holyoke College*, 106.

67. Sarah J. Burnham to Elizabeth P. Dodge, February 20, 1842, Sarah J. Burnham's Papers, folder Burnham, LD, 7096.6, X1844, MHCASC.

68. Cole, *Hundred Years of Mount Holyoke College*, 57.

69. G. J. Web and Lowell Mason, *The Odeon: A Collection of Secular Melodies, Arranged and Harmonized for Four Voices, Designed for Adult Singing Schools, and for Social Music Parties* (Boston: J. H. Wilkins and R. B. Carter, 1841), xxv.

70. Thomas Hastings and Wm. B. Bradbury, *The Psalmodist; A Choice Collection of Psalm and Hymn Tunes, Chiefly New; Adapted to the Very Numerous Metres Now in Use, Together with Chants, Anthems, Motets, and Various Other Pieces; Choirs, Congregations, Singing Schools and Musical Associations: Most of Which Are Now for*

the First Time Presented to the American Public (New York: Mark H. Newman, 1844), 33.

71. See chapter 8 for a discussion of the repertoire performed at Mount Holyoke.

72. Isaac Watts and Samuel Worcester, *The Psalms, Hymns, and Spiritual Songs of the Rev. Isaac Watts, D.D. to Which Are Added, Select Hymns from Other Authors; and Directions for Musical Expression, by Samuel Worcester, D.D. Late Pastor of the Tabernacle Church, Salem, Mass.* (Boston: Samuel T. Armstrong, 1823); Asahel Nettleton, *Village Hymns, for Social Worship. Selected and Original. Designed as a Supplement to the Psalms and Hymns of Dr. Watts* (New York: E. Sands, 1828).

73. Webb and Mason, *Odeon*; A. N. Johnson, *The Key-Stone Collection of Church Music: A Complete Collection of Hymn Tunes, Anthems, Psalms, Chants, etc., to Which Is Added the Physiological System; for Training Choirs and Teaching Singing Schools; and the Cantata, The Morning of Freedom* (Lancaster City, PA: J. H. Sheaffer, 1868); *The Jubilee* includes a section titled "The Study of Singing," by [Luigi] Lablache, which contains some of the same instructions found in *The Odeon* and *The Key-Stone Collection*. William B. Bradbury, *The Jubilee: An Extensive Collection of Church Music for the Choir, the Congregation, and the Singing-School. New Edition, Containing Additional Anthems, Opening and Closing Pieces. Etc.* (New York: Mason Brothers, 1858), 50–52.

74. Johnson, *Key-Stone Collection*, 44.

75. "Diary of Charlotte Sheldon," [July] 6, 1796, [September] 8, 1796, series 2, folders 84 and 85, CLHS.

76. Ibid.

77. According to the 1843 catalog, every student was taught the science of music and the singing of sacred music.

78. *Catalogue of the Members of Troy Female Seminary, for the Academic Year, Commencing September 16, 1829, and Ending August 4, 1830. Together with the Conditions of Admittance, etc.* (n.p., n.d.), 8, EWSA.

79. See chapter 8 for a discussion of the repertoire performed on programs.

80. "Concert Given by the Pupils of the Troy Female Seminary Assisted by their Teachers, February 19, 1850" and "Concert Given by the Teachers and Pupils of the Troy Female Seminary, under the Direction of Prof. Thorbecke, June 26, 1855," folder "Troy Female Seminary—Musical Programs," box "MSS#6, Middlebury Academy, Waterford Academy, Troy Female Seminary Records, Articles, Pictures," EWSA. All of the musical programs are housed in this box unless otherwise noted. Names of the performers are not given on the programs; however, teachers assisted the students; the male parts would have been sung by teachers.

81. No extant circular gives the name of a vocal instructor until 1863, though by 1857 the names of the faculty are provided along with the instruments taught.

82. *Thirty-First Annual Circular of Music Vale Seminary*, 5, MVSA.

83. Since George F. Root was a visitor at Music Vale, along with such noted musicians as Lowell Mason and Louis Moreau Gottschalk, it seems likely that Orramel

Whittlesey would have used Root's book as an instruction method. Sarah Augusta Shoner, "Articles Pertinent to Her Story," in "KBW," part 4, 37. See "KBW," part 3, 39. Music Vale used Richardson's piano method.

84. "Opinions of the Press and of Distinguished Gentlemen," *Gleaner of the Vale* (1874), MVSA.

85. A[ugustus] Backus, comp., *History, Theory, and Analysis of Music: Designed for the Music Department of the Troy Female Seminary* (Troy, NY: Tuttle, Belcher and Burton, 1839), 17–19.

86. Ibid., 84–108.

87. Cole, *Hundred Years of Mount Holyoke College*, 144. No mention is made of these events as open to the public, but this would likely have been the case, since this was common at such other schools as Troy and the Moravian Young Ladies' Seminary in Bethlehem, Pennsylvania.

88. "Concert. A Concert will be given at the Troy Female Seminary, by the Music Teachers and Pupils, Assisted by Several Gentlemen from the City," (V Cannon Place: Johnson & Davis, Steam Press Printers, n.d.), folder "Troy Female Seminary—Musical Programs," EWSA.

89. An article in the *Gleaner of the Vale* indicates that two concerts were given weekly. I have found no other indication of concerts being given more than once a week. "Self-Reliance," *Gleaner of the Vale* [2, no. 1 (1859)], MVSA.

90. See chapters 7 and 8 for a discussion of the concerts.

91. CHICK, "Music Vale," MVSA.

92. Ibid.

93. "Mt. Holyoke Female Seminary. Order of Exercises for Public Examination, Tuesday, July 23, 1861," MHCASC.

94. George F. Whicher, ed., *William Gardiner Hammond: Remembrance of Amherst, an Undergraduate's Diary 1846–1848* (New York: Columbia University Press, 1946), 162.

95. "For the Gleaner," *Gleaner of the Vale* (1874), MVSA.

96. *Catalogue of the Officers and Pupils of the Troy Female Seminary, for the Academic Year, Commencing September 19, 1849, and Ending July 24, 1850*, 27, EWSA.

97. "Troy Female Seminary," *Troy Daily Whig* (Troy, NY), July 11, 1855.

98. Ibid. Mdme Stephani and Miss Bayeau were also music professors. The gentlemen were most likely acquaintances living in the area. The report mentions that two or three gentlemen amateurs aided in the performances, thus suggesting these men were not members of the music faculty. No documentation exists to provide any further explanation.

99. "Music Vale Seminary. Thirty-Second Annual Examination. June Twenty-Ninth, 1871," MVSA.

100. Holbrook, "Music Vale Seminary," MVSA.

101. It appears the concert was given at the local church (also called the "meetinghouse"). Cole, *Hundred Years of Mount Holyoke College*, 96. Various events ("be-

nevolent and secular enterprises—lecture, concerts, political rallies") were held at the church during the week. Elizabeth Alden Green, *Mary Lyon and Mount Holyoke: Opening the Gates* (Hanover, NH: University Press of New England, 1979), 241.

102. Cole, *Hundred Years of Mount Holyoke College*, 96.

103. The performers do not appear to have been connected with the school or were touring musicians. Since Litchfield was a thriving cultural community, perhaps some of the citizens were well-trained musicians.

104. "Journal of Lucy Sheldon," February 7, 1803, series 2, folder 4, CLHS.

105. "Diary of Charlotte Sheldon, 1796," series 2, folders 84 and 85, CLHS.

106. "Journal of Eliza Ogden, 1816–1818," series 2, folder 23, CLHS.

107. *Catalogue of the Officers and Pupils of the Troy Female Seminary for the Academic Year, Commencing September 15, 1847, and Ending July 26, 1848*, 18, EWSA.

108. "Fireman's Concert," January 8, 1846, folder "Troy Female Seminary—Musical Programs," EWSA.

109. Ibid.

110. "Programme of Gustave Blessner's Farewell Concert at Apollo Hall, Troy, Tuesday Evening, May 14, 1850," folder "Troy Female Seminary—Musical Programs," EWSA. E. P. Jones is the only performer who was not a member of the faculty. Perhaps he was a local musician or a friend of Blessner.

111. Ibid. Blessner dedicated "The Empire State Quick Step" (Troy, NY: William Hall and Son, 1850) to fellow teacher John C. Andrews. http://imslp.org/wiki/Empire_State _Quick_Step_(Blessner,_Gustav).

112. E. D. Mansfield, "Personal Memories," quoted in Vanderpoel, *Chronicles of a Pioneer School*, 258.

113. Mary Lyon to Miss Backus, January 30, 1846, MHCASC.

114. *Calisthenic Exercises*, 4. Folder Ix83M.M8ca. c.1, MHCASC.

115. Ibid.

116. Ibid. The manual also includes *Variations of the Triple Spring* on the same page.

117. Quoted in Lord, *Life of Emma Willard*, 123.

118. John C. Andrews composed "My Own Sunny France" (Troy, NY: John C. Andrews, 1837), with text by Emma Willard. http://imslp.org/wiki/My_Own_Sunny_France _(Andrews,_John_C.). Lafayette was highly impressed with the seminary and with Emma Willard, and this visit, along with another one a year later, established a strong mutual friendship. He invited Willard to visit France, which she did on an extended trip to Europe with her son during a sabbatical in 1830. Their welcome was as warm as Lafayette's had been at the seminary. Alma Lutz, *Emma Willard: Daughter of Democracy* (Boston: Houghton Mifflin, 1929), 102–6, 135–44.

119. "Journal of Eliza Ogden, 1816–1818," series 2, folder 23, CLHS.

120. Anne E. Walker to her brother James, October 1, 1849, folder "Anne E. Walker," Papers, MHCASC. Cole suggests that the "Mason like" reference was probably due to Lowell Mason's influence on choral singing; he had organized the Boston Academy of Music in 1833. Cole, *Hundred Years of Mount Holyoke College*, 366n57.

121. Lydia French to her sister, February 27, 1855, folder "Lydia French's" Papers, MHCASC.

Chapter 7. Instrumental Music at the Seminaries

1. Except for meager information in some students' diaries, no primary source material survives documenting the music studied and performed at Litchfield. Lucy Sheldon's four music books, all dated 1818, along with her diaries, provide the best information. Lucy Sheldon was a student there from 1803 to 1805. Her music books, however, date from 1818. Lucy Sheldon's Music Books 1–4, CLHS. Linda Hocking, curator of the library and archives at the Litchfield Historical Society, confirms that Lucy lived on North Street in Litchfield her entire adult life. Further, Lucy's brother attended the academy in 1816 (although it was a women's institution, some men were admitted). Given Lucy's association with the academy and life in Litchfield, Hocking argues that her music books can be considered as representative of music studied and performed at the school, although Lucy attended earlier. Email to author from Linda Hocking, October 15, 2014.

2. Sarah Augusta Shoner, "Karolyn Bradford Whittlesey: 1843–1928," part 3, 18, 19, unpublished notebook (hereafter, "KBW)," MVSA.

3. Sarah Victoria, Orramel Whittlesey's second daughter, attended Troy Female Seminary from 1834 to 1836. Undoubtedly Whittlesey knew of the prestigious music department at Troy. *Catalogue of the Members of Troy Female Seminary Commencing March 5, 1834, and Ending February 18, 1835*, (n.p.), folder "TFS Catalogues 1835"and *Catalogue of the Members of Troy Female Seminary Commencing March 4, 1835, and Ending February 17, 1836. Together with the Conditions of Admittance, etc."* (n.p.), folder "TFS Catalogues 1836," box "Troy Female Seminary Catalogues, 1820–1895," EWSA. All of the catalogs are housed in folders according to years in this box.

4. "Troy Female Seminary," *Troy Daily Budget* (Troy, NY), February 24, 1848, folder, "Newspaper Clippings," box "Troy Female Seminary," EWSA. All references from the Troy newspaper are preserved in this folder unless otherwise noted. The report covered the semiannual examinations held in February. The examining committee consisted of seven to ten invited guests—men and women of various professions such as law, education, and clergy—from different states and areas of New York. There is no mention that the examiners were musicians or that students were graded on their performances. See chapter 5 for more discussion of examinations at Troy Female Seminary.

5. "Troy Female Seminary," *Troy Daily Whig* (Troy, NY), March 9, 1852, EWSA. The report was for the semiannual examinations held in February.

6. Emily Noyes Vanderpoel, comp., *Chronicles of a Pioneer School from 1792 to 1833 Being the History of Miss Sarah Pierce and Her Litchfield School*, ed. Elizabeth C. Barney Buel (Cambridge, MA: University Press, 1903), 294.

7. See chapter 8 for a discussion of vocal music.

8. From 1844 to 1846 piano was offered upon request. See chapter 6 for more information. *Second Annual Catalogue of the Mount Holyoke Female Seminary, in South Hadley, Mass., 1838–39* (n.p., n.d.), 9. All of the Mount Holyoke Female Seminary catalogs are housed in the MHCASC. They are also online in the Mount Holyoke College Library Digital Collections: "Catalogs, Registers and Directories, Annual Catalogs only, 1837–1900," http://clio.fivecolleges.edu/mhc/catalogs.

9. Litchfield and Troy held these exercises twice yearly; the first apparently coinciding with the end of the first semester. The exhibition occurring at the end of the year undoubtedly drew the larger crowd, since parents and guardians would have come to take their daughters or wards home for the summer.

10. "[Examination] Report," in *Catalogue of the Officers and Pupils, of the Troy Female Seminary, for the Academic Year, Commencing September 9, 1857, and Ending June 30, 1858. Together with the Conditions of Admittance, etc.* (Troy, NY: A. W. Scribner, 1858), 36, folder "TFS Catalogue 1858," EWSA.

11. Music Vale Seminary, "Thirtieth Annual Examination," June 24, 1869, 2–3, MVSA.

12. Young Ladies' Annual Concert Announcement, Music Vale Seminary, "Thirtieth Annual Examination," June 24, 1869, 4, MVSA.

13. Troy included musical performances during the examination exercises to relieve tension, as well as holding separate concerts. See chapter 6, "Music Performances."

14. "Notice of Semi-Annual Exhibition. 'Female Academy,'" *Litchfield County Post*, April 24, 1828, quoted in Vanderpoel, *Chronicles of a Pioneer School*, 270, 271.

15. Shoner, "KBW," part 3, 38.

16. Ibid., 37.

17. Ibid., 38.

18. Concert Program, Troy Female Seminary, February 1, 1853, folder "Troy Female Seminary Musical Programs," EWSA. Some concert programs include students' and teachers' names as well.

19. See chapters 3, 4, and 5 for more information on Reeve's law school and its association with the Litchfield Academy.

20. The two piano performances were Beethoven's Sonata No. 12 and Theodore Oesten's *Fantaisie Dramatique*. Composers of vocal music include Felix Mendelssohn, Robert Topliff, Franz Wilhelm Abt, Christian Heinrich Rinck, and Faustina Hodges. Given that the students performed vocal music by such contemporaries, it can be assumed the pianists also played compositions by these or other composers of equivalent status. "Mount Holyoke Female Seminary. Order of Exercises for the Thirty-Second anniversary. 1869," MHCASC.

21. Shoner, "KBW," part 3, 38.

22. Ibid., 17.

23. Ibid., 39, 40. Shoner suggests that "doubtless, the Whittlesey daughters who had studied meanwhile in Boston and in New York, had influenced the selections chosen for Music Vale students." It is possible that Eliza Whittlesey, who was then

slightly over twenty-one, had studied in New York with Dr. William Mason, "her idol all her lifetime, as regarded musicianship and ability as a teacher." Ibid., 39.

24. "First Impressions of the Vale," *Gleaner of the Vale*, 2, no. 1 (1873), MVSA.

25. "Concert Given by the Teachers & Pupils of the Troy Female Seminary, under the Direction of M. Philippi, July 22d, 1851," folder "Troy Female Seminary, Musical Programs"; box "MXX #6: Middlebury Academy, Waterford Academy, Troy Female Seminary: Records, Articles, Pictures," EWSA.

26. Handel is only included in Lucy Sheldon's music books. Perhaps this is indicative of the English influence, since Litchfield was founded in the late eighteenth century.

27. Given the emphasis on music training at Troy, it is surprising that there is a disparity between the two schools. Perhaps missing programs provide an explanation.

28. Names of composers commonly performed at Music Vale include Beethoven, Czerny, Gottschalk, Wilhelm Kuhe, Mendelssohn, Louis Plaidy, Julius Schulhoff, Fritz Spindler, Thalberg, and Hermann Adolph Wollenhaupt, while those favored at Troy were Auber, Blessner, Herz, and Thalberg.

29. The only exception is a set of variations on a theme by Pleyel, composed by Faustina H. Hodges, teacher at Troy Seminary.

30. This could suggest Lucy Sheldon's pianistic ability.

31. Perhaps this is a result of missing programs. Such a conclusion seems logical given the type and level of literature found on Troy's extant programs.

32. Founded in 1742, the Moravian Young Ladies' Seminary is the second-oldest known female boarding school in the United States. It achieved renown for its music and academic education before Troy or Music Vale came into existence. For a discussion of the piano repertoire studied and performed at the Moravian Young Ladies' Seminary, see my book *Music, Women, and Pianos in Antebellum Bethlehem, Pennsylvania: The Moravian Young Ladies' Seminary*, chapter 5, "Piano Literature for a Young Lady" (Bethlehem, PA: Lehigh University Press, 2008).

33. J. Bunker Clark, *The Dawning of American Keyboard Music* (New York: Greenwood Press, 1988), 231.

34. Ibid., 234.

35. Orramel Whittlesey was impressed when he heard this piece performed. Sarah Augusta Shoner, biographer of an unpublished collection of memoirs concerning the Whittlesey family, notes that in 1871 Agnes Iveagh, a granddaughter of Whittlesey, wrote to her mother: "Miss Scott played the Battle of Prague for Grandpa. He thinks it is elegant." Shoner, "KBW," part 3, 40.

36. "Poet and Peasant," "The Chime of Silvery Sabbath Bells," "Fairy Fingers," and "The Harp Eolienne" were performed at Music Vale; "Les Belles de l'Amérique" was performed at Troy. "Jefferson's Whim" and "The Opera Neel" are in Lucy Sheldon's Music Book 1, CLHS; no composer is given.

37. Louis Moreau Gottschalk, *Notes of a Pianist*, ed., with a prelude, a postlude, and explanatory notes, Jeanne Behrend (New York: Da Capo Press, 1979), 166–67.

Gottschalk's brief encounter implies that Whittlesey is an alcoholic and that Apollo (Greek god of music, among other things) was not a major influence. However, Whittlesey was no doubt pleased that his students could hear Gottschalk's performance. Gottschalk's comments are entertaining, if not entirely factual.

38. S. Frederick Starr recalls how *The Last Hope* became synonymous with Gottschalk: "Soon *The Last Hope* began to dog Gottschalk mercilessly. He admitted that 'even my paternal love for *The Last Hope* has succumbed under the terrible necessity of meeting it at every step, of playing it every evening, and hearing it played every day.' When he deleted it from the program in a small Wisconsin town, someone passed up a note from the audience asking, 'Will Mr. Gottschalk oblige *thirty-six* young ladies who have studied *The Last Hope* by playing said piece?' Soon he abandoned himself to fate and accepted the fact that *The Last Hope* was 'one among other inevitable afflictions of my life.'" *Bamboula: The Life and Times of Louis Moreau Gottschalk* (New York: Oxford University Press, 1995), 195.

39. Ibid., 196, 295. Concerning *La Gallina*, Starr noted Harold Schonberg's description of this piece: "'The effect is highly Ivesian, even though Charles Ives had as yet not been born.'" Ibid., 295.

40. George W. Warren's "La Fête des Fées," op. 13 (Boston: George P. Reed, 1832), mm. 46–61, in New York State Library, Albany, New York.

41. Sigismond Thalberg, "Home! Sweet Home!," Air Anglais, op. 72 (New York: C. Breusing, 1857), mm. 37–41, in Albert and Shirley Small Special Collections Library, University of Virginia, Charlottesville.

42. James M. Wehli, "Home Sweet Home. For the Pianoforte, Transcribed for the Left Hand Only: As Played by the Author at His Concerts in America" (New York: Hamilton S. Gordon, 1905–7), title page, in Albert and Shirley Small Special Collections Library, University of Virginia, Charlottesville.

43. Ibid., mm. 73–81.

44. *Lee and Walker's Musical Almanac for 1869. For the Use of Seminaries, Professors of Music, and the Musical Public. Being a Condensed Catalogue; to Which Is Added a List of Our Latest and Best Publications* (Philadelphia: Lee and Walker, 1869), 116.

45. I have been unable to find a given name for Zungmann.

46. Oscar Comettant, "Gabrielle: Etude d'Expression pour Piano" (New York: Horace Waters, 1853), mm. 45–57, in the Library of Congress, https://www.loc.gov/item/sm1853.531990.

47. Wilhelm Iucho, "Third Calisthenic Rondo" (New York: Firth and Hall, 1833). Iucho wrote at least four rondos to accompany calisthenics. Whittlesey had high regard for Iucho, inviting him to serve on the Board of Examiners. He held this position at least in 1857 and likely other undocumented years. *Board of Examiners*, MVSA.

48. Rudolphe Kreutzer, "The Celebrated Overture to *Lodoïska*," mm. 81–111, Lucy Sheldon's Music Book 3, CLHS.

49. *Lee and Walker's Musical Almanac for 1869*, 116, 117.

50. Brinley Richards, "Cottage by the Sea" (New York: William A. Pond, 1859), mm. 19–36, University of Tennessee Library, Digital Collection, Sheet Music Collection, http://diglib.lib.utk.edu/utsmc/main.php?bid=1002.

51. Charles Grobe, "Smile On: Brilliant Variations on Wallace's Beautiful Melody, 'Katie Strang'" (New York: William Hall and Son, 1838), var. 2, mm. 1–17, Digital Collection: Nineteenth Century Music, University of North Carolina at Chapel Hill, Music Library, http://dc.lib.unc.edu/cdm/ref/collection/sheetmusic/id/36082.

52. This was Herz's "most popular work written in America." R. Allen Lott, *From Paris to Peoria: How European Piano Virtuosos Brought Classical Music to the American Heartland* (New York: Oxford University Press, 2003), 82.

53. "Pleyel's Favorite German Hymn," var. 3, var. 4, Lucy Sheldon's Music Book 3, CLHS.

54. S. B. Mills, "Saltarello," op. 26 (New York: William A. Pond, 1871), mm. 149–87, in Albert and Shirley Small Special Collections Library, University of Virginia, Charlottesville, Virginia.

55. This is not noted on the handwritten copy in Lucy's book, but it is printed on the sheet music for "The Celebrated One Finger'd Sliding Waltz" (Baltimore: F. D. Benteen, 1840), mm. 1–18, in the Albert and Shirley Small Special Collections Library, University of Virginia, Charlottesville.

56. [Muzio Clementi,] "Clementi's Favorite Waltz," mm. 1–55, Lucy Sheldon's Music Book 4, CLHS.

57. The catalogs do not list the instruments the faculty taught until 1848, when Blessner is listed as a violin instructor. However, he was a member of the faculty in 1847, so it can be assumed he also offered violin that year.

58. I have been unable to find given names for Spinaleo and Holland.

59. Further, none of the programs at Troy include any organ performances. Since organ instruction was offered beginning in 1849, it seems likely that students would have performed organ works. Perhaps a paucity of programs offers an explanation.

60. Perhaps this is William Bradbury.

61. I have been unable to find a given name for La Port.

62. See the "Ensemble Music" section above for a discussion of other pieces that include violin.

63. See the discussion of vocal music in chapter 8.

Chapter 8. Singing Ladies: Vocal Repertoire at the Seminaries

1. Undoubtedly Sarah Pierce was referring to the practice of the time when singing masters would teach note reading and psalm singing.

2. See chapter 7 for more information on Orramel Whittlesey. Frances Hall Johnson claims that Whittlesey's first songs were published in 1849; however, a brochure

from around 1851 detailing the terms, expenses, etc., of Music Vale, possibly sent to prospective students, includes titles of several of his songs; some were already in their fifth or sixth edition: "Dying Soldier of Buena Vista" (5th ed.), "Farewell to My Home" (6th ed.), "Warrior's Rest" (4th ed.), and "Wild Roses" (6th ed.). Johnson, *Music Vale Seminary: 1835–1876*, published for the Tercentenary Commission (New Haven, CT: Yale University Press, 1934), 17; "Salem Normal Academy of Music" [1851]. All primary source material for Music Vale Seminary is located in the MVSA.

3. Johnson, *Music Vale Seminary*, 17.

4. The only exception is Whittlesey's opera *Ralvo, or the Pirate of the Gulf*, apparently performed at the close of the annual examination exercises several years in succession.

5. "Salem Normal Academy of Music" [1851], MVSA.

6. Orramel Whittlesey, "Harp of the Wild Wind" (Boston: Oliver Ditson, 1851), title page, in William L. Clements Library, University of Michigan, Ann Arbor, Michigan.

7. Ibid., mm. 29–45.

8. "Salem Normal Academy of Music" [1851], MVSA.

9. "Programme of a Concert at the Troy Female Seminary, December 16, 1847"; "Programme of a Concert, Given at the Troy Female Seminary, June 20, 1850"; "Programme of a Concert to Be Given at the Troy Female Seminary," June 29, 1849, folder "Troy Female Seminary Musical Programs," box "MSS#6, Middlebury Academy, Waterford Academy, Troy Female Seminary: Records, Articles, Pictures," EWSA. All programs are in this folder and box unless otherwise noted.

10. According to the title page of "Farewell to the Alps," Mary Ely, member of the seminary music faculty from 1845 to 1850, sang this ballad; however, as also noted on the title page, Gustave Blessner composed and dedicated it to Jane A. Andrews.

11. The only composers given are R. Taylor for "Psalm CV" and Pleyel for "Pleyel's Favorite German Hymn." Lucy Sheldon's Music Books 1 and 3, CLHS. See chapter 7n1 for information on Lucy Sheldon's music books.

12. Asahel Nettleton, *Village Hymns for Social Worship, Selected and Original: Designed as a Supplement to Dr. Watts's Psalms and Hymns* , 2nd ed. (Hartford, CT: Goodwin, 1824), preface.

13. Isaac Watts, comp., *The Psalms, Hymns, and Spiritual Songs, of the Rev. Isaac Watts, D.D., to Which Are Added, Select Hymns, from Other Authors; and Directions for Musical Expression. by Samuel Worcester, D.D.* New edition. The Selection Enlarged, and the Indexes Greatly Improved by Samuel M. Worcester (Boston: Crocker and Brewster, 1836), 4. Special Collections, Princeton Theological Seminary Library, Princeton, New Jersey.

14. A "Key of Expression" explained the symbols: a—very slow; e—slow; *a*—very soft; *e*—soft; p—slow and soft; g—slow and loud; o—quick; u—very quick; *o*—loud; *u*—very loud; b—quick and soft; s—quick and loud; d—variously distinctive. The prose included an explanation and terms for sentiments given in the "Key": *Pathetic* (p)—slow and soft; *Beautiful* (b)—quick and soft; *Spirited* (s)—quick and loud; and

Grand (g)—slow and loud (omitted from the "Key"). In some instances no change from the common is required, except "either a peculiar *distinctness* of utterance, or some peculiar *distinction* in the tone or modulation of voice." The letter "d" was used to denote this expression. A short dash after any other symbol indicates that the passage should be sung in a normal manner. Ibid., 4, 5; "Hymn 66," ibid., 547.

15. The meter is given at the top of the hymn, followed by the tune name. For instance, in the hymn in example 8.2., "C.M." is an abbreviation for "Common Meter," and the tune name is "York."

16. Lowell Mason, Edwards Amasa Park, and Austin Phelps, eds., *The Sabbath Hymn and Tune Book: For the Service of Song in the House of the Lord* (New York: Mason Brothers, 1859); George F. Root, *The Sabbath Bell, a Collection of Music for Choirs, Musical Associations, Singing-Schools, and the Home Circle, Consisting of Part I.—Singing-School Music. Part II.—Church Music. Part III.—Occasional and Concert Music* (New York: Mason Brothers, 1857).

17. Lowell Mason, *The Boston Academy's Collection of Church Music: Consisting of the Most Popular Psalm and Hymn Tunes, Anthems, Sentences, Chants, &c. Old and New: Together with Many Beautiful Pieces, Tunes and Anthems, Selected from the Masses and Other Works of Haydn, Mozart, Beethoven . . . and Other Distinguished Composers, Arr. and Adapted to English Words Expressly for This Work, Including, Also, Original Compositions by German, English and American Authors* (Boston: J. H. Wilkins and R. B. Carter, 1839).

18. Lowell Mason, comp., *Carmina Sacra; or Boston Collection of Church Music, Comprising the Most Popular Psalm and Hymn Tunes in General Use. Together with a Great Variety of New Tunes, Chants, Sentences, Motetts, and Anthems, Principally by Distinguished European Composers; the Whole Constituting One of the Most Complete Collections of Music for Choirs, Congregations, Singing Schools, and Societies, Extant.* 2nd ed. (Boston: J. H. Wilkins and R. B. Carter, 1841). Lowell Mason addressed the significance of new publications in the preface to the *Carmina Sacra*, arguing that they "facilitate the progress of music itself." Further, he claimed that a "new book of Church Music . . . founded on correct principles of science and taste" will broaden the awareness of the art. Mason emphasized the importance for choirs to regularly obtain modern music in order to progress. While old music is worthy of repetition, new publications "may possess some value . . . not found in their predecessors." Ibid., preface.

19. Ibid.

20. Springfield is approximately thirteen miles from South Hadley, the location of Mount Holyoke Female Seminary. Thus, the *Springfield Daily Republican* would have been one of the main newspapers of the area.

21. "Mount Holyoke Female Seminary," *Daily Republican*, Springfield, Massachusetts, August 1, 1845.

22. I. B. Woodbury, ed., *The Anthem Dulcimer: Constituting a Large and Choice Variety of New Tunes, Chants, Anthems, Motets, etc., from the Best Foreign and American Composers, with All the Old Tunes in Common Use; Together with a New and*

Greatly Improved Elementary Course, and a Choice Collection of Original Anthems. The Whole Comprising the Most Complete Collection of Sacred Music Ever Published (New York: F. J. Huntington, 1856). Mount Holyoke used *The Anthem Dulcimer* from 1850 through 1858.

23. A. N. Johnson, *The Key-Stone Collection of Church Music: A Complete Collection of Hymn Tunes, Anthems, Psalms, Chants, etc., to Which Is Added the Physiological System; for Training Choirs and Teaching Singing Schools; and the Cantata, The Morning of Freedom* (Lancaster City, PA: J. H. Sheaffer, 1868). See chapter 6 for more information on this book.

24. Other vocal selections included "He Was Despised" from Handel's *Messiah* and "God of Israel," "I Waited for the Lord," and "Salvation to Our God" (composers unidentified). "Mt. Holyoke Female Seminary. Order of Exercises for Public Examination, Commencing Monday, July 20, 1863," MHCASC.

25. Bradbury, *The Jubilee.*

26. "The Anniversary on Thursday. Mount Holyoke Female Seminary. The Annual Anniversary Exercises," *Springfield Daily Republican*, Springfield, Massachusetts, July 20, 1866. All four parts of this piece are written in the treble clef; however, the parts are notated as "1st Treble, 2d Treble, 1st Tenor, Bass." John Braham, "Through Forest and Meadow," *The Social Choir. Designed for a Class Book, and the Social Circle. Consisting of Selections from the Most Distinguished Composers, among Whom Are the Names of Rossini, Bellini, Von Weber, Auber, Herrold, Myerbeer, Weigl, and Many Others, with Several Compositions of the Editor. The Poetry Has Generally Been Selected with Care, and with Particular Reference to Moral Sentiment. The Music Is Arranged as Songs, Duets, Trios, and Quartettes, with an Accompaniment for the Piano Forte,* ed. George Kingsley, 5th ed. (Boston: Crocker and Brewster, 1847), 191. This is the earliest edition I was able to locate. Perhaps this was the typical designation for SSAA voice parts.

27. Given the emphasis on religious studies, it seems likely that all students would have sung hymns during devotional times at the school. Perhaps missing programs offers an explanation for the omission of more sacred literature than appears on surviving programs.

28. Emma Willard, "Rock'd in the Cradle of the Deep" (New York: C. E. Horn, ca. 1840), 3–7, in Albert and Shirley Small Special Collections, University of Virginia, Charlottesville, Virginia.

29. According to the "Stephen Collins Foster: Collection of American Popular Songs," it was published by C. E. Horn, New York, in 1840. http://www.stephen-foster -songs.de/amsong42.htm.

30. "Programme of Concert, To Be Given by the Teachers and Pupils of the Troy Female Seminary, Thursday Evening, February 9, 1854," EWSA.

31. "Programme of Concert, To Be Given by the Teachers and Pupils of the Troy Female Seminary Tuesday Evening, June 27, 1854, Edward Thorbecke, Director,"

EWSA. This might seem unusual given the title, since Easter would have occurred several weeks earlier. Most of the foreign titles were sung in English; this piece was "translated from the German of Tiedge."

32. "Consider the Lilies" was performed during the anniversary exercises of August 14, 1873. It was performed four years earlier on the examination exercise program at Mount Holyoke. "Mount Holyoke Female Seminary. Order of Exercises for the Thirty-Second Anniversary [July 12–15], 1869," MHCASC. It is listed on the Mount Holyoke program as a "recitative and Air." Miss Jane A. Andrews had sung this song during the "Firemen's Concert" in Troy, New York, on July 9, 1846. Topliff also composed "Ruth and Naomi," performed at Mount Holyoke's examination exercises, on July 20, 1863. Student M. Davis performed "Rock'd in the Cradle of the Deep" as the penultimate number on the morning session of the twenty-fourth examination exercises, July 8, 1863. MHCASC.

33. Examples include "Mother Can This the Glory Be?" by Stephen Ralph Glover; "Who Will Care for Mother Now?" by Charles Carroll Sawyer; Whittlesey's "Rest Warrior, Rest"; and "March Away Boys, March Away Cheerily," "The Girls at Home," "Take Your Gun and Go, John," and "Brave Boys Are They" (no composer is identified for the last four songs).

34. The Battle of Buena Vista on February 23, 1847, was possibly the most severe combat of the U.S.-Mexican War. "War (1846–1848): Battles of the War. The Battle of Buena Vista," PBS, http://www.pbs.org/kera/usmexicanwar/war/buena_vista.html.

35. "Mt. Holyoke Female Seminary. Order of Exercises for Public Examination, Commencing Tuesday, July 23, 1861"; "Mt. Holyoke Female Seminary. Order of Exercises for Public Examination, Commencing Monday, July 20th, 1863," MHCASC.

36. Two examples are "Hark the Goddess Diana" (no composer is given) and "The Minute Gun at Sea" by Matthew P. King. Both are noted as "A Favorite Duett." "Hark the Goddess Diana" was made famous as sung by Messrs. Hodgkinson and Williamson at the Anacreontic Society. The subject matter in both duets would not have been appropriate for female singers. ("Hark the Goddess Diana" is a hunting song, and "The Minute Gun at Sea" reflects the lifeboat man and his crew battling a storm to save an endangered ship.) Since the academy did admit a few males, including Lucy Sheldon's brother and Lyman Beecher's son, perhaps Lucy included such songs for their benefit. Lucy Sheldon's Music Books 3, 4, CLHS.

37. "There's More Luck about the House," Lucy Sheldon's Music Book 1, CLHS.

38. See chapter 7 for a discussion of the "Battle of Prague"; Dr. George K. Jackson, "A Winter's Evening," Lucy Sheldon's Music Book 2, CLHS.

39. Thomas Thompson, "Orphan Bess and Beggar Girl" (New York: I. and M. Paff, n.d.); James Hewitt, "Sadi the Moor: A Favorite New Song" (New York: J. Hewitt's Musical Repository, 1803).

40. For example, the score for "The Invitation" includes a German flute part that can be substituted for the violin. No composer is given for this song.

41. G. J. Webb and Lowell Mason, *The Odeon: A Collection of Secular Melodies, Arranged and Harmonized for Four Voices, Designed for Adult Singing Schools, and for Social Music Parties* (Boston: J. H. Wilkins and R. B. Carter, 1841).

42. Ibid., 138–46, 248–51, 303–4. No composer is named for "Hail Columbia."

43. Well-known composers include Bellini, J. B. Cramer, C. M. von Weber, Mozart, and Franz Hünten; some lesser-known names are T. H. Bailey, Miss Brown, S. Nelson, S. Lover, G. Kiallmark, C. E. Horn, M. P. King, and Carl Keller. While George J. Webb and Lowell Mason compiled this book, Webb's name appears several times as composer, but Mason's is not mentioned. "Friendship," "Erin! The Tear and the Smile in Thine Eyes," and "The Harp, that Once through Tara's Halls" all include "Irish Melody" instead of composers' names. Webb and Mason, *The Odeon*, 16, 245, 295.

44. Kingsley, *The Social Choir*.

45. With the exception of "Ruth and Naomi" by Topliff and "Song of David" (the composer or arranger is unidentified; [Thomas] Moore wrote the poetry), all other pieces are secular.

46. Kingsley, *The Social Choir*, title page.

47. Edward W. Hooker, *Music, as a Part of Female Education* (Boston: T. R. Marvin, 1843), 12–13.

48. George F. Root and Wm. B. Bradbury, *The Festival Glee Book: A Collection of Part Songs, Accompanied and Harmonized Melodies and Glees, A New Edition, Revised and Enlarged* (New York: Mason Brothers, 1859).

49. "The Crystal Stream," a temperance glee by Root; "When All Is Hushed," a Boat Song (glee) originally composed by Rudolphe Kreutzer and altered by Root; and John Blockley's "List, to the Convent Bells," arranged by Root.

50. Nicholas E. Tawa, *Sweet Songs for Gentle Americans: The Parlor Song in America, 1790–1860* (Bowling Green, OH: Bowling Green University Popular Press, 1980), 3.

51. "Salem Normal Academy of Music," [1851], brochure detailing the terms and conditions of Music Vale Seminary, MVSA.

52. Tawa, *Sweet Songs for Gentle Americans*, 75.

53. Vauxhall Gardens (1661–1859) was a major attraction in central London, especially for the arts; many singers became well-known names in the professional world. http://www.vauxhallgardens.com/vauxhall_gardens_briefhistory_page.html. For more information, see David Coke and Alan Borge, *Vauxhall Gardens: A History* (New Haven, CT: Yale University Press, 2011).

54. The name of the accompanist is not provided on the program; possibly it was a faculty member.

55. Tawa claims it was not unusual for Irish and Scottish musicians to compose songs using their native musical style and text with the intent of earning support from their native citizens. *Sweet Songs*, 70.

56. Samuel Lover, Esq., "True Love Can Ne'er Forget: A Favorite Ballad," *Songs of the Legends and Traditions of Ireland* (New York: Atwill's Music Saloon [1834–1847]), 2.

57. Maria Caterina Rosalbina Caradori-Allan (1800–1865), a native of Milan, enjoyed a highly successful career as a vocalist. Trained exclusively by her mother, Caradori-Allan began her career out of necessity as a means of support after her father's death. She toured Europe performing Italian opera; later in life she became recognized for singing oratorio and concert literature. *The New Grove Dictionary of Music and Musicians*, 2nd ed., s.v. "Caradori-Allan, Maria (Caterina Rosalbina)." Caradori-Allan also performed and toured in the United States. See Katherine K. Preston, *Opera on the Road; Traveling Opera Troupes in the United States, 1825–60* (Urbana: University of Illinois Press, 1993), 28, 39–40, 384n90.

58. An untitled glee by Lover was performed on the first half of this concert.

59. The title page of "The Flower Queen" advertises Mrs. Edward Loder and Miss Julia L. Northall as singers of this composition. In 1831 Eliza Watson married British composer Edward J. Loder and sang as Mrs. Loder in Bath, England, throughout the 1830s. After a short-lived marriage, she emigrated with her mother and siblings to America in 1840 to begin a new career. A young and "extravagantly puffed" prima donna, Northall likewise achieved popularity for her vocal ability. Vera Brodsky Lawrence, *Strong on Music: The New York Music Scene in the Days of George Templeton Strong*, vol. 1, *Resonances: 1836–1849* (Chicago: University of Chicago Press, 1988), 84, 279.

60. "The Old English Gentleman" was published around 1836 and performed at the seminary on March 23, 1838.

61. This is obviously British musician Henry Russell (1812/1813–1900), who achieved recognition for composing and singing some of the favored songs of the early nineteenth century (for example, "The Old Arm Chair") while living in America. Tawa, *Sweet Songs*, 70.

62. Ibid., 92. A minstrel song, "The Fine Old Colored Gentleman" by Dan Emmett, published in 1843, uses the same melody. "'The Old English Gentleman' A Popular English Ballad. As Sung by Mr. H. Russell" (New York: Atwill's Music Saloon, n.d.), title page, in Lester S. Levy Collection of Sheet Music, Sheridan Libraries, Johns Hopkins University, Baltimore, Maryland.

63. W[illiam] V[incent] Wallace, "Why Do I Weep for Thee?" (Macon, GA: John S. Screiner and Son, 1863), 2–3.

64. "Programme of Gustave Blessner's Farewell Concert at Apollo Hall, Troy, Tuesday Evening, May 14, 1850," EWSA.

65. John C. Andrews, "Somebody's Coming, but I'll Not Tell Who. Sung with Great Applause by Miss Jane A. Andrews. Written, Composed, Dedicated to Miss Eveline Hayner" (New York: Firth Pond, 1849). The title page does not mention this as a ballad, but it fits the description.

66. I have chosen to identify the pitches as C = middle C; thus here E is the third above middle C. John C. Andrews, "O Love Is Like the Rose, Rosalie," mm. 9–25. Johns Hopkins University, Levy Sheet Music Collection, box 102, Item. http://jhir.library .jhu.edu/handle/1774.2/32267.

67. Tawa, *Sweet Songs*, 183–84. See this source for a discussion of the harmonic construction of "Kathleen Mavourneen."

68. Ibid., 184–85.

69. Four editions of this song were published between 1838 and 1860. http://www.worldcat.org/identities/lccn-nr95045664.

70. Tawa, *Sweet Songs*, 9.

71. Jenny Lind, the "Swedish Nightingale," arrived in New York, September 1850, "to a veritable frenzy of excitement . . . similar to her reception by London audiences from 1847 through 1849," and continued "almost undiminished until her departure from North America in May 1852." Preston, *Opera on the Road*, 159. Eckert's "Swiss Song" was written for Henriette Sontag, who performed it widely in the United States (including Germania Musical Society concerts). See Vera Brodsky Lawrence, *Strong on Music: The New York Music Scene in the Days of George Templeton Strong*, vol. 2, *Reverberations: 1850–1856* (Chicago: University of Chicago Press, 1995).

72. It seems unusual that the seminary included "Swiss Song" on this program, since all of the other vocal pieces were sacred compositions. "Programme of Concert, To Be Given by the Teachers and Pupils of the Troy Female Seminary, Thursday Evening, February 9, 1854, Edward Thorbecke, Director," EWSA. Karl Anton Florian Eckert, "The Celebrated Swiss Song" (New York: William Hall & Son, 1852), mm. 46–56, in Sibley Music Library, Eastman School of Music, University of Rochester, Rochester, New York. Although the score contains two soprano lines (the first line "simplified"), it is unknown which version was performed on February 9, 1854.

73. See note 57 above for more information on Caradori-Allan. Pixis also composed a theme and variations on this theme for piano duet ("Brilliant Variations for Two Performers on One Piano Forte, on the Favorite Subject The Swiss Boy, or Der Schweizerbue, as Sung by Madlle. Sontag, Made. Carador and the Rainer Family" [London: I. Willis, 1800s]), title page.

74. Missing programs undoubtedly account for omissions. Jenny Lind's popularity preceded her arrival in 1850.

75. Faustina Hasse Hodges, "The Alp Horn" (New York: Firth Pond, n.d.), mm. 11–24, Albert and Shirley Small Special Collections Library, University of Virginia, Charlottesville, Virginia.

76. The edition I was able to obtain is for solo voice.

77. At least two versions of this trio exist: one published by Oliver Ditson in 1866, translated as "Stars of the Night Shine O'er Us," and one published by G. Schirmer in 1871 ("Fountain of Love Eternal"). It is unknown which edition the young women performed.

78. For example, see "Good Night" from Flotow's *Martha* in the discussion of opera in this chapter.

79. "Report," *Catalogue of the Officers and Pupils of the Troy Female Seminary, for the Academic Year, Commencing September 10, 1856, and Ending June 24, 1857. Together*

with the Conditions of Admittance, etc. (Troy, NY: A. W. Scribner, 1857), 28, folder "TFS Catalogues, 1857," EWSA.

80. This is undoubtedly Euphrosyne Parepa(-Rosa) (1836–1874), a prominent nineteenth-century Scottish soprano. Preston, *Opera on the Road*, 382n50; "The Bateman Concerts," *American Art Journal* 6, no. 1 (1866): 3, http://www.jstor.org.proxy.libraries .uc.edu/stable/25306511.

81. This is the sole piece by Mozart or any classical composer on extant programs. Misses Irvin, DeVine, and O[ra] Maginnis performed this piece on June 29, 1871.

82. The title of the quartet is not given on the program.

83. The only copy of Auber's "El Jaleo de Xeres" I was able to obtain was in English, arranged and adapted by Theodore Victor Giubilei, "El Jaleo de Xeres: A Popular Air Composed by Auber. As Sung with Great Applause by Mrs. Seguin & Miss Poole. Arranged & Adapted by Theodore Victor Giubilei. The Words by F. W. Rosier, Esq." (New York: Wm. DuBois, 1841), title page. Soprano Anne Seguin and her husband, Edward, "played an important role in the cultivation of English opera" in the United States during the 1840s. Preston, *Opera on the Road*, 51. Contralto Clara Poole performed with the Seguins in Philadelphia and New York. Ibid., 41.

84. Madame Bishop made "Je suis la Bajadere" popular, singing it in French. (See note 93 for more information on Madame Bishop.) No composer's name is given on the program for "Tu Sandunga," but Signor Blanco is commonly given as the composer. Robert Nicholas-Charles Bochsa, arr., "I Am the Bayadere [Je Suis la Bajadere]: Tambourine Song" (New York: Firth Pond, 1843); Signor Blanco, "Tu Sandunga [What Enchantment]: The Celebrated Spanish Song" (New York: Firth, Pond, and Hall, 1848). Although the English translation is also given on the scores for both songs, foreign titles on the program indicate that the performers sang these songs in the original languages.

85. Pico performed in the United States during the 1840s. Preston, *Opera on the Road*, 127, 128, 396n109.

86. Another of Abt's songs was performed in 1873: "Amor der Spotter." Abt toured the United States in 1872, which may have prompted the seminary to continue having students sing his songs. Possibly missing programs recorded other performances of Abt's songs.

87. Francis Lynch and James Power, "Dearest Mae: A Celebrated Ethiopian Song Sung by the Harmoneons" (Philadelphia: A. Fiot, 1847), 5. The Harmoneon Family Singers was a Negro minstrel group. Sometime between 1843 and 1844, the Harmoneons became known as the "Albino Minstrels" and the "Albino Family." Their concerts satirized the seriousness of the popular performing Hutchinson Family Singers: "the albino makeup [symbolized] a purity of rectitude that ran counter to the audience's expectation of blackness and its gleefully derogatory chaos and good-natured fun." The extant playbills from 1846 to 1851 denote the concerts performed as "Whites and Blacks": "the first half performed [with whitened faces and flaxen wigs]

as 'Citizens,' the second in blackface as 'Ethiopians.'" Charles D. Martin, *The White African American Body: A Cultural and Literary Exploration* (New Brunswick, NJ: Rutgers University Press, 2002), 89.

88. Reginald Spofforth, "Hail! Smiling Morn," mm. 26–40. National Library of Australia.

89. No composer is named for *Paul and Virginia*. It is likely Jean-François Lesueur's *Paul et Virginie*.

90. The program on February 1, 1853, for example (fig. 7.1), opened with the overture to Hérold's *Zampa* arranged for eight hands. The fourth performance on part 1 was a duo for harp and piano on airs from Bellini's *La Sonnambula*, arranged by Théodore Labarre. A potpourri for two pianos on airs from *I Puritani*, arranged by Johann Georg Lickl, opened the second half of the program; and Thalberg's arrangement of "La Serenade de Don Pasquale" as a *fantaisie* for piano was number four. No given name for Lickl is included on the program. See chapter 7 for more information on concerts that included operatic overtures arranged for piano ensemble, or arias set as theme and variations for piano solo, airs arranged as a *fantaisie* for piano, etc.

91. Gustave Blessner taught violin during the 1849–1850 school year. There is no evidence that violin instruction continued to be offered after he left. Perhaps some current students played violin as well as cello and flute before coming to Troy, or other faculty were proficient on these instruments. Another possibility is that the school hired local artists, given the musical climate of the town. The opening number on the concert was the second movement of a G major trio by Beethoven for piano, violin, and cello.

92. William Michael Rooke, "To the Vine Feast Song Sung by Mrs. W. Penson, in the Grand Opera of *Amilie, or The Love Test*, Performed at the National Theatre" (New York: Firth, Pond, n.d), in New York State Library, Albany, New York. Mrs. William Penson, soprano, was the wife of the orchestra leader at the National Theatre. Preston, *Opera on the Road*, 52, 54.

93. See note 84 for more information on Mrs. Anna Bishop. Preston, *Opera on the Road*, 233. "The Banks of the Guadalquiver, Composed by L. Lavenu, as Sung by Mrs. Bishop, in the Opera of Linda di Chamounix" (New York: Joseph F. Atwill, 1847).

94. Additional trios and quartets appeared in the non-operatic repertoire.

95. Duets from operas by Bellini, Rossini, Verdi, and Wallace were also part of the repertoire. Examples include untitled duets from *Montecchi e Capuletti* and *Norma* by Bellini, "Giorno d'orroe" from Rossini's opera *Semiramide*, "Qui mi trasse" from Verdi's *Ernani*, and "Holy Mother" from Wallace's *Maritana*.

96. William Michael Rooke, "Rest, Spirit, Rest: Hymn Sung by Miss Shirreff & Chorus, in the Grand Opera *Amilie, or The Love Test*, Performed at the National Theatre" (New York: Firth and Hall, n.d.), mm. 45–56, in Sterling Memorial Library, Yale University. Jane Shirreff's and John Wilson's concert tour of 1839 included Troy, New York. See map in Preston, *Opera on the Road*, 79.

97. Sarah Augusta Shoner, "Karolyn Bradford Whittlesey: 1843–1928," part 3, 37, 31, unpublished notebook (hereafter, "KBW"), MVSA.

98. Florence Whittlesey Thompson, "Music Vale," *Connecticut Quarterly* 3, no. 1 (1897): 21, MVSA.

99. Shoner, "KBW," part 3, 37.

100. Ibid., 41. Shoner suggests that "inmates" indicated that Whittlesey was involved in writing the opera. Whittlesey spared no expense in elaborate productions. According to the thirtieth annual examination program, June 24, 1869, the price of admission was still one dollar. I have not found evidence of other operas produced at Music Vale, although it seems likely given the elaborate facility.

101. Pierce, *Ruth*, quoted in Emily Noyes Vanderpoel, comp., and Elizabeth C. Barney Buel, ed., *Chronicles of a Pioneer School from 1792 to 1833 Being the History of Miss Sarah Pierce and Her Litchfield School* (Cambridge, MA: University Press, 1903), 84–100; *Jephthah's Daughter*, quoted in *Chronicles of a Pioneer School*, 119–145.

102. Vincenzo Pucitta, "Strike the Cymbal: Song of Rejoicing for the Conquest of Goliath by David," mm. 1–44, no. 23 of Carr's *Musical Miscellany* (Baltimore: J. Carr, [1814]), 98, in Ohio State University Library, Columbus, Ohio. This song was "one of the most admired pieces performed at the Oratorio given in the Church of St. Augustine on the 13th of April 1814 for the Orphan Asylum of Philadelphia." Ibid., 97.

103. Male music faculty and guests occasionally participated in the concerts at Troy.

Afterword

1. R. K. Buehrle, "Educational Position of the Pennsylvania Germans," *Pennsylvania-German Society Proceedings and Addresses* 4 (n.d.): 128, quoted in Mabel Haller, "Early Moravian Education in Pennsylvania," *Transactions of the Moravian Historical Society* (Nazareth, PA: Moravian Historical Society, 1953), 15:230n94.

2. There is no indication that Orramel Whittlesey's view of women's intelligence or need of education differed from that of Emma Willard, Sarah Pierce, or Mary Lyon. Since he focused on music, his name is not relevant to this area of the discussion.

3. Robert Winthrop Marsh, "The Higher Education of Woman," *Potter's American Monthly* 10, no. 73 (1878): 1, ProQuest.

4. S., "Article 2—No Title ["Female Seminaries"], *New York Mirror: A Weekly Gazette of Literature and the Fine Arts* 10, no. 21 (1832): 167, ProQuest. The author may have been referring to Emma Willard, whose school opened in 1821 and is later referred to in the same article.

5. Marsh, "Higher Education of Woman," 1.

6. S., "Article 2—No Title," 167.

Bibliography

Primary Archival Sources

Collection of the Litchfield Historical Society, Litchfield, Connecticut (CLHS).
Emma Willard School Archives (Troy Female Seminary), Emma Willard School, Troy, New York (EWSA).
Mount Holyoke College Archives and Special Collections, South Hadley, Massachusetts (MHCASC).
Music Vale Seminary Archives, Salem, Connecticut (MVSA).

Secondary Sources

Abell, Mrs. L. G. *Woman in Her Various Relations: Containing Practical Rules for American Females*. New York: R. T. Young, 1853.
Adams, Abigail, to John Adams, August 14, 1776. In *Adams Family Correspondence*, edited by L. H. Butterfield. Cambridge, MA: Belknap Press, 1963.
Adams, Abigail. *Letters of Mrs. Adams, the Wife of John Adams*. Boston: C. C. Little and J. Brown, 1840. Gale.
Adams, Daniel. *Adam's New Arithmetic; Arithmetic, in Which the Principles of Operating by Numbers Are Analytically Explained and Synthetically Applied*. Keene, NH: J. Prentiss, 1827.
"An Address of Female Education, delivered in Portsmouth, New Hampshire, October 26, 1827." *American Journal of Education* 3, no. 1 (1828): 52–58. ProQuest.
"Advantages of Musical Instruction." *Musical Visitor* 2, no. 8 (1841): 58–59. ProQuest.
Alcott, [William]. "Female Education: Young Woman's Guide." *Musical Reporter* 5 (May 1841): 218. ProQuest.
Allmendinger, David F., Jr., "Mount Holyoke Students Encounter the Need for Life-Planning, 1837–1850." *History of Education Quarterly* 19, no. 1 (1979): 27–46. doi: 10.2307/367808.

Amicus. "The Influence of a Musical Education." *The Family Minstrel: A Musical and Literary Journal* 1, no. 22 (1835): 170–71. ProQuest.

Arthur, T. S. *Advice to Young Ladies on Their Duties and Conduct in Life*. Boston: Phillips and Sampson, 1848.

———. "The Young Music Teacher." *Arthur's Ladies' Magazine of Elegant Literature and the Fine Arts* (October 1844): 191–97. ProQuest.

Astell, Mary. *A Serious Proposal to the Ladies, for the Advancement of Their True and Greatest Interest. In Two Parts. By a Lover of Her Sex*. London, 1697 [1701]. Eighteenth Century Collections Online. Gale.

Backus, A[ugustus], comp. *History, Theory, and Analysis of Music: Designed for the Music Department of the Troy Female Seminary*. Troy, NY: Tuttle, Belcher, Burton, 1839.

Barnard, Henry, ed. *Educational Biography, Pt. 1. Teachers and Educators*. Vol. 1. *United States: Memoirs of Teachers, Educators, and Promoters and Benefactors of Education, Literature, and Science*. 2nd ed. New York: F. C. Brownell, 1859.

"The Bateman Concerts." *American Art Journal* 6, no. 1 (1866): 3. ProQuest.

"The Beauties of Music." *Ladies' Garland and Family Wreath Embracing Tales, Sketches, Incidents, History, Poetry, Music* 1, no. 4 (1837): 62. ProQuest.

Boas, Louise Schutz. *Woman's Education Begins; The Rise of Women's Colleges*. New York: Arno Press, 1971.

Boers, David. *History of American Education Primer*. New York: Peter Lang Publishing, 2007.

Brickley, Lynne Templeton. "Sarah Pierce's Litchfield Female Academy, 1792–1833." EdD diss., Harvard University, 1985.

Buehrle, R. K. "Educational Position of the Pennsylvania Germans." *Pennsylvania-German Society Proceedings and Address* 4 (n.d.): 128. Quoted in Mabel Haller, "Early Moravian Education in Pennsylvania." Vol. 15 of *Transactions of the Moravian Historical Society*. Nazareth, PA: Moravian Historical Society, 1953.

Burnap, George W. *Lectures on the Sphere and Duties of Woman and Other Subjects*. Baltimore: John Murphy, 1841.

Campbell, Jennifer E. P. "Music Education at the Troy Female Seminary: 1817–1904." PhD diss., University of Mississippi, 2016.

Chase, Gilbert. *America's Music: From the Pilgrims to the Present*. Rev. 3rd ed. Urbana: University of Illinois Press, 1992.

Clark, J. Bunker. *The Dawning of American Keyboard Music*. New York: Greenwood Press, 1988.

Clinton, DeWitt. "1819. January. Legislature, Forty-Second Session: Opening Speech." In *State of New York: Messages from the Governors Comprising Executive Communications to the Legislature and Other Papers Relating to Legislation from the Organization of the First Colonial Assembly in 1683 to and Including the Year 1906. With Notes*, edited by Charles Z. Lincoln. Vol. 2. Albany: J. B. Lyon, 1909.

Cogan, Frances B. *All-American Girl: The Ideal of Real Womanhood in Mid-Nineteenth-Century America*. Athens: University of Georgia Press, 1989.

Coke, David, and Alan Borge. *Vauxhall Gardens: A History.* New Haven, CT: Yale University Press, 2011.

Colburn, Warren. *Intellectual Arithmetic upon the Inductive Method of Instruction.* Bellows-Falls, VT, 1829.

Colby, Frederick Myron. "Emma Hart Willard and Her Work." *Potter's American Monthly* 13, no. 96 (1879): 436–41. ProQuest.

Cole, Arthur C. *A Hundred Years of Mount Holyoke College: The Evolution of an Educational Ideal.* New Haven, CT: Yale University Press, 1940.

Cott, Nancy F. *The Bonds of Womanhood: Women's Sphere in New England, 1780–1835.* New Haven, CT: Yale University Press, 1978.

Crawford, Richard. *America's Musical Life: A History.* New York: W. W. Norton, 2001.

Cross, Barbara, ed. *The Autobiography of Lyman Beecher.* Vol. 1. Cambridge: Belknap Press of Harvard University Press, 1961.

Curti, Merle. *The Social Ideas of American Educators, with New Chapter on the Last Twenty-Five Years.* Paterson, NJ: Pageant Books, 1959.

DePauw, Linda Grant, and Conover Hunt, with the assistance of Miriam Schneir. *Remember the Ladies: Women in America, 1750–1815.* New York: Viking Press, 1976.

Dexter, Elizabeth Williams Anthony. *Career Women of America, 1776–1840.* Francestown, NH: M. Jones, [1950].

DuBois, Ellen Carol, and Lynn Dumenil. *Through Women's Eyes: An American History with Documents.* Vol. 1. 2nd ed. Boston: Bedford/St. Martin's, 2009.

Edmonds, Anne Carey. *A Memory Book: Mount Holyoke College, 1837–1987.* South Hadley, MA: Mount Holyoke College, 1988.

"Emma Willard." *Journal of Education* 27, no. 6 (1893): 1–2.

Fairbanks, Mary J. Mason, ed. *Emma Willard and Her Pupils, or Fifty Years of Troy Female Seminary: 1822–1872.* New York: Mrs. Russell Sage, 1898.

Fennelly, Catherine. "Sarah Pierce." In *Notable American Women, 1607–1950: A Biographical Dictionary.* Vol. 3, 67–68, edited by Edward T. James, Janet Wilson James, and Paul S. Boyer. Cambridge, MA: Belknap Press, 1971.

Fisk, Fidelia. *Reflections of Mary Lyon, with Selections from Her Instructions to the Pupils in Mt. Holyoke Female Seminary.* Boston: American Tract Society, 1866. Reprint, Los Olivos, CA: Olive Press Publications, 1995.

Fitzpatrick, Edward A. *The Educational Views and Influence of DeWitt Clinton.* New York: Teachers College, Columbia University, 1911. Reprint, New York: Arno Press, 1969.

Fowler, Henry. "Educational Services of Mrs. Emma Willard." In *Memoirs of Teachers, Educators, and Promoters and Benefactors of Education, Literature, and Science.* 2nd ed., edited by Henry Barnard. New York: F. C. Brownell, 1859.

Goodsell, Willystine. *Pioneers of Women's Education in the United States: Emma Willard, Catharine Beecher, and Mary Lyon.* New York: AMS Press, 1970. Reprint of the 1931 edition.

Gordon, Ann D., and Mari Jo Buhle. "Sex and Class in Colonial and Nineteenth-Century America." In *Liberating Women's History: Theoretical and Critical Essays*, edited by Berenice A. Carroll. Urbana: University of Illinois Press, 1976.

Gottschalk, Louis Moreau. *Notes of a Pianist*, edited, with a prelude, a postlude, and explanatory notes, by Jeanne Behrend. New York: Da Capo Press, 1979.

Green, Elizabeth Alden. *Mary Lyon and Mount Holyoke: Opening the Gates.* Hanover, NH: University Press of New England, 1979.

Guilford, L[inda] T[hayer], comp. *The Use of a Life: Memorials of Mrs. Z. P. Grant Banister.* New York: American Tract Society, [1851].

Hale, Sarah Josepha Buell. *Manners, or, Happy Homes and Good Society.* New York: Arno Press, 1972. First published 1868 by J. E. Tilton (Boston).

———. "Emma Willard." In *Woman's Record; or Sketches of All Distinguished Women, from the Creation to A.D. 1868. Arranged in Four Eras. With Selections from Authoresses of Each Era.* 3rd ed. Revised with additions. New York: Harper and Brothers, 1870. Gale.

Hamilton, Gail. "An American Queen." *North American Review* 143, no. 359 (1886): 329–44. ProQuest.

———. *Gala-Days.* Boston: Ticknor and Fields, 1863.

Hamm, Charles. *Music in the New World.* New York: W. W. Norton, 1983.

Historical Sketch of Mount Holyoke Seminary. Springfield, MA: Clark W. Bryan, 1878.

History's Women: The Unsung Heroines. http://www.historyswomen.com/thearts/MaryAbigailDodge.html.

Hitchcock, Edward, comp. *The Power of Christian Benevolence Illustrated in the Life and Labors of Mary Lyon.* New Edition. New York: American Tract Society, 1858.

Hitchcock, H. Wiley. *Music in the United States: A Historical Introduction*, with a final chapter by Kyle Gann, 4th ed. Upper Saddle River, NJ: Prentice Hall, 2000.

Hooker, Edward W. *Music as a Part of Female Education.* Boston: T. R. Marvin, 1843. Reprint of "Music as a Part of Female Education." *Musical Reporter*, no. 9 (September 1841). ProQuest.

Johnson, Frances Hall. *Music Vale Seminary: 1835–1876.* New Haven, CT: Yale University Press, 1934.

Keene, James A. *A History of Music Education in the United States.* 2nd ed. Centennial, CO: Glenbridge Publishing, 2009.

Kelley, Mary. *Learning to Stand and Speak: Women, Education, and Public Life in America's Republic.* Chapel Hill: University of North Carolina Press, 2006.

Kendall, Elaine. *Peculiar Institutions: An Informal History of the Seven Sister Colleges.* New York: G. P. Putnam's Sons, 1976.

Kerber, Linda K. *Women of the Republic: Intellect and Ideology in Revolutionary America.* Chapel Hill: University of North Carolina Press, 1980.

Kimber, Marion Wilson. *The Elocutionists: Women, Music, and the Spoken Word.* Urbana: University of Illinois Press, 2017.

"Ladies Department: The Use and Abuse of Music." *Western Christian Advocate* 7, no. 27 (1840): 108. ProQuest.

Lansing, Marion, ed. *Mary Lyon through Her Letters*. Boston: Books, 1937.

Lawrence, Vera Brodsky. *Strong on Music: The New York Music Scene in the Days of George Templeton Strong*. Vol. 1, *Resonances: 1836–1849*. Chicago: University of Chicago Press, 1988.

———. *Strong on Music: The New York Music Scene in the Days of George Templeton Strong*, Vol. 2, *Reverberations: 1850–1856*. Chicago: University of Chicago Press, 1995.

Lee and Walker's Musical Almanac for 1869. For the Use of Seminaries, Professors of Music, and the Musical Public. Being a Condensed Catalogue; to Which Is Added a List of Our Latest and Best Publications. Philadelphia: Lee and Walker, 1869.

Lerner, Gerda. *The Woman in American History*. Menlo Park, CA: Addison-Wesley, 1971.

Llamarada, The. South Hadley, MA: Mount Holyoke College, 1915.

Loesser, Arthur. *Men, Women, and Pianos: A Social History*. New York: Simon and Schuster, 1954.

Lord, John. *The Life of Emma Willard*. New York: D. Appleton, 1873.

Lott, R. Allen. *From Paris to Peoria: How European Piano Virtuosos Brought Classical Music to the American Heartland*. New York: Oxford University Press, 2003.

Lutz, Alma. *Emma Willard: Daughter of Democracy*. Boston: Houghton Mifflin, 1929.

Maclean, Sydney R. "Lyon, Mary." In *Notable American Women 1607–1950: A Biographical Dictionary*. Vol. 2, 443–47, edited by Edward T. James, Janet Wilson James, and Paul S. Boyer. Cambridge, MA: Belknap Press, 1971.

Mark, Michael L., and Charles L. Gary. *A History of American Music Education*. New York: Rowman and Littlefield Education, 2007.

Marsh, Robert Winthrop. "The Higher Education of Woman." *Potter's American Monthly (1875–1882)* 10, no. 73 (1878): 1–15. ProQuest.

Martin, Charles D. *The White African American Body: A Cultural and Literary Exploration*. New Brunswick, NJ: Rutgers University Press, 2002.

McDannell, Colleen. *The Christian Home in Victorian America, 1840–1900*. Bloomington: Indiana University Press, 1986.

Mechanic, T., and A. W. Farmer. "Music in Common Schools: Number Two." *Boston Musical Gazette; A Semimonthly Journal, Devoted to the Science of Music* 1, no. 9 (1838): 68. ProQuest.

———. "Miscellaneous: Music in Common Schools: Number Three." *Boston Musical Gazette; A Semimonthly Journal, Devoted to the Science of Music* 1, no. 10 (1838): 74–75. ProQuest.

"Music, as a Branch of Common Education." *American Annals of Education* 1, no. 2 (1831): 64–67. ProQuest.

"Music, as a Branch of Common Education." *American Annals of Education* 1, no. 6 (1831): 269–73. ProQuest.

"Music in Common Schools." *Boston Musical Visitor* 3, no. 4 (1842): 52. ProQuest.

Nash, Margaret A. *Women's Education in the United States, 1780–1840*. New York: Palgrave Macmillan, 2005.

Naylor, Natalie A. "Emma Hart Willard." In *Women Educators in the United States, 1820–1993: A Bio-bibliographical Sourcebook*, edited by Maxine Schwartz Seller. Westport, CT: Greenwood Press, 1994.

Nixon, William. "A Guide to Instruction on the Pianoforte." *American Musical Journal* 1, no. 12 (1835): 283–85. ProQuest.

———. *A Guide to Instruction on the Piano-forte: Designed for the Use of Both Parents and Pupils; In a Series of Short Essays, Dedicated to the Young Ladies of the Musical Seminary*. Cincinnati: Josiah Drake, 1834.

"On Cultivation of Taste." *Ladies' Garland and Family Wreath Embracing Tales, Sketches, Incidents, History, Poetry, Music, etc.* 1, no. 1 (April 15, 1837): a12. ProQuest.

Osborne, William. *Music in Ohio*. Kent, OH: Kent State University Press, 2004.

Perry, Ruth. *The Celebrated Mary Astell: An Early English Feminist*. Chicago: University of Chicago Press, 1986.

Phelps, Almira. *The Female Student; or Lectures to Young Ladies on Female Education. For the Use of Mothers, Teachers, and Pupils*. New York: Leavitt, Lord, 1836.

Preston, Katherine K. *Opera on the Road: Traveling Opera Troupes in the United States, 1825–60*. Urbana: University of Illinois Press, 1993.

"Progress of Female Education." *American Journal, and Annals of Education and Instruction* 1, no. 7 (1830): 421–23. ProQuest.

Rowson, Susan. *Mentoria*. Philadelphia, 1794. Quoted in Judith Tick, *American Women Composers before 1870*. Ann Arbor, MI: UMI Research Press, 1983. Reprint, Rochester, NY: University of Rochester Press, 1995.

Rush, Benjamin. *Thoughts upon Female Education, Accommodated to the Present State of Society, Manners, and Government in the United States of America. Addressed to the Visitors of the Young Ladies' Academy in Philadelphia, 28 July 1787, at the Close of the Quarterly Examination*. Philadelphia: Prichard and Hall, 1787. Gale.

Rush, Dr. [Benjamin]. "Use of Vocal Music." *The Euterpeiad; An Album of Music, Poetry & Prose* (1830–1831) 1, no. 2 (1830): 9. ProQuest.

Ryan, Mary P. *Womanhood in America: From Colonial Times to the Present*, 3rd ed. New York: Franklin Watts, 1983.

S. "Article 2—No Title" ["Female Seminaries"]. *New York Mirror: A Weekly Gazette of Literature and the Fine Arts* 10, no. 21 (1832): 167. ProQuest.

Scott, Anne Firor. *Making the Invisible Woman Visible*. Urbana: University of Illinois Press, 1984.

Senex [Rev. William Woodbridge]. "Female Education in the Last Century." *American Annals of Education* 1, no. 11 (1831): 522–26. ProQuest.

Sigourney, L[ydia] H[oward]. *Letters to Young Ladies*, 3rd ed. New York: Harper and Bros., 1837.

Sizer, Theodore, et al. *To Ornament Their Minds: Sarah Pierce's Litchfield Female Academy, 1792–1833*, edited by Catherine Keene Fields and Lisa C. Kightlinger. Litchfield, CT: Litchfield Historical Society, 1993.

Smith, Jewel A. *Music, Women, and Pianos in Antebellum Bethlehem, Pennsylvania: The Moravian Young Ladies' Seminary*. Bethlehem, PA: Lehigh University Press, 2008.

———. "Music, Women, and Pianos: The Moravian Young Ladies' Seminary in Antebellum Bethlehem, Pennsylvania (1815–1860)." PhD diss., University of Cincinnati, 2003.

Solie, Ruth A. "'Girling' at the Parlor Piano." Chap. 3 in *Music in Other Words: Victorian Conversations*. Berkley: University of California Press, 2004.

Solomon, Barbara Miller. *In the Company of Educated Women*. New Haven, CT: Yale University Press, 1985.

Sophia, "Article 2—No Title." *Evening Fire-side; or, Literary Miscellany* 1, no. 17 (1805): 5–6. ProQuest.

Starr, S. Frederick. *Bamboula: The Life and Times of Louis Moreau Gottschalk*. New York: Oxford University Press, 1995.

Stow, Sarah D. [Locke]. *History of Mount Holyoke Seminary, South Hadley, Mass. during Its First Half Century, 1837–1887*. South Hadley, MA: Mount Holyoke Female Seminary, 1887.

"Suggestions to Parents on Female Education: Accomplishments." *American Journal of Education* 3, no. 5 (1828): 276–83. ProQuest.

Tawa, Nicholas E. *Sweet Songs for Gentle Americans: The Parlor Song in America, 1790–1860*. Bowling Green, OH: Bowling Green University Popular Press, 1980.

Tick, Judith. *American Women Composers before 1870*. Ann Arbor, MI: UMI Research Press, 1983. Reprint, Rochester, NY: University of Rochester Press, 1995.

"Thoughts on Music." *American Annals of Education* (February 1837): 81–82. ProQuest.

Tocqueville, Alexis de. *Democracy in America*. Translated by Henry Reeve, with original preface and notes by John C. Spencer, 4th ed. Vol. 2. New York: J. and H. G. Langley, 1841.

"TROY FEMALE SEMINARY: Method of Government Studies Pursued Examination Domestic Training—Manners, Morals, and Health General Remarks." *American Ladies' Magazine; Containing Original Tales, Essays, Literary & Historical Sketches, Poetry, Criticism, Music, and a Great Variety of Matter Connected with Many Subjects of Importance and Interest (1834–1836)* 8, no. 12 (1835): 700–711. ProQuest.

Vanderpoel, Emily Noyes, comp., and Elizabeth C. Barney Buel, ed., *Chronicles of a Pioneer School from 1792 to 1833 Being the History of Miss Sarah Pierce and Her Litchfield School*. Cambridge, MA: University Press, 1903.

Vanderpoel, Emily Noyes, comp. *More Chronicles of a Pioneer School from 1792 to 1833 Being Added History on the Litchfield Academy Kept by Miss Sarah Pierce and Her Nephew, John Pierce Brace*. Cambridge, MA: University Press, 1927.

Vidi, Ipse. "Musical Talent." *American Annals of Education* 1, no. 11 (1831): 518–21. ProQuest.

Vitz, Robert C. *The Queen and the Arts: Cultural Life in Nineteenth-Century Cincinnati*. Kent, OH: Kent State University Press, 1989.

"Vocal Music." *The Euterpeiad; An Album of Music, Poetry, and Prose* 2, no. 1 (1831): 4–5. ProQuest.

"War (1846–1848): Battles of the War. The Battle of Buena Vista." PBS. http://www
.pbs.org/kera/usmexicanwar/war/buena_vista.html.

Welter, Barbara. "The Cult of True Womanhood: 1820–1860." *American Quarterly* 18 (1966): 151–74.

Whicher, George F., ed. *William Gardiner Hammond: Remembrance of Amherst, an Undergraduate's Diary, 1846–1848*. New York: Columbia University Press, 1946.

Willard, Emma. *Astronography or Astronomical Geography, with the Use of the Globes*. Troy, NY: Merriam Moore, 1854.

———. "Mrs Willard on Female Education: An Address to the Public; Particularly to the Members of the Legislature of New York, Proposing a Plan for Female Education 'Defects in the Present Mode of Female Education, and Their Causes' of the Principles by Which Education Should Be Regulated; Sketch of a Female Seminary Benefits of Female Seminaries." *American Ladies' Magazine; Containing Original Tales, Essays, Literary and Historical Sketches, Poetry, Criticism, Music, and a Great Variety of Matter Connected with Many Subjects of Importance and Interest*, 7, no. 4 (1834): 163–73. ProQuest.

Wollstonecraft, Mary. *A Vindication of the Rights of Woman: With Strictures on Political and Moral Subjects*. London, 1792.

Woloch, Nancy, comp. *Early American Women: A Documentary History, 1600–1900*. 2nd rev. ed. Boston: McGraw-Hill, 2002.

———. *Woman and the American Experience*. New York: Alfred A. Knopf, 1984.

Woodbridge, William C. "On Vocal Music as a Branch of Common Education: Communicated to the American Lyceum." *American Annals of Education* 3, no. 5 (1833): 193–212. ProQuest.

Woody, Thomas. *A History of Women's Education in the United States*. 2 vols. New York: Science Press, 1929.

Musical Scores and Collections

Andrews, John C. "My Own Sunny France." Troy, NY: John C. Andrews, 1837.

———. "Somebody's Coming, But I'll Not Tell Who. Sung with Great Applause by Miss Jane A. Andrews. Written, Composed, Dedicated to Miss Eveline Hayner." New York: Firth, Pond, 1849.

Blanco, Signor. "Tu Sandunga [What Enchantment]: The Celebrated Spanish Song." New York: Firth, Pond, and Hall, 1848.

Blessner, Gustave. "The Empire State Quick Step." Troy, NY: William Hall and Son, 1850.

Bochsa, Robert Nicholas-Charles, arr. "I Am the Bayadere [Je Suis Le Bajadere]: Tambourine Song." New York: Firth, Pond, 1843.

Bradbury, William B. *The Jubilee: An Extensive Collection of Church Music for the Choir, the Congregation, and the Singing-School. New Edition, Containing Additional Anthems, Opening and Closing Pieces. Etc.* New York: Mason Brothers, 1858.

Campana, Fabio. "Madre del Sommo Amore" (translated as "Stars of the Night Shine O'er Us"). Boston: Oliver Ditson, 1866.

———. "Madre del Sommo Amore" (translated as "Fountain of Love Eternal"). New York: G. Schirmer, 1871.

"The Celebrated One Finger'd Sliding Waltz." Albert and Shirley Small Special Collections Library, University of Virginia, Charlottesville, Virginia.

Comettant, Oscar. "Gabrielle: Etude d'Expression pour Piano." New York: Horace Waters, 1853.

Eckert, Karl Anton Florian. "The Celebrated Swiss Song." New York: William Hall and Son, 1852. Sibley Music Library, Eastman School of Music, University of Rochester, Rochester, New York.

Giubilei, Theodore Victor, arr. "El Jaleo de Xeres: A Popular Air Composed by Auber. As Sung with Great Applause by Mrs. Seguin & Miss Poole. Arranged & Adapted by Theodore Victor Giubilei. The Words by F. W. Rosier, Esq." New York: Wm. DuBois, 1841.

Grobe, Charles. "Smile On: Brilliant Variations on Wallace's Beautiful Melody, 'Katie Strang.'" New York: William Hall and Son, 1838. Digital Collection: Nineteenth Century Music, University of North Carolina at Chapel Hill, Music Library.

Hastings, Thomas, and Wm. B. Bradbury. *The Psalmodist; A Choice Collection of Psalm and Hymn Tunes, Chiefly New; Adapted to the Very Numerous Metres Now in Use, Together with Chants, Anthems, Motets, and Various Other Pieces; Choirs, Congregations, Singing Schools and Musical Associations: Most of Which Are Now for the First Time Presented to the American Public.* New York: Mark H. Newman, 1844.

Hewitt, James. "Sadi the Moor: A Favorite New Song." New York: J. Hewitt's Musical Repository, 1803.

Hodges, Faustina Hasse. "The Alp Horn." New York: Firth, Pond, n.d. Albert and Shirley Small Special Collections Library, University of Virginia, Charlottesville, Virginia.

Iucho, Wilhelm. "Third Calisthenic Rondo." New York: Firth and Hall, 1833.

Johnson, A. N. *The Key-Stone Collection of Church Music: A Complete Collection of Hymn Tunes, Anthems, Psalms, Chants, etc., to Which Is Added the Physiological System for Training Choirs and Teaching Singing Schools; and the Cantata, The Morning of Freedom.* Lancaster City, PA: J. H. Sheaffer, 1868.

Kingsley, George, ed. *The Social Choir. Designed for a Class Book, and the Social Circle. Consisting of Selections from the Most Distinguished Composers, among Whom Are the Names of Rossini, Bellini, Von Weber, Auber, Hérold, Meyerbeer, Weigl, and Many Others, with Several Compositions of the Editor. The Poetry Has Generally Been Selected with Care, and with Particular Reference to Moral Sentiment. The Music Is Arranged as Songs, Duets, Trios, and Quartettes, with an Accompaniment for the Piano Forte.* 5th ed. Boston: Crocker and Brewster, 1847.

Lavenu, L. "The Banks of the Guadalquiver, Composed by L. Lavenu, as Sung by Mrs. Bishop, in the Opera of Linda di Chamounix." New York: Joseph F. Atwill, 1847.

Lover, Samuel, Esq. "True Love Can Ne'er Forget: A Favorite Ballad from the *Songs of the Legends and Traditions of Ireland*. Sung by Madame Caradori-Allan." New York: Atwill's Music Saloon, 1834–1847. University of Tennessee Library, Digital Collection, Sheet Music Collection.

Lynch, Francis, and James Power. "Dearest Mae: A Celebrated Ethiopian Song Sung by the Harmoneons." Philadelphia: A. Fiot, 1847.

Mason, Lowell, ed. *The Boston Academy's Collection of Church Music: Consisting of the Most Popular Psalm and Hymn Tunes, Anthems, Sentences, Chants, &c. Old and New: Together with Many Beautiful Pieces, Tunes and Anthems, Selected from the Masses and Other Works of Haydn, Mozart, Beethoven . . . and Other Distinguished Composers, Arr. and Adapted to English Words Expressly for This Work, Including, also, Original Compositions by German, English and American Authors*. Boston: J. H. Wilkins and R. B. Carter, 1839.

Mason, Lowell, comp. *Carmina Sacra; or Boston Collection of Church Music, Comprising the Most Popular Psalm and Hymn Tunes in General Use. Together with a Great Variety of New Tunes, Chants, Sentences, Motetts, and Anthems, Principally by Distinguished European Composers; the Whole Constituting One of the Most Complete Collections of Music for Choirs, Congregations, Singing Schools, and Societies, Extant*. 2nd ed. Boston: J. H. Wilkins and R. B. Carter, 1841.

Mason, Lowell, Edwards Amasa Park, and Austin Phelps, eds. *The Sabbath Hymn and Tune Book: For the Service of Song in the House of the Lord*. New York: Mason Brothers, 1859.

Mills, S. B. "Saltarello," op. 26. New York: William A. Pond, 1871. Albert and Shirley Small Special Collections Library, University of Virginia, Charlottesville, Virginia.

Nettleton, Asahel. *Village Hymns for Social Worship, Selected and Original: Designed as a Supplement to Dr. Watts's Psalms and Hymns*. 2nd ed. Hartford, CT: Goodwin, 1824.

"The Old English Gentleman." A Popular English Ballad. As Sung by Mr. H. Russell. New York: Atwill's Music Saloon, n.d. Lester S. Levy Collection of Sheet Music, Sheridan Libraries, Johns Hopkins University, Baltimore, Maryland.

Pixis, Johann Peter. "Brilliant Variations for Two Performers on One Piano Forte, on the Favorite Subject The Swiss Boy, or Der Schweizerbue, as Sung by Madlle. Sontag, Made. Carador and the Rainer Family." [London: I. Willis, 1800s].

Pucitta, Vincenzo. "Strike the Cymbal: Song of Rejoicing for the Conquest of Goliath by David," no. 23 of Carr's *Musical Miscellany*. Baltimore: J. Carr, [1814]. Ohio State University Library, Columbus, Ohio.

Richards, Brinley. "Cottage by the Sea." New York: William A. Pond, 1859. University of Tennessee Library, Digital Collection, Sheet Music Collection.

Richardson, Nathan. *The Modern School for the Piano-Forte: Composed and Compiled from the Works of the Most Eminent Modern and Classical Authors and Teachers, Comprising a Complete Course of Instruction, Based Upon a New Principle, Pro-*

gressive in Its Character, with Anatomical Illustrations of the Hands, Thoroughly Explained, Showing the Use of Their Muscles and Tendons in Playing the Piano. Boston: O. Ditson, 1856.

Rooke, William Michael. "Rest, Spirit, Rest: Hymn Sung by Miss Shirreff & Chorus, in the Grand Opera *Amilie, or The Love Test*, Performed at the National Theatre." New York: Firth and Hall, 1838. Sterling Memorial Library, Yale University.

———. "To the Vine Feast: Song Sung by Mrs. W. Penson, in the Grand Opera of *Amilie, or The Love Test*, Performed at the National Theatre." New York: Firth, Pond, n.d. New York State Library, Albany, New York.

Root, George F. *The Sabbath Bell, a Collection of Music for Choirs, Musical Associations, Singing-Schools, and the Home Circle, Consisting of Part I.—Singing-School Music. Part II.—Church Music. Part III.—Occasional and Concert Music.* New York: Mason Brothers, 1857.

Root, George, and Wm. B. Bradbury. *The Festival Glee Book: A Collection of Part Songs, Accompanied and Harmonized Melodies and Glees, A New Edition, Revised and Enlarged.* New York: Mason Brothers, 1859.

"Stephen Collins Foster: Collection of American Popular Songs." http://www.stephen-foster-songs.de/amsong42.htm.

Thalberg, Sigismond. "Home! Sweet Home!" op. 72, 1857. Albert and Shirley Small Special Collections Library, University of Virginia, Charlottesville, Virginia.

Thompson, Thomas. "Orphan Bess and Beggar Girl." New York: I. and M. Paff, n.d.

Wallace, W[illiam] V[incent] "Why Do I Weep for Thee?" Macon, GA: John C. Schreiner and Son, 1863.

Warren, George W. "La Fête des Fées," op. 13. Boston: George P. Reed, 1852. New York State Library, Albany, New York.

Watts, Isaac, comp., *The Psalms, Hymns, and Spiritual Songs, of the Rev. Isaac Watts, D.D., to Which Are Added, Select Hymns, from Other Authors; and Directions for Musical Expression. By Samuel Worcester, D.D.* New Edition, The Selection Enlarged, and the Indexes Greatly Improved by Samuel M. Worcester. Boston: Crocker and Brewster, 1836. Special Collections, Princeton Theological Seminary Library, Princeton, New Jersey.

Webb, G. J., and Lowell Mason. *The Odeon: A Collection of Secular Melodies, Arranged and Harmonized for Four Voices, Designed for Adult Singing Schools, and for Social Music Parties.* Boston: J. H. Wilkins and R. B. Carter, 1841.

Wehli, James M. "Home Sweet Home, for the Pianoforte, Transcribed for the Left Hand Only," ca. 1905. Albert and Shirley Small Special Collections Library, University of Virginia, Charlottesville, Virginia.

Whittlesey, Orramel. "Harp of the Wild Wind." Boston: Oliver Ditson, 1851. William L. Clements Library, University of Michigan, Ann Arbor, Michigan.

———. "Music Vale Seminary Quickstep." New York: Horace Waters, 1855. Lester S. Levy Collection of Sheet Music, Sheridan Libraries, Johns Hopkins University, Baltimore, Maryland.

Willard, Emma. "Rock'd in the Cradle of the Deep." New York: C. E. Horn, ca. 1840. Charlottesville: Albert and Shirley Special Collections Library, University of Virginia, Charlottesville, Virginia.

Woodbury, I. B., ed. *The Anthem Dulcimer: Constituting a Large and Choice Variety of New Tunes, Chants, Anthems, Motets, etc., from the Best Foreign and American Composers, with All the Old Tunes in Common Use; Together with a New and Greatly Improved Elementary Course, and a Choice Collection of Original Anthems. The Whole Comprising the Most Complete Collection of Sacred Music Ever Published.* New York: F. J. Huntington, 1856.

Index

Note: *Italicized* page numbers indicate material in tables, figures, and musical examples. Page numbers followed by "n" indicate numbered endnotes.

Abell, Mrs. L. G., 29

Abt, Franz Wilhelm: "Amor der Spotter," 235n86; "The Chime of Silvery Sabbath Bells," 123; "Golden Chimes," 129; "Ich Bin Der Klein Postillon," 164

academic curricula, 72, 74–82; comparative, *82*; at Litchfield, 72–82, *82*; at Mount Holyoke, 27, 72–82, *82*; at Music Vale, 72; at Troy, 27, 72–82, *82*

academic year for schools, 67–68, 202–3n67

"academy," as term, 175n1, 182n4

Academy Vocalist, The (Root), 104

"accomplishment," music education as, 25–28, 35, 56–57

Adams, Abigail, 17–18

Adams, John, 17

Adams Female Academy (Derry, NH), 49–50

"Addio" (F. Curschmann), 161

"Address of the Queen," 90

Address to the Public, An (E. H. Willard), 45–46

admission and retention requirements, 67–71; domestic work, 69, 71, 73; fees (*see* fees and expenses)

"adventure" schools, 13

aesthetics curricula, 80

ages of students, 65–66, 92

Alcott, William, 29

Allen, Abby, 99, 219n52

"Alp Horn, The" (Hodges), 161, *162*

"America," 153

American Annals of Education, 20, 26, 31

"American Eagle" (O. Whittlesey), 96, 152

American Institute of Instruction, 20

American Journal of Education, 20

American Ladies' Magazine, 92

American Revolution, 4, 7, 12, 15–16, 24

Amherst Academy (Amherst, MA), 49

Amherst College, 205n93

Amicus (author), "The Influence of a Musical Education," 32

Amilie, or the Love Test (Rooke), 167, *168*

"Amor der Spotter" (Abt), 235n86

Andrews, Jane A., 110, 146–47, 157, 158, 228n10, 231n32, 233n65

Andrews, John C., 95, 110; "He Tells Me He Loves Me, or Aileen Mavourneen," 158; "Jennie with Her Bonnie Blue E'e," 146–47; "My Own Sunny France" (with E. H. Willard), 111–12, 222–23n118; "O Love Is Like the Rose, Rosalie," 158; "Somebody's Coming, but I'll Not Tell Who," 158

anniversary exercises. *See* public examination exercises

annual examinations. *See* public examination exercises

Anthem Dulcimer, The (Woodbury, ed.), 149
"Araby's Daughter" (Kiallmark), 153
Arditi, Luigi, "L'Estasi," 159
Arthur, T. S., 33
art songs, 159–66
Ascher, Joseph, 119, 132; "Concordantia, Andante et Allegro Marziale," 128
assistant teachers, 60, 62–63, 93–94, 198n27
Astell, Mary, 18
Astor, George, 100, 219n58
Astor, John Jacob, 219n58
astronography, 77
Atwood, Thomas, "Hark! The Curfew," 165
Auber, Daniel-François-Esprit, 138–39, 235n83; *Fra Diavolo*, 120, 130, 139; "El Jaleo de Xeres" / "The Evening Dance," 164, 235n83; *Masaniello [La muette de Portici]*, 130, 167; "Overture to *Masaniello* for Eight Hands, Performed on Two Pianos," 130
Auguera, Antonio de, 141
"Ave Maria" (Schletterer, arr.), 151
"Ave Regina" (Tadolini), 150

Backus, Augustus, 104–5
Bacon, Mary Ann, 99, 100
Baker, Nettie, 109
Baldwin, Ashbel, 39
Balfe, Michael William, 104, 167–68
ballads, 152, 154–59, 166–67
Bancroft, Grace, 109
"Banks of the Guadalquiver, The" (Lavenu), 167
"Barcarola" (Campana), 163
Barnard, Henry, 19, 20
Barnekov, Kjell Volmar: "Fantaisie for Piano," 95; "Valse à La Fantaisie," 95
Bateman Concert Company, 163
"Battle of Prague for the Piano Forte, The" (Koczwara), 122, 153
battle pieces, for piano, 122, 153
Bayeau, Miss, 108
Beecher, Catharine, 172
Beecher, Rev. Lyman, 7, 76, 80, 196n17, 212n82, 231n36
Beethoven, Ludwig van, 128, 130, 137, 138, 140
Bellak, James, 132
"Belles d l'Amerique, Les" (Blessner), 123
Bellini, Vincenzo, 153, 236n95; *La Sonnambula*, 139, 164, 167–68, 236n90; "The Wedding Chorus," 164, 167

Benedictus (Mozart), 150
benefits of music education, 28–33, 173. *See also* employment of women
Berg, Albert, 120, 128, 132
Bible reading, 12
Bishop, Anna, 167
Blanco, Signor, "Tu Sandunga" / "What Enchantment," 164, 235n84
"Blessed Are the Peacemakers" (Bradbury), 149
Blessner, Gustave: "Les Belles d l'Amerique," 123; "Commencement March," 139; "Daguerre," 95, 138; *Les Echos de l'Europe*, 133–34; farewell concert (1850), 110, 130, 137, 140, 146–47; "Farewell to the Alps," 147, 157, 228n10; "Florida March," 124–28; as head of Troy Seminary music department, 95, 157; "I Have Got the Blues," 157; "The Last Rose of Summer" (harmony), 166; "Nanny's Mammy," 157–58; as violin instructor, 97, 140, 218n43, 227n57, 236n91
Blockley, John, 232n49
boarding schools, 13–14, 39, 40, 43, 44, 54, 55, 70, 114; Litchfield Academy as, 64; Mount Holyoke Seminary as, 64, 65; Music Vale Seminary as, 64–65; transition to female seminaries and academies, 14, 64–65, 178–79n17; Troy Seminary as, 65
board of examiners, Music Vale Seminary, 88, 94, 106, 108–9
board of trustees/visitors: Litchfield Academy, 59–60; Mount Holyoke Seminary, 51, 59–60, 61, 90, 98, 191n85, 191n87; Music Vale Seminary, 59–60, 195n3; Troy Seminary, 59–60
Bochsa, Robert Nicholas-Charles, 138–39, 164, 235n84
Bohemian Girl (Balfe), 167
bookkeeping curricula, 81
Boston Academy, The (L. Mason), 147–48
Boston Musical Gazette, 30
Brace, James, 77
Brace, John P.: academic curriculum at Litchfield, 78–79, 81–82; as co-principal at Litchfield, 60, 61, 73, 74, 76; joins faculty of Litchfield, 60, 73, 78, 82, 215n4; leaves Litchfield, 79
Brace, Mrs. L. E., 61
Bradbury, William B.: "Blessed Are the Peacemakers," 149; *The Festival Glee Book* (with Root), 154, 166; *The Jubilee*, 102, 149, 220n73

Bradford, Karolyn ("Katie") Whittlesey, 60, 62, 192–93n103, 195n8, 196–97n18
Brickley, Lynne Templeton, 81–82, 89, 210n49
"Bright Star of Hope" (Halévy), 138
Bronk, Catharine, 96, 217–18n37
Brooks, M. L., 128
Brown, Mary Q., 63
Brown, O. R., 140
Brunner, Christian Traugott, 120
Buckingham, William A., 57
Bull, Ole (Bornemann), "Variations Fantastique," 140
Burnap, Rev. George, 29–30
Burnham, Sarah, 101
Burroughs, Charles, 19, 20
Byfield Female Seminary (near Newburyport, MA), 20, 49, 192n93

Cahoon, E. A., 99
"Calabrese, La" (Gabussi), 161–62
Caldwell, Eunice, 60, 68
calisthenics/gymnastics, 29, 83, 84–85, 87, 110–11, 133, 212n82, 227n47
Campana, Fabio: "Barcarola," 163; "Madre del Sommo Amore," 161
Canawahoo, or The Perils of the Wilderness (Music Vale students), 90, 168, 237n100
canzonets, 155
Caradori-Allan, Maria Caterina Rosalbina, 159, 233n57; "Lay of the Sylph" / "Sono il Silfo," 155
Carmina Sacra (L. Mason, compiler), 148–49, 229n18
Catherine the Great (Russia), 19
cavatinas, 166–67
"Celebrated One Finger'd Sliding Waltz, The," 134–35, *136*
"Celebrated Overture to *Lodoïska*, The" (Kreutzer), 130, *131*
"Celebrated Rondo Finale, The" (Donizetti), 167
"Celebrated Swiss Song, The" / "The Swiss Song" (Eckert), 159, *160*, 164
certificates and diplomas, 89–90, 201n59
Chamberlin, Ella, 108–9
Chapin, Mary W., 61
character formation, music education in, 31–32
character pieces, for piano, 122–24
Cherubini, Luigi, 165
Chester, Mary, 201n51

Child, Lydia Maria, *The Frugal Housewife*, 22
"Chime of Silvery Sabbath Bells, The" (Abt), 123
Chopin, Frédéric, 128, 138
choruses, 164–65
chronography, 77
Church, Edward, 81
church/sacred music, 112–13, 139–40, 147–51
Civil War, 3, 58, 63, 64, 152, 156–57
Clapisson, Antoine-Louis, 165
Clark, J. Bunker, 122
class, socioeconomic. *See* social class
class singing instruction. *See* voice class
Clementi, Muzio, 135
Clinton, DeWitt, 19–20, 45
Colman, George, 166
Combe, George, 189n43
Comettant, Oscar, "Gabrielle: Etude d'Expression pour Piano," 128, *129*
"Comme à vingt ans" (Durand), 164
"Commencement March" (Blessner), 139
common schools, 4, 14–15, 31, 33, 72, 73, 91
"Concordantia, Andante et Allegro Marziale" (Ascher), 128
"Consider the Lilies" (Topliff), 151
contra dance, 29
Cornelia (mother of the Gracchi), 19
Cramer, Johann Baptist, 119
Crawford, Mrs. (lyricist for "Kathleen Mavourneen"), 158
Creation, The (Haydn), 150, 164
Crouch, Frederick N., 158
"cult of true womanhood," 22
curricula of female seminaries and academies, 72–91; academic, 72, 74–82; calisthenics, 84–85, 110–11, 212n82; comparison of schools, *82*; graduates and graduation requirements, 87, 88–90; level of, 73; organization of, 73–74; prizes, certificates, and diplomas, 89–90. *See also* instrumental instruction and performance (generally); music education (generally); ornamental arts; public examination exercises; semiannual examinations; vocal music instruction and performance
Curschmann, Friedrich, "Addio," 161
Curschmann, Karl, 163
Curschmann, Michael, 146
Czerny, Carl, 119–20, 130

"Daguerre" (Blessner), 95, 138

dame schools, 12, 39
dance instruction and performance, 29, 83, 84–85
dance pieces, for piano, 133–36, 138
Davidson, Lucretia, 85–87
Day, Jeremiah, 207n12
"Dearest Mae: A Celebrated Ethiopian Song," 164–65
De Bériot, Charles, 140
de Bruyn Kops, Gertrude, 211n66
Declaration of Independence, 15, 17–18
Demar, John, "Hunting Tower or When Ye Gang Awa, Jamie," 163
Descartes, René, 13
Dickinson, Emily, 68
diplomas and certificates, 89–90, 201n59
Ditson, Oliver, 56, 87
Dodge, Mary Abigail (Gail Hamilton), 35, 186n60
domestic work of students, at Mount Holyoke Seminary, 69, 71, 73
Donizetti, Gaetano: L'elisir d'amore, 166; Linda di Chamounix, 167; Lucia di Lammermoor, 104, 130, 132, 167
Dow, Howard Malcolm, 140
"Down in the Dewy Dell" (Smart), 163
dramatic works, 76, 168–70
drawing, 83, 84
Durand, Emile, "Comme à vingt ans," 164
Dutton, Henry, 57
Duvernoy, Jean-Baptiste, 128
"Dying Soldier of Buena Vista, The" (O. Whittlesey), 96, 152

Early Republic, 16, 19
Easter Morning, The (von Neukomm), 151
Eaton, Amos B., 49, 78, 79, 190n66, 210n48, 210n52
"Ecco ridente" (Rossini), 166
Echos de l'Europe, Les (Blessner), 133–34
"Echo—Waltzes" (Philippi), 120
Eckert, Karl Anton Florian, "The Celebrated Swiss Song," 159, 160, 164
Egghard, Jules, 129
L'elisir d'amore (Donizetti), 166
Elizabeth I (England), 19
elocution, 31, 76, 85, 207–8n25
Ely, Mary, 228n10
Emerson, George B., 19, 20, 180n54
Emerson, Rev. Joseph, 19, 20, 49, 180n54, 192n93

Emerson, Luther Orlando, "Flower Girl," 146
Emma Willard School. See Troy Female Seminary (Troy, NY)
emotional well-being, and music education, 26, 28, 29–30, 32, 171, 173
employment of women: American Revolution and, 15; female seminaries and, 3, 4, 7, 14, 23, 115; music education and, 1, 7, 32–33, 57, 115; in postcolonial period, 12; as school teachers, 23, 39 (see also female seminaries and academies; and names of specific institutions); woman's sphere vs., 11
English and literature curricula, 75–76, 82
English Classical School (Boston), 20
Enlightenment, 13
ensemble music, 120–21, 137–39
entrance examinations, at Mount Holyoke Seminary, 68, 73
equality, and Declaration of Independence, 15, 17–18
Ernst, Louis, 87
"L'Estasi" (Arditi), 159
etudes, for piano, 128
Evening Fire-side; or, Literary Miscellany, 16
examining committee: Music Vale Seminary, 90, 100–101, 161; Troy Seminary, 31–32, 78, 80, 87, 94–95, 107–8, 115, 116, 184n54, 223–24n4
exhibitions. See public examination exercises
expenses. See fees and expenses

faculty and staff: characteristics of, 60–63, 93–95; faculty composers, 95–96, 118, 143, 146–47 (see also names of specific composers); at Litchfield, 60–63, 93, 94, 198n28 (see also Brace, John P.); at Mount Holyoke, 60–63, 93, 94, 105, 149, 197–98n20, 198–99nn29–30; at Music Vale, 53, 58, 60–63, 93–94, 96, 108–9, 197–98n20; at Troy (see Troy Female Seminary: faculty and staff)
Fairbanks, Mary J. Mason, 90, 196n14
"Fantaisie for Piano" (Barnekov), 95
"Farewell to My Home" (O. Whittlesey), 96
"Farewell to the Alps" (Blessner), 147, 157, 228n10
fees and expenses, 69–71; age of student and, 92; music education, 33–34, 96–97;

for piano use, 97, 99, 205n91; private music lessons, 34, 97, 103; tuition, 50, 51, 217–18n37

female seminaries and academies: "academy," as term, 1, 175n1, 182n4; admission and retention of students, 67–68; assistant teachers, 60, 62–63, 93–94, 198n27; domestic duties of students, 69, 71, 73; employment of women and, 3, 4, 7, 14, 23, 115; faculty and staff characteristics, 60–63; finishing schools vs. (*see* finishing/fashionable schools); importance of, 1–2, 3, 4–5, 7, 9; as launching pads for degree programs, 1–2; precursors to, 6, 19, 24, 37, 40–41, 58, 74, 172–74; "seminary," as term, 1, 45, 175n1, 178–79n17, 182n4; social class of students, 21, 23, 64–67, 71, 181n76; student body characteristics, 64–67. *See also* board of trustees/visitors; curricula of female seminaries and academies; fees and expenses; *and names of specific institutions*

female seminary movement: expansion of, 24; groundwork for, 1; importance of, 1–2, 9, 172–74; Litchfield Academy as precursor, 6, 19, 40–41, 74, 172–74; origins of, 177n17; *A Plan for Improving Female Education* (E. H. Willard), 5, 7–8, 21, 44–46, 65. *See also names of specific institutions*

Festival Glee Book, The (Root & Bradbury), 154, 166

"Fête des Fées, La" (Warren), 124, *125*

finishing/fashionable schools: as business ventures, 4–5, 59; French language instruction, 81; music education in, 7, 25–28, 35–36, 57, 92, 98, 172, 173, 176n8, 211n69; and the ornamental arts, 83, 91, 92, 98; reputation of, 4–5; role of, 7, 14, 72

"First Day of Spring, The" (Mendelssohn), 161

Fisk, Fidelia, 191n81

Fitch, Susannah, 33

Five College Women's Studies Research Center (FCWSRC), xi

"Florida March" (Blessner), 124–28

Flotow, Friedrich von, 167, 234n78

"Flower Girl" (L. O. Emerson), 146

"Flower Queen, The" (C. Glover), 155

foreign languages: in academic curricula, 81–82; and finishing/fashionable schools, 81; and vocal music, 164

"Forest Song" (Philippi), 96, 166

Fowler, Joseph A., 134

Fra Diavolo (Auber), 120, 130, 139

Fraser, Donald A., 192–93n103

French, Lydia, 113

French language instruction, 81

Frugal Housewife, The (Child), 22

Fuller, Sallie, 109

Gabriel, Mary Ann Virginia, "When the Pale Moon Arose Last Night," 162

"Gabrielle: Etude d'Expression pour Piano" (Comettant), 128, *129*

Gabussi, Vincenzo, 146; "La Calabrese," 161–62; "I Pescateri," 163

Gallaudet, Thomas, 19, 20

"Gallenberg Waltz" (Neuland), 134, 138

Ganz, Wilhelm, "The Nightingale's Trill," 162–63

Gardiner, Sarah D., 202n62

Gary, Charles L., 2, 176n4

gender: education of male vs. female students, 39, 42–43, 184n34; Enlightenment philosophers and, 13; of faculty and staff, 60–63, 93–95; of students, 66, 67, 195–96n10, 231n36; and woman's sphere, 6, 11, 17–19, 21–23, 42, 44, 72, 90, 177–78nn3–4

geographic diversity, of students, 64–65

geography and history curricula, 76–77, *82*

Getze, Jacob Alfred, 123

Giosa, Nicola de, "I Tamburelli I Campanelli" / "Now Sounds the Tambourine," 159–60

Gleaner of the Vale (newsletter), 104, 120

glees, 154, 165–66

Gleffer, J. E., "Music Comes with Various Power," 161

"Glöcklein im Thale" (von Weber), 166–67

Glover, Charles, 146; "The Flower Queen," 155

Glover, Stephen, 146, 231n33; "What Are the Wild Waves Saying?," 155

Godey's Lady's Book, 35, 43

"Golden Chimes" (Abt), 129

Gottschalk, Louis Moreau, 119, 120–21, 123–24, 128, 226nn37–38

Gould, John E., 56, 87

Gounod, Charles François, 138

graduation, 87, 89–90. *See also* public examination exercises

Grant, Zilpah, 49–50, 172, 190n71

Great Awakening, 12
"Great Big House, A" (O. Whittlesey), 143
Grobe, Charles, 120–21; "Smile On: Brilliant Variations on Wallace's Beautiful Melody, 'Katie Strang,'" 132
"Guide to Instruction on the Pianoforte, A" (Nixon), 30
guitar instruction and performance, 57, 93, 97, 98, 120, 134, 137, 138, 139, 140–41
Gumbert, Ferdinand, 163
"Gut Nacht, Far Wol" (F. W. Kücken), 164
gymnastics. See calisthenics/gymnastics

"Hail! Smiling Morn" (Spofforth), 165–66
Hale, Sarah J., 22, 35, 43
Halévy, F. Barclay, 138
Hamilton, Gail (Mary Abigail Dodge), 35, 186n50
Hammond, William Gardiner, 107
Handel, George Frederick, 120, 133; Messiah, 149–50, 230n25
Hansen, Lucy, 159
"Hark! The Curfew" (Atwood), 165
Harmoneons (Harmoneon Family Singers), 164–65, 235–36n87
harp instruction and performance, 57, 97, 98, 138, 139
"Harp of the Wild Wind" (O. Whittlesey), 96, 143, 144, 145, 162–63, 193n110
Harris, Harry, 123
Hart, Emily, 93
Hastings, Thomas, 102, 140
Hawes, Harriet, 93
Hawks, Rev. Roswell, 51, 191n87
Hayden, Winslow L., 141
Haydn, Franz Joseph: The Creation, 150, 164; "The Heavens Are Telling," 150, 164
Hayner, Eveline, 233n65
"Heavens Are Telling, The" (Haydn), 150, 164
Herbert, George R., 61, 93
Hérold, Louis Joseph Ferdinand, 130, 236n90
Herz, Henri, 121, 140; "The Last Rose of Summer" (arr.), 132–33, 227n52
"He Sleeps in Yonder Dewy Grave," 152
"He Tells Me He Loves Me, or Aileen Mavourneen" (J. C. Andrews), 158
Hewitt, James, 121, 146; "Sadi the Moor," 153
Hidden, Fanny M., 166

Hill, G. C., 31
Hinsdale, Nancy, 61
history and geography curricula, 76–77, 82
History of American Music Education, A (Mark & Gary), 2
History of Music Education in the United States (Keene), 2
History of Women's Education in the United States (Woody), 2
History, Theory, and Analysis of Music (Backus), 104–5
Hitchcock, Rev. Dr. Edward, 48, 50, 52, 79
Hodges, Faustina Hasse, 110, 132, 146, 159, 163, 225n29; "The Alp Horn," 161, 162; "The Holy Dead," 95, 150; "Maiden Fair," 95; "O'er the Alps," 161; "Speed Away," 95; "Variations—on an Air of Pleyel," 95
Holbrook, S. T., 88, 100, 108–9, 212n86
Holbrooke, Madame, 167
"Holy Dead, The" (Hodges), 95, 150
Home! Sweet Home! (Thalberg), 109, 124, 126
"Home Sweet Home" (Wehli), 124, 127
Hook, James, 146; "Willy's Rare and Willy's Fair," 154
Hooker, Rev. Edward W., 26, 28, 32, 34, 35, 153–54
Horn, August, 120
"How Lovely Are the Messengers" (Mendelssohn), 150
Hudson, Sarah L., 61, 196n14
Hudson, Theodosia, 61, 198n23
"Hunting Tower or When Ye Gang Awa, Jamie" (Demar), 163
"Huntsman's Song, The" (Philippi), 166
Hymn of Praise, A (Mendelssohn), 150

"Ich Bin Der Klein Postillon" (Abt), 164
"If With All Your Hearts" (Mendelssohn), 150
"I Have Got the Blues" (Blessner), 157
Industrial Revolution, 4, 16, 24
instrumental instruction and performance (generally), 114–41; comparison of female seminaries, 98; ensemble music, 120–21, 137–39; at finishing/fashionable schools, 83; guest performances, 87, 109–10; guitar, 57, 93, 97, 98, 120, 134, 137, 138, 139, 141; harp, 57, 97, 98, 138, 139; at Litchfield, 99–100, 115, 117; melodeon, 57, 98; at Mount Holyoke, 8–9, 98, 98–99, 115, 116; musical

entertainments, 116–19; music courses, 104–5; at Music Vale, 8, *98*, 100–101, 104, 114–15, 116, 137–40, 141; organ, 57, 97, *98*, 120, 137, 139–40, 151; piano (*see* piano instruction and performance); student performances, 88–89, 105–9 (*see also* public examination exercises); at Troy, 8, *98*, 100, 115, 116, 137–39, 140, 141; violin, 97, *98*, 138, 139, 140, 218n43, 227n57, 236n91; vs. vocal music instruction and performance, 27, 28, 34, 98–99
intellectual benefits, of music education, 30–31
"Invisible Chorus," 90
"I Pescateri" (Gabussi), 163
Ipswich Female Seminary (Ipswich, MA), 23, 49–50, 62, 71, 73, 98, 190n71, 191n86
"Isle of the Syrens," 90
"I Tamburelli I Campanelli"/ "Now Sounds the Tambourine" (Giosa), 159–60
Iucho, Wilhelm, 128–29
"I Waited for the Lord" (Mendelssohn), 150

Jackson, George K., "A Winter's Evening," 153
"Jaleo de Xeres, El" / "The Evening Dance" (Auber), 164, 235n83
J. E. Gould and Company, 56
"Jennie with Her Bonnie Blue E'e" (J. C. Andrews), 146–47
Jenny Lind Club, 160–61
Jephthah's Daughter (S. Pierce), 169–70
"Je suis la Bajadere" / "I Am the Bayadere" (Bochsa, arr.), 164, 235n84
Johnson, A. N.: *The Key-Stone Collection of Church Music*, 102, 149, 220n73; *The Morning of Freedom*, 149
Johnson, Frances Hall, 143, 192–93n103, 194n130
Journal of Education, 43
"Joy of Saints" (Watts), *148*
Jubilee, The (Bradbury), 102, 149, 220n73
junior (first-year grade level), 65–66, 68, 73–77, 79, 101

"Kathleen Mavourneen" (Crouch), 158
Keene, James A., 2, 176n5
Kelley, Mary, 2
Kelly, Michael, "When Pensive I Thought on My Love" (with Colman), 166

Kevney, Eleanor, 211n66
"Key of Expression," 229n14
Key-Stone Collection of Church Music, The (A. N. Johnson), 102, 149, 220n73
Kiallmark, G., "Araby's Daughter," 153
Kimber, Marion Wilson, 207–8n25
Kimberly, Maretta, 93
King, Matthew P., "The Minute Gun at Sea," 153
Kingsley, George, *The Social Choir*, 153–54
Knight, Eliza P., 218n46
Knight, Joseph, "Rock'd in the Cradle of the Deep" (with E. H. Willard), 151
Koczwara, Franz, "The Battle of Prague for the Piano Forte," 122, 153
Kreutzer, Rudolphe, 232n49; "The Celebrated Overture to *Lodoïska*," 130, *131*
Kücken, Friedrich Wilhelm: "Gut Nacht, Far Wol," 164; "Swallow's Farewell," 162
Kücken, L., "We Met by Chance," 147
Kuhe, Wilhelm, transcriptions for piano, 130

Labarre, Théodore, 138–39, 236n90
Lablache, Luigi, 104, 220n73
"La Calabrese" (Gabussi), 161–62
Lachner, Franz, 128
Ladies' Garland and Family Wreath Embracing Tales, Sketches, Incidents, History, Poetry, Music (anonymous), 26
Ladies' Loyal Union League, 58
Lafayette, General, 47, 111, 222–23n118
Lafont, Charles, 140
language curricula, 81–82
"La Serenade" (Philippi), 96
La Sonnambula (Bellini), 139, 164, 167–68, 236n90
"Last Hope, The" (Gottschalk), 123–24
"Last Rose of Summer, The" (Blessner, harmony), 166
"Last Rose of Summer, The" (Herz, arr.), 132–33, 227n52
Latin grammar schools, 12
Latin instruction, 81–82
Lavenu, Louis Henry, "The Banks of the Guadalquiver," 167
law school (Litchfield, CT), 7, 39–40, 64, 84, 119, 168, 208n29
"Lay of the Sylph" / "Sono il Silfo" (Caradori-Allan), 155
Learning to Stand and Speak (Kelley), 2

Lee and Walker's Musical Almanac for 1969, 125–28, 132
L'elisir d'amore (Donizetti), 166
"L'Estasi" (Arditi), 159
Lickl, Johann Georg, 236n90
Lincoln, Almira Hart. *See* Phelps, Almira Hart Lincoln
Lind, Jenny, 159–61, 234n71
Linley, George, 156–57
Litchfield County Post, 89, 99, 117
Litchfield Female Academy (Litchfield, CT), 38–41, *41*; academic curricula, 72–82, *82*; academic year, 67–68, 202–3n67; admission and retention requirements, 67; board of trustees, 59–60; church/sacred music, 112; closing, 6, 82; faculty and staff, 60–63, 93, 94, 198n28; fees and expenses, 69–71, 96, 97; founding, 5, 7, 19, 24, 40–41, 74, 83, 187n15; funding sources, 40; graduation prizes, 89; guest performances, 109–10; instrumental instruction and performance, 99–100, 115, 117 (*see also* Litchfield Female Academy: piano instruction and performance); law school near, 7, 39–40, 64, 84, 115, 119, 168, 208n29; male students, 66, 231n36; musical entertainments, 119; music use in seminary life, 110–11; naming of, 40; ornamental curricula, 83, 84, 85; philosophy of music education, 26, 28–33, 34, 41, 92, 103, 115, 142, 170; piano instruction and performance, 119, 120, 121, 122, 130, 133, 134–37; plays, 76, 168–70; as precursor to female seminary movement, 6, 19, 24, 40–41, 74, 172–74; public examination exercises, 67, 85, 87, 89, 99, 214n113, 224n9; semiannual examinations, 67, 85, 89, 99, 224n9; students and student characteristics, 64, 65, 66, 99–100, 103, 109–10, 112, 198n28 (*see also* Sheldon, Lucy); vocal music instruction and performance, 9, 101, 102–3, 142, 146, 147, 152–53, 154, 166, 168–71. *See also* Pierce, Sarah
literature and English curricula, 75–76, *82*
Llamarada, The (Mount Holyoke College yearbook), 215n5
Locke, John, 13
logic curricula, 80–81, *82*
Longfellow, Henry Wadsworth, 158
Lord, John, 4–5, 44, 206n2
"Lord Is Nigh, The," 149

Lord's Prayer, 12
Lover, Samuel, "True Love Can Ne'er Forget," 155
Lucia di Lammermoor (Donizetti), 104, 130, 132, 167
Lutz, Alma, 66, 206n4
Lyon, Mary, 47–52, *48*; academic curricula at Mount Holyoke, 27, 72–82, *82*; as assistant to Zilpah Grant, 49–50; death in 1849, 61, 62, 93; duties at Mount Holyoke, 60, 61, 62; early career, 48–50; education and family background, 48–50; founding of Mount Holyoke, 5, 6, 7, 8, 51–52, 60–61; at Ipswich Female Seminary, 23, 49–50, 73, 98; lack of music education, 27, 142; and middle-class students, 21, 34, 50–52, 61, 66, 67, 70–71, 83, 115; ornamental curricula at Mount Holyoke, 83, 84–85; philosophy of music education, 26, 27, 28–33, 34, 101–2, 111, 115, 142, 170, 171; and Emma Willard, 50, 51; and women's higher education, 50–51. *See also* Mount Holyoke Female Seminary

"Madre del Sommo Amore" (Campana), 161
Maeder, James Gasper, 146
Maginnis, Eliza. *See* Whittlesey, Eliza Tully Maginnis (Mrs. John T. Maginnis)
Maginnis, Jennette ("Nettie") Whittlesey (Mrs. William Henry Maginnis), 62, 196–97n18
Maginnis, John T., 58, 196–97n18
Maginnis, Ora, 109
Maginnis, William Henry, 196–97n18
"Maiden Fair" (Hodges), 95
"Maid of Lodi, The," 154
male students: education compared with that of female students, 39, 42–43, 184n34; at established educational institutions, 19; at Litchfield, 66, 231n36
Mann, Horace, 19, 20
Mansfield, E. D., 110–11
marches, for piano, 124–28
"March of the Amazons," 90
Maretzek, Max, 167
Mark, Michael L., 2, 176n4
marriage: neglect of music after, 34–35; role of finishing/fashionable schools and, 7, 14 (*see also* finishing/fashionable schools). *See also* woman's sphere
Martha (Flotow), 167, 234n78

Masaniello (Auber), 130, 167
Mason, Lowell, 101, 112, 140; advice to
Mary Lyon, 27, 98; *The Boston Academy*,
147–48; *Carmina Sacra*, 148–49, 229n18;
as founder of public school music edu-
cation, 2; as lecturer at Mount Holyoke
Seminary, 94; *The Odeon* (with G. J.
Webb), 102, 153, 220n73
Mason, William, 225n23
Massachusetts Bay Colony, 12
Masters, Susan, 70
mathematics curricula, 77–78, *82*
Mazzinghi, Joseph, 146
McCurdy, Charles J. M., 152
McDannell, Colleen, 44
McNary, Abbie, 159
melodeon instruction and performance,
57, *98*
Mendelssohn, Felix, 132, 140; "The First Day
of Spring," 161; "How Lovely Are the Mes-
sengers," 150; *A Hymn of Praise*, 150; "If
With All Your Hearts," 150; "I Waited for
the Lord," 150; "On the Sea," 161; "O Praise
the Lord," 150; "Wedding March," 128
Mercandante, Saverio, 130
Merrill, Dr., 45, 188n39
Merwin, Lula, 109
Messiah (Handel), 149–50, 230n25
metronome, 100
Meyer, Philippe-Jacques, 138
Meyerbeer, Giacomo, 119, 130, 167
Middlebury College, 7, 42–43
Middlebury Female Academy, 42, 43, 45
middle class (grade level), 68, 73–74, 79–80,
166
middle class (socioeconomic), 21–23, 101,
115; and Mary Lyon/Mount Holyoke Fe-
male Seminary, 21, 34, 50–52, 61, 66, 67,
70–71, 83, 115; and music education, 28;
and new nineteenth-century woman,
21–22
Mills, S. B., 123; "Saltarello," 109, 133, *134, 135*
Milton, John, 75, 76
minstrel songs, 164–65
"Minute Gun at Sea, The" (King), 153
Modern School for the Piano-Forte, The
(Richardson), 56, 88
Mœlling, Theodore, 132
Molter, Johann Melchior, 141
monitress, 63
"Moonlight Sonata" (Beethoven), 137

Moore, Abigail, 81
Moore, Hannah, 19
Moore, Thomas, 146, 161
Moravian Young Ladies' Seminary (Beth-
lehem, PA), 121, 172, 178–79n17, 185n51,
186n1, 225n32; founding, 5, 14, 37, 58; as
precursor to female seminary movement,
19, 24, 37, 58
Morgan, Charlotte Maconda (Mrs. Orramel
Whittlesey), 53, 58, 60
Morning of Freedom, The (A. N. Johnson),
149
Morse, Jedidiah, 25
Moscheles, Ignas, 132
Mount Holyoke College, 2, 215n5. *See also*
Mount Holyoke Female Seminary
Mount Holyoke Female Seminary (South
Hadley, MA), 47–52, *52*; academic curricula, 27, 72–82, *82*; academic year, 67–68,
202–3n67; admission and retention requirements, 67–68; board of trustees, 51,
59–60, 61, 90, 98, 191n85, 191n87; church/
sacred music, 112–13; diplomas for course
work, 89, 90; domestic duties of students, 69; entrance examinations, 68, 73;
faculty and staff, 60–63, 93, 94, 105, 149,
197–98n20, 198–99nn29–30; fees and
expenses, 69–71, 97; in female seminary
movement, 6, 172–74, 177n17; founding, 5,
6, 7, 8, 51–52, 60–61; funding sources, 51–
52, 191n86; graduation requirements, 89–
90; guest performances, 109; instrumental instruction and performance, 8–9, *98*,
98–99, 115, 116 (*see also* Mount Holyoke
Female Seminary: piano instruction and
performance); musical entertainments,
119; music courses, 104; music use in seminary life, 111; naming of, 52; ornamental
curricula, 83, 84–85; philosophy of music
education, 26, 27, 28–33, 34, 101–2, 111, 115,
142, 170, 171; piano instruction and performance, 119, 121, 133, 137; probationary
period, 68; public examination exercises,
67, 85, 87, 106–7, 115, 119, 148–49, 212n82,
214n113; student performances, 105,
106–7; students and student characteristics, 33, 64, 65–66, 67, 98–99, 101, 112–13,
195–96n10, 198–99nn29–30, 202n65; vocal music instruction and performance,
8–9, 27, *98*, 101–2, 142, 147–50, 152, 153–54,
166, 170–71. *See also* Lyon, Mary

Mozart, Wolfgang Amadeus, 108, 120, 121, 163; *Benedictus*, 150; piano sonatas, 109, 137

Müller, Wilhelm, 140

Murray, Judith Sargent, 18

musical entertainments, 116–19

Musical Reporter, The, 28

"Music Comes with Various Power" (Gleffer), 161

music education (generally), 92–113; as "accomplishment," 25–28, 35, 56–57; arguments for and against, 33–36; benefits for women, 28–33, 173; church/sacred music, 112–13, 139–40, 147–51; comparison of female seminaries, *98*; employment opportunities and, 1, 7, 32–33, 57, 115; faculty composers, 95–96, 118; fees and expenses, 33–34, 96–97; in female seminary movement, 1, *98*, 173–74; at finishing/fashionable schools, 7, 25–28, 35–36, 57, 92, 98, 172, 173, 176n8, 211n69; guest performances, 87, 109–10; music courses, 104–5; music teachers, 93–95; origins of public school music programs, 2; and the ornamental arts, 1, 14–16, 24, 28; role of music use in seminary life, 110–12; and social class, 28, 33, 35–36, 200n45; student performances, 88–89, 105–9 (*see also* public examination exercises; semiannual examinations). *See also* instrumental instruction and performance (generally); philosophies of music education; vocal music instruction and performance

Music Vale Seminary (Salem, CT), 53–58, 56, 97–98; academic curricula, 72; academic year, 67–68, 202–3n67; admission and retention requirements, 67–68; board of examiners, 88, 94, 106, 108–9; board of visitors, 59–60, 195n3; campus, 54–56; closing, 58, 194n130; concerts and staged productions, 55, 56; diplomas, 90; ensemble music, 137–39; examining committee, 90, 100–101, 161; faculty and staff, 53, 58, 60–63, 93–94, 96, 108–9, 197–98n20; faculty composers, 95, 96, 143 (*see also* Whittlesey, Eliza Tully Maginnis; Whittlesey, Orramel, works); farm, 55; fees and expenses, 69–71, 97; in female seminary movement, 6, 172–74; fire of 1868, 55, 194n129; as first U.S. music conservatory, 6, 53; founding, 6, 7, 8, 54, 100, 192–93n103; graduation requirements, 88–89, 90; instrumental instruction and performance, 8, *98*, 100–101, 104, 114–15, 116, 137–40, 141 (*see also* Music Vale Seminary: piano instruction and performance); Liberty Pole, 58; musical entertainments, 116–17; music courses, 6, 104; naming of, 54; as normal school/teacher preparation school, 54, 57; philosophy of music education, 26, 28–33, 56–57, 100–101, 114–15, 117, 142, 170, 171; piano instruction and performance, 57, 116, 119–20, 121, 122–24, 128–29, 130, 132–33, 134, 137–39; Piano Teachers' Graduating Course, 57; public examination exercises, 85, 87–90, 94, 96, 100–101, 105–9, 116–17, 120, 124, 128, 139, 143–46, 163, 168, 214n113; student performances, 105–6, 107, 108–9, 124, 128; students and student characteristics, 64–65, 66–67, 108–9, 158; and town of Salem, 54–58; vocal music instruction and performance, 9, *98*, 101, 142–46, 151, 152, 154, 158–59, 161–65, 168, 170–71. *See also* Whittlesey, Orramel

"Music Vale Seminary Quick Step" (O. Whittlesey), 96, 138

"My Own Sunny France" (E. H. Willard & J. C. Andrews), 111–12, 222–23n118

"Nanny's Mammy" (Blessner), 157–58

Nash, Margaret A., 2

needlework, 83, 85

Nelson, Sydney, "The Winds Are Up—The Stars Are Out," 155

Nettleton, Rev. Asahel, *Village Hymns for Social Worship*, 102, 147

Neuland, Wilhelm, "Gallenberg Waltz," 134, 138

New England Singing School, 102

New York Mirror, 173

Nicolai, Valentino, 137

"Nightingale's Trill, The" (Ganz), 162–63

"Nights of Music" (Philippi), 96, 161

"Night Thoughts" (Young), 81

Nixon, William, "A Guide to Instruction on the Pianoforte," 30

Norcross, Emily, 33

normal schools, 54, 57, 206n4

Odeon, The (Webb & Mason), 102, 153, 220n73

"O'er the Alps" (Hodges), 161

Oesten, Theodore, 121

Ogden, Eliza, 110, 112

"O Hail Us" (Verdi), 167
"Old English Gentleman, The," 155–56, 156
Oliver Ditson's music store (Boston), 56
"O Love Is Like the Rose, Rosalie" (J. C. Andrews), 158
"On the Sea" (Mendelssohn), 161
operas, 166–68
"O Praise the Lord" (Mendelssohn), 150
organ instruction and performance, 57, 97, 98, 120, 137, 139–40, 151
ornamental arts, 1, 14–16, 24; "accomplishment" vs., 25–28; calisthenics/gymnastics, 29, 83, 84–85, 87, 110–11, 133, 212n82, 227n47; curricula in female seminaries and academies, 72, 83–85; curricula in finishing/fashionable schools, 25–28; dancing, 29, 83, 84–85; defined, 26; drawing, 83, 84; needlework, 83, 85; painting, 83, 84. See also instrumental instruction and performance (generally); vocal music instruction and performance
"Orphan Bess and the Beggar Girl" (T. Thompson), 153
"Our Country" (Verdi), 96, 167
"Our Harp and Banner" (O. Whittlesey), 139, 143, 165
"Overture to Masaniello for Eight Hands, Performed on Two Pianos" (Auber), 130

painting, 83, 84
Palmer, Miss F., 124
Paradise and the Peri (R. Schumann), 163
Paradise Lost (Milton), 75, 76
Parepa(-Rosa), Euphrosyne, 163, 235n80
parlor songs, 154–59
parsing, 75
patriotic music, 152
Peck, Mary W., 61
penmanship, 75–76, 83
Perkins, J. Deming, 40
"Pescateri, I" (Gabussi), 163
Pestalozzi, Johann Heinrich, 189–90n58
Pestalozzian dialogue, 189–90n58
Peters, Miss, 60
Petrikin, Henry, 152
Phelps, Almira Hart Lincoln, 21, 31, 32, 35–36, 61, 78, 210n48
Philadelphia Academy (Pennsylvania), 16–17, 19
Philbrick, John D., 207–8n25
Philippi, Matthieu, 134, 146, 159; arrangement of "Our Country" (Verdi), 96, 167;

"Echo—Waltzes," 120; "Forest Song," 96, 166; as head of Troy Seminary music department, 95–96, 167; "The Huntsman's Song," 166; "Nights of Music," 96, 161; "La Serenade," 96; "Sounds from the Heart," 120
philosophies of music education, 25–36, 114–16; arguments for and against, 33–36; benefits for women, 28–33; at finishing schools vs. female academies, 7, 25–28, 57; and Mary Lyon/Mount Holyoke, 26, 27, 28–33, 34, 101–2, 111, 115, 142, 170, 171; and Sarah Pierce/Litchfield, 26, 28–33, 41, 92, 103, 115, 142, 170; vocal vs. instrumental music, 27, 28, 34, 98–99; and Orramel Whittlesey/Music Vale, 26, 28–33, 56–57, 100–101, 114–15, 117, 142, 170, 171; and Emma Hart Willard/Troy, 26, 27, 28–33, 36, 47, 92, 115, 116–17, 142, 170, 171
philosophies of women's education, 11–24; American Revolution impact, 15–16; colonial period, 4, 11–12; Enlightenment philosopher views, 13; mid- to late eighteenth century, 13–15; new nineteenth-century woman, 21–22; postcolonial progression, 12; postrevolutionary, 16–21; rationales and reforms in, 22–23; women's advocates, 5–6, 16–23
philosophy and religion curricula, 79–80, 82
physical health, and music education, 28–29
piano instruction and performance, 2–3, 9, 93, 98, 98–101, 119–39; battle pieces, 122, 153; character pieces, 122–24; dances, 133–36, 138; ensemble music, 120–21, 137–39; etudes, 128; fees for piano use, 97, 99, 205n91; at Litchfield, 119, 120, 121, 122, 130, 133, 134–37; marches, 124–28; at Mount Holyoke, 119, 121, 133, 137; at musical entertainments, 116–19; at Music Vale, 57, 116, 119–20, 121, 122–24, 128–29, 130, 132–33, 134, 137–39; rondos, 128–29; sonatas, 137; student performances, 88–89, 105–9 (see also public examination exercises); themes and variations, 132–33; transcriptions, 130–32; at Troy, 98, 119, 120–21, 124–28, 130, 133–34, 137–39; vs. vocal music instruction and performance, 27, 28, 98–99
Pico, Rosina, 164
Pierce, Anna, 60
Pierce, John, 39, 186n4, 186–87n7
Pierce, Mary, 40, 60

Pierce, Sarah, *38*, 38–41; academic curricula at Litchfield, 72–82, *82*; duties at Litchfield, 60, 61, 62–63; education and family background, 38–39; founding of Litchfield, 5, 7, 19, 24, 40–41, 74, 83, 187n15; lack of music education, 41, 47, 93, 102–3, 142, 215n4; ornamental curricula at Litchfield, 83, 84, 85; philosophy of music education, 26, 28–33, 41, 92, 103, 115, 142, 170; plays written by, 76, 168–70; as textbook author, 77. *See also* Litchfield Female Academy

Pierce, Susan, 60

Pitt, William, II, 57

Pixis, Johann Peter, "Swiss Boy," 159

Plan for Improving Female Education, A (E. H. Willard), 5, 7–8, 21, 44–46, 65

plays, 76, 168–70

Pleyel, Ignaz, 95, 121; "Pleyel's Favorite German Hymn," 133, 146, 147, 228n11

Poullain de la Barre, François, 13

Powell, Mr., 103

Pratt, Eva, 109

Pratt, George, 196–97n18

Pratt, Sarah Whittlesey. *See* Whittlesey, Sarah (Mrs. George Pratt)

private schools, 13–14, 20, 39, 72, 83

probationary period, at Mount Holyoke, 68

"Psalm CV," 147

Psalms, Hymns, and Spiritual Songs, The (Watts & Worcester), 102, 147

public examination exercises, 224n9; comparison of, 85–90; at Litchfield, 67, 85, 87, 89, 99, 214n113, 224n9; at Mount Holyoke, 67, 85, 87, 106–7, 115, 119, 148–49, 212n82, 214n113; at Music Vale, 85, 87–90, 94, 96, 100–101, 105–9, 116–17, 120, 124, 128, 139, 143–46, 163, 168, 214n113; at Troy, 67, 85–88, 89–90, 94–95, 107–8, 116–17, 214n113, 223–24n4, 224n9. *See also* semiannual examinations

Pucitta, Vincenzo, 170, 237n102

Ralvo, the Pirate of the Gulf (O. Whittlesley), 90, 168

Reeve, Tapping, 7, 39–40, 64, 84, 115, 119, 168, 187n15, 208n29

Reichardt, Johann Friedrich, "Thou Are So Near and Yet So Far," 163

religious training: music education and, 32; reading in, 12; religion and philosophy curricula, 79–80, 82

Rensselaer Polytechnic Institute, 78, 190n66

Republican Motherhood, 19, 23, 24

"Rest, Spirit, Rest" (Rooke), 168

Revolutionary War, 4, 7, 12, 15–16, 24

rhetoric, 75

Richards, Brinley, 132

Richardson, Nathan, 87; *The Modern School for the Piano-Forte*, 56, 88

Ries, Ferdinand, 128

"Rock'd in the Cradle of the Deep" (E. H. Willard & J. Knight), 150–51

Romberg, Andreas Jacob, *The Transient and the Eternal*, 105, 151

rondos, for piano, 128–29

Rooke, William Michael, 236n92; "Rest, Spirit, Rest," 168; "To the Vine Feast," 167

Root, George F., 221n83; *The Academy Vocalist*, 104; *The Festival Glee Book* (with Bradbury), 154, 166

Rossini, Gioachino, 120, 166, 167, 168, 236n95

Rousseau, Jean-Jacques, 13

Rowson, Susanna, 180n52; Young Ladies Academy (Boston), 19, 30

Rubinstein, Anton, 123

Rush, Benjamin, 16–17, 19, 28–29, 34, 178–80nn37–41

Russell, Henry, 155–56, *156*, 233n61

Russell, William, 19, 20

Ruth (S. Pierce), 168–69

"Ruth and Naomi" (Topliff), 149, 231n32

Sabbath Bell, The, 147

Sabbath Hymn Book, The, 147

sacred/church music, 112–13, 139–40, 147–51

"Sadi the Moor" (Hewitt), 153

"Salem Quick Step" (O. Whittlesey), 96

"Saltarello" (Mills), 109, 133, *134*, *135*

Sanderson Academy (Ashfield, MA), 49

Schletterer, Hans Michael, "Ave Maria" (arr.), 151

Schonberg, Harold, 226n39

Schubert, Franz, 130, 138, 140, 163

Schumann, Robert, *Paradise and the Peri*, 163

science curricula, 78–79, 82

Scott, Anne Firor, 79, 206n2, 210n48

Second Great Awakening, 22

secular music, 152–54

"select" schools, 13

semiannual examinations: at Litchfield, 67, 85, 89, 99, 224n9; at Troy, 67, 85, 223–24n4, 224n9

"seminary," as term, 1, 45, 175n1, 178–79n17, 182n4

seminary and academy structures, 59–71; admission and retention, 67–71; faculty and staff, 60–63; student body, 64–67. See also board of trustees/visitors

senior class (grade level), 66, 68, 73–74, 79, 101

sentimentality, and music education, 31–32

"Serenade, La" (Philippi), 96

Shaurman, Emily T., 158

Sheldon, Charlotte, 103, 109–10

Sheldon, Lucy (Litchfield Academy student), 99–100, 109; brother at Litchfield, 231n36; music books, 114, 115, 119, 121, 122, 124, 130, 131, 133, 134–37, 146, 147, 152–53, 154, 166, 223n1, 225n26, 226n36, 228n11; pianistic skills, 137; piano at school, 100, 219n58

Shoner, Sarah Augusta, 192–93n103, 225–26n35

Sigourney, Lydia, 29

singing. See vocal music instruction and performance

Smart, Henry, 163

"Smile On: Brilliant Variations on Wallace's Beautiful Melody, 'Katie Strang'" (Grobe), 132

Smith, Sydney, 123

Smith, Theodore, 146

Social Choir, The (Kingsley, ed.), 153–54

social class, 66–67; and advocates for women, 16–23; and the American Revolution, 15–16; Enlightenment standards for refinement, 13; and female seminaries and academies, 21, 23, 64–67, 71, 181n76; and music education, 28, 33, 35–36, 200n45; and the new nineteenth-century woman, 21–22. See also finishing/fashionable schools; middle class (socioeconomic)

"Somebody's Coming, but I'll Not Tell Who" (J. C. Andrews), 158

sonatas, for piano, 137

"Song of the Pirates," 90

Songs of the Legends and Traditions of Ireland, 155

Sonnambula, La (Bellini), 139, 164, 167–68, 236n90

Sontag, Henriette, 159

"Sounds from the Heart" (Philippi), 120

"Speed Away" (Hodges), 95

Spofforth, Reginald, "Hail! Smiling Morn," 165–66

Sporle, Nathan James, "The Star of Glengary," 158–59

Springfield Daily Republican, 148–49

Stafford, Daniel, 98

"Star of Glengary, The" (Sporle), 158–59

Starr, S. Frederick, 226n38

Start, Sarah A., 98

Steinway and Sons, 163

Stephani, Madame, 108

Stoddard, Sophia D., 61

Stowe, Harriet Beecher, 73, 213n96

Strakosch, Maurice, 130

Streabbog, Louis, 128

student body characteristics, 64–67; ages, 65–66, 92; gender, 66, 67 (see also gender); geographic diversity, 64–65; social class, 66–67 (see also middle class [socioeconomic]; social class). See also names of specific institutions

"Swallow's Farewell" (F. W. Kücken), 162

"Swiss Boy" (Pixis), 159

"Swiss Song, The [Celebrated]" (Eckert), 159, 160, 164

Tadolini, Giovanni, "Ave Regina," 150

Taft, William Howard, 204–5n84

"Take Care!" (O. Whittlesey), 158

"Tamburelli I Campanelli, I" / "Now Sounds the Tambourine" (Giosa), 159–60

Tawa, Nicholas, 154, 158

Taylor, Joseph C., 110

Taylor, R., 228n11

teachers, assistant, 60, 62–63, 93–94, 198n27. See also faculty and staff

Thalberg, Sigismond, 121, 236n90; Home! Sweet Home!, 109, 124, 126; transcriptions for piano, 130

themes and variations, for piano, 132–33

"These Moments of Pleasure" (Donizetti), 166

Thomas, J. R., 132

Thompson, Charles F., "Who Will Care for Mother Now?," 146

Thompson, Thomas, "Orphan Bess and the Beggar Girl," 153

Thorbecke, E., 108

"Thou Are So Near and Yet So Far" (Reichhardt), 163

Thurston, Miss, 93

Tirrell, Almeda N., 94

Tocqueville, Alexis de, 21–22

Topliff, Robert: "Consider the Lilies," 151; "Ruth and Naomi," 149, 231n32

Torrey, Louisa M. (mother of William Howard Taft), 204–5n84

"To the Vine Feast" (Rooke), 167

transcriptions, for piano, 130–32

Transient and the Eternal, The (Romberg), 105, 151

Troy Female Seminary (Troy, NY), 42–47, *47*; academic curricula, 27, 72–82, *82*; academic year, 67–68, 202–3n67; admission and retention requirements, 67–68; board of trustees, 59–60; certificates/diplomas for course work, 89, 90, 201n59; Committee of Ladies, 60; examining committee, 31–32, 78, 80, 87, 94–95, 107–8, 115, 116, 184n54, 223–24n4; faculty and staff, 60–63, 94–97, 108, 110–12, 146–47, 157, 167, 198n23, 198n27; faculty composers, 95–96, 118, 146–47 (*see also* Andrews, John C.; Blessner, Gustave; Hodges, Faustina Hasse; Matthieu, Philippi); fees and expenses, 92, 96–97; in female seminary movement, 6, 172–74, 177n17; as forerunner to normal school, 206n4; founding (Middlebury, VT), 5, 7–8, 60; funding sources, 45–46, 187n15, 189n44; guest performances, 110; instrumental instruction and performance, 8, *98*, 100, 115, 116, 137–39, 140, 141 (*see also* Troy Female Seminary: piano instruction and performance; move to Troy, 46–47, 60, 61, 62; move to Waterford, NY, 45–46; musical entertainments, 116–18, *118*; music courses, 104; music use in seminary life, 111–12; ornamental curricula, 62, 84–85; philosophy of music education, 26, 27, 28–33, 36, 47, 92, 115, 116–17, 142, 170, 171; piano instruction and performance, *98*, 119, 120–21, 124–28, 130, 133–34, 137–39; public examination exercises, 67, 85–88, 89–90, 94–95, 107–8, 116–17, 214n113, 223–24n4, 224n9; semiannual examinations, 67, 85, 223–24n4, 224n9; "seminary," as term, 45; student performances, 105, 107–8; students and student characteristics, 61, 64, 65, 67, 85–87, 108, 159, 196n14, 198n27; vocal music instruction and performance, 9,

98, 101, 103–4, 142, 146–47, 150–51, 154–58, 159–61, 164–68, 170–71. *See also* Willard, Emma Hart

Troy Lyceum of Natural History (Troy, New York), 46

"True Love Can Ne'er Forget" (Lover), 155

tuition, 50, 51, 217–18n37. *See also* fees and expenses

"Tu Sandunga" / "What Enchantment" (Blanco), 164, 235n84

Ursuline Convent (New Orleans, LA), 14, 24, 178–79n17

"Valse à La Fantasie" (Barnekov), 95

Van Schoonhoven, Jacobus, 45

"Variations Fantastique" (Bull), 140

"Variations—on an Air of Pleyel" (Hodges), 95

"venture" schools, 13

Verdi, Giuseppe, 167, 236n95

Vidi, Ipse, 26

Village Hymns for Social Worship (Nettleton), 102, 147

Vindication of the Rights of Woman (Wollstonecraft), 18, 46

violin instruction and performance, 97, *98*, 138, 139, 140, 218n43, 227n57, 236n91

vocal music instruction and performance, 8–9, 57, 101–4, 142–71; art songs, 159–66; choruses, 164–65; classes, 97, *98*; comparison of female seminaries, *98*; composers and genres (overview), 143–47; at finishing/fashionable schools, 8–9; glees, 154, 165–66; guest performances, 87, 109–10; *versus* instrumental instruction and performance, 27, 28, 34, 98–99; at Litchfield, 9, 101, 102–3, 142, 146, 147, 152–53, 154, 166, 168–71; at Mount Holyoke, 8–9, 27, *98*, 101–2, 142, 147–50, 152, 153–54, 166, 170–71; music books, 102, 103, 115; music courses, 104–5; at Music Vale, 9, *98*, 101, 142–46, 151, 152, 154, 158–59, 161–64, 165, 168, 170–71; operas, 166–68; parlor songs, 154–59; patriotic music, 152; and plays, 76, 168–70; sacred music, 147–51; secular music, 152–54; student performances, 88–89, 105–9 (*see also* public examination exercises); at Troy, 9, *98*, 101, 103–4, 142, 146–47, 150–51, 154–58, 159–61, 164–68, 170–71

voice class, 97, *98*

von Neukomm, Sigismund Ritter, *The Easter Morning*, 151
Von Suppé, Franz, 123
von Weber, Carl Maria, 128, 130; "Glöcklein im Thale," 166–67
Voyer, Jane, 25

Wagner, Wilhelm Richard, 165
Walker, Anne, 112
Wallace, William Vincent, 121, 132, 156–57, 161, 236n95
War of 1812, 43
Warren, Rev. George W., 140; "La Fête des Fées," 124, *125*
"Warrior's Rest" (O. Whittlesey), 96
Washington, George, 37
Waterford Academy for Young Ladies (Waterford, NY), 45–46, 60, 189n44
Watts, Rev. Isaac, 204n77; "Joy of Saints," *148*; *The Psalms, Hymns, and Spiritual Songs* (with S. Worcester), 102, 147
W. B. B. (composer), 140
Webb, Catherine Cebra, 100
Webb, George J., 101; *The Odeon* (with L. Mason), 102, 153, 220n73
Webster, Daniel, 208n35
"Wedding Chorus, The" (Bellini), 164, 167
"Wedding March" (Mendelssohn), 128
Weekly Democrat, 94
Wehli, James M., "Home Sweet Home," 124, *127*
"Welcome to Music Vale" (O. Whittlesey), 96, 143, 165, 217n35
"We Meet Again" (E. Whittlesey), 96, 146
"We Met by Chance" (L. Kücken), 147
Westminster Catechism, 12
"What Are the Wild Waves Saying?" (S. Glover), 155
"When Pensive I Thought on My Love" (Kelly & Colman), 166
"When the Pale Moon Arose Last Night" (Gabriel), 162
White, Hannah, 69
Whitefield, George, 12
Whitman, Mary C., 61
Whittlesey, Charlotte Maconda Morgan (Mrs. Orramel Whittlesey), 53, 58, 60
Whittlesey, Eliza Tully Maginnis (Mrs. John T. Maginnis), 58, 62, 95, 143, 196–97n18, 225n23; as vice principal at Music Vale Seminary, 60; "We Meet Again," 96, 146; "Why Weep for the Dead," 96, 146

Whittlesey, Henry, 53
Whittlesey, Jennette ("Nettie") Maginnis (Mrs. William Henry Maginnis), 62, 196–97n18
Whittlesey, John, 53
Whittlesey, Karolyn ("Katie") Bradford, 60, 62, 192–93n103, 195n8, 196–97n18
Whittlesey, Orramel, *53*, 53–58, 237n2, 237n100; duties at Music Vale Seminary, 60, 61–65, 94, 196–97n18; education and family background, 53, 94; founding of Music Vale Seminary, 6, 7, 8, 54, 100, 192–93n103; and Gottschalk, 123–24; legal and political activities, 56, 58; marriage to Charlotte Maconda Morgan, 53, 58, 60; philosophy of music education, 26, 28–33, 56–57, 100–101, 114–15, 117, 142, 170, 171; pianistic skills, 152; piano-building family, 53, *54*, 94. *See also* Music Vale Seminary
—works, 56, 95, 143–46, 228n2; "American Eagle," 96, 152; "The Dying Soldier of Buena Vista," 96, 152; "Farewell to My Home," 96; "A Great Big House," 143; "Harp of the Wild Wind," 96, 143, *144*, *145*, 162–63, 193n110; "Music Vale Seminary Quick Step," 96, 138; "Our Harp and Banner," 139, 143, 165; *Ralvo, The Pirate of the Gulf*, 90, 168; "Salem Quick Step," 96; "Take Care!," 158; "Warrior's Rest," 96; "Welcome to Music Vale," 96, 143, 165, 217n35; "Wild Roses," 96
Whittlesey, Sarah (Mrs. George Pratt), 62, 194n130, 196–97n18, 223n3; as head of Music Vale, 58; as vice principal of Music Vale, 60
"Who Will Care for Mother Now?" (C. Thompson), 146
"Why Do I Weep for Thee?" (Wallace), 156–57
"Why Weep for the Dead" (E. Wittlesey), 96, 146
Wilcox, Harriet, 99
Wilcox, Jeremiah, 99
Wilder, Eliza, 93–94, 105, 142, 149–50, 171
"Wild Roses" (O. Whittlesey), 96
Willard, Emma Hart, 23, *42*, 42–47, 237n4; academic curricula at Troy, 27, 72–82, *82*; certificates for student course work, 89; duties at Troy, 59, 60, 61, 62; education and family background, 42–43; founding of Troy Female Seminary, 5, 7–8, 60;

Willard, Emma Hart (*continued*): lack of music education, 47; and Mary Lyon, 50, 51; marriage to John Willard, 42–43; and Middlebury College, 42–43; and Middlebury Female Academy, 42, 43, 45; move to Troy, NY, 46–47, 60, 61, 62; ornamental curricula at Troy, 83, 84, 85; philosophy of music education, 26, 27, 28–33, 36, 47, 92, 115, 116–17, 142, 170, 171; sabbatical in Europe (1830), 61, 133–34, 150; visit of General Lafayette, 47, 111, 222–23n118; and Waterford Academy for Young Ladies, 45–46, 60, 189n44. *See also* Troy Female Seminary
—works, 87–88; *An Address to the Public*, 45–46; "My Own Sunny France" (with J. C. Andrews), 111–12, 222–23n118; *A Plan for Improving Female Education*, 5, 7–8, 21, 44–46, 65; "Rock'd in the Cradle of the Deep" (with J. Knight), 150–51; textbooks, 77
Willard, John (husband of Emma), 42–43, 46, 61
Willard, John H. (son of Emma), 61
Willard, Sarah Hudson (Mrs. John H. Willard), 61, 198n23
"Willy's Rare and Willy's Fair" (Hook), 154
"Winds Are Up—The Stars Are Out, The" (Nelson), 155
"Winter's Evening, A" (Jackson), 153
Wolcott, Elizabeth, 87

Wollstonecraft, Mary, 18, 19, 46
woman's sphere, 6, 11, 17–19, 21–23, 42, 44, 72, 177–78nn3–4
women's education: advocates for, 5–6, 16–23; new era in, 37–38, 177n17; restrictions on, 11–12. *See also* female seminaries and academies; finishing/fashionable schools; music education (generally); philosophies of women's education; *and names of specific institutions*
Women's Education in the United States, 1780–1840 (Nash), 2
Wood, Frances M., 199n29
Wood, T., 140
Woodbridge, Rev. William C., 19, 20, 29, 32, 33, 77
Woodbury, I. B., 149
Woody, Thomas, 2, 175n3
Worcester, Samuel, *The Psalms, Hymns, and Spiritual Songs* (with Watts), 102, 147
working women. *See* employment of women
Wright, Daniel, 33
Wrighten, Mary Ann, 154
writing, 75

Young, Alexander, "Night Thoughts," 81
Young Ladies Academy (Boston), 19, 30

Zinzendorf, Beningna, 178–79n17

JEWEL A. SMITH serves on the musicology faculty at the University of Cincinnati's College-Conservatory of Music and is the author of *Music, Women, and Pianos in Antebellum Bethlehem Pennsylvania: The Moravian Young Ladies' Seminary.*

MUSIC IN AMERICAN LIFE

Only a Miner: Studies in Recorded Coal-Mining Songs   *Archie Green*
Great Day Coming: Folk Music and the American Left   *R. Serge Denisoff*
John Philip Sousa: A Descriptive Catalog of His Works   *Paul E. Bierley*
The Hell-Bound Train: A Cowboy Songbook   *Glenn Ohrlin*
Oh, Didn't He Ramble: The Life Story of Lee Collins, as Told to Mary Collins
     Edited by Frank J. Gillis and John W. Miner
American Labor Songs of the Nineteenth Century   *Philip S. Foner*
Stars of Country Music: Uncle Dave Macon to Johnny Rodriguez
     Edited by Bill C. Malone and Judith McCulloh
Git Along, Little Dogies: Songs and Songmakers of the American West   *John I. White*
A Texas-Mexican *Cancionero*: Folksongs of the Lower Border   *Américo Paredes*
San Antonio Rose: The Life and Music of Bob Wills   *Charles R. Townsend*
Early Downhome Blues: A Musical and Cultural Analysis   *Jeff Todd Titon*
An Ives Celebration: Papers and Panels of the Charles Ives Centennial
     Festival-Conference   *Edited by H. Wiley Hitchcock and Vivian Perlis*
Sinful Tunes and Spirituals: Black Folk Music to the Civil War   *Dena J. Epstein*
Joe Scott, the Woodsman-Songmaker   *Edward D. Ives*
Jimmie Rodgers: The Life and Times of America's Blue Yodeler   *Nolan Porterfield*
Early American Music Engraving and Printing: A History of Music Publishing
     in America from 1787 to 1825, with Commentary on Earlier and Later
     Practices   *Richard J. Wolfe*
Sing a Sad Song: The Life of Hank Williams   *Roger M. Williams*
Long Steel Rail: The Railroad in American Folksong   *Norm Cohen*
Resources of American Music History: A Directory of Source Materials from Colonial
     Times to World War II   *D. W. Krummel, Jean Geil, Doris J. Dyen,
     and Deane L. Root*
Tenement Songs: The Popular Music of the Jewish Immigrants   *Mark Slobin*
Ozark Folksongs   *Vance Randolph; edited and abridged by Norm Cohen*
Oscar Sonneck and American Music   *Edited by William Lichtenwanger*
Bluegrass Breakdown: The Making of the Old Southern Sound   *Robert Cantwell*
Bluegrass: A History   *Neil V. Rosenberg*
Music at the White House: A History of the American Spirit   *Elise K. Kirk*
Red River Blues: The Blues Tradition in the Southeast   *Bruce Bastin*
Good Friends and Bad Enemies: Robert Winslow Gordon and the Study of American
     Folksong   *Debora Kodish*
Fiddlin' Georgia Crazy: Fiddlin' John Carson, His Real World, and the World of His
     Songs   *Gene Wiggins*
America's Music: From the Pilgrims to the Present (rev. 3d ed.)   *Gilbert Chase*
Secular Music in Colonial Annapolis: The Tuesday Club, 1745–56   *John Barry Talley*
Bibliographical Handbook of American Music   *D. W. Krummel*
Goin' to Kansas City   *Nathan W. Pearson Jr.*

"Susanna," "Jeanie," and "The Old Folks at Home": The Songs of Stephen C. Foster from His Time to Ours (2d ed.)   *William W. Austin*

Songprints: The Musical Experience of Five Shoshone Women   *Judith Vander*

"Happy in the Service of the Lord": Afro-American Gospel Quartets in Memphis
Kip Lornell

Paul Hindemith in the United States   *Luther Noss*

"My Song Is My Weapon": People's Songs, American Communism, and the Politics of Culture, 1930–50   *Robbie Lieberman*

Chosen Voices: The Story of the American Cantorate   *Mark Slobin*

Theodore Thomas: America's Conductor and Builder of Orchestras, 1835–1905
Ezra Schabas

"The Whorehouse Bells Were Ringing" and Other Songs Cowboys Sing
Collected and Edited by Guy Logsdon

Crazeology: The Autobiography of a Chicago Jazzman   *Bud Freeman,*
as Told to Robert Wolf

Discoursing Sweet Music: Brass Bands and Community Life in Turn-of-the-Century Pennsylvania   *Kenneth Kreitner*

Mormonism and Music: A History   *Michael Hicks*

Voices of the Jazz Age: Profiles of Eight Vintage Jazzmen   *Chip Deffaa*

Pickin' on Peachtree: A History of Country Music in Atlanta, Georgia
Wayne W. Daniel

Bitter Music: Collected Journals, Essays, Introductions, and Librettos   *Harry Partch;*
edited by Thomas McGeary

Ethnic Music on Records: A Discography of Ethnic Recordings Produced in the United States, 1893 to 1942   *Richard K. Spottswood*

Downhome Blues Lyrics: An Anthology from the Post–World War II Era
Jeff Todd Titon

Ellington: The Early Years   *Mark Tucker*

Chicago Soul   *Robert Pruter*

That Half-Barbaric Twang: The Banjo in American Popular Culture   *Karen Linn*

Hot Man: The Life of Art Hodes   *Art Hodes and Chadwick Hansen*

The Erotic Muse: American Bawdy Songs (2d ed.)   *Ed Cray*

Barrio Rhythm: Mexican American Music in Los Angeles   *Steven Loza*

The Creation of Jazz: Music, Race, and Culture in Urban America   *Burton W. Peretti*

Charles Martin Loeffler: A Life Apart in Music   *Ellen Knight*

Club Date Musicians: Playing the New York Party Circuit   *Bruce A. MacLeod*

Opera on the Road: Traveling Opera Troupes in the United States, 1825–60
Katherine K. Preston

The Stonemans: An Appalachian Family and the Music That Shaped Their Lives
Ivan M. Tribe

Transforming Tradition: Folk Music Revivals Examined   *Edited by Neil V. Rosenberg*

The Crooked Stovepipe: Athapaskan Fiddle Music and Square Dancing in Northeast Alaska and Northwest Canada   *Craig Mishler*

Traveling the High Way Home: Ralph Stanley and the World of Traditional Bluegrass
Music   *John Wright*

Carl Ruggles: Composer, Painter, and Storyteller   *Marilyn Ziffrin*

Never without a Song: The Years and Songs of Jennie Devlin, 1865–1952
Katharine D. Newman

The Hank Snow Story   *Hank Snow, with Jack Ownbey and Bob Burris*

Milton Brown and the Founding of Western Swing   *Cary Ginell, with special
assistance from Roy Lee Brown*

Santiago de Murcia's "Códice Saldívar No. 4": A Treasury of Secular Guitar Music
from Baroque Mexico   *Craig H. Russell*

The Sound of the Dove: Singing in Appalachian Primitive Baptist Churches
Beverly Bush Patterson

Heartland Excursions: Ethnomusicological Reflections on Schools of Music
Bruno Nettl

Doowop: The Chicago Scene   *Robert Pruter*

Blue Rhythms: Six Lives in Rhythm and Blues   *Chip Deffaa*

Shoshone Ghost Dance Religion: Poetry Songs and Great Basin Context
Judith Vander

Go Cat Go! Rockabilly Music and Its Makers   *Craig Morrison*

'Twas Only an Irishman's Dream: The Image of Ireland and the Irish in American
Popular Song Lyrics, 1800–1920   *William H. A. Williams*

Democracy at the Opera: Music, Theater, and Culture in New York City,
1815–60   *Karen Ahlquist*

Fred Waring and the Pennsylvanians   *Virginia Waring*

Woody, Cisco, and Me: Seamen Three in the Merchant Marine   *Jim Longhi*

Behind the Burnt Cork Mask: Early Blackface Minstrelsy and Antebellum American
Popular Culture   *William J. Mahar*

Going to Cincinnati: A History of the Blues in the Queen City   *Steven C. Tracy*

Pistol Packin' Mama: Aunt Molly Jackson and the Politics of Folksong   *Shelly Romalis*

Sixties Rock: Garage, Psychedelic, and Other Satisfactions   *Michael Hicks*

The Late Great Johnny Ace and the Transition from R&B to Rock 'n' Roll
James M. Salem

Tito Puente and the Making of Latin Music   *Steven Loza*

Juilliard: A History   *Andrea Olmstead*

Understanding Charles Seeger, Pioneer in American Musicology   *Edited by Bell Yung
and Helen Rees*

Mountains of Music: West Virginia Traditional Music from *Goldenseal*
Edited by John Lilly

Alice Tully: An Intimate Portrait   *Albert Fuller*

A Blues Life   *Henry Townsend, as told to Bill Greensmith*

Long Steel Rail: The Railroad in American Folksong (2d ed.)   *Norm Cohen*

The Golden Age of Gospel   *Text by Horace Clarence Boyer;
photography by Lloyd Yearwood*

Aaron Copland: The Life and Work of an Uncommon Man   *Howard Pollack*

Louis Moreau Gottschalk   *S. Frederick Starr*
Race, Rock, and Elvis   *Michael T. Bertrand*
Theremin: Ether Music and Espionage   *Albert Glinsky*
Poetry and Violence: The Ballad Tradition of Mexico's Costa Chica
    John H. McDowell
The Bill Monroe Reader   *Edited by Tom Ewing*
Music in Lubavitcher Life   *Ellen Koskoff*
Zarzuela: Spanish Operetta, American Stage   *Janet L. Sturman*
Bluegrass Odyssey: A Documentary in Pictures and Words, 1966–86
    Carl Fleischhauer and Neil V. Rosenberg
That Old-Time Rock & Roll: A Chronicle of an Era, 1954–63   *Richard Aquila*
Labor's Troubadour   *Joe Glazer*
American Opera   *Elise K. Kirk*
Don't Get above Your Raisin': Country Music and the Southern Working Class
    Bill C. Malone
John Alden Carpenter: A Chicago Composer   *Howard Pollack*
Heartbeat of the People: Music and Dance of the Northern Pow-wow   *Tara Browner*
My Lord, What a Morning: An Autobiography   *Marian Anderson*
Marian Anderson: A Singer's Journey   *Allan Keiler*
Charles Ives Remembered: An Oral History   *Vivian Perlis*
Henry Cowell, Bohemian   *Michael Hicks*
Rap Music and Street Consciousness   *Cheryl L. Keyes*
Louis Prima   *Garry Boulard*
Marian McPartland's Jazz World: All in Good Time   *Marian McPartland*
Robert Johnson: Lost and Found   *Barry Lee Pearson and Bill McCulloch*
Bound for America: Three British Composers   *Nicholas Temperley*
Lost Sounds: Blacks and the Birth of the Recording Industry, 1890–1919   *Tim Brooks*
Burn, Baby! BURN! The Autobiography of Magnificent Montague
    Magnificent Montague with Bob Baker
Way Up North in Dixie: A Black Family's Claim to the Confederate Anthem
    Howard L. Sacks and Judith Rose Sacks
The Bluegrass Reader   *Edited by Thomas Goldsmith*
Colin McPhee: Composer in Two Worlds   *Carol J. Oja*
Robert Johnson, Mythmaking, and Contemporary American Culture
    Patricia R. Schroeder
Composing a World: Lou Harrison, Musical Wayfarer   *Leta E. Miller
    and Fredric Lieberman*
Fritz Reiner, Maestro and Martinet   *Kenneth Morgan*
That Toddlin' Town: Chicago's White Dance Bands and Orchestras,
    1900–1950   *Charles A. Sengstock Jr.*
Dewey and Elvis: The Life and Times of a Rock 'n' Roll Deejay   *Louis Cantor*
Come Hither to Go Yonder: Playing Bluegrass with Bill Monroe   *Bob Black*
Chicago Blues: Portraits and Stories   *David Whiteis*
The Incredible Band of John Philip Sousa   *Paul E. Bierley*

"Maximum Clarity" and Other Writings on Music   *Ben Johnston,*
   edited by Bob Gilmore
Staging Tradition: John Lair and Sarah Gertrude Knott   *Michael Ann Williams*
Homegrown Music: Discovering Bluegrass   *Stephanie P. Ledgin*
Tales of a Theatrical Guru   *Danny Newman*
The Music of Bill Monroe   *Neil V. Rosenberg and Charles K. Wolfe*
Pressing On: The Roni Stoneman Story   *Roni Stoneman, as told to Ellen Wright*
Together Let Us Sweetly Live   *Jonathan C. David,*
   with photographs by Richard Holloway
Live Fast, Love Hard: The Faron Young Story   *Diane Diekman*
Air Castle of the South: WSM Radio and the Making of Music City
   Craig P. Havighurst
Traveling Home: Sacred Harp Singing and American Pluralism   *Kiri Miller*
Where Did Our Love Go? The Rise and Fall of the Motown Sound   *Nelson George*
Lonesome Cowgirls and Honky-Tonk Angels: The Women of Barn Dance
   Radio   *Kristine M. McCusker*
California Polyphony: Ethnic Voices, Musical Crossroads   *Mina Yang*
The Never-Ending Revival: Rounder Records and the Folk Alliance   *Michael F. Scully*
Sing It Pretty: A Memoir   *Bess Lomax Hawes*
Working Girl Blues: The Life and Music of Hazel Dickens   *Hazel Dickens*
   and Bill C. Malone
Charles Ives Reconsidered   *Gayle Sherwood Magee*
The Hayloft Gang: The Story of the National Barn Dance   *Edited by Chad Berry*
Country Music Humorists and Comedians   *Loyal Jones*
Record Makers and Breakers: Voices of the Independent Rock 'n' Roll Pioneers
   John Broven
Music of the First Nations: Tradition and Innovation in Native North America
   Edited by Tara Browner
Cafe Society: The Wrong Place for the Right People   *Barney Josephson,*
   with Terry Trilling-Josephson
George Gershwin: An Intimate Portrait   *Walter Rimler*
Life Flows On in Endless Song: Folk Songs and American History   *Robert V. Wells*
I Feel a Song Coming On: The Life of Jimmy McHugh   *Alyn Shipton*
King of the Queen City: The Story of King Records   *Jon Hartley Fox*
Long Lost Blues: Popular Blues in America, 1850–1920   *Peter C. Muir*
Hard Luck Blues: Roots Music Photographs from the Great Depression
   Rich Remsberg
Restless Giant: The Life and Times of Jean Aberbach and Hill and Range Songs
   Bar Biszick-Lockwood
Champagne Charlie and Pretty Jemima: Variety Theater in the Nineteenth
   Century   *Gillian M. Rodger*
Sacred Steel: Inside an African American Steel Guitar Tradition   *Robert L. Stone*
Gone to the Country: The New Lost City Ramblers and the Folk Music Revival
   Ray Allen

The Makers of the Sacred Harp   *David Warren Steel with Richard H. Hulan*
Woody Guthrie, American Radical   *Will Kaufman*
George Szell: A Life of Music   *Michael Charry*
Bean Blossom: The Brown County Jamboree and Bill Monroe's Bluegrass
    Festivals   *Thomas A. Adler*
Crowe on the Banjo: The Music Life of J. D. Crowe   *Marty Godbey*
Twentieth Century Drifter: The Life of Marty Robbins   *Diane Diekman*
Henry Mancini: Reinventing Film Music   *John Caps*
The Beautiful Music All Around Us: Field Recordings and the American
    Experience   *Stephen Wade*
Then Sings My Soul: The Culture of Southern Gospel Music   *Douglas Harrison*
The Accordion in the Americas: Klezmer, Polka, Tango, Zydeco, and More!
    Edited by Helena Simonett
Bluegrass Bluesman: A Memoir   *Josh Graves, edited by Fred Bartenstein*
One Woman in a Hundred: Edna Phillips and the Philadelphia Orchestra
    Mary Sue Welsh
The Great Orchestrator: Arthur Judson and American Arts Management
    James M. Doering
Charles Ives in the Mirror: American Histories of an Iconic Composer   *David C. Paul*
Southern Soul-Blues   *David Whiteis*
Sweet Air: Modernism, Regionalism, and American Popular Song
    Edward P. Comentale
Pretty Good for a Girl: Women in Bluegrass   *Murphy Hicks Henry*
Sweet Dreams: The World of Patsy Cline   *Warren R. Hofstra*
William Sidney Mount and the Creolization of American Culture
    Christopher J. Smith
Bird: The Life and Music of Charlie Parker   *Chuck Haddix*
Making the March King: John Philip Sousa's Washington Years, 1854–1893
    Patrick Warfield
In It for the Long Run   *Jim Rooney*
Pioneers of the Blues Revival   *Steve Cushing*
Roots of the Revival: American and British Folk Music in the 1950s   *Ronald D. Cohen
    and Rachel Clare Donaldson*
Blues All Day Long: The Jimmy Rogers Story   *Wayne Everett Goins*
Yankee Twang: Country and Western Music in New England   *Clifford R. Murphy*
The Music of the Stanley Brothers   *Gary B. Reid*
Hawaiian Music in Motion: Mariners, Missionaries, and Minstrels   *James Revell Carr*
Sounds of the New Deal: The Federal Music Project in the West   *Peter Gough*
The Mormon Tabernacle Choir: A Biography   *Michael Hicks*
The Man That Got Away: The Life and Songs of Harold Arlen   *Walter Rimler*
A City Called Heaven: Chicago and the Birth of Gospel Music   *Robert M. Marovich*
Blues Unlimited: Essential Interviews from the Original Blues Magazine
    Edited by Bill Greensmith, Mike Rowe, and Mark Camarigg

Hoedowns, Reels, and Frolics: Roots and Branches of Southern Appalachian
    Dance   *Phil Jamison*
Fannie Bloomfield-Zeisler: The Life and Times of a Piano Virtuoso
    Beth Abelson Macleod
Cybersonic Arts: Adventures in American New Music   *Gordon Mumma,*
    edited with commentary by Michelle Fillion
The Magic of Beverly Sills   *Nancy Guy*
Waiting for Buddy Guy   *Alan Harper*
Harry T. Burleigh: From the Spiritual to the Harlem Renaissance   *Jean E. Snyder*
Music in the Age of Anxiety: American Music in the Fifties   *James Wierzbicki*
Jazzing: New York City's Unseen Scene   *Thomas H. Greenland*
A Cole Porter Companion   *Edited by Don M. Randel, Matthew Shaftel,*
    and Susan Forscher Weiss
Foggy Mountain Troubadour: The Life and Music of Curly Seckler   *Penny Parsons*
Blue Rhythm Fantasy: Big Band Jazz Arranging in the Swing Era   *John Wriggle*
Bill Clifton: America's Bluegrass Ambassador to the World   *Bill C. Malone*
Chinatown Opera Theater in North America   *Nancy Yunhwa Rao*
The Elocutionists: Women, Music, and the Spoken Word   *Marian Wilson Kimber*
May Irwin: Singing, Shouting, and the Shadow of Minstrelsy   *Sharon Ammen*
Peggy Seeger: A Life of Music, Love, and Politics   *Jean R. Freedman*
Charles Ives's *Concord*: Essays after a Sonata   *Kyle Gann*
Don't Give Your Heart to a Rambler: My Life with Jimmy Martin, the King of
    Bluegrass   *Barbara Martin Stephens*
Libby Larsen: Composing an American Life   *Denise Von Glahn*
George Szell's Reign: Behind the Scenes with the Cleveland Orchestra
    Marcia Hansen Kraus
Just One of the Boys: Female-to-Male Cross-Dressing on the American Variety
    Stage   *Gillian M. Rodger*
Spirituals and the Birth of a Black Entertainment Industry   *Sandra Jean Graham*
Right to the Juke Joint: A Personal History of American Music   *Patrick B. Mullen*
Bluegrass Generation: A Memoir   *Neil V. Rosenberg*
Pioneers of the Blues Revival, Expanded Second Edition   *Steve Cushing*
Banjo Roots and Branches   *Edited by Robert Winans*
Bill Monroe: The Life and Music of the Blue Grass Man   *Tom Ewing*
Dixie Dewdrop: The Uncle Dave Macon Story   *Michael D. Doubler*
Los Romeros: Royal Family of the Spanish Guitar   *Walter Aaron Clark*
Transforming Women's Education: Liberal Arts and Music in Female
    Seminaries   *Jewel A. Smith*

The University of Illinois Press
is a founding member of the
Association of American University Presses.

Composed in 10.5/13 Minion
with Plantin Std display
by Lisa Connery
at the University of Illinois Press
Cover designed by Jennifer S. Fisher
Cover illustration: Members of the Banjo and Mandolin Clubs
posing for a formal portrait, ca. 1898–1899. Photo by George H.
Van Norman. Mount Holyoke College Collections / Archives and
Special Collections / Student Organizations Records.

University of Illinois Press
1325 South Oak Street
Champaign, IL 61820-6903
www.press.uillinois.edu